Understanding Manga and Anime

Understanding Manga and Anime

Robin E. Brenner

A Member of the Greenwood Publishing Group

Westport, Connecticut • London

Library of Congress Cataloging-in-Publication Data

Brenner, Robin E., 1977-
    Understanding manga and anime / Robin E. Brenner.
      p. cm.
    Includes bibliographical references and index.
    ISBN 978-1-59158-332-5 (alk. paper)
    1. Libraries—Special collections—Audio-visual materials.
2. Libraries—Special collections—Comic books, strips, etc.
3. Young adults' libraries—Collection development. 4. Libraries
and teenagers. 5. Animated films—Japan—History and criticism.
6. Animated television programs—Japan—History and criticism.
7. Animated videos—Japan—History and criticism.
8. Comic books, strips, etc.—History and criticism. I. Title.
Z692.A93B74   2007
025.2'187626—dc22   2007009773

British Library Cataloguing in Publication Data is available.

Library of Congress Catalog Card Number: 2007009773
ISBN: 978-1-59158-332-5

First published in 2007

Libraries Unlimited, 88 Post Road West, Westport, CT 06881
A Member of the Greenwood Publishing Group, Inc.
www.lu.com

Printed in the United States of America

∞

The paper used in this book complies with the
Permanent Paper Standard issued by the National
Information Standards Organization (Z39.48-1984).

10 9 8 7 6 5 4 3 2 1

Contents

Acknowledgments

I would never have even contemplated writing this book were it not for the prompting, support, and encouragement from all my professional colleagues and fellow graphic novel librarians. Thanks to all of you who inspire me, including but not limited to Mike Pawuk, Kat Kan, Michele Gorman, Kristin Fletcher-Spear, Beth Gallaway, Christine Jenkins, everyone on the Graphic Novels in Libraries (GNLIB-L) listserv, and all of my readers over at No Flying, No Tights. All of my coworkers at Cary Memorial Library in Lexington and my new colleagues at the Brookline Public Library in Brookline deserve piles of thanks for letting me be a bit crazy at work, especially my fellow "floaters," Janice Franca and Cynthia Johnson.

All of the members of Club Otaku, Cary Library's manga and anime club, have been invaluable in fueling my own enthusiasm while sharing their own. You are all amazing, and I can't wait to see your comics in print!

All of the publishers who were so helpful in my quest to get image permissions must be acknowledged for their tireless pursuit of example images on my behalf both here in the United States and in Japan. I would especially like to thank David Wise, Audry Taylor, Amelia Cantlay, Rachel Livingston, Chris Oarr, Dallas Middaugh, Susan Hale, Charles Babb, Evelyn Dubocq, Dudley Jahnke, and Jane Lui. Also on the publisher side of things, thanks go out to all of the publisher representatives and editors including but not limited to Lillian Diaz-Pryzbyl, Holly Smith, Alan Payne, Alicia Wilson, and Rich Johnson as well as all of the creators who have given me a moment of their time at conferences.

This book would not have been possible without the support of my friends, especially the Dinner crowd. Special thanks go out to Jennifer Webb, Alison Kotin, Katie Morrissey, Jennifer Giordano, Jennifer Pectol, Eva Volin, Jessica Smith, and Wil Dalphin, and Snow Wildsmith for help in brainstorming and editing along the way. Piles of thanks, hugs, and good chocolate go out to Petra Beunderman, housemate and editor extraordinaire, not to mention the person who kept the apartment neat, me fed, and put up with endless discourse on manga and watching anime at any time of day or night. She deserves all kinds of chocolate for reading this as many times as she did.

My family always has my thanks: to my sister, who read me stories when I was little; to my mother, who taught me about art and science and everything in between; and to my father, who always knew I could be a cartoonist if I set my mind to it. Thanks for teaching me to always ask why, and even more important, what if?

Thanks must also go out to my editor, Barbara Ittner, who wrangled this first-time author with wit and eloquence, keeping me focused on what we all hoped the book could and should be. Elizabeth Budd and Emma Bailey were both invaluable, and I thank all of the people at Libraries Unlimited who were involved in the production of this book.

Introduction

If you go to your local Barnes and Noble bookstore and survey the vast sprawl of shelves, you will soon spy the now-ubiquitous graphic novel section. You'll notice that despite a long history of U.S. comics dominated by superheroes and Peanuts strips, you now may have to go to the bottom shelf to find your favorite Spider-Man or Batman title. Lining the shelves, running down the aisle and in special display racks, a very different kind of comic dominates, in neat, seven-inch paperback volumes. Japanese *manga,* or print comics, are steadily taking over. No doubt a few local readers, from young teens to thirty-somethings, are lounging between the shelves reading the latest volume of their favorite series. U.S comics, once very much a specialty comic store and "guy's domain," now have popular competition, drawing in every kind of reader and boosting the visibility of female comics readers dramatically.

Graphic novels as a format are still struggling for acceptance as literature and everything that label implies, but progress is being made. But when media —from the *New York Times Book Review* to *Entertainment Weekly*—has begun featuring and reviewing the latest titles, it can be said that the format has arrived.

Ever since the 1950s, when Senate investigations erroneously blamed comics for juvenile delinquency and other unsavory conditions, the medium has struggled with negative associations. The resulting backlash from those investigations encouraged a confusing mish-mash of national cultural memories and stereotypes: it's all porn; it's just for kids; it's all superheroes; it's only literary if it deals with history and memoir; there's no way it's art or literature; it's just ephemeral trash with no quality content.

Happily, librarians and libraries, alongside comics authors, publishers, reviewers, and other advocates, are finally making headway in proving the quality and reputation of their medium of choice. Although we may all tire of yet another headline that proclaims "Comics! Not for Kids Anymore!" the growing recognition of the variety and quality of work that is produced in the medium is heartening.

Japanese manga, however, is a different story. The same old stereotypes rear their heads again: it's all porn, it's damaging to kids, it's not literature. The fact that manga are by definition of foreign origin signals the exotic factor, making these titles even more "the other," filled with different values and obscure customs. The unfamiliar stories, conventions, and references make the whole kit and caboodle puzzling to many adults—just as they make it fascinating to younger readers in search of something new, complex, and—always a bonus—outside their parents' realm of understanding.

This guide to Japanese manga is intended especially for those new to the format and desperate for some understanding. Readers may include librarians selecting titles for their collections, parents purchasing for their children, or simply new readers wondering what those giant sweat drops appearing above characters' heads are all about. There are already a number of excellent titles on Japanese manga, their history and meaning in Japan, and their cultural origins. This guide is a bit different—although some history is included—because it is written by someone who started from the same place you are now occupying: blithe ignorance. Although I cannot claim to be an expert on Japanese culture, nor have I ever set foot in Japan itself, as a fan, a librarian, and a researcher, I have knowledge and experience to share. This book, then, is here to illuminate manga and anime from just those points of view—as a fan, certainly, but also as an outsider, a librarian, and a reader.

Manga and anime represent a growing reading and viewing trend in U.S. pop culture, and as younger readers, especially teens, embrace these media, many adults are feeling more and more adrift among traditions, symbols, and stories they do not recognize. Rather than simply recommending this new format, this book is intended to foster understanding and appreciation and to bring novices up to speed on the traditions, cultural road bumps, and joys of reading manga.

Why Manga and Anime?

Recently, numerous articles have been published speculating on why U.S. readers have embraced Japanese manga. One of the simplest reasons is the "coattail effect" derived from the general success of graphic novels. As comics and graphic novels blip higher on the pop culture radar, from winning Pulitzers to inspiring Hollywood filmmakers, they pave the way for a wider audience and for more variety in the format.

Traditional comics are still customarily produced as serials in the familiar thirty-two-page comic books before they are bound together to form a paperback or hardbound volume. The U.S. audience was, and still is, more accustomed to seeing comics in this format—relatively cheap story segments that continue from week to week or month to month, easily digestible and disposable. The rise of graphic novels, however, has changed both the attitude of the reader and of the publishers. While in the past twenty years the comics industry focused on collectors who seek that number one issue or build up collections for storage, the current market is a reader's market. The overall graphic novel market in North America has been growing consistently, from $75 million in 2000 to $245 million in 2005. The bookstore market in 2001 accounted for $32 million of the graphic novel market. By 2005, they accounted for $167 million, almost five times the previous amount and twice as much as the once-dominant specialty and comic book stores. Manga's popularity continues to grow within the market as a whole, sales increasing by 25 percent between 2004 and 2005 in bookstores where the bulk of manga are now sold. In October 2005, manga titles made up forty-seven of the fifty top-selling graphic novels in bookstores (Griepp 2006, n. 13). People who currently buy comics and graphic novels are less concerned with the worth of the object they are holding than the content inside—they want to read it, not own it, and they don't particularly care if it's in a comic book or a book.

The audience for manga was and is different than the traditional comics readership in the United States. Part of the reason manga took a while to find its audience in the West is that manga is produced and mainly available in book form. In Japan, manga is first published and read as installments of different stories in weekly and monthly magazines of three hundred or more pages, but there was no such counterpart for consumption in the United States. When a few manga comic books were first published here, none succeeded with the comic book audience. Further, bound manga volumes were much more expensive than either comic books or mass-market paperbacks. As graphic novels and readers have gained influence over the comics market and the attitude of comics readers began to shift toward the content rather than the object, manga readership in the United States began to explode.

Another factor that has contributed to the popularity of manga comes from an unanticipated and often unacknowledged source: video games. Gaming is a huge industry here in the United States. According to the 2005 Pew Internet and American Life report on Teens and Technology, 81 percent of teens go online to game—up from 52 percent in 2000—which represents around 17 million teens (Pew Internet Life and American Life Project 2005, July). The bulk of video games are from Asian creators, and the links between manga, anime, and video games are inextricable, both in terms of market and in appeal. The design of characters, the environments, the history, and the goals of heroes in video games and manga are undoubtedly parallel. In addition to these surface similarities, the literacy required to succeed in video games is closely linked to the literacy required to read manga: an understanding of the combination of text and image and the ability to follow cinematic structure and navigate through symbols and clues, and follow extended story arcs. Additionally, gaming and manga share the distinction of befuddling previous generations—both are entertainment that parents and teachers stereotypically undervalue.

Manga publishing is a vibrant and substantial market in Japan, making up 30 percent of the entire publishing market, and although it has been available in the United States for decades, the cultural mind-set had to catch up to the format before manga could catch the general public's attention. The sheer number of titles ready-made for this new market dwarfs the titles produced by Western comics publishers.

Manga's popularity with readers, especially with teen readers, is the primary reason libraries acknowledge and collect Japanese manga and anime. In a recent survey conducted on my own Web site, No Flying, No Tights (http://noflyingnotights.com), I asked teen readers whether they read only U.S. comics, Japanese comics, or both. More than 60 percent responded that they only read Japanese manga, and another 30 percent read both; only 10 percent read only U.S. comics (NFNT Reader Survey 2006). One of the largest U.S. publishers of translated manga, Tokyopop, recently found that over 70 percent of their teen readers are young women (personal communication with Lillian Diaz-Przybyl 2005–2006). Publishers, reviewers, and the book industry at large have taken notice simply because of manga's commercial success. Likewise, librarians see the boost in circulation statistics and are familiar with the merits of comics from years of collecting and defending graphic novels. If we, as librarians, continue to collect graphic novels, we need to follow the audience's demand. We need to begin reading and understanding manga ourselves—not simply to keep up with our audience but also to ensure we select and maintain our collection wisely. Manga, like romance novels, comics, and television before it, does and will continue to suffer from being seen as an "inferior" art form. But as this book aims to illuminate, manga is diverse and has a complexity that rivals any other format.

In my experience, manga fans are an intelligent and adventurous community. These readers research mythology and history; discuss the details of plot, costume, and acts of cultural significance; learn to read, write, and speak Japanese; long to visit the shrines and bustling cities of Japan; and mine each volume read for information about story, place, and period. They decipher each new symbol or reference they don't know, often conferring with other fans, and they try to figure out why their own sense of humor is different from the writers and readers in Japan. These readers are aware that although we are living in a global culture, there are still attitude differences, at the surface and deeper, between cultures that intrigue, amuse, and enlighten those who take notice of them.

Literacy in Manga and Anime

While he was studying literacy and the value of voluntary reading, researcher Stephen Krashen discovered that comics were an unrecognized mine of vocabulary, literary devices, and encouragement for the simple pleasure of reading. Starting with the memory of former Marvel Comics editor-in-chief Jim Shooter, who recalled wowing his second-grade teacher with vocabulary learned from Uncle Scrooge in a Donald Duck comic, Krashen discovered that comics not only provided pleasurable and unofficial reading for kids but also included close to 20 percent more rare vocabulary than a typical chapter book for children and 40 percent more than a typical conversation between a child and an adult. Krashen knew from his own work the value that self-selected reading has for kids' confidence and reading enjoyment, and in comics he found a natural starting place (Krashen 1993). In comics, images help readers who struggle with description or context, allowing them to feel they are accomplishing understanding without the intimidation of dense prose. When teen librarian Michele Gorman further researched the connections between graphic novels and literacy, she concluded that graphic novels will only continue to engage readers, reluctant or not, by encouraging literacy and the active reading in making connections between text and panels (Gorman 2003). The visible literary devices of flashback and point of view make it easier for children and teens to identify the same devices used in prose (Versaci 2001).

There is no doubt that we live in a multimedia world. Kids and teens grow up with skills that older generations lack, from navigating a computer with instinctive ease to creating a story from the jump-cuts and flashing images of two-minute music videos. While their parents might sit and struggle to read the numerous acronyms in instant messaging, teens can't imagine a world without them. Instant communication, video games, and the vast reaches of the Internet are a large part of how they live their lives and how they read and tell their stories. Eighty-seven percent of teens are online, and eighty-one percent go online to play games (up from 56 percent in 2000) (Pew Internet Life and American Life Project 2005, July). Fifty-seven percent of those teens create content online, with two out of five sharing self-authored content such as blogs and Web pages, and one in five remixing content from other online sources. Traditional reading has a lot of competition with all these media, and teens are learning to pick and choose what they love in terms of storytelling (Pew Internet Life and American Life Project 2005, November).

Comics and graphic novels require a distinct kind of literacy. The ability to connect description, dialogue, image, symbols, and the sequence of panels into a coherent story is neither a passive nor a simple act (McCloud 1993): ask anyone who's tried to read a manga title for the first time. First-time readers will come out of the story confused and unsure of what exactly happened, who was who, or why and how things happened. Give that same volume to a visual learner, and he or she will adapt more quickly, pulling out the necessary information and visual cues to create the story from the page, but there is still a learning curve. Elementary school librarian Allyson Lyga and comic industry insider Barry Lyga discussed the types of learners to whom graphic novels especially appeal in her book *Graphic Novels in Your Media Center*. She identified children with linguistic intelligence (and strong vocabularies), spatial intelligence (those who think in images and pictures), and interpersonal intelligence (those who react to body language and are strong communicators). All of these talents are reflected in graphic novels' high vocabulary level and their visuals and symbols; further, graphic novels require readers to interpret expression and gesture into a story (Lyga 2004). In the end, adaptation revolves around what previous experience the reader has had with visual media. Visual literacy is a newly developing field of study; it has become of interest in great part because younger generations are so at ease with visual signals while their elders are left wondering how all the different input creates a readable story.

Comics and graphic novels are excellent examples of a melding of visual literacy with traditional text-based literacy. Comics literacy, or the act of seeing what's going on in between the panels, is a new literacy that combines both visual and textual clues. Reading comics is a learned activity for many but is more and more an instinctive understanding for children and teenagers growing up in a world that combines text and image all the time. The divide between comprehension and confusion is not so much a generation gap but dependent on whether readers have had previous experience reading comics. If they grew up reading comics, then readers new to reading manga will be a step ahead of a reader trying sequential art for the first time. Although people who grew up in the 1940s through the 1960s read comics en masse as children, the later generations, especially from the 1980s on, had far less access to or recommendations for reading comic books and graphic novels. Reading comics became a cult activity, and many readers dismissed the medium after childhood, if they ever read them at all. Today's teens are growing up on video games, television, and the Internet, all of which require a visual literacy more complex than the media of their parents' generation (Gorman 2003), and so today's youth are more inclined to embrace new formats like Japanese manga than their parents were.

Manga readers in Japan are famous for reading manga everywhere—on their commutes or as a break from the intense pressure of school or corporate life—and at a rapid rate. As Frederik Schodt noted in his landmark book *Manga! Manga! The World of Japanese Comics,* these readers typically spend twenty minutes reading a magazine of three hundred or more pages, which breaks down to four seconds per page. This seems impossible to a prose reader, or even a U.S. comics reader—how could they get any information off a page in just four seconds? Manga obviously reads differently from U.S. comics, and as Western teens speed through volume after volume of the latest manga series, it seems they are on track to catch up with their fellow fans in Tokyo.

While all comics rely on a familiar visual language to tell their stories, from speech bubbles to sound effects to art conventions, manga uses a larger and entirely different set of cues that were never intended for a foreign audience. Just as we all know what a light bulb above a head means in a cartoon, Japanese readers know what a nosebleed means (see Chapter 4 for the answer), but both are incomprehensible occurrences to readers outside the culture of origin. One of the biggest barriers to understanding manga is these very instances of cultural divergence, and there is a steep learning curve for new U.S. readers to begin to decipher a story.

Manga, and more obviously their animated counterparts in anime, are also much more closely related to cinematic language than to the language of comic strips and print cartoons. As manga originated from creators drenched in the traditions of animation and Hollywood movies of the 1930s and 1940s, their presentation is distinctly more filmic than most U.S. comics. To truly comprehend manga we must look to films, television, and comics to find the roots of the story.

Remember that none of these new media replace books or traditional reading—they just add to the pile of what's available. If teens find valuable narrative in formats librarians rarely read, how are we to connect with newer generations? We must meet teens halfway, and one of those steps toward connection is to understand and collect graphic novels and specifically Japanese manga.

Why Libraries?

In their heyday in the 1940s, comic books were available almost everywhere, from the grocery store to the newsstand to the corner store. As the audience grew up and the market shifted, comic books slowly disappeared from general view, finally ending up being available only through specialty comic stores aimed at collectors and fans, although perhaps an occasional title might be found in a corner store. Eventually kids and teens had no obvious source for comics, and while many parents and grandparents may remember with fondness their clandestine collections of *Archie* and *Batman* comics, their kids growing up in the 1970s and 1980s had no access to comics except through the Sunday funnies. These kids grew up with comic strip collections such as *Garfield* and *Calvin and Hobbes* mixed in with the occasional *Archie*. Books, television, and films are where they got their long story arcs. Comics were never again to be the booming, kid-oriented business that they were in the Golden Age of the 1940s or the Silver Age of the 1960s.

When graphic novels began to pick up steam again in the late '90s and at the beginning of this millennium, they started in comics stores. They were also picked up by innovative libraries and finally broke into bookstores. Suddenly a whole new generation of kids and teens saw that comics could be used to tell all kinds of stories, from the adventures of superheroes to the memoirs of Holocaust survivors. Still, not many realized that what they were reading were essentially comics—comics were outside their experience.

Forward-thinking librarians have been collecting graphic novels for decades with one simple, original aim—to attract boys and young men back to the library. Boys tend to drop reading when they hit puberty, and in an effort to draw boys back to reading and to appeal to what they already enjoyed and didn't think of as "real reading," libraries started small collections of graphic novels to see whether they could recapture some of their lost audience.

The plan worked, and over the years libraries across the country have built up graphic novel collections for teenagers, children, and adults. As it turned out, graphic novels had a much wider audience than originally targeted—from parents who remembered the comics they loved to read as children and teens to those fans who never stopped reading comics delighted that their local library supported their reading habits.

As graphic novels arrived, so did Japanese manga, and it began to make its presence felt in libraries with circulation statistics and the fact that most volumes never stayed on the shelf; a similar trend was seen in bookstores. Teens are excited to see libraries once again adapting to their tastes and acknowledging their way of reading, not to mention saving them the money of buying each book of a thirty-volume series at ten bucks a pop. On top of that, many of the teens who read graphic novels and Japanese manga otherwise would rarely come into the library. The bulk of teens who attend special manga and anime events are not the "library geeks"—the teens who customarily hang out in the local library. These are teens who don't come to the library except when a school project forces them to do so. In one workshop I recently gave on the history of Japanese manga and anime, the librarian was ecstatic to see teens she had known from years before in the Children's Room but had never seen after they entered their preteens. As with any other population, these fans are happy to find other teens, let alone an adult, who speak their language and validate their interests. Any librarian gets excited when a patron is inspired to read, and the exuberance of manga and anime fans for their media is exciting. The more they read, the more they seek to explore—what else could a librarian ask of readers?

The Appeal of Manga and Anime

The dominance of the superhero subgenre has had continuing impact on U.S. production, although recently comics are diversifying in the kind of story they tell as well as how the sequential art form itself is used. Nonetheless, the bulk of comics are limited to select genres, partly because of the success of superheroes and partly as a result of the squelching of many genres due to the mid-1950s uproar over comics' content generated by Frederick Wertham's *Seduction of the Innocent* and the resulting hearings in the U.S. Senate.

Happily, the market is growing and diversifying, featuring more titles every month, but diversity of genre has yet to be a driving force in the market. Comics are still overwhelmingly aimed at (and created by) men. Female fans are beginning to be acknowledged, and although there were efforts in the past to attract girls to comics with romance themes, these lines died out in the late 1970s. There are always exceptions, of course: independent publishers have contributed unmeasured diversity to comics production and led the way toward more literary genres with titles such as Art Speigelman's *Maus* and David Clowes's *Ghost World*. The major publishers, however, stick with what sells:

superheroes, crime, and horror, with a bit of science fiction and fantasy thrown in for good measure.

Japanese manga on the other hand, to paraphrase one of library pioneer S. R. Ranganathan's five laws of libraries, has a manga for every reader. The sheer variety of manga is a large part of its appeal. Although we still only see a small percentage of the many genres available in Japan, the fantasies, melodramas, slice-of-life comedies, and hard science fiction, not to mention the memoirs, histories, and mysteries already outstrip U.S. comics. The U.S. industry is currently changing and producing an increasing variety of work, but Japan's manga industry passed that phase of growth thirty years ago and currently produces manga on everything from pachinko (a favorite Japanese pastime like a vertical pinball game) to fairy tales to the corporate world. In the United States, the comics industry is still behind in attracting female readers and tends not to pursue them, whereas since the 1970s, manga publishers have aggressively pursued girls and women as readers. This has led to many U.S. articles trumpeting how manga has girls reading comics—and despite the fact that girls and women have always read comics, they are suddenly a visible, and thus moneymaking, audience to target.

The fact is that kids and teenagers have no qualms about embarking into new formats, nor do they hold the stereotypes associated with comics as firmly in mind. All of these factors have made manga a format perfectly suited for today's teens. Manga represents an unexplored country where few adults or professionals have ventured. It represents an innovative, complicated, and culturally different puzzle for teenagers to decipher, and as with much of today's media, from Internet sites to video games to multimedia, they must read carefully, research, and connect with other fans to truly understand their reading. Every volume they read not only tells an appealing story but illuminates that much more of a language obscure to a casual reader, and those who understand the details and signals feel the thrill of a secret code.

In the end, it comes down to a very simple fact: teens love manga, and the more we can understand it, the better we can understand and support teen reading.

How to Use This Guide

This guide covers the essential issues involved in reading, collecting, and promoting Japanese manga and anime. Because far more titles exist to advise on Japanese anime, a majority of the discussions and examples here concentrate on manga. Nonetheless, anime is an inextricable part of the industry and fans' activities, and so it is also referenced and represented. The guide is intended to work together as a whole, with sections progressing from the most basic questions to the less obvious differences represented by cultural context and comfort zones. The initial sections show where manga comes from and how it is identified. Later chapters address more complex questions from what kinds of subjects will raise concerns to how to advertise and promote manga collections. Suggested title lists relevant to each topic are included throughout the guide.

The guide begins with basic information about Japanese manga and anime as formats. This section includes a brief history of the formats and profiles of the industries and creators in Japan and the United States today. The end of this section provides a guide to the basic format and construction of a manga title accompanied by advice on how to determine intended audiences and how to maintain collections in terms of shelving, labeling, and cataloging.

Next the conventions of manga and anime storytelling are explained. This information ranges from basic terms and vocabulary to identifying intended audiences, pacing, and storytelling tropes. The complex task of translating the Japanese language for U.S. audiences is addressed, as are common visual elements such as character design, symbols, and layout elements that bring the stories to life. Manga covers a diverse array of genres including those familiar to Western readers as well as genres unique to Japan. Chapter 3 provides descriptions and title lists for the most common genres, concentrating on those unique to the format.

Throughout the text, there are booklists of recommended titles. These titles are annotated to indicate the titles publishing information, intended audience and appeal, genre, and related media. Each title lists the publisher's assigned aged rating as well as my own assessment of an age recommendation: M (middle, grades 6–8), J (junior, grades 7–9), S (senior, grades 9–12), and A (adult). For more information on how the annotations are formatted, please see page 206 for the key to the annotations.

Once readers are equipped with the basics, they can dive into the cultural references that make manga a fascinating but occasionally confusing read. Because manga has never been created specifically for export, the potential for cross-cultural confusion is high. In Chapter 4, common causes for disconnects between readers and manga, or viewers and anime, are identified and explained.

Manga and anime fans create and participate in their fandom in a variety of ways. In Chapter 5, the full range of fan activities is explored with a focus on how the community can benefit readers and libraries including programming ideas and plans.

Drawing on years of reading, viewing, and working with this community, the final chapter is my annotated list of the top recommended titles of both manga and anime for younger, teen, and school audiences. Suggested reading for additional exploration is provided, and manga publishers, anime distributors, and production companies are included in the indexes.

Readers may choose to read chapters out of order or in sequence. Each chapter depends and builds on concepts and information presented in the previous sections, but readers with previous knowledge of the topic should be able to read whatever section answers their questions.

Please note that within this book, Japanese names are given in the Japanese order, with the surname first and the given name second. Because currently neither readers nor publishers make a pointed distinction, both Japanese manga and Korean manhwa are discussed as part of the same comic continuum, but of course the Korean titles reflect their culture of origin.

References

Gorman, Michele. *Getting Graphic! Using Graphic Novels to Promote Literacy with Preteens and Teens*. Worthington, OH: Linworth, 2003.

Griepp, Milton, ed. *ICv2 Retailers Guide to Graphic Novels*, 2006.

Krashen, Stephen. *The Power of Reading: Insights from the Research*. Westport, CT: Libraries Unlimited, 2004.

Lenhard, Amanda, and Mary Madden. "Pew Internet Life Survey: Teen Content Creators and Consumers." November, 2005. Washington, DC: Pew Internet and American Life Project. Available at http://www.pewinternet.org.

Lenhard, Amanda, and Mary Madden. "Pew Internet Life Survey: Teens and Technology." July, 2005. Washington, DC: Pew Internet and American Life Project. Available at http://www.pewinternet.org.

Lyga, Allyson, and Barry Lyga. *Graphic Novels in Your Media Center: A Definitive Guide*. Westport, CT: Libraries Unlimited, 2004.

McCloud, Scott. *Understanding Comics: The Invisible Art*. Northampton, MA: Kitchen Sink Press, 1993.

"NFNT Teen Reader Survey." Conducted by Robin Brenner, April, 2006. A report prepared by No Flying, No Tights, Arlington, MA. Available at http://www.noflyingnotights.com.

Versaci, Rocco. "How Comic Books Can Change the Way Our Students See: Literature: One Teacher's Perspective." *English Journal* (November 2001): 61–67.

Chapter One

Short History of Manga and Anime

Not unlike Western comics, manga and anime developed from historical art traditions in Japanese culture, although their influences and predecessors arguably reach back farther than their Western counterparts. The creation of both forms has many parallels, including political and governmental influences on the growth of the medium and a definite break away from juvenile origins to "grow up" as a storytelling format. Due to certain twists of fate, the development of the Japanese industry is an accelerated version of the growth of the Western industry. The evolution of their industry may be an indication of the direction the U.S. industry will take toward reaching acceptance as one format among many, rather than a strictly cult medium. In this chapter, I take a brief tour of the major events in the creation of manga, from feudal-era Buddhist monks to the explosion of manga and anime as the cultural forces they are today, ending with a portrait of the current manga and anime industries both in Japan and the United States.

Origins

Twelfth-Century Scrolls

The format that defines and shapes all comics, from comic strips to graphic novels, is sequential art. Sequential art is a narrative created from images, and often but not always text, presented in sequence across a page (Eisner 1994; McCloud 1993). Although it is difficult to identify the exact date when manga emerged, many credit the beginning of sequential art in Japan with the creation of scrolls of illustrations by Buddhist monks in the twelfth century. The most famous example of this art is the *Chōju Giga,* or "animal scrolls" created by a monk known as Bishop Toba. The *Chōju Giga* feature a lengthy sequence of expressive and humorous scenes of animals, including monkeys,

1

foxes, rabbits, and toads, acting out the activities and pastimes of members of the clergy and the nobility. A parody and critique of the religious hierarchy, the *Chōju Giga* also shows the particularly Japanese way of using space and carefully considered calligraphic lines to create eloquent movement, expressions, and figures. The scrolls reach as long as eighty feet and are viewed from right to left. Most important to the history of manga, they follow a definite sequence across the page to tell their story and thus lay the pattern for the sequential storytelling to come. Picture scrolls, often religious in nature, were produced for hundreds of years on a variety of topics, from religious cautionary tales and ghost stories to men indulging in farting contests (when not subject to religious constraints). Zen pictures marked a simpler offshoot, as an activity intended to focus the mind as much as to produce a piece of art, and it is here that the economy of line can be seen most clearly in the artistic tradition (Schodt 1983).

These cartoons, as part of religious study and culture, were rarely seen by the public but soon made their way into the culture of the common people, who quickly sought out cartoons in the style. Pictures that began as Buddhist amulets for travelers soon included a variety of subjects—from demons to beautiful women to warriors—and were dubbed *Otsu-e* because of their emergence and popularity near the city of Otsu around the middle of the seventeenth century (Schodt 1983).

Woodblock Printing

The next important shift in art came in the sixteenth and seventeenth centuries, when artists began producing a particular style of illustration known as *ukiyo-e*, or "pictures of the floating world." The relative peace of the Tokugawa Era (1600–1867), after hundreds of years of constant warfare, allowed artists to create and refine art objects for mass consumption, particularly using woodblock printing. The *ukiyo-e* panels of illustration, full of studied layout, line, and now splashes of vibrant color and pattern, documented the life and activities of the "floating world" of Yoshiwara. Yoshiwara was the decadent corner of capital city Edo where teahouses, restaurants, traditional theater, and high-class brothels provided escape and fantasy for well-to-do customers. Yoshiwara was the center of nightlife and provided a rich pageantry for any artist. Although panels were not specifically used, the tradition of style and observation from life turned into stylized beauty is still an evident part of manga's visuals. It is during the ukiyo-e boom that many visual traditions were created that continue in today's manga, from caricature to the stylized blood splatters of battle to the erotic art that continues in today's *ero* manga (Schodt 1996).

The Arrival of "Manga"

Artist Hokusai Katsuhika (1760–1849) coined the term "manga." Hokusai is responsible for one of the most famous images of Japanese art, the brilliant and precise woodblock print known as *The Great Wave off Konnagawa* featuring elegantly curling waves threatening Japanese fishermen, with Mt. Fuji visible in the distance. Hokusai was a master of many arts. His ability to capture a person or scene with a few fluid lines led to collections of what, around 1815, he called manga, meaning whimsical pictures or sketches. Collections of this kind of illustration, plus the continued popularity of ukiyo-e, provided ample foundation for variant art forms (Schodt 1983).

These traditions had two popular spin-offs that preceded manga's booming business. Around Osaka at the turn of the eighteenth century, bound books of twenty to thirty cartoons appeared, dubbed *Toba-e* after the legendary *Chōju Giga* creator, and sold by the thousands. Soon *kibyoshi,* or yellow-covered books, arrived. These were bound books with a strong story line that grew from a tradition of children's books based on fables, although the tales were decidedly adult in nature. Kibyoshi featured everyday stories of town life, often satirized and thus often banned by the strict government of the Tokugawa regime (Schodt 1983).

Western Influence

Opening to the West

A few years after Hokusai's death came the event that would change Japan forever. In 1853, U.S. Commodore Matthew Perry arrived on Japanese shores at Gorahama and, representing American and Western political pressure, strong-armed the already faltering Japanese government into opening its ports to trade with the West. From that time until the turn of the nineteenth century, Japan's culture was in turmoil. Society descended into a political and cultural civil war between those who wished to maintain Japanese tradition at all costs and those who embraced the West with what many considered an indecent fervor. This splintering of culture led to sudden and often violent changes, especially as Japan struggled to catch up with Western technology to maintain a position of power in this new world. This period of history, stretching from the Tokugawa Era (1600–1867) into the Meiji Era (1868–1912), is the setting for innumerable Japanese stories and is perhaps best known for the struggle between the Western-leaning emperor, the powerful politicians behind the throne, and the final stand of those mythic warriors, the samurai.

The Arrival of Cartoons

The influx of new Western art and traditions immediately influenced Japanese art, and the younger generations of artists were fascinated by styles and formats they had seen previously only in carefully edited excerpts. The relatively new cartoon caricature was represented by London's famous humor and cartoon magazine *Punch*. The existence of a few comic strips hit the illustration scene quickly, and within a few years, Japanese artists had adopted this Western style of political and cultural critique in their own magazine, *The Japan Punch*. *The Japan Punch* was started in 1862 by British citizen Charles Wirgman but was eventually taken over by Japanese editors and artists, and a later magazine, called *Marumaru Chimbun* from 1877, surpassed *The Japan Punch* in inventiveness. Many of the original comics poked fun at the very Westerners who had brought the format east, and for many years, these magazines were full of artistic skewers rivaling their inspiration's creations (Schodt 1983).

In all of these adoptions of Western style, though, Japanese artists immediately incorporated their own styles and traditions to create a hybrid art form. Some of the early cartoons of Westerners carousing with Japanese representatives are an illuminating look at how the Japanese saw Westerners—big nosed, gangly, monstrous—compared with their own graceful and fine-featured representations. Right in line with London's *Punch,* though, were the clever and pointed critiques of the government, the upper classes, and the industrialists who controlled the country. Even as the illustration and cartoon styles became more Westernized, mimicking comic strips such as *The Yellow Kid* and the new stylized art deco magazine illustrations from Paris and New York, the simplicity of layout and inventiveness of point of view derived from ukiyo-e and other Japanese illustrative predecessors kept the images distinctly Japanese (Schodt 1983). One notable difference from Western comic traditions is the awareness of how a background affects the overall image, especially in deciding when to make it particularly detailed to show place, and when to use a dramatic obliteration of all background to set off the key figure in action sequences.

From Newspapers to Magazines

In the beginning of the twentieth century, Japanese comic strips and comics began to multiply, and they were immediately popular with the public in the same way the ukiyo-e had been in the last century. Political cartoons and the tradition of political humor magazines soon gave way to more popular and less obviously politically charged comic strips. By the end of the 1920s, numerous cartoon strips were read across Japan. Many of these comics were read in children's magazines, the most popular of which, *Shōnen Club,* is still in publication today. Originally *Shōnen Club* and its rivals were collections of short articles, comics, and games meant to appeal to young boys, but slowly comics began to take over the pages of the magazines. When comic strips from comics magazines were bound into hardcover books, they became immediate best-sellers and signal one of the major differences between U.S. comics and Japanese manga—the quick shift to publishing as a book rather than a magazine. This sequence of publishing—serializing in a magazine to be later published in a book—is part of what has given manga series the measured pace and extended story arcs that are far from the norm in U.S. comics (Schodt 1983; Gravett 2004).

Even today in Japan, many adults read comic strips in newspapers and magazines and are as avid fans as their children. *Norakuro,* a comic strip that ran from 1931 through 1941, followed the journey of a small black dog through Japanese society. *Fuku-chan,* or Little Fuku, ran from 1938 through 1971 in *Shōnen Club*, following the madcap adventures of a little boy whose mischievous, sunny attitude and ability to extricate himself from scrapes is reminiscent of similar Western strips including *Dennis the Menace* and *Family Circus* (Gravett 2004).

The Impact of World War II

Now we arrive at the second major event in modern Japanese history that affected the comics world as well as all other parts of Japanese life—World War II. As idealistic militarism and nationalism increased across the country before the outbreak of war, the comics that had originally been a voice of dissension were suppressed by an increasingly tyrannical government. Artists and editors were threatened with a variety of punishments for disobeying the government's idea of what their work should be —patriotic, inspirational, and unifying. The deal was clear: either work for the government, producing comics propaganda for both the home front and the enemy front, or be pressured out of a job, exiled, or even arrested. A few artists simply stopped working during the war, while many others buckled under the pressure and worked for the government's propaganda machine. Still others fled the country to continue their critique from afar or even to produce propaganda comics for the Allies. The result was a devastating halt in the creativity and variety of the comics available in Japan, and the comics industry took a good while to recover from the bitterness of such oppression as leading artists had to come to terms with their decision to either flee or abandon their ideals under pressure (Schodt 1983).

The other undeniable impact on culture and history came with the nuclear bombings of Hiroshima and Nagasaki. Whatever the circumstances behind the use of these weapons against Japan, their detonation still reverberates through every aspect of Japanese culture. Many of the most common themes in manga and anime today can be traced back to the war and the bombs, from the examination of the conflict between man and technology to the threat of apocalypse in many stories. Most notably, of course, are the strong antiwar messages often found in postwar anime and manga—the Japanese experienced the full sweep and consequences of a militaristic society and remain the only country to experience such a devastatingly focused "apocalypse" in modern history (Drazen 2003; Murakami 2005). As they recovered from the war, these moments in history would become the touchstones for the creators about to reinvigorate the manga industry. Most manga and anime creators then and now still prefer to discuss the themes of the war through other stories and other places. Authors avoid directly depicting World War II except in showing innocent civilians caught up in war, as with Nakazawa Keiji's *Barefoot Gen* and Takahata Isao's later anime film *Grave of the Fireflies*.

War could not keep comics down for long, and in postwar Japan, comics started reappearing almost immediately, this time bound as small, red books. These comics were cheap and not always of the caliber the first postwar creators thought necessary to prove the format's worth, but the destruction of the old structure of the comics industry allowed many innovative younger artists to break into the industry and thus reinvigorate the comics scene with ambitious ideas about what the medium could accomplish.

Tezuka Osamu, Grandfather of Japanese Comics

One of these red book artists was Tezuka Osamu, now heralded as the grandfather of Japanese comics. Tezuka and many of his fellow artists who started in the red book comic world would become some of the most influential artists in the manga magazines about to explode on the scene. Tezuka influenced every manga creator that came after him, whether following in his footsteps or reacting against his style, and he single-handedly defined many of the major characteristics of modern manga (Schodt 1983; Gravett 2004).

Cinematic Inspiration

Tezuka believed that the format of comics could be used far more creatively than it had been previously, and the relative freedom of the red book comics allowed him to experiment with technique. Unlike the artists influenced by styles from comics and traditional illustration, Tezuka's major influences were from the cinema. He grew up absorbing motion pictures like a sponge, and he was particularly drawn to the early animated cartoons of the Fleischer brothers—creators of Betty Boop and Popeye the Sailor Man—and of Walt Disney. He was entranced by the drama that editing lent to cinematic storytelling and began to use the panels on his page like the view out of a film camera. He implemented cinematic techniques including pans, zooms, and jump cuts by using the space in between the panels like the break between film frames. His awareness of cinema didn't stop at the visual, however, and he pushed the use of sound effects in comics to lend realism not only to fights but also to everyday sounds, from the rustling of fabric to the dripping of water. The use of cinematic techniques also expanded the stories Tezuka created to hundreds and even thousands of pages, far longer than had previously been attempted and thus started the convention of extended storytelling still prevalent in manga and anime (Schodt 1996).

Stories of Any Kind

Tezuka was convinced that the format could be used to tell every kind of story, from adventure to comedy to serious drama. He began by telling stories that featured long story arcs and in-depth character development, notably paying attention to the passage of time. *Kimba the White Lion*, for example, shows a lion cub growing up and becoming an adult lion rather than remaining a cub for an unnaturally static existence akin to *Fuku-chan*'s eternal little boy or superheroes perpetually stuck in their early thirties. *Astro Boy*, an imaginative science fiction adventure starring a boy robot hero, sparked the action/science fiction genre today known as mecha, complete with questions of the conflict between man and machine and the potential dangers of technology overtaking society's morals and resources. 1953's *Princess Knight* is a road map for trends still prevalent in shōjo manga, featuring a wide-eyed but spunky heroine disguised as a knight to save her kingdom.

On top of that, Tezuka mimicked the artistic style of early Western animators, including the overly large eyes found on Betty Boop and Mickey Mouse. From there, however, he created his own curved, simplistic style that incorporated the traditions from Japan's past, including the dramatic use of space seen in ukiyo-e. The design of manga characters started with Tezuka, though every artist has his own interpretation of manga conventions. His early work, from 1952's *Astro Boy* to 1954's *Jungle Emperor*, known in the United States as *Kimba the White Lion*, show the revolution already in progress in his use of a simple style paired with carefully edited images (Schodt 1983).

Tezuka's cinematic inspirations led him to animation, and in the 1960s, he once again revolutionized a medium. He first adapted his own work, *Astro Boy*, and after its 1963 release, it became one of the most popular television shows in Japan. Each addition to his work in anime cemented his genius as a director and storyteller (Schodt 1996). The serial nature of comics and television shows are part of what has defined both manga and anime in the story arcs and episodic storytelling that dominate both media (Napier 2000).

Manga Grows Up

In the 1950s, as readers grew less inclined to keep reading the more juvenile storylines and began to look for comics that would feed their need for more adult drama, the original venues for many comics, the shōnen magazines, began to lose business. In keeping with Tezuka's belief that manga could tell any story, new comics began to be published as volumes bought through pay library subscriptions. These stories, dubbed *gekiga* or drama pictures, appealed specifically to the young men now too old for shōnen comics. Featuring men as heroes instead of boys, these comics told adult stories, leaving behind the black-and-white view of the world presented in shōnen manga. These comics did not shy away from violence, sex, or crime, and they embraced antiheroes as protagonists. Legendary samurai comic, Koike Kazuo's *Lone Wolf and Cub*, emerged from this market. All of these began what we now know as *seinen* manga, or comics for young men from older teenagers on up, and established that comics were no longer solely for the juvenile market (Schodt 1983)

Manga Anthology Magazines Set the Standard

At this point in manga's history, the market realigned into today's manga market. In 1959, publishing giant Kodansha issued *Shōnen Magazine*, the first magazine devoted solely to comics, and the magazine rapidly grew to a 300-page anthology of stories. As other publishers leapt into the fray, the demand never seemed to wane, and many magazines adopted a weekly format instead of monthly. By contrast, U.S. comics started with sixty-four pages in the 1930s, but by the 1950s the page count had shrunk to thirty-two pages, where it remains today (Gravett 2004). The increase in volume was undoubtedly hard on the artists—they suddenly had four times as much work to do in the same amount of time. The pay library market collapsed with the emergence of the new magazines, and most of those creators working for that market moved into the magazine industry (Schodt 1983).

The Ladies Arrive

Although Tezuka acknowledged the female audience for manga with *Princess Knight* and other ventures, shōjo comics were created by men, and they were not as popular as shōnen comics. As their shōjo sales flagged, the creators realized there was a simple solution—invite women into the profession because women would certainly know what girls and women wanted to read. From this obvious but nonetheless inspired conclusion, a new subgenre of manga began to emerge, and by the 1970s shōjo manga became a force all its own. The new female creators did intuit what female readers wanted and created stories of exciting melodrama, elaborate settings, and costumes with dramatic and often dark psychology (Schodt 1983).

Perhaps more than other manga artists, the first female shōjo creators embraced the idea of manga as escape as they spun tales of a fairy-tale European past vivid with details. They ignored realism and adherence to historical fact in favor of drama, romance, tragedy, and fabulous costumes. Some of the most influential creators are known as the Fabulous 49ers (or, the Fabulous 24 Group, as they were all born in the 24th year of Showa era, or 1949 in Western reckoning). Ikeda Ryoko's *Rose of Versailles* displays many of now the standard conventions of shōjo manga.

Early Established Shōjo Conventions

- a girl dressed as a boy
- lithe and beautiful heroes and heroines nearly indistinguishable in their beauty
- gender-bending romance
- giant and multistarred eyes
- the exuberant use of flowers, feathers, and other objects to divide panels

---

These women did not limit themselves to the traditionally feminine genres of romance and historical epic—Takemiya Keiko's *To Terra* tackled science fiction on a multigenerational scale. The intended audience divides in comics do still exist, reflecting their readers' interests, but many manga break down the barriers and address issues that in the beginning were not considered interesting to one audience or the other (Gravett 2004). Minekura Kazuya's *Saiyuki* combines shōnen action with a bevy of young men designed according to shōjo bishōnen, or beautiful young men, designs. CLAMP's *Tsubasa: RESERVoir CHRoNICLE*, Takahashi Rumiko's *Inuyasha*, and Konomi Takashi's *Prince of Tennis* all appeal to both genders equally.

In the 1970s, shōnen manga regained their former glory and became the dominant seller once again. Still intended for boys, these stories nonetheless became more varied and addressed more serious issues than had ever been attempted in the prewar society. In 1973, Nakazawa Keiji explicitly tackled the nuclear bombings in *Barefoot Gen*, a four-volume series following a young teenage boy, Gen, and his mother who were caught in the bombing of Hiroshima and their struggle to survive in the aftermath. Long considered a classic for its unflinching look at a recent historical event, *Barefoot Gen* is one of the few manga or anime to address directly the war and was originally serialized in *Shōnen Jump* (Schodt 1983; Gravett 2004).

Today's shōjo manga, as seen here in *Tenshi Ja Nai!!*, still uses flowers and shifting gray tones, created with screen tones, to break panels and soften edges.

Journey to the West

By the 1970s, manga and anime both were experiencing countrywide popularity. The hundred- and thousand-page manga magazines that are now common started in this decade, and the public's seemingly unquenchable appetite for manga of all kinds led to the variety of titles and genres represented in separate magazine titles for boys, for girls, and for young women and young men. Manga continued to develop as a format as well. It was in this decade that Tezuka Osamu started his epic biography of *Buddha*. Miyazaki Hayao launched his landmark manga and anime *Nausicaä of the Valley of the Wind*, starting with the manga, then stopping to create the anime feature film, and going back to complete his twelve-year mission of completing the complex and carefully constructed four-volume manga series (Schodt 1996).

Manga and Anime Underground

During this decade, anime and manga also started appearing in the underground of Western culture, often untranslated or translated by fans. Edited and dubbed versions of anime series, most notably the landmark mecha series *Macross* and *Mach Go! Go! Go!*, renamed *Robotech* and *Speed Racer,* respectively, in the United States, made their way onto American television (Amazing Anime 1999). Soon fans were seeking out more of this engaging and different style of storytelling. They were often frustrated by the difficulty in acquiring media, as well as by U.S. distributors who would edit or otherwise drastically alter the manga and anime they released believing the American public would not adapt to the storytelling style (Schodt 1996).

In 1988, the film *Akira* hit like a cultural bomb in U.S. art house movie theaters. *Akira*, an elaborate science fiction drama featuring a post-apocalyptic Tokyo, rival motorcycle gangs, and a mysterious and mutilating government experiment gone awry, marked the first major arrival of anime in the United States. Most who watched it for the first time remember both the extreme violence and the dark vision of the future defined by government control and genetic tinkering. Although much of the story was so mysterious as to confuse many American viewers, the brilliant visual style and weighty issues this "cartoon" addressed was shocking, exhilarating, and left audiences wanting more (Napier 2000). Fans became a more solid subculture and started importing all manner of manga and anime to feed their desire for more of this newly discovered entertainment.

By the 1990s, the American fan culture was substantial, and it became obvious to U.S. companies that there was a business in importing, translating, and distributing both manga and anime. In 1995, another major film hit the U.S., Shirow Masamune's *Ghost in the Shell*, and drew in a new generation of anime fans. This time the film hit more than just the art house filmgoers. Soon films with more mainstream appeal, especially the fantasies of Miyazaki Hayao (*My Neighbor Totoro* and *Princess Mononoke*) and the realistic history in Takahata Isao's *Grave of the Fireflies* proved that the popularity of anime was not a blip on the radar but a growing trend (Napier 2000). The glimpse of animation used to make films that in the United States would be live-action films intrigued many Western viewers and proved that animation, as a medium, could be for adults.

Anime and Television: A Perfect Match

The arrival of anime on television is a big part of what led to the current manga boom. In the early 1980s, a few subtitled anime shows were broadcast via UHF channels, and soon edited and dubbed shows were making regular appearances on television including *Star Blazers* and *Robotech*, actually a combination of three anime series aired with an entirely new English script. When VCRs arrived on the scene, fans had the opportunity to rewatch and share their favorites. A fan network based on watching and fan subtitling, or fansubbing, the recordings began to take shape, and the popular demand for anime began a steady ascent toward the mainstream. At the same time in the comics world, older fans were looking for alternatives to the superhero comics on which the U.S. market still concentrated, and publishers Dark Horse and VIZ brought curious readers classic titles such as *Lone Wolf and Cub*, *Akira*, and *Barefoot Gen* (Schodt 1996). Once a few titles were available, demand grew, and manga publishers stepped up to meet readers' expectations.

Manga was being translated and making its way into specialty stores, but the true manga boom didn't hit until the end of the 1990s. At first, manga was translated only through the arduous and expensive process of being "flipped" so that it read the Western way, left to right, which involved not only flipping the image but translating all of the sound effects and retouching the artwork. Publishers were concerned that their audiences would not be able to make the shift to reading right to left. However, in the late 1990s, U.S. publisher Tokyopop began releasing titles in the traditional Japanese format, and fans adapted to this without difficulty. Tokyopop also began publishing equal quantities of shōjo (girls) and shōnen (boys) manga (Reid 2004).

The Manga Boom

The teens and twenty-somethings of the first decade of the twenty-first century were not intimidated or confused by the leaps they had to make to read manga—reading right to left, the cultural differences, the art style—and soon showed their market power by tearing through title after title. The diversity of genres available attracted previously untapped audiences for comics—most notably the interest of teenage girls, a population still too often ignored by the

U.S. comics industry. Although previous generations certainly appreciated manga, their group force was never quite enough to convince the business side of publishing that manga would be worth the trouble, but by 2000 the market began to outstrip other entertainment media and soon, as with any money-maker, new publishers, translators, and distributors started appearing on the scene.

Book publishers finally dove in, led by Random House's Del Rey's imprint in 2004. New smaller manga companies, including Go Comi, Seven Seas, and Aurora, are building up title lists. Korean manhwa publishers, including Netcomics, Ice Kunion, and Infinity Studios, are now working to bring more and more titles to the United States. Many publishers have also begun tapping the younger generations' desire to create manga themselves by publishing manga-style graphic novels. These titles range from original works as produced by Tokyopop to manga inspired by current hot properties such as Meg Cabot's immensely popular prose novels, which HarperCollins has announced plans to produce (ICv2, March 28, 2006). Similarly, manga series in Japan can derive from or inspire prose novels. U.S. publishers have begun translating manga- and anime-related novels derived from *Fullmetal Alchemist*, *.hack*, *Gravitation*, *Vampire Hunter D*, *Love Hina*, and *Only the Ring Finger Knows*. These novels have proved successful thus far, with a number of titles cracking the top twenty-five graphic novels of 2005 (Griepp 2006a).

The Manga and Anime Market Today

In Japan

The manga industry is not a cult or specialty market—it's a major part of the publishing industry. Manga magazines and their collected book editions account for close to 40 percent of the entire publishing market in terms of volume.

- 38.4% boys' or shōnen magazines
- 37.7% men's or seinen magazines,
- 8.8% shōjo magazines
- 6.7% josei magazines
- 8.4% other audiences, including sports and hobbies, boys' love, pachinko, and gag-driven manga

Shōnen Jump circulates more than 3 million copies a week and the manga magazine industry accounts for over $3 billion, or one-sixth of the entire magazine industry (Gravett 2004).

In terms of bang for your buck, a thirty-two-page comic book in the United States today costs around $3, whereas a four-hundred-page volume of *Shōnen Sunday* costs 220 yen, or around $2. Manga magazines are seen as entirely ephemeral—read to take a break, kill time, chill out, and then easily discarded on the train or into the trash. When a particular story grabs a reader, they will then move on to collecting the tankobon, or bound paperback volumes clocking in at about two hundred pages, and this is the smaller, more permanent edition that Japanese readers keep in their homes (Gravett 2004). This version of manga is what has truly arrived in U.S. bookstores—the kind of volume found on bookshelves in the bookstore rather than as a periodical on a newsstand.

Bang for Your Buck

United States:
Thirty-two-page comic book = $3

Japan:
Four-hundred-page Shōnen Sunday = 200 yen or about $2

In Japan manga can be purchased almost anywhere, in convenience stores as well as bookstores and the common specialty stores that market to particular audiences and tastes. Since about 1990, new establishments called manga cafes are the place to go to read manga—open twenty-four hours, they provide free Internet access and shelf after shelf of manga volumes to read for a small hourly fee compared with the price of purchasing titles. The latest shift of manga being beamed directly to cell phones is already having an impact on the market, as are the cell phone and handheld video games that are rivaling reading manga as a solitary, unobtrusive pastime, but the manga industry is in no danger of disappearing any time soon (Gravett 2004).

Profile of a Manga Artist

Being a manga creator today is an intense and solitary existence. While upward of twenty people may be involved in creating a U.S. comic book, from the artist to writer to inker to colorist to letterer to editor, most manga artists work intimately with their editor and support staff to create the entire work. Manga creators own their creations, or co-own them with their publishers, so manga creators are in control of their own series. In the U.S. comics market, characters are owned by publishers and are kept vibrant by moving series from writer to writer and artist to artist with stories that never reach a true end. Manga creators, on the other hand, rarely feel compelled to continue stories beyond their envisioned end, and the ability to shift through personal interests, target audiences, and genres allows the creators the relative freedom to create when and where they are inspired.

A Day in the Life of a Manga-ka: CLAMP

9:00 AM: Start work

11:00 AM: Brunch

3:00 PM: Break for lunch

6:00 PM: Break for dinner, perhaps a shower

1:00 AM: Bedtime

Repeat every day for three weeks, take a day off, and start over again

CLAMP, of course, is in high demand and must produce upward of 120 finished pages a week (Lehmann 2005).

Manga creators' schedules are exhausting: almost all of their time is and must be devoted to the creation of manga. At Anime Boston 2005, when *Chrono Crusade*'s creator Moriyama Daisuke was asked about his hobbies, his answer was that his favorite thing to do was to take walks. When pressed, he insisted that walking was his primary pastime other than manga creation, and a welcome one that got him outside and moving in a life that is usually sedentary and closed off. Manga art is still done largely by hand, with computer assistance limited to creating buildings and technology, screen tones, backgrounds, or to clean up work (Lehmann 2005).

How Much Manga per Week?

CLAMP (*Tsubasa: RESERVoir CHRoNICLE*): 120 pages

Asamiya Kia (*Nadesico*): 70 pages

Inoue Takehiko (*Slam Dunk*): about 40–50 pages

Sakurazawa Erica (*Between the Sheets*): 40–50 pages

(Lehmann 2005)

In terms of the actual process of production, U.S. artists are left comparatively free of interference once hired for a particular project or series, usually having previously established their talent and style in either other comics series or in the less visible positions of inker or colorist. In manga publishing, editors are inextricably involved in every step of the manga's production, from story ideas to final production. Editors are famous in manga circles for doing everything from providing feedback on storylines to pitching in with background art to cooking for their artists so they can continue working. Given the highly pressurized schedule for production, editors are also the whip-crackers when it comes to meeting deadlines, sometimes sleeping over at their artists' homes to ensure that the pages are finished in time.

The other unsung allies for many manga artists are the teams of assistants who commonly support the credited major artist. Assistants finish inking; draw panel borders, balloons, and sound effects; create the photo-based background images; and apply the numerous black-and-white and grayscale screen tones that create the depth and shading so expertly used in manga in place of color. Being an assistant can be a stepping-stone to becoming a manga artist, but the high demand for an assistant's specialized talents can also keep these artists in the ranks of anonymous helpers (Gravett 2004).

All of these factors explain the volume of production compared with United States artists but also explain the variation and sense of individuality that manga series maintain. Rather than being created by committee, manga series are created by a small group of people often over a period of many years, and thus their creations are a product of a focused and individual imagination.

Profile of the Anime Industry

Once Tezuka began creating animation and established the qualities that have spelled out its success—long storylines, cinematic storytelling—the Japanese demand for more animation never waned. Today television studios produce around fifty anime television series and original video animations (OVA) per year (Napier 2000). Anime has been called Japan's chief export since the 1990s, and anime films account for at least half of movie tickets sold in the country (Amazing Anime 1999). In 1997, *Princess Mononoke* became the top grossing film of all time in Japan, surpassed later only by *Titanic* (Napier 2000).

Major Anime Companies in Japan

The major anime production companies currently producing in Japan include the following:

BONES (*Cowboy Bebop, Scrapped Princess, Fullmetal Alchemist*)

Gainax (*Neon Genesis Evangelion, Kare Kano: His and Her Circumstances*)

GONZO (*Samurai 7, Gankutsuou: The Count of Monte Cristo, Chrono Crusade*)

Madhouse (*Trigun, Ninja Scroll, Tokyo Godfathers*)

Production I.G. (*Ghost in the Shell, Blood the Last Vampire*)

Studio DEEN (*Fruits Basket, GetBackers, Maison Ikkoku*)

Studio Ghibli (*Spirited Away, Baron: The Cat Returns*)

Studio Pierrot (*Bleach, Saiyuki, Ceres: Celestial Legend*)

SUNRISE (*Cowboy Bebop, Planetes, Witch Hunter Robin*)

Toei Animation (*Dragon Ball, Sailor Moon, Yu-Gi-Oh!*)

Japan has more than 430 anime production companies, the bulk of which concentrate on making television series and OVAs. Television production itself usually doesn't bring in a profit, but DVD and media tie-in sales do. In recent years anime companies have started outsourcing anime work to other countries including China and South Korea. Because most animators learn their craft growing up in the industry, though, animation companies are concerned that this trend will eventually halt Japanese creators' progress and expertise in the format.

Anime companies and other media companies often work together to produce individual series or works to fund more complex projects effectively. In creating *Spirited Away*, for example, Studio Ghibli partnered with a publishing house, a television network, and another anime company to produce the final product. In 2001, eight times as many films were produced in Japan than in 1998. In 2003, more than eighty anime television titles aired on television. Animation accounted for around 7% of the film market. In comparison, live action films accounted for 4.6%, and documentaries accounted for 55.6%. In the DVD market, however, anime titles accounted for almost 70% of total sales. Given the growing popularity of anime in overseas markets, more anime are produced with an international market in mind (Japan External Trade Organization 2004).

In the United States

In recent years the graphic novel market in North America has been consistently growing, from $75 million in 2000 to $245 million in 2005. Perhaps more important, that shift has been into the bookstore market—whereas in 2001 bookstores accounted for $32 million of the graphic novel market, in 2005 they accounted for $167 million, almost twice as much as the once-dominant specialty and comic book stores. Manga continues to grow within the market as a whole, with sales increasing by 25 percent over 2005 in bookstores where the bulk of manga are now sold. One question currently posed is whether the manga boom will stop once the market hits its saturation point. No doubt, the rapid growth of the manga market is already slowing after years of exponential growth when it was increasing almost 200 percent per year, and if you measure by volume, the market finally stabilized at the end of 2005. Industry watchers are predicting this lull may be temporary, as new publishers and producers are edging into the market, and 2006 may prove to be the most competitive year yet in terms of new publishers arriving and older publishers maintaining their hold on the market (Griepp 2006a).

From 2000 on, dubbed anime television shows have been shown in the United States for kids, on the WB and other networks, and for adults, on Cartoon Network's successful *Adult Swim* programming block. The importance of anime infiltrating network and cable television cannot be overemphasized, especially relating to teen favorites. Anime films still outsell television series, but five of the top-ten-selling anime titles and four of the top-ten-selling manga of 2005 are anime titles recently aired on the Cartoon Network. In addition, American-produced cartoons have now adopted Japanese style, most successfully in shows such as the *Powerpuff Girls*, *Samurai Jack*, and *Teen Titans Go!* (Griepp 2006b).

The Power of TV

Five of the top-ten-selling anime titles and four of the top-ten-selling manga titles of 2005 were anime titles recently aired on the Cartoon Network, including *Fullmetal Alchemist*, *Ghost in the Shell: Stand Alone Complex*, *Samurai Champloo*, and *Inuyasha*.

Even though Miyazaki Hayao's *Spirited Away* won the 2003 Academy Award for Best Animated Film, the anime business in the United States consists mostly of DVD sales rather than theatrical showings. As with the movie and DVD industry as a whole, DVD sales in terms of units sold show little increase over the course of the year. Competition from a number of other venues, from video on-demand services provided by cable companies to illegal video downloading, continue to have an impact on DVD sales. Furthermore, U.S. anime production companies and distributors are still constrained by high licensing fees and the expense of dubbing, keeping the price of individual DVDs and series relatively high. Progress is being made with companies like Central Park Media and ADV Films providing legal downloads, but it's unclear how these new developments will compare to the success of Apple's iTunes in the music industry (Griepp 2006b). The effect of the combination of high prices and the temptation of illegally available downloads has not been measured quantitatively, so the long-term booms in the anime market is yet to be determined.

Despite the fact that the anime industry is not peaking in the way the manga industry is, a number of TV series, including *Fullmetal Alchemist* and *Samurai Champloo*, sold very well in the DVD market. Movies including *Nausciaä of the Valley of the Wind*, the *Inuyasha* movies, and *Ghost in the Shell: Innocence* sold even better. The increased presence of anime on TV, from the established segments of *Toonami* for kids and *Adult Swim* for teens and adults on the Cartoon Network to ADV Films' Anime Network means that anime is continuing to permeate U.S. pop culture. As anime's influence continues to infiltrate general mass culture, the manga and anime markets are starting to cross over in a way they always have in Japan, leading anime fans to the related manga and vice versa. Add video games to the mix, and you have a powerful synergy across markets, with stories flooding across multiple mediums and gaining audiences from a variety of sources (see more about the connections between the markets in Chapter 3) (Griepp 2006b).

Japanese manga has also paved the way for comics of other origins, including Korean comics or *manhwa* and Chinese comics or *manhua* to begin penetrating the U.S. market. Korean manhwa are often lumped in with Japanese products by fans as the style and storylines are similar. Chinese manhua are produced in color and thus easily recognizable, but aside from a few titles like the adaptations of *Crouching Tiger, Hidden Dragon*, most manhua have not yet made a major impact on the U.S. market or audience.

U.S. creators have started creating manga style comics as well. These titles, dubbed Amerimanga or original English language manga, draw their inspirations from Japanese and other Asian comics. As soon as manga appeared on U.S. comics' creators radar, U.S. artists were influenced by manga's storytelling and art style, but recently more and more artists have consciously mimicked the art, symbols, and language of Japanese manga. Tokyopop's line of original English language manga has made impressive inroads into this market and promises many such titles in the future. The best titles make use of manga conventions while maintaining their own style and voice, but many also seem to adopt the style without using the elements correctly. Selective or inaccurate use of manga's language jars readers used to the original Japanese conventions, but ultimately the combination wins or loses depending on the quality of the story.

Anatomy of a Manga

When purchasing manga and anime, there are a number of considerations to take into account before making your selection: intended audience, appeal, quality, popularity, length of series, and the longevity of the physical volume itself.

Basic Cataloging Information

Manga publishers provide vital information on the back of the title page, or the verso of the title page. Remember, however, that manga's presentation, similar to children's books, may require that the colophon and other publishing information be moved to a page at the end of the book, as with ADV Manga's *Full Metal Panic!* The verso is where to check the English language publishing date, the original publishing date, and the list of creators both on the Japanese side as well as the translators, editors, and designers working on the U.S. side. Volume numbers are also usually listed on the verso and printed on the cover and spine of a manga volume.

Manga Are Serials, Not Monographs!

In terms of cataloging, one of the most common mistakes in cataloging manga is that they are catalogued as monographs. In fact, they are serial products, not individual books. Manga series should be catalogued on one serial bibliographic record, distinguished by volume numbers, rather than individually on separate monograph records. More and more libraries are adjusting to this medium and correctly cataloging titles as serials or serial monographs, but it's important to encourage librarians and cataloguers to follow this method. This approach makes it easier to locate individual volumes, and it prevents slight differences in individual cataloging of volumes causing librarians and patrons to miss volumes while searching.

Intended Audience

When considering a title's age range, it is always useful to check the publishers' ratings, always keeping in mind your own readers' preferences and community standards. Publishers' ratings are usually published on the back cover of a volume, often with a visual symbol and a print listing the intended audience, such as "Teens 13+." Publishers work hard to rate their series consistently, and each has its own definition for what falls into each category (see the Appendix for examples of publishers' rating systems).

In anime, most titles are officially unrated, but many anime companies provide ratings in line with U.S. TV ratings. In considering the audience and appropriateness, however, remember that many titles are still being published in Japan, and U.S. publishers may not realize that content may be forthcoming that would, for example, push a series rated teen into their older teen category. If this happens, publishers will go back and rerate the series, but this won't necessarily help a collector if he or she started with the original volumes. Ratings can be tricky—they are not standardized, and the content and age range ratings will vary from publisher to publisher, so use your judgment and knowledge of your own community.

Example Ratings: Tokyopop

A (All Ages)

Suitable for ages six and up. May contain cartoon violence and potty humor.

Y (Youth, ages 10+)

Suitable for ages ten and up. May contain mild language, fantasy violence, and bullying.

T (Teen, ages 13+)

Suitable for ages thirteen and up. May contain infrequent and mild profanity, mild violence and gore, crude humor, mild sexual language and themes, nondescript nudity, and mild fan service, as well as references to tobacco, alcohol, and illegal drug use.

OT (Older Teen, ages 16+)

Suitable for ages 16 and up. May contain profanity and strong language, moderate violence and gore, moderate sexual themes and sexual violence, nudity, moderate fan service, and alcohol and illegal drug use.

M (Mature, ages 18+)

Suitable for ages eighteen and up. May contain excessive profanity and language, intense violence, excessive gore, explicit sexual language and themes, and explicit fan service.

What Magazine Originally Serialized the Title?

Another way to check a series' intended audience is to check which magazine the series was originally published in, keeping in mind that the Japanese standards for intended audiences differ from ours. However, as a general rule of thumb, if the original magazine title contains the word shōnen, as in *Shōnen Jump* or *Shōnen Sunday*, then the magazine and thus the series is intended for boys and teenage guys from ages eight to sixteen. If the magazine title contains the word "young," as in *Young Sunday* or *Young Champion*, then the magazine is intended for older teens, college-aged men and up, or young men aged sixteen and up. Most manga list the publisher on the verso of the title page, but not the original magazine; however, if you check the title on the *Anime News Network*'s manga encyclopedia online, you can often discover the original publishing information.

Original Magazine Source

To check the original magazine, a generally reliable web resource is the *Anime New Network*'s manga encyclopedia (http://www.animenewsnetwork. com/encyclopedia/manga.php). Look up the title, and often at the very top of the entry will be a notation "serialized in ...," followed by a link to the original magazine. Scanning a magazine's past and current titles will give you a sense of the intended audience and potential content of the manga.

Endnotes and Instructions

Most manga printed today also have a final page, often the flyleaf at the end of the book, which warns unsuspecting English readers that if they have opened to the expected English front page, they are starting at the wrong end of the book. Most of these warning pages feature instructions for the uninitiated on how to read a manga page in the traditional Japanese format. Of equal usefulness are the now standard inclusions of explanatory notes in most manga series. Most publishers include textual notes of some sort, from sections as simple as an index for untranslated sound effects or as complex as historical and cultural notes accompanied by reprints of the annotated panels. Language notes usually include an explanation of honorifics in Japanese names, especially if honorifics are left untranslated, and can also include indexes of sound effects and unique vocabulary or slang used. More complex notes provide comments on translation. Translation is certainly an art, and often translators will give customs or food cultural context, explain a pop culture reference, or explain how they adjusted a joke funny only in Japanese also to be funny in English.

Common sections found in manga books include the following:

- Indexes (sound effects)
- "How to Read This Book" page
- Explanation of honorifics
- Translation notes
- Side stories
- Author's notes
- Previews
- Advertisements

Side Stories

Side stories are often included in series and can run anywhere from a page long to more than forty pages, depending in the intention of the volume. Most often side stories feature tales of the series' characters that don't fit in to the series' timeline and can be presented to add historical context, profile a character, or explain a plot point. Occasionally the side stories get wilder, featuring a fantastical alternate storyline whipped up for the comic effect of imagining favorite characters in completely different roles and settings or allowing an author to let go completely and make fun of his or her own manga, mocking conventions and characters with gleeful abandon.

Author's Notes

Akin to these side stories, creators frequently include notes in manga. Depending on the original format of the manga's presentation, author's notes may appear in their own column down the side of one page, or they may appear in comic form at the end of each volume. Almost all author's notes begin with thanking the readers for choosing to read their manga, and from there the author may talk about anything, from research for the manga to tales of studio work to completely unrelated subjects such as their new pets or culinary likes and dislikes.

Within the story itself, side comments written in tiny letters may appear around the edges of panels or within a sequence, almost like a footnote. These notes are most often a humorous aside or comment on the character's behavior or the artist's own dissatisfaction with the final drawing. In *Descendants of Darkness*, for example, when the characters progress toward intimate clinches, the manga creator will often write along the edge of a scene an exclamation, "You can't do that! This is a shōjo manga! Youngsters might be reading this!" Of course, the characters rarely enter into explicit romance, as would make sense with the intended audience, but the feeling that the creator cannot necessarily control her character's impulses adds a level of distance and humor that lightens the whole mood of the manga. These chatty and often entertaining notes are part of the fun of reading manga and occasionally provide intriguing snippets of background about the story as well as the creator's inspirations and intentions with the series.

Context for a Title

It is always important for a manga or anime series to be placed in context. Are there related series in other media? Does it have sequels, or spin-offs? Publisher's websites can be helpful in providing certain information, but can be limited by the fact that while they may publish the beginning of one series, another publisher may have snapped up rights to the sequel or related series. Currently the most informative place to trace the connections of a manga to other manga series or to other media is the *Anime News Network*'s encyclopedias for manga and anime titles. Not only does this resource list the origins of the manga in terms of what magazine it was originally serialized in, it also lists at a glance the related anime and manga series in order of their place within the series timeline, clearly indicating adaptations, sequels, and prequels. For example, the entry for the *Rurouni Kenshin* manga series lists the adaptation of the *Rurouni Kenshin* television series, the three *Samurai X* OVAs (two sequels and one prequel), and a spin-off manga series following a side character currently printed only in Japan. These entries also show the number of volumes released in Japan, usually a reasonable indicator of how many volumes will be released in the United States, even if the series is not complete.

Author Takeuchi Mick's notes for *Her Majesty's Dog* present short snippets of her process as a manga creator.

Standard Format and Shelving

The standard manga format aids collectors in both labeling and shelving. Most manga series have a consistent style of cover per series, allowing for easy recognition of different series by spine color and layout. Manga are generally printed in a standard size of 4.5 × 7.5 inches, and the size makes it very easy to shelve them together as well as fit them in most shelving designed for paperbacks. Consider how to shelve your manga in relation to your other graphic novels. Many libraries do not separate the collections into two sections, one for manga, one for non-manga—and for good reason: manga readers may find titles they might enjoy in the Western style, and Western comics readers may discover manga titles they might not have considered without the side-by-side shelf arrangement.

In my own public library's collection, we have separated manga from the Western graphic novels simply because of size and space. Intermingling the manga with the much larger and thinner Western graphic novels led to messy shelves and tilted volumes, and because we happened to have a paperback spinning rack available right next to our regular graphic novel shelving, we moved the manga over to that separate but near and visible location. All of our graphic novels circulate almost immediately, so we rarely have to worry about overcrowded shelves, although in the future, more shelving may be necessary to accommodate the multivolume nature of all series.

In the end, manga readers will find manga wherever you shelve it, but making it visible and advertising it well can and will draw in a larger readership. Once I had a teen bemoan the fact that there was no rent-by-mail service, a recent shift for DVD rentals, for manga, so that she didn't have to buy so much manga and could pass her manga on to another fan when she was done with it. I agreed, considered the problem, and then realized that libraries could be just that. We may never meet the demand as promptly—networks and libraries can only afford so many copies of every manga series—but as a goal, modeling manga library service on rental-by-mail services may well help us reach out to our teens and establish lasting ties with them as library users.

References

"Amazing Anime: Princess Mononoke and Other Wildly Imaginative Films Prove that Japanese Animation Is More Than Just *Pokémon*." *Time* 154, no. 21 (1999): 94.

Drazen, Patrick. *Anime Explosion: The What? Why? & Wow! of Japanese Animation*. Berkeley, CA: Stone Bridge Press, 2003.

Eisner, Will. *Comics and Sequential Art*. Tamarac, FL: Poorhouse Press, 1994.

Gravett, Paul. *Manga: Sixty Years of Japanese Comics*. London: Laurence King, 2004.

Griepp, Milton, ed. *ICv2 Retailers Guide to Graphic Novels* 7 (2006a).

———. *ICv2 Retailers Guide to Anime and Manga* 13 (2006b).

———. "Tokyopop Signs Alliance with HarperCollins for Co-Publishing and Distribution." http://www.icv2.com/articles/news/8430.html March 28, 2006 (accessed April 28, 2006).

Japan External Trade Organization. "Japanese Animation Goes Global." http://www.jetro.go.jp/en/market/trend/topic/2004_07_anime.html (accessed April 28, 2006).

Lehmann, Timothy. *Manga: Masters of the Art*. Scranton, PA: Collins Design, 2005.

McCloud, Scott. *Understanding Comics: The Invisible Art*. Northampton, MA: Kitchen Sink Press, 1993.

Murakami, Takashi, ed. *Little Boy: The Arts of Japan's Exploding Subculture*. New Haven, CT: Yale University Press, 2005.

Napier, Susan J. *Anime from Akira to Princess Mononoke: Experiencing Contemporary Japanese Animation*. New York: Palgrave, 2000.

Reid, Calvin. "Manga Sells Anime—and Vice Versa." *Publishers Weekly* 251, no. 42 (October 2004): 30. http://www.publishersweekly.com/article/CA472167.html (accessed April 18, 2007).

Schodt, Frederik L. *Manga! Manga! The World of Japanese Comics*. Tokyo: Kodansha International, 1983.

———. *Dreamland Japan: Writings on Modern Manga*. Berkeley, CA: Stone Bridge Press, 1996.

Chapter Two

Manga and Anime Vocabulary

One of the most obvious features of manga but also one of the most off-putting for new readers is the distinct style and symbolism that all manga and anime artists rely on to telegraph meaning to their readers and viewers. As readers from outside the culture, most of us did not grow up learning the traditions and signals of comic art in Japan, so we are left adrift in a sea of implied meaning. This chapter seeks to clarify some of the basic vocabulary and visual cues of manga and anime.

Read Manga! And Then Read More

Of course, one of the best ways to learn this information is simply to read manga. New readers should be encouraged to press on and take what they can from context and storyline. The more you read, the more you see the connections and understand the methods of storytelling that make manga so appealing. Once you've become accustomed to the rhythm and style of manga, you can then move on to researching the details. Casual fans and official experts alike find part of the fun of reading manga is in deciphering these foreign symbols, traditions, and meanings.

Remember that manga is meant to be read at great speed, so much of what might be described in a book or detailed in a Western comic's artist's rendering will be absent. Instead, manga creators rely on an established set of symbols, sound effects, and stylistic changes in art to give the reader the necessary information or background for the scene. For readers accustomed to either the rich description of novels or the more detailed work in Western comics, the apparent lack of detail may make the story seem incomplete. Manga relies on certain visual cues, especially to convey emotions. Once a reader learns those cues, manga begins to work on multiple levels.

Character Design Is Their Personality

In the world of manga, a character's clothing, hair, and appearance say as much about him or her as the text. For example, a handsome young man with wide eyes, thick eyebrows, an easy smile, and a spiky hairdo is recognizable as the hero of many shōnen (boys') manga. His enemy is usually older, leaner, dressed in a more elaborate way, wears jewelry, and has narrow eyes fixed in a menacing glare. These are stereotypes, and characters may and do break the visual mold, but these clues are strong indicators of a character's nature. In modern stories, photorealistic background images are also often used, and the reader is expected to recognize a building and understand where the scene is set. When the background drops away or a character suddenly changes into an exaggerated version of their usual appearance, the images of the story are changing in ways that are vital to understanding the progression of characters and plot.

Emotion Is the Key

Because everything happens on a melodramatic scale in manga, every aspect of the art is used to heighten the drama. For example, in a fight scene, the background dissolves away into action lines showing both the character's momentum and intense concentration. In comedy, wildly exaggerated reactions, motions, and changes in appearance are all part of the laughs; they give manga the manic quality that some readers find difficult to accept. In drama, the pacing most often sets the tone, allowing for long silences within the story to extend the tension and accentuate the inner struggle of the characters. All of these techniques are used to highlight the story's emotional life, and although Western comics use similar tactics, they have never been as consistent or inherent a part of the medium as in Japan.

Basic Vocabulary

Before you read on, familiarize yourself with these common terms used both throughout this book and within discussions of manga and anime. Further vocabulary can be found in Appendix A at the back of this guide.

Vocabulary List

Anime—Anime refers to the animated films produced in Japan for a Japanese audience. The word itself comes from the word *animeshon*, a translation of the English word "animation." This term encompasses all animated titles including feature films, television shows, and original video animation (OVA) released to the home entertainment market.

Chibi, **or super-deformed (SD)**—The exaggerated and simplified form characters take on in a heightened emotional state. From the noun *chibi*, which is a slang term referring to a short person or child (similar to the English runt).

Dōjinshi—Comics produced by fans outside of the traditional publishing industry.

Fan service—The tradition of including content that appeals to fans rather than advancing the plot or developing characters. Examples include pin-up poses and outfits or, in science fiction tales, extensive shots of spaceships and machinery.

Manga—Print comics in Japan. The word simply translates as comics, and covers all printed matter from three-hundred-page magazines printed weekly and monthly to the *tankobon*, or bound volumes, available at newsstands, manga stores, and bookstores.

Manga-ka—The title given to all manga creators.

Otaku—In the past, this term referred to a very formal address for "you," similar to the French *vous* or German *sie*. At this point in Japan, the term means an obsessive fan or geek and has a negative spin. In the United States, this term has been adopted and reclaimed by anime and manga fans without the negative connotation and is frequently used for self-identification with pride.

OVA—Acronym for original video animation, or those anime released in the home video market rather than via television or as films. OVAs are often, but not always, titles that are not expected to have the popular acceptance and demand that produce feature films or television shows and may feature the more risqué and cult genres and stories.

Shōjo—Literally, girl(s). This term distinguishes the audience for girls', or shōjo, manga. Shōjo manga is usually defined by a concentration on emotion and relationships. As with the counterpoint shōnen manga, shōjo manga has its own set of character types, conventions, and typical genres, ranging from romance to science fiction.

Shōnen—Literally, boy(s). This term distinguishes the audience for boys', or shōnen, manga. Shōnen manga is often distinguished by storylines that concentrate on action, humor, honor, and social obligation.

Tankobon—The bound collections of manga originally serialized in magazine form. Essentially the same as the trade paperbacks or graphic novels collected from U.S. comics originally printed in comic book form.

Intended Audiences

In the United States since the creation of the Comics Code in 1954, most comics have been aimed at a younger, male audience. Superhero comics have always appealed to boys, and although the industry has grown up and diversified over the past half-century, the prominence of the superhero genre, as well as the simple fact that men still dominate the industry as creators, editors, executives, and readers, means that most stories still appeal primarily to adult men or teenage boys. This is by no means always true, but it is the nature of the industry at large in the United States. There are few titles aimed at girls or women and even fewer titles for children.

Part of the reason manga is now growing in popularity among teenagers and adults is that it has titles that appeal to both genders, and its much touted appeal to girls is not exaggerated (ICv2, April 4, 2006).

How to Tell Whether You're Reading a Shōnen Manga or a Shōjo Manga

Wondering what kind of manga you're reading? The hard and fast rule, both a joke and the truth, is as follows:

- If there are buxom girls, men with heavy eyebrows, panty jokes, and lots of slapstick, then you're reading a shōnen manga.

- If there are lots of slender, beautiful people of both genders, bursts of flowers, and parades of fashion, then you're reading a shōjo manga.

One thing that distinguishes Japan's comic industry is that it has developed different genres for distinct audiences. Whereas comics in the United States are not specifically aimed at boys or girls, men or women, Japan divides its manga into categories defined by gender as well as age. Different ages and genders may enjoy any genre, but a general rule of thumb is that manga for the female population emphasizes emotion and relationships whereas manga for men emphasizes action and humor.

It's a Format, Not a Genre

Remember when considering any format, including graphic novels and animation, that they are formats, not genres, and can be used to tell any story. Any genre may appear in the comic format.

In the United States, manga is not necessarily advertised as intended for one gender or another. VIZ Media is the one current manga publisher distinguishing its titles by gender with the *Shōnen Jump* line for boys and the *Shōjo Beat* line for girls. Most other publishers do not indicate up front the gender of the intended audience, although readers can usually tell from the style of art, the main characters, and other external signals. Most publishers do give a genre description on the back of their titles or within the imprint, such as VIZ's action line or Tokyopop's genre listings of romance, drama, or sports along with age ratings designed to signal the target audience in terms of content.

Kodomo Manga

Kodomo manga are titles created for children, especially for new readers under ten years of age. At this point, no kodomo manga have been translated, but noted titles include *Doraemon* and *Hamtaro*.

Shōnen Manga—Boys' Comics

Shōnen manga traditionally indicates titles aimed at boys and young men, aged from twelve to eighteen years. Shōnen also refers to typical story conventions including a concentration on action, battles and fighting, humor, honor, heroism, and family or group obligations. The common genres within this category include historical drama, fantasy, mysteries, and space adventures. *Mecha*, or "boy and his robot" stories, are often shōnen manga as are many samurai epics, adventure stories, and sports sagas. Shōnen titles are exemplified by those titles that appear in VIZ's *Shōnen Jump* magazine.

Shōnen Manga Checklist

If a manga contains three or more of the following, then it's likely a shōnen manga:

- Teen guys dealing with teen concerns
- Action/sports sequences
- Slapstick humor
- Protagonist traits include heavy eyebrows, a "never-say-die" attitude, and a rakish grin
- Themes of honor, heroism, determination, and teamwork
- Female characters with hourglass figures, skimpy outfits, and a lot of jiggle, otherwise known as fan service

---

As shōnen readers grow up, titles will contain increasingly mature content. Shōnen starts with stories such as *Shaman King*, a gung-ho adventure story for older elementary school boys. Middle school titles include *Hikaru no Go* and *Yu Gi Oh!* Older titles show a less black-and-white view of the world, starting with the darker morality tales such as *Death Note* and *Fullmetal Alchemist*. Stories intended for older male teens are being labeled by the publisher VIZ as *Shōnen Jump Advanced*, indicating more complex, ambiguous stories as well as the potential for more explicit violence and sensuality. *Shōnen Jump*'s regular titles, including *Naruto*, *Rurouni Kenshin*, *Bleach*, *Tenchi Muyo*, and *Inuyasha*, all display the traditional shōnen traits and involve everything from ninjas, samurai, demons, ghosts, and historical drama, to mythology and, of course, plenty of action. Slapstick humor is common even in essentially dramatic titles. These stories are akin to the hero's quest found all over the Western canon, from E. B. White's *The Once and Future King* to J. K. Rowling's *Harry Potter* series. Shōnen titles appear from every publisher, including the thief adventure comedy *Jing King of Bandits*, magical adventure *Elemental Gelade*, romantic comedy *Oh My Goddess!*, and slapstick military high school spoof *Full Metal Panic! Negima*, *Air Gear*, and *Pastel* contain all the action and humor of shōnen titles but, like the *Shōnen Jump Advanced* line, contain content aimed at older readers.

On the other hand, the line between shōnen and shōjo manga (girl's comics) blurs a bit in titles like Takahashi Rumiko's *Maison Ikkoku* and *Inuyasha*, titles featuring male leads that are also about relationships and romance. If a reader tells you a story is "too shōnen," they usually mean there's too much action and too little character development.

Shōnen Grows Up

Grades 3–5
> *Beyblade*
> *Shaman King*
> *Beet the Vandel Buster*

Grades 6–9
> *Yu Gi Oh!*
> *+ANIMA*
> *Hikaru no Go*
> *Dragon Ball Z*

Grades 10–12
> *Death Note*
> *Bleach*
> *Air Gear*
> *Great Teacher Onizuka* (GTO)

Crossover Titles

Shōnen to Shōjo
  Angelic Layer
  Inuyasha
  Prince of Tennis
  Rurouni Kenshin
  Saiyuki
Shōjo to Shōnen
  D.N.Angel
  Fushigi Yugi
  Here Is Greenwood
  Tsubasa: RESERVoir CHRoNICLE

Seinen Manga—Men's Comics

Seinen Manga Checklist

If a manga contains three or more of the following, then it's likely a seinen manga:

- Action/combat sequences

- Adult characters dealing with adult concerns

- Hero traits include heavy eyebrows, a stoic attitude, and a murky past

- Themes of honor, heroism, sacrifice, and obligation

- Female characters with hourglass figures and a lot of jiggle, more likely to be nude at some point

- Sensual or sexual content

- Explicit violence

Seinen manga is the older equivalent of shōnen manga. Seinen manga is more mature both in visual content and in addressing topics of interest to adult men, including tales of married life, work life, sex comedies, and morally ambiguous war and crime stores. Seinen titles are for young men out of their teens, going into college, and beyond. These titles started appearing in the late 1960s as *gekiga* manga, or dramatic manga, and continue to focus on stories of action, honor, outsiders, and violence (Gravett 2004). Common genres include action, mystery, suspense, and historical drama. These stories often revolve around icons of masculinity including samurai, *yakuza* (Japanese organized crime syndicates), assassins, spies, and snipers. Seinen manga also include many of the humorous and raunchy manga aimed at businessmen from office comedies to manga focused entirely on pachinko, a kind of upright pinball game that is the stress reliever of choice for many businessmen. Seinen manga titles include the landmark *Golgo 13*, *Lupin III*, *Akira*, and the epic samurai classic *Lone Wolf and Cub*. Given the age range at which these titles are aimed, they are more likely to include sexual and violent content on par with an R-rated film.

Recommended Seinen Titles

Lone Wolf and Cub by Kazuo Koike
Akira by Otomo Katsuhiro
Ghost in the Shell by Shirow Masamune
Saikano by Takahashi Shin
Please see annotations in Chapter Three.

Shōjo Manga—Girls' Comics

Shōjo Manga Checklist

If a manga contains three or more of the following, then it's likely a shōjo manga:

- Teen girls dealing with teen concerns

- Lithe, beautiful young men (a.k.a. *bishōnen*)

- Focus on relationships, especially romantic

- Heroine traits include kindness, determination, empathy, and a girl-next-door beauty

- Elaborate and detailed outfits

Representing the other half of the population, shōjo manga features titles aimed at girls and young women from aged twelve through eighteen. Shōjo's conventions include a concentration on relationships (often leading to melodrama), romance, honor, family or group obligations, peer pressure, and heroism. Shōjo genres are as diverse as shōnen genres, ranging from science fiction, to historical drama, to sports stories, to fantasy adventures. Heroes' quests are equally as prevalent in shōjo manga as in shōnen, leading to the running joke about how all shōjo manga is about how "big eyes save the world." Shōjo manga also covers the full range of ages, starting with titles appropriate for older elementary school girls and ending with titles for older high school girls.

As with shōnen manga, shōjo manga can defy expectations and be hard science fiction or brutal action drama. What defines these titles as shōjo is the primacy of relationships, including romantic entanglements, and the focus is on family and friends. Typical shōjo titles include *Mars*, *Fruits Basket*, *Nana*, and *Kare Kano*. As with shōnen manga, there are titles that challenge the conventions. For example, the violent action woven throughout *X/1999* and *Clover* and the heroine who refuses to fall in line with beauty and behavior standards in *The Wallflower* flout standard shōjo content and messages. "Too shōjo" for readers means there's too much relationship mush and not enough plot or action in the story for the reader.

Shōjo Grows Up

Grades 3–5
> *Yotsuba&!*
> *Cardcaptor Sakura*
> *Ultra Maniac*

Grades 6–8
> *Fruits Basket*
> *Land of the Blindfolded*
> *D.N.Angel*

Grades 9–12
> *Ceres: Celestial Legend*
> *Hana-Kimi*
> *Her Majesty's Dog*

Josei Manga—Women's Comics

Josei Manga Checklist

If a manga contains three or more of the following, then it's likely a josei manga:

- Adult women dealing with adult concerns
- Sexy, attractive men (a.k.a. *biseinen*) with a bit more bulk than typical *bishōnen*
- Focus on relationships, especially romantic and sexual
- Heroine traits include growing confidence, independence, sensuality, and restlessness
- Explicit sensual or sexual content

Josei comics are the grown up versions of shōjo manga, for young women entering their twenties and beyond. They also concentrate on relationships but are often less fantastical and more matter of fact than their shōjo counterparts; and they can be brutally honest about romance and sex. Common genres for this age range include the typical shōjo genres of romance, fantasy, science fiction, and historical drama plus topics of interest to adult women including company and office work, single and married life, and family sagas including that particular nemesis of many housewives, an overbearing mother-in-law. These slice-of-life titles are no less explicit than seinen titles, and female *manga-ka* are noted for exploring darker and more exotic sexual territory than their male counterparts. Fewer *josei* works have been translated into English, but Sakurazawa Erica's titles, such as *Between the Sheets* and *Angel*, provide excellent examples of the type. Most dōjinshi and *yaoi* titles would be either josei or *ero*, depending on how explicit they get.

Recommended Josei Titles

Nodane Cantabile
Nana
Tramps Like Us
Our Everlasting (BL/yaoi)

Dōjinshi—Fan Comics

Dōjinshi, or fan comics, are a huge industry in Japan. A lot of dōjinshi operate like fan fiction authors in the United States—they fill in, continue, or reimagine stories, relationships, and adventures fans wish had happened in a published manga. Japanese copyright law allows anyone to write or draw a story based on a published work with no threat that the original creator will lose his or her copyright. Because of this setup, dōjinshi comics are prevalent and quite a lot of fun. Published manga creators are known to create dōjinshi for their own work, featuring a scene edited out of the original or too raunchy for the publishers or intended audience. At this time, the bulk of dōjinshi comics are created by women for other women, and much of it is *yaoi*, or romances between two male leads with different levels of explicitness (Thorn 2004). Male fans are beginning to partake in fandom in the same way by creating *shōjo-ai* and *yuri*, or romances between two female characters, although they are still in the minority. A growing trend in current dōjinshi are the more disturbing *moe* or *loli-con* dōjinshi, or stories featuring sensual or sexual situations starring prepubescent girls. Dōjinshi manga, like fan fiction, has led to all manner of fascinating studies and conclusions about fandom, gender, and sexuality, but because most are not readily available in the United States, no dōjinshi titles are discussed in this book. The community is large and enthusiastic, however, and is definitely mirrored by the U.S. teen fan fiction/fan art communities. Matt Thorn has written a number of articles on the dōjinshi market, found at his Web site (http://www.matt-thorn.com), while Patrick Macias talks about dōjinshi fandom extensively in his fan guide to Tokyo, *Cruising the Anime City*. In *Dreamland Japan*, Fredrik Schodt tells of his first time attending Comiket, the largest dōjinshi fan convention.

American Dōjinshi?

Tokyopop's brand new Web site (http://www.tokyopop.com) now contains a section entirely for budding manga artists to post their own manga-style comics. A quick search on the Internet for online manga opens up a world of original manga-style comics by U.S. artists and those from other countries. Fan art is where most of the dōjinshi-esque comics created stateside can be seen—check out *Deviant Art* (http://www.deviantart.com/) for an extensive series of collections divided by series titles and characters.

Underground or Experimental Comics

Specialist publishers outside of dōjinshi create manga and anime that would be considered underground or independent comics in the United States. These manga titles do not follow the popular and regimented rules of the booming mainstream manga industry. Here is where manga artists explore matters outside the mainstream, ranging from surreal autobiographies to erotic manga for every taste. The bulk of these titles have not been translated into English, but as the manga boom continues, readers can hope to see more arriving in translation than the mainstream titles. One title that is closer to our own literary comics that has recently been published in the United States is Tatsumi Yoshihiro's *The Push Man and Other Stories*, a collection of melancholy, troubling, and introspective short stories of men coping with joyless urban lives.

Ero or Hentai—"Perverted" or Pornographic Comics

In keeping with the general Japanese lack of shame about sex and sexuality as entertainment, ero or hentai comics are as common in Japan as magazines such as *Playboy* and *Hustler* are in the United States. They are fantasies intended for adults, not children or teens, although unfortunately their existence has led to misunderstandings about what manga and anime contain. We in the United States have our share of pornography, including cartoon pornography, but it is not nearly as visible or accepted a part of life as similar works are in Japan. Those who consume pornography or erotica here usually partake in it as a relatively clandestine interest and keep it strictly in the private realm. In Japan, it is part of being an adult, especially an adult man, and sexual content and humor can be found everywhere from daily newspapers to adult manga (Schodt 1983). Within this book, no specific hentai or ero manga are discussed but such titles do exist and are a vibrant part of the manga world. Paul Gravett's book *Manga: Sixty Years of Japanese Manga* explains the history and current world of ero and hentai manga, and Frederik Schodt's older but still informative *Manga! Manga! The World of Japanese Comics* also speculates on the origins and nature of ero and hentai.

Do the Gender Divisions Hold Up Here?

With all of these divisions, you may wonder if these gender and age demarcations apply to U.S. and Western audiences. Many people may disagree with or even be distressed by the idea of gendering comics because it is based on generalizations and stereotypes of both genders. In some ways, Japanese age ranges may not fit U.S. standards. The nudity or sexual humor and slapstick the Japanese consider appropriate for younger readers would be considered vulgar or risqué here. In Japan, such incidents are considered part of human nature, not to be ashamed of, and often provide ripe targets for jokes (discussed more in Chapter Three's Humor section).

In reading comics originally intended for boys or girls, adults may be unnerved or shocked by the content included. Publishers try to rate series appropriately by Western standards and generally succeed. Because of the broad age ranges used and the fact that a reader in urban San Francisco and a reader in a small town in Maine may have very different ideas of appropriateness, be aware that manga can be as varied as any book or film. Manga and anime should be judged according to the age standards applied to book and video collections, although U.S. age guidelines may not always be in sync with the original intended audiences in Japan. For example, the age of majority across most of Japan is sixteen, leading to heroes and heroines who would be considered minors in the United States taking on adult responsibilities and pastimes. Middle school starts at age twelve, whereas high school starts at fifteen, leading to fifteen year-old freshmen.

As to the gender assignments, anecdotally these stereotypes do hold up more often than not. Girls and young women in the West are drawn to the shōjo manga intended for young women, and boys and young men gravitate toward shōnen manga. Some series were specifically created to appeal across gender lines, as with Minekura Kazuya's *Saiyuki*, a raucous action adventure series aimed at older teen boys that features a group of heroes on a quest. The difference is in the character design—instead of simply following usual shōnen character traits, the artist decided to make the four main characters into bishōnen, or the beautiful young men so often admired in shōjo comics, and now *Saiyuki* has a notable female following who openly admit to following the series for the hot guys.

In my own discussions with a variety of teens at manga clubs and workshops, most U.S. teens are dubious about the strict demarcations of gendered audiences. Most of them insist that they don't care what gender assignment a title is given—they'll read it if it seems like a good story. If you look at what they read, however, the gender divisions are visible. Boys do not tend to read the classic shōjo manga genres including romances, school dramas, and fantasies. Girls are more likely to read titles from the shōnen side as well as the shōjo manga they enjoy, but they will draw the line at whatever offends them most: a lack of relationships or the overabundance of scantily clad women.

Gender Crossover

It is widely acknowledged in Japan and in the United States that there are many crossover readers who flit from series to series without paying attention to its intended audience. In Japan, middle-aged businessmen sheepishly admit that they enjoy reading shōjo titles and teenage girls follow shōnen titles as faithfully as the boys (Gravett 2004). In the United States, the same is true. Because most publishers do not make a special attempt to identify titles for one audience or the other, readers may not know a title's category unless it fits the stereotype.

The category with the fewest crossover readers is romance manga. Romance, as in the United States, is a genre aimed at women, and although there are titles that are essentially romantic titles for boys or young men (Takahashi Rumiko's *Maison Ikkoku* being a prime example), shōnen romance titles are few and far between. From my own observations, I have found that teen male readers do not tend to read the melodramatic romances intended for girls, such as *Mars* or *Peach Girl*, while middle school and high school girls devour them.

There has been a lot of attention paid in recent media to the fact that girls read manga, as evidenced by the *New York Times Book Review*'s article "Manga for Girls" by Sarah Glazer, *Time Magazine*'s "Drawing in the Girls" by Andrew Arnold, and *Cosmo Girl*'s decision to acquire a manga-style comic strip for monthly publication. For a U.S. audience accustomed to the stereotype of boys and men reading comics while girls read prose, this is indeed news. It is also true that many girls read manga who otherwise would not read comics at all; those who do read manga find little appealing in U.S. comics, a trend noted by Tokyopop editor Lillian Diaz-Przybyl (Diaz-Przybyl 2006) and backed up by teen girl responses to an online survey conducted on my own Web site. When asked why they preferred Japanese manga to Western comics, the most common answers were the art, the complex plots, the characters, the consistency of creative teams, and the "realistic" stories. A few even made uncharitable digs at U.S. comics, reporting that they liked manga because "it's cooler than American comics," and "they know how to draw" (No Flying, No Tights 2006). This is a trend that should be acknowledged by U.S. publishers. Girls read manga because, quite simply, they tell the stories girls want to read: stories that emphasize emotion and character development. The major comics that people recognize, like Batman and Spiderman, do have women writers and strong female characters, but even when well written, the women are drawn to be pinups for the male audience. Female fans end up reading U.S. comics despite the fact the nagging awareness that they are not the intended audience.

Character Design

People unfamiliar with manga and anime often note the most obvious differences between Japanese and Western character design—the giant, glistening doe eyes, the exaggerated body shapes, the elaborate hairstyles, and the imaginative and physics-defying outfits. What they may not know is that these physical details are not just a style. In a world where a character's emotional life is key, their nature is made manifest in their appearance.

U.S. comics have their own visual signals that work almost subliminally on the public. A hero is classically identified as having broad shoulders, a muscled torso, a square jaw, and a stoic mien. A weak character will have little or no chin, whereas a snobbish or scheming character often has heavily lidded eyes. Just imagine if a creator tried to cast a sidekick or comic relief character, like Le Fou from Disney's *Beauty and the Beast* or Edna "E" Mode from *The Incredibles*, as the romantic or action hero. These signals are so ingrained in our visual culture that we barely notice them. Likewise, Japanese manga have their own set of symbols that Japanese readers are deeply familiar with, but we are at a loss to notice or identify without help.

Visual Character Traits in Manga

There is some truth to the comment that manga characters are told apart mostly by their hairstyles and clothing. Most manga characters are drawn with an economy of line—compared with the dense style of traditional superhero comics, manga characters are almost empty of detail. Part of this simplicity arises from expediency—if the artists need to turn out thirty pages a week, they have to be able to draw and finish their art quickly. In terms of skill, this simplicity can be deceptive. The fewer lines an artist works with, the more the placement of each line makes a difference in the finished drawing, requiring an expert sense of space and line within each drawing. Shift a line too far in one direction and a character may suddenly look ten years older, or even change into another character. A certain type of jawline, the length of the face, and the size of the eyes define a character's age. Individual characters are signaled by hairstyles that vary strand-by-strand, customary clothing choice, and accessories.

Blood Type

Another character indicator in manga that is often included as part of a character description or even discussed in conversation is blood type. In Japan, blood type is similar to one's astrological sign in the United States. It denotes personality and likely strengths and weaknesses, and it is used to predict compatibility with other people. Everyone knows their blood type, and characters follow the predicted traits (Poitras 1999). Here is a brief overview of blood-type traits (Nomi 1983):

Type A: A team player, industrious, trustworthy, needs leadership, can be inflexible

Type B: Independent, creative, honest, emotional, can be irresponsible

Type O: Ambitious, a planner, romantic, focused on status, can be superficial

Type AB: Diplomatic, organized, sensible, moral, can be unforgiving

---

In Japanese storytelling and culture, emotion is the key to all stories, and the eyes are the most important way to determine any character's emotional state. The Japanese consider themselves a "wet" (or emotional) culture compared to the dry (cerebral) Western point of view. They value emotion and all of the signals thereof, including tears and sweat, as most important to understanding any story. Our stories, by comparison, are more distant and conservative in their handling of emotion and thus dry (Schodt 1983; Poitras 1999). Manga and anime characters tear up, blush, and generally burst with emotion far more dramatically than Western comics characters—no clenched jaw will suffice in Japanese manga.

Eyes

Eyes are the most obvious feature in any character, and for good reason. The giant eyes so common in manga and anime originated in Western cartoons, including Betty Boop and Mickey Mouse, so Americans have plenty of experience with suspending disbelief to accept and identify with an unnaturally wide-eyed character.

It's All in the Eyes

Large, round eyes = innocence, purity, and youth

Medium, oval eyes = still a good guy, but with a shady past

Narrow, squinty eyes = evil, sadistic, and vicious

Large irises = hero or heroine

Small irises or no irises = the bad guys

The larger and more star-filled the eyes, the more innocent and pure the character. Traditionally, women and girls have larger eyes than their male counterparts, indicating their traditional role as the purer sex, although young male heroes often have eyes that are almost as large. These large eyes show their internal goodness and purity of spirit. Villains of either gender, on the other hand, almost always have extremely wide but squinty eyes with much smaller irises. If a reader encounters a character with relatively narrow eyes, including a hero, this usually indicates a certain level of amorality. These characters have elements of both good and bad traits and may well end up the protagonist of the story, but they always have a dark or damaged past (Poitras 1999).

The action manga *GetBackers*, follows this code scrupulously. The two protagonists, Ban and Ginji, specialize in retrieving any lost item for a price. Ginji, the more naïve and exuberant of the pair, has the wide eyes of a traditional hero. Ban, though still a hero, hides a darker, more brutal past, and his eyes accordingly are medium sized, wide enough to call him a hero but squinted enough to indicate his checkered past. The main villain of the series, Dr. Jackal, fits the classic villain profile: sadistic, melodramatic, and icily beautiful. His eyes, by comparison, narrow down to slits with small irises indicating at his first appearance that no matter how solicitous he may seem, this guy is bad news.

Ban and Ginji from *GetBackers* display the various eye types for heroes: Ginji the classic wide-eyed hero, Ban the shadier man with a past eye shape.

© YUYA AOKI * RANDO AYAMINE * KODANSHA/TEAM Get Backers.

Body Type

Outside of facial structure, characters' body types also show their character as well as the intended audience for the manga. If you see a busty female character dressed in an impractical but revealing outfit and a spunky hero with heavy eyebrows and a wide grin, you're reading a shōnen manga (boy's comic). If you see tall, absurdly and identically beautiful young men and women, then you're reading a shōjo manga (girl's comic). Forget the plot, which may be hard science fiction or a wacky fantasy adventure—if the character designs fit, you know the manga is primarily intended for one audience.

Stunning young men are known as *bishōnen*, which literally translates as a beautiful young man from about fourteen to nineteen years old (older examples of male beauty would be *biseinen*, aged twenty and up). Bishōnen are stock characters in manga and anime, and although they are more likely to populate shōjo manga as objects of affection, they certainly appear in shōnen manga as well. They are so common that the character type is occasionally mocked, as in *Inuyasha*, where the character Hotohori is such a bishōnen that he is constantly mistaken for a woman and repeatedly trips over his own hair. In *Ouran High School Host Club*, head host King Tamaki is undoubtedly a bishōnen, but his beauty is only rivaled by his obliviousness to anyone but himself.

Stock Characters: Emotionally Distant Hottie

More usually men than women, these characters are drop-dead attractive, stoic, and unattainable. Confident, arrogant, often emotionally damaged, they are accomplished in whatever skill they pursue and are key allies. Ideal romantic idols in shōjo manga. Examples: Tsume in *Wolf's Rain*, Yuki in *Gravitation*, Kusanagi Motoko in *Ghost in the Shell*.

Most character types are identifiable by their design, and it is rare that characters step outside of the form they're given. In manga and anime, you act the way you are drawn. These types are so ingrained that they are also satirized in comedies, including *Fushigi Yugi*, the anime series *Magical Play*, and *otaku* favorite manga and anime series *Excel Saga*. The frequent use of conventional visual cues is deliberate to make each story a quick read for commuting or a quick break.

Stock Characters: Bespectacled Genius

Calm, cool-headed, brilliant, and the keeper of knowledge. Usually, but not always, wears glasses. May or may not be as intelligent as he thinks he is. An offshoot of this character type is the genius mechanic or tinkerer who can fix any machine and provides invaluable support to the main characters. Examples: Winrie in *Fullmetal Alchemist*, Yukito in *Cardcaptor Sakura*.

Heroes and Heroines

Stock Characters: Hero

Strong in body, pure of heart, steadfast, courageous. In shōnen manga, he's usually an adventurer with a bit of goofball mixed in. In shōjo manga, he will be handsome, admirable, and most often a bit unattainable. Examples: Edward and Alphonse Elric in *Fullmetal Alchemist*, Beet in *Beet the Vandel Buster*.

The wide eyes of purity and honesty mark heroes. Their body types range from a gangly youth to a muscle-bound martial arts master; as mentioned earlier, the more slender and beautiful the youth, the more likely you are reading a shōjo manga. Heroes tend to be decent, honorable, and hardworking souls, although they may indulge in raucous humor or childish fits of pique. The particularly Japanese traits of a hero are usually present, including loyalty to ideals and family or the group, sticking to your guns in a fight even to the death, and honorable behavior at all times whether in work or play (Drazen 2003).

Stock Characters: Lecherous Rake

Although usually an expert in their chosen profession (fighter, baker, etc.), these characters are concerned solely with collecting dates. Good at heart, loyal to their friends, but often distracted by pretty conquests. Examples: Gojyo in *Saiyuki*, Mugen in *Samurai Champloo*.

As manga diversified in the 1960s and 1970s, these character traits became less standardized and more complex. In gekiga (dramatic) manga, the antihero rose in popularity; the character design shifted to follow, leading to the smaller eyes and less heroic physical build exemplified by Ogami in *Lone Wolf and Cub* (Schodt 1983). Where once heavy eyebrows and a muscled physique immediately cued a hero, today more manga heroes are less obviously strong or good and may inhabit a shady middle ground with narrowing eyes and dubious skills—until tested. One of the most famous examples of this reluctant hero type appears in the manga and anime of *Cowboy Bebop*, as embodied by the reckless bounty hunter Spike Spiegel. As the slender Spike shuffles around in an ill-fitting suit, smoking up a storm, his medium-sized eyes and laissez-faire stance do not adhere to the usual conventions of a hero. When tested in action, he is a deadly master of martial arts, an excellent marksman, and a daring pilot; despite his dark past and bitter heart, he usually ends up on the side of good. Other examples of protagonists so close to villains as to be almost indistinguishable include Ororon in *The Demon Ororon* and Light in *Death Note*.

Stock Characters: Antihero

Strong and often steadfast, these guys usually have a dark past and are more willing to bend the moral and legal rules to attain their goals. May be at peace with their dark side or struggling with their demons. Examples: Spike Spiegel in *Cowboy Bebop*, Cain Hargreaves in *Godchild*.

Heroines have followed a less varied path. Again, large eyes dominate a heroine's face. Body types vary with intended audience and expected moral stance—the younger, more naïve heroines most often have a realistic if slender figure and tend to be the stars of shōjo manga. The older, more experienced heroine appears with an hourglass shape provocatively displayed, and tends to appear more in shōnen manga. Most female heroines are marked by their purity more than anything else—they may be spunky, foul-mouthed, awkward, or sassy, but they are always in essence good, and determined to represent and fight for the side of justice and harmony. Although many female manga characters are less idealized, these women are not the heroines. Male heroes are allowed to be more complicated, and it is rare for a female character of equally shady character or sensuality to be held up as the heroine of a story. In shōjo manga, in fact, many more dangerously sensual or psychologically dark men are admired, desired, and pursued. No such female counterpart is ever admired —she is always the villain, and although she may be momentarily attractive, she is not redeemable.

Stock Characters: Heroine

Pure in spirit, determined, cute rather than beautiful. In most comedies and shōjo, she will be spunky and quick to emotional outbursts. In shōnen manga, she may be sexier and wear less clothing, but usually maintains the same level of humor and talent. Examples: Kaoru in *Rurouni Kenshin*, Alice in *Alice 19th*, Sister Rosette in *Chrono Crusade*.

Enemies and Villains

So enter the villains of manga and anime—those forced or willing to turn to darker, unscrupulous means to achieve their goal. It is noteworthy that in Japanese pop culture, enemies are not always villains. It is acknowledged that an enemy is simply the person fighting for the other side of the conflict and that if the story were told from his point of view, he would be the hero of the tale. When the reader is introduced to opponents, they are distinguished visually as to whether they are an enemy or a true villain.

Enemies vs. Villains

Enemies will look a lot like the hero in character design. They are the antagonists but are also the hero on the other side of a conflict.
Villains will have elaborate hair, outfits, jewelry, and weapons. They are vicious, sadistic, dishonorable, and excessively violent—their actions make them monstrous rather than just an opposing force.

This kind of conflict is most apparent in historical dramas where real historical figures battle, such as the Meiji Era (1868–1912) conflicts presented in *Rurouni Kenshin*, *Peacemaker Kurogane*, or in *Kaze Hikaru*. In the conflict between the Shogunate and the samurai, a side is often chosen as a point of view for the story, and all men involved are heroes in displaying their adherence to group loyalty, their mission, and an honorable code. In *Rurouni Kenshin*, Kenshin is a wandering samurai devoted to the cause of keeping the peace, on the side of the emperor and against the Shogunate and samurai resisting the opening to the West. In Kenshin's own past as an assassin for the Choshu clan, he fought against those known as the *Shinsengumi*. The Shinsengumi, literally the new recruits, were the local force in Kyoto loyal to the Shogunate, deadly fighters all, and most died in battle or by ritual suicide before age twenty-five. They are a legendary group, often vilified in retrospect for their opposition to the emperor and the admired samurai, but they, too, fit the Japanese ideal of the hero. They were young, incredibly strict in their loyalties and honor, and proven fighters. Taking the opposite point of view as the Kenshin series, the Shinsengumi are the heroes of *Peacemaker Kurogane* and *Kaze Hikaru*.

A villain, as opposed to an enemy, will have narrowed eyes and more fantastic hair, dress, and accessories that indicate more drama and evil in his heart. In some manga, the more jewelry you have, the more evil you are likely to be. Villains of both genders are also almost always more overtly sexual, displaying their charms or beauty to that purpose and backing up their threats with sexually confrontational behavior. Barus in *Clover* follows this type, as does Muraki in *Descendants of Darkness* and both Aki and Ceres in *Ceres: Celestial Legend*. While enemies and heroes alike work within the accepted rules of society and of war, villains have no qualms about crossing lines in behavior or tactics.

Stock Characters: Nefarious Villain

Vicious, selfish, relentless, obsessed with power or their opponent (or both), and prone to delivering dramatic speeches. Often physically beautiful, but have few, if any, feelings or morals. May or may not have a glimmer of goodness in their past before being twisted toward dark ends. The ultimate betrayer. Examples: Darcia in *Wolf's Rain*, Vicious in *Cowboy Bebop*, Lust in *Fullmetal Alchemist*.

Stock Characters: Wizened Old Man or Crone

Depending on the circumstances, an older advisor to the main characters, usually the key provider of exposition and background for any adventure or quest. A common offshoot of this character is the lecherous old man who, while still remaining valuable as a resource, is also usually used for comic relief in how relentlessly he pursues glimpses of panties or naked girls. Examples: "Elder" Edward Hamilton of *Chrono Crusade*, Zeniba from *Spirited Away*.

Sidekicks and Comic Relief

Stock Characters: Best Friend

Loyal, encouraging, good humored. Often a sounding board for the plot of the story. In lighter stories, he or she may provide comic relief and inexhaustible cheeriness. In darker stories, has a hidden agenda and is often the perpetrator of a betrayal of the hero, often unexpected and especially damaging. Examples: Hiro in *Gravitation*, Tomoyo in *Cardcaptor Sakura*.

Stock Characters: Loyal Warrior

Strong, devoted, unparalleled in skill. An excellent ally whose quiet demeanor often hides emotional depths. Can be a hero, as in *Lone Wolf and Cub*, or may be an ally. Examples: Ogami in *Lone Wolf and Cub*, Batou in *Ghost in the Shell*.

Sidekicks usually follow the character design of the leads best friends and lackeys will be designed along the same lines of the hero and villain, respectively. Best friends and allies tend to be either cuter, bouncier versions of the hero or a more serious, studious foil for a hero's impulsive bravery.

Stock Characters:
Cute Sidekick of Indeterminate Origin

You know who they are—those chirping cute creatures that accompany the hero. Frequently endowed with magic or tools destined to help the hero, they are often used as comic relief. Examples: Mokona from *Magic Knight Rayearth*, *Tsubasa: RESERVoir CHRoNICLE,* and *XXXholic*, Nyozeka from *Alice 19th*, Wizu from *D.N.Angel*.

Comic relief characters are often presented with the most distortion from traditional proportions, and are often squat figures with caricatured faces. A character like the housekeeper in *Ceres: Celestial Legend* is a prime example of this type, with her almost lewd sense of humor and thick-lipped face. Again, this tradition is not unfamiliar to Western comics and animation, especially within the icons of Disney comic relief. Take a look at the character design of many Disney side characters, including Le Fou in *Beauty and the Beast*, and you will see similar distortion and simplification for comic effect. Lackeys and thugs on the villainous side tend to be more radical in their appearance, with distortions of anatomy and features creating fearsome or ugly faces and forms. In CLAMP's *Tsubasa: RESERVoir CHRoNICLE*, for example, an evil king has the narrowed eyes, distorted features, and devilish face to match his personality, while his son, a massive fighter at his father's beck and call, has the mountainous form and boorish attitude befitting a thug. As the hero travels through a story encountering resistance, he may run into all manner of villains, but I have observed that that the primary enemy will look most like the hero, a visual sign that the most threatening enemies may also be those akin to the hero.

Bumbling Goofball

Good humored but clumsy, dim, and exuberant to the point of causing scenes. Occasionally the hero or heroine, especially in comedies. Examples: Luffy in *One Piece*, Goku in *Dragon Ball*.

Visual Symbols

Picture this: you're enjoying a traditional fantasy manga complete with a magical schoolgirl, a chirping sidekick, and a strapping young hero journeying through a mythical landscape. For whatever reason—a sudden gust of wind, a snagging tree branch, or a clumsy fall—the heroine manages to lose her shirt, revealing her charms to the world. Her companion fighter, caught unawares, starts in surprise, cannot help but ogle her, and is then launched out of the panel and across the countryside by a nosebleed of extraordinary force.

Um … what!? You scan the panels for more information, perhaps a previously unnoticed blow from an enemy a few panels back. Nothing.

When first confronted with this very common convention in manga, Western readers are usually puzzled, and, while understanding the extreme reaction is meant to be funny, they don't quite get the joke. As the scene is repeated again and again, with varying degrees of outrageousness, readers will clue in to the connection: nosebleeds signal arousal. Depending on how exaggerated the particular comic wants to be, the poor boy may be afflicted with a trickle of blood or he may be launched out of the panel by the force of the gushing stream. This visual gag is similar to the Western convention of male cartoon characters' eyes bugging out when they see a sexy woman saunter by.

Cultural Shorthand

As previously noted, one of the most common stumbling blocks in understanding manga is the cultural shorthand found in every story. Nosebleeds played for giggles are an excellent example. They occur in every manga genre, from science fiction to high school melodramas, and across gender, because girls are just as susceptible as boys. These kinds of signals, which will often pass by in a panel or two without any explanation or comment from the author, are all over manga and are intended to add detail and depth to a story that is told swiftly and without cumbersome textual description.

These signals also remind readers that manga remains essentially Japanese, written for a Japanese audience. On the surface, Japanese culture seems deceptively similar to our own. Both the United States and Japan have a powerful international presence economically and politically, are technologically advanced, and have a strong connection with their own history that resonates in their current way of life. Japanese and Western culture seem to have much in common. The similarity of genres—science fiction, fantasy, romance, and horror, to name but a few—lull many new readers into seeing only the surface differences in style and pacing. The deeper you go into the Japanese imagination, the more cultural differences you will encounter. For some these differences make manga alluring, but for others they are the obstacles to enjoying the story.

One of the most powerful tropes in American history is that of the Old West. Cowboys, the conflict between order and lawlessness, and the vanishing prairie are the meat and potatoes of much of American pop culture. Think, however, of how confusing it would be to see a visual gag about a shootout at high noon—two men in ten gallon hats, one in white and one in black, stalking down a street—if you'd never even heard of cowboys. A white hat and a single star pin signify nothing to you. For a Western audience, Japanese manga and anime are chock-full of cultural vocabulary that readers sense but miss the meaning of, no matter how many times they read it through. It is not, of course, necessary to research all of Japanese history and literature to watch anime and manga, but as readers learn the cues meant to be obvious to Japanese readers, understanding increases exponentially.

Focus on Emotion

A Quick Guide to Common Visual Symbols

- Sweat drop(s) = nervous
- Pulsing vein near forehead = anger
- Blush = embarrassed
- Prominent canine tooth = animalistic behavior, losing control
- Dog ears/tail = begging
- Drool = leering
- Ghost drifting away from the body = fainting
- Snot bubble = asleep
- Shadow over face = extreme anger
- Glowing eyes = intense glare
- Nosebleed = aroused
- Ice/snow = on the receiving end of cold or cruel behavior
- Chibi/super-deformed character = extreme emotional state

To maintain absolute realism, a creator may discard some of the more common distortions used to indicate emotion, but many artists use these conventions even in the middle of serious dramas. Often characters' faces will pop from their usual shape into a dramatically simple representation of surprise, laughter, or embarrassment only to immediately return to their previous proportions in the next panel. Creators use these expression changes to relay information quickly.

As shown in a panel from *Her Majesty's Dog*, characters' faces will distort in surprise, and a glare is shown with shadows, piercing eyes, and a sound effect.

Blushing

Blushing is one of the most common shifts in appearance for manga characters. It is indicated by a sequence of diagonal lines across the characters' cheekbones and nose and is usually accompanied by a mortified expression with a small, frowning mouth and enormous embarrassed eyes. Manga characters blush frequently, from embarrassment, from surprise, from awkwardness, from feeling caught up in inappropriate emotions of any sort. Does this mean that the Japanese blush more than other nationalities? Doubtful. The blush is a useful indicator of a change in emotional state and is frequently used to emphasize a joke or slapstick moment in the text.

Sweat Drops

Related to the common blush, nervousness and embarrassment are represented by a sweat drop either on a character's face or hovering near their head. The more nervous or embarrassed they are, the bigger the sweat drop, and if they are especially mortified, the sweat drop may dominate their whole expression.

Hikaru in Tenshi Ja Nai! displays the trademark sweat drops.

Anger

Anger is also indicated by a distortion of the face, especially an impending angry outburst. A character's face will suddenly lose all distinctiveness and will be represented with either no mouth or a growling line as the entire top half of their face is shadowed over as if by their own private thundercloud. This visual can also signal envy combined with anger, and will always lead to an explosion. This face is often accompanied by the specific symbol for anger, a character that looks like the outlines of a plus sign, minus the final capping lines at the end of each arm of the plus. The symbol originates from the pulsing blood vessels at the temple when ire is raised, and the symbol will thus appear either above the character's head or near their temple.

In Dramacon, creator Svetlana Chmakova uses the traditional symbol for anger to emphasize Christie's state of mind.

© SVETLANA CHMAKOVA 2005 COURTESY OF TOKYOPOP.

Drooling and Leering

Leering is indicated by characters' mouths, suddenly expanding beyond the confines of their face to spread, oblong shaped, beyond their cheeks, marked by a small break in their bottom lip indicating a drop of drool hanging down. Not a pleasant image, but certainly an evocative one.

Tory in Off*beat flushes with embarrassment, signaled by traditional, manga-style blush lines.
© JEN LEE QUICK 2005 COURTESY OF TOKYOPOP.

Animal Characteristics

Another favorite technique that manga artists use is giving characters animal traits that indicate their mood. The most common of these is a wolfish set of ears and tail to accompany a leer, or a perky set of dog ears, curled up paws, and a wagging tail paired with giant, pleading eyes to indicate begging.

Chibi or Super-Deformed

When a character is given over to a strong emotion, particularly anger, fear, begging, or romantic swooning, their entire form will shrink and be represented by what is called a super-deformed, or chibi, form. The term chibi originates from a word for children, akin to our own "runt," and this is what characters resemble in this distortion. The character's hair is often their most unique feature and caps off the chibi's form to make clear who it is, but the figure is stylized to the point of making the character look like a short, squat starfish with hair. Wildly gesturing or moving through the frame, their features are drastically simplified—heavy, furrowed eyebrows a slashing "v" and a squiggle of a line for a mouth in anger, for example—and the symbols indicating whatever state they are in, the anger sign or a giant sweat drop hovering above their head, complete the image. In some ways, the chibi forms are the most expressive of any manga because they eloquently express emotion with only a few lines. Many creators, in their titles side and endnotes, represent themselves in chibi forms.

In Off*beat, artist Jen Lee Quick uses the convention of chibi character design to amplify the embarrassment and goofiness of the interaction between Tory and his mom.
© JEN LEE QUICK 2005 COURTESY OF TOKYOPOP.

Slapstick and Pratfalls

Actions are also often simplified for emotional impact, especially in reactions to events or people. When manga characters are shocked, they literally fall over so that in the next panel, all the reader can see is a foot sticking up into the panel. The movement is often accompanied by a "fwump" noise, indicating their sudden faint. By the next panel, they are usually on their feet again, but the impact of the shock is immediate. Similarly, when one character is particularly excited and affectionate in greeting another person, he or she barrels that person over with a hug, usually landing on top of them with a "glomp" noise.

Symbolism

In manga, numerous symbols provide the reader with emotional cues. These symbols generally come from mythology and national culture and are used frequently to indicate everything from a character's intent to the importance of a location. One of the most potent symbols for the Japanese are the flowers of the cherry tree, or the *sakura*. These delicate pink flowers appear again and again in imagery and can indicate a variety of ideas at once. They may simply be used to signal spring, the season when they bloom. Sakura refer to delicate beauty, but a beauty tinged with the knowledge that it is fleeting: because cherry blossoms only bloom for a short period, they are considered even more precious and beautiful for their brief appearance. This is certainly in keeping with the general Japanese ideal that romance is all the more poignant if it is tinged with tragedy.

Sakura can also refer to early and untimely death, as they are used to exemplify Sakurazukamori Seishirou in *X/1999*. Here is a character by no means delicate, although certainly beautiful, who uses as his key symbol and tool the sakura flower. A shower of sakura petals precedes his magic or arrival, and his assassinations provide gruesome meals to feed the magical hunger for souls of one sinister, eternally blooming sakura tree. Although readers can glean tragedy and beauty from the story itself, the special resonance of the sakura petals may be lost without the awareness of the position sakura hold in the Japanese imagination.

In a less sinister appearance, blooming cherry trees surround the Ministry of Hades where Tsuzuki and Hisoka work in Descendants of Darkness, once again representing death and an eternal springtime.

In addition to flowers, names often function as symbols. Names are powerful indicators of a character's intended role or personality, especially if they refer to Japan's mythological past or the religious stories of Shintōism. All of the "Gokus" running around, from *Saiyuki* to *Dragon Ball*, are intentional references to the Monkey King from *The Journey to the West*. Kamui in *X/1999* literally means the mind of god, an apt name for a young man who holds the fate of the world in his hands.

Although manga is most often black and white, the indications of colors can be important. Some references are simply assumed to be known—for example, white is the color of mourning and death and can be the trademark color of a villain, as it is with Aion in *Chrono Crusade*. In *Descendants of Darkness*, Tsuzuki is considered unnatural because of his brilliant purple eyes commented on by other characters. In anime, of course, colors are much more immediately important.

Brunette or Blond?

One of the more confusing aspects of manga art is the shifting color of characters' hair from black to white depending on what panel they are in. In general, manga readers know everyone's hair is dark, whether it's a shade of black or brown or a deep red. Some characters in a Japanese setting are represented with white or light hair, like Rei in the *Mars* series or Mayura in *Alice 19th*—this is either because the artist decided to take a shortcut and not fill in the black or to separate that character from another in the same manga. It does not mean the character has suddenly gone blond. It's a given that the hair remains black, even if it's not always shown that way.

Pacing

When the Hayao Miyazaki's anime *Nausicaä of the Valley of the Wind* was originally released in the United States in 1985, under the title *Warriors of the Wind*, the distributors decided that American viewers would not be able to deal with the length and pacing of the story and proceeded to cut a full twenty minutes out of the original film. Most of the cut scenes were slow, meditative moments. Viewers were unaware of the missing scenes, but many noted the jumpy quality to the film, and now this release is widely considered a butchery of the original film (Schodt 1996). The growing popularity of Miyazaki's films in the Western world indicates that many viewers just don't care about different pacing, but even as recently as 2004, twenty minutes were edited from the English dubbed version of Otomo Katsuhiro's *Steamboy*. Viewers had to attend the subtitled version to see the full Japanese release.

In this sequence from After School Nightmare, the deliberate framing and pacing of each page rachets up the disorientation and hyperawareness of the lead Ichijo, primed for a fight.

© 2005 Setona Mizushiro/AKITASHOTEN. English text (c) 2006 Go! Media Entertainment LLC. Used by permission.

"Being There Over Getting There"

In most stories told in manga or anime, everything simply takes more time. The Japanese concentration on emotion, which influences everything from their art style to their genres, also means that they spend a substantial part of their stories building character and establishing the setting. Much of this tendency goes back to the fact that manga's creative inspiration initially came from cinema rather than from Western comics. By using the panels more like a camera's eye, Japanese storytellers focus on images of the environment to establish a scene and will spend a number of panels this way. They are giving the reader a break, a quiet moment, to take in the scene and appreciate the telling details of the surroundings. Nothing is presented without having a purpose, but creators' tendency to stop and ponder their environments can leave readers who are accustomed to swift action champing at the bit. Authors also use apparently unrelated images—a pinwheel spinning or a water fountain—to focus attention on the dialogue or underscore a moment of contemplation for the stars of their story. Symbols are used lavishly, and many of these foci might have weightier meaning for a character or story, but they can just be a visual beat within the story allowing the reader to take a breath.

Shishi-Odoshi: "Deer Chasers"

One of the most common objects focused on during a pause in manga or anime is the shishi-odoshi or deer chaser, a bamboo contraption placed in gardens to frighten hungry deer from private gardens. The hollow clunk as the length of bamboo dumps its fill of water and snaps back to its upright position is everywhere in anime, even when you don't see the source and indicates a relatively wealthy household with a garden.

Drawing out the Tension

In the original English language manga Psy-Comm, the artist adopts Japanese style action lines to indicate movement.
© JASON HENDERSON AND SHANE GRANGER 2005 COURTESY OF TOKYOPOP.

This kind of pacing is not limited to the quiet times of the story. Fight scenes in manga are known to last for entire chapters or even books, panel after panel, featuring detailed and extended depictions of every angle or gesture of hand-to-hand combat. Backgrounds disappear, and every line focuses on a character's movement. This is the equivalent of slow motion and quick editing in film—creators use their panels to extend the emotional moment and to increase the tension as long as they can. As any fan of action can tell you, nothing is more disappointing than a shoddy climactic battle between hero and villain that is too muddy to understand and too short to provide any emotional satisfaction. There is a definite talent to balancing the swiftness of fighting with the need for an emotional climax, and creators are always striving for new ways to bring such conflicts to life so as to satisfy both needs within the story.

In a fight from Peacemaker Kurogane, the quick moves and surprise of an ambush are rendered with heavy use of action lines, sound effects, and an increasing number of panels.

© Nanae Chrono 2003 KODANSHA.

In both the manga and anime versions of *Peacemaker Kurogane*, the fight sequences are extended and exciting, with many pages of fighting and a complex sequence of panels indicating every incident of a confrontation. At the same time, the emotional impact of any action is the most important piece. When Yamanami Keisuke, judged to be a traitor to his fellows and thus expected to commit ritual suicide, forces his comrades to mete out his execution, the creator spends an equal amount of time on the flashing movement of blades and the tortured faces of the characters.

In the soccer series *Whistle!,* soccer games take place over the course of several volumes, detailing every small victory and failure as well as the players' individual journeys across the field, spectators' reactions to the game, and the downtime during timeouts. The soccer games replace battle sequences, and showing every move, tactic, and game ratchets up the excitement and makes the payoff that much more satisfying.

Endings

Manga and anime endings sometimes leave Western readers wondering whether they missed the conclusion of the story. The stories also often leave the endings open. Series end with characters continuing their journeys, usually having defeated a villain or resolving a conflict in their life, but their lives may well be just as precarious as they were when the story started. There is a tendency to leave everything implicit, as many creators do with aspects of the story all along. While authors give the viewers the necessary information to draw their own conclusions about the story, they do not spell it out.

That's the Ending?

In the more plot-driven genres of science fiction, mystery, and fantasy, this tendency can be even more frustrating because a series may end without any of the promised conclusions about characters' true identities, crimes, or destinies. Even when an ending is inevitable, as with many of the apocalyptic fantasy tales in which a climactic battle is par for the course, individual characters are often left adrift in the aftermath, and death seems to be the only certain ending a character can claim.

In *Wolf's Rain*, for example, the question throughout the story has been whether the wolf heroes will in fact find Paradise as they are destined to do. What Paradise truly is, what will happen if the wolves find it, and why the villains of the series are so desperate to find it, are never revealed. In the anime version, Paradise is left amorphous and unclaimed. Although we see the final showdown between the wolves and their antagonist, the cruel noble Darcia, the consequences of the wolves' victory are unclear.

In the anime version of *Fullmetal Alchemist*, the original goal of the Elric brothers—to make amends for their past mistakes by restoring one body and repairing another—is discarded but replaced with another equally ambitious goal. Their experiences from the story's beginning to end have taught them an enormous amount, and the journey has indeed been the point of the entire story. By-products of their mission include debunking alchemy's perceived rules, revealing government corruption, restoring a homeland to refugees, and reuniting with their own father. Their ultimate goal is never reached, and it's doubtful it ever will be—the sacrifice is too great; this is the real lesson they have learned.

Different Formats, Different Versions

Another more practical aspect for the unresolved storylines is that many manga or anime stories are also told in a variety of other formats, from anime to manga to video games to popular drama CDs (full cast recordings of manga and anime scripts on compact disc) to radio programs and novels. Drama CDs often spring from manga but may continue the story beyond the original manga with their own extended storylines. Anime series and OVAs are particularly famous for simply choosing a story from a manga and telling it with only a cursory background or summary of the story before or after the particular incident depicted. In Japan, especially in OVAs, it is presumed that the only viewers interested in these releases are readers of the manga, who thus need nothing explained. In the same way, an anime may only tell the beginning of a story, knowing that fans of the anime will be able to read the manga to finish it. This can be frustrating for Western readers and viewers because although the multiple formats of the story may be available to the Japanese consumer, they are often only available in one form for Western audiences.

Even more confusing is the tendency for creators to allow different versions of their stories. One of the most contrary examples available in the West is the marked difference between the film of the manga series *X/1999*, titled *X* (Madhouse Studios 1996) and the television series *X* also from Madhouse Studios airing in 2001–2002. Manga author team CLAMP has still not finished the original *X/1999* manga series. Kadokawa Shoten in Japan and VIZ in the United States have each published up to volume 18, but the authors themselves have stopped working on the series with no immediate plans to continue. When the *X* movie was made, CLAMP was only up to volume 8 in the manga, and the studio selected the threads of the story it found compelling for the two-hour movie format. Although the main characters' conflicts remained essentially the same, many side characters met different fates than they did in the manga, and the final conflict between best friends ended up with one friend beheading another. The TV series was made when the manga had hit volume 16 and faithfully follows the manga up to that point. Intriguingly, the television series ends with almost precisely the opposite ending of the film.

Layout

Pastry chef Ono gets ready for a day of baking in Antique Bakery. This
particular page is also a fine example of how manga artists highlight negative
space and everyday gestures.

© FUMI YOSHINAGA/SHINSHOKAN 2001.

One aspect of manga that is hard to pin down but definitely inherent to the
form is the way the layout acts as storyteller. Starting with Tezuka Osamu's
cinematic style in the 1950s, manga has generally been more experimental in
layout than Western comics. The use of the panels on the page to mimic a camera's eye is immediately apparent, and manga contain many of the shots and
patterns of cinema including close-ups, pans, jump-cuts, and irising (using a
circular frame to zero in on a subject as lenses originally "irised" in
filmmaking). The way creators frame each panel (or don't, letting the image
bleed across the page) is often more fragmentary than Western convention al-

lows and expects more work from the reader to put the images together into a coherent narrative (McCloud 1993). The key point to remember is that whereas Western comics artists can trace their influences back to comic strips and their linear sequence of storytelling, Japanese manga are powerfully influenced by cinema and draw more from film than from the panels in comic strips.

More Panels, More Leaps in Story

As Scott McCloud expertly summarized it in his landmark work, *Understanding Comics*, Japanese artists emphasize "being there over getting there." A big part of this is in how the panels are used on a page. Japanese artists use more panels than Western artists, requiring more work from their readers to put the story together, and their layout uses more "aspect to aspect" associations between panels, splintering a scene into parts of a whole instead of using panels mainly for different places, people, or actions.

All sequential art requires that the reader make the narrative out of combinations of art, text, and panels. Scott McCloud, in his landmark text *Understanding Comics*, noted the various kinds of transitions between panels that are common in sequential art, including subject to subject, action to action, and aspect to aspect. U.S. comics use action to action and subject to subject transitions most often. For example, a superhero might swing his fist in a punch, and in the next panel the villain reels back: action to action. When two characters are speaking back and forth, the panels typically switch from one face to another in a shift from subject to subject. McCloud noted that although Japanese comics rely on subject-to-subject and action-to-action shots, they also use a much higher percentage of aspect to aspect transitions, or those shifts from panel to panel that highlight particular sections or movements within one scene. In considering Japanese layouts, McCloud also noticed that Japanese creators typically use many more panels per page than are used in Western comics, a kind of layout that requires more attention and work on the reader's part to order and make sense of the sequence of panels (McCloud 1993). This expectation of visual literacy is key to reading manga, and the learning curve for building coherent meaning is one of the common hurdles for new readers.

To show an argument in a Western comic, artists tend to lay the page out in alternating panels, showing the speakers' back and forth, moments of silence, and expressions. They can be cinematic, running down the page like a film moves across a screen, but they often stick to the set pattern of back and forth. In manga, the entire page represents the emotional force of the argument. Instead of simply focusing on the characters at a middle distance, manga artists may choose to show the basic conflict at the center and splinter panels off to-ward the edge showing details like an edit and closeup in film. Manga artists use panels to show necessary information to highlight the emotional story arc or summarize background, even if it doesn't immediately follow within the scene's progress. These side panels tend to focus on aspects of the scene and thus might highlight a clenched fist or a tearful eye. The panel groups are often presented in starlike patterns with triangular edges slicing into the central image.

In *Beyond My Touch*, Mizuno looks around his empty apartment searching for a friend. His movements across the page and through the panels are an excellent example of aspect-to-aspect transitions on a page.

© TOMO MAEDA/SHINSHOKAN 2003.

Panels are not always clearly defined in manga—they are often bordered by thin lines or may have no border at all. The boundaries of panels may be crossed, especially if smaller panels surround a main figure or scene. Shōjo comics are the most famous in pushing these frame boundaries, dissolving the lines altogether, using flower petals and feathers to break up the page, or including wide dramatic images that roll across an entire two-page spread. Experimentation with borders and layout can make the page confusing, especially to readers accustomed to the straightforward comic-strip setup, but as readers grow more familiar with the method, and as younger generations recognize the patterns present in music videos and more and more feature films, the narrative flows more easily.

Speech Bubbles and Backgrounds

Aside from the most obvious traits of panels and design, manga artists have developed a range of visual codes that subtly define a narrative, and which many readers may not even notice unless they are pointed out. New manga readers do notice that the speech bubbles look different—whereas most Western comics' text and thought bubbles clearly designate the speaker or thinker with a "tail" pointing toward the character, in manga these same tails are small, delicate, or even absent. Instead, bubbles representing different characters' speech feature different edge designs. One character's dialogue might be inside perfectly oval speech bubbles, while their companion's dialogue falls inside a geometric shape. If a character is upset, the text bubble may become jagged, displaying pointed edges, to reflect the tone of voice. When characters are thinking, their thoughts appear without any bubble at all and may simply float in air or be shaded with a different screentone applied to the background.

Another convention working subtly through pages of manga is the use of a flashback within a story. Flashbacks are indicated by a shift in scene and the different age of the characters involved, but often the background literally changes color as well. If a manga starts with a white background, as most do, then a flashback sequence will have a black background to indicate that the panels are not taking place in the same timeline. This device can be seen in action in *Antique Bakery* and in *Tsubasa: RESERVoir CHRoNICLE*, to name but a few instances.

How a character is perceived is also indicated by elements in the background. As shōjo comics experimented with panels and boundaries, they also introduced the tradition of using flowers, feathers, and other objects to surround a character and show them from a particular point of view and emotional state. Most often, romantic visions of a character are presented surrounded by a spray of blooming flowers or brilliant stars, indicating an idealized or romantic point of view. When a cheerful character grins or generally brightens the mood of a scene, he or she may be accompanied by sparkles and glints.

Manga pages often challenge readers, but the challenge is part of the fun and enjoyment of the story for many readers. Once you relax into the style, it also heightens the emotional impact and rapidly propels the story forward.

In *Our Everlasting*, Shouin thinks back upon first meeting boyfriend Horyu. The variety of text bubbles show thoughts and speech, and the background fading toward black leads us into the coming flashback.

© Toko Kawai 2000.

Language

U.S. publishers are increasingly careful about including endnotes, translation notes, and panel-by-panel translations of sound effects to ensure that Western readers are not lost in prose translation with manga's already busy visual presentation. However, there are many language clues that can be learned ahead of time to help any reader navigate the textual landscape.

The Complex Task of Translation

One thing to keep in mind at all times is that manga and anime are translations. The dialogue and text contain many shades of meaning that may or may not be easily understood by word choice or implied in tone of voice. Each translator decides how to go about his or her task, and publishers may have strict guidelines—either their own internal guidelines or ones insisted upon by the original Japanese producers. Translation rules direct how much freedom translators have to deviate from a strict translation of the text. Some of the common difficulties include how to translate pop culture references or puns and jokes that would have little resonance for Western readers, as well as how to get across the societal significance of vocabulary and forms of address that do not exist in American speech. In anime translation, these tasks become even more complex when dubbing and trying to make sure the translation matches the movements of the character's mouth. There are longstanding debates among fans about the best translations and the type of translation.

There is a continuing debate about whether a phrase or word makes more sense directly translated into another language or whether the translator should choose a different term with similar impact. This is especially true with slang and pop culture references, both common in manga. If a famous pop star is referenced, for example, the name would mean little to most English-speaking readers, but if the name is changed to a U.S. idol, a similar understanding would be triggered.

The more delicate negotiations come in the social meaning of a phrase, or the tenor of a reaction in a conversation. Every language has accepted rules for formal and informal discussions as well as words with meanings that change depending on the circumstances and audience. Manga uses all of these vocabularies, and the quality of the translation can be judged both by its faithfulness and its ability to transform the story's dialogue and description into a whole that conveys the same spirit and meaning as the original tale. The shades of translation can easily shift, however, as any viewer can see by noting the differences between a dubbed track and the subtitling on a foreign language DVD. When a language is structured as differently as Japanese is to English, the process of translation becomes more complicated and more of a concern for fans.

Sound Effects: To Translate or Not to Translate?

In manga, for example, one editor may leave the Japanese sound effects intact in the original script, providing an index of sound effects at the back of the title; another editor may tuck a tiny lettered translation of the sound effect into each panel next to the Japanese lettering; yet other titles go through the trouble of blocking out the original Japanese text and replacing it with an English translation in the same spot and approximate font. Every editor and reader has a different preference—the translations included on the page make it easier to read, but purists often prefer seeing the original Japanese text within the panels.

Many readers do not notice the subtle differences between the original Japanese texts and the English translations. Some manga readers, however, are inspired to learn Japanese, and many fans begin to see the contrast between how an English sentence reads and how a similar sentiment might be expressed in Japanese. These differences are most notable in situations when the social rules are disparate—Japanese etiquette uses language and gestures that seem awkward in English translation. Fans debate the quality of translations, often preferring one company to another. Even when a reader does not understand the original language, poor translations leave readers feeling they missed something.

Translators must deal with more than just dialogue. Manga uses a more varied list of sound effects than Western comics, inspired again by the use of sound in film. While we have certain words we all recognize, from the "bam!" of knockouts to the "twang" of a released bow string, the Japanese have thousands more words indicating sound. They use a sound effect to indicate silence, *shin*, often extended as shiiiiiiin across the panel. They have sound effects for all manner of activities, including, to name but a few, *ba* for a sudden impact such as thump or bang, *bari bari* for crunching (like eating potato chips), *piku* for blinking and noticing something, *jiro* for a hard look or glare, *su* for a sigh, *suru* for cloth sliding against skin, and *po* for blushing (Oop-ack.com 2006). Instead of using noises solely for emphasis, sounds in manga are a part of the everyday world and simply add depth to the panels.

Honorifics

Honorific language, or *keigo*, is another troublesome aspect of translation. Its social meaning can be complicated and varies depending on the situation and the speakers. In Japan, honorifics are most commonly used at the end of a person's name to indicate the age, gender, and social standing of the addressee and his or her relative position to the speaker. There are two major types of speech that affect verb structure: the informal plain speech and the customary polite speech. Plain speech is most often used with immediate family members, close friends, and children. In addition, there are the traditional three levels of honorifics added on to names and nouns. There is *sonkeigo* (exalted terms), *kenjōgo* (humble terms), and *teineigo* (polite terms). Exalted terms are most often used in reference to the addressee, including their families, possessions, and house, whereas humble terms are used in reference to the family, possessions, and house of the speaker. Polite terms are used without reference to either participant in the conversation and are more common in formal conversation (Suzuki 2001; Kodansha International 1999).

Honorifics at a Glance

Honorifics are most frequently used at the end of a last name (formal) or at the end of a first name (less formal):

- san: toward any older person, usually a man
- kun: toward anyone of equal status, most common among males
- chan: toward younger, usually female, friends; has a sense of a diminutive
- sama: carries greater weight than -san, used with very distinguished, noble classes, especially historically

(no honorific): only used between intimate friends or spouses; indicates a very close relationship

---

Honorifics in Manga and Anime

In actual use, a younger man almost always addresses an older acquaintance of either gender with the addition of -san to the end of their surname. So in *Descendants of Darkness*, Tsuzuki becomes Tsuzuki-san. In response, an older or more senior person addresses a younger person with the familiar honorific -kun, if the addressee is male, and perhaps -chan if the addressee is female. If Tsuzuki were speaking with Kurosaki Hisoka, his subordinate, he would call him Kurosaki-kun.

Among teens or young men of equal age, the most common honorific is the familiar -kun, used among equals. The -chan honorific is usually used for younger girls and among girls or to girls from boys, and can be a diminutive. Among students and teachers, there are specific honorifics indicating position: *sensei*, *kōhai*, and *sempai*. Sensei is reserved for masters of their art, including instructors and teachers, as Westerners may recognize from martial arts films. Upperclassmen are referred to as sempai, and underclassmen are addressed by upperclassmen as kōhai. Relationships established in schools extend into adult life—so much so that an underclassman can expect help in advancing their career from any upperclassmen of the same school, even if the two students have never met. These same terms are used to indicate superior and inferior status within corporations and businesses.

If two friends are speaking with each other, rather than to acquaintances or strangers, they may switch from using the person's surname to their given name; for example, as Tsuzuki and Hisoka grow closer, they begin to address each other as Asato-san and Hisoka-san, or even Asato-kun and Hisoka-kun.

An entirely different type of respectful prefix is exchanged with friends' family members and family acquaintances, usually including adding an "o" onto the beginning of a person's name or relation to indicate affection. If a younger person encounters an elderly woman he does not know, he may well address her as *obaasan*, or the polite equivalent of grandmother. A brother is addressed as *niisan*, but a beloved brother would be *oniisan* (Suzuki 2001).

Traditionally even close friends do not refer to each other by only their given names, as is the custom in the West. Addressing someone only by his or her first name is a level of intimacy reserved for close family members, most specifically, spouses and lovers. The lack of an honorific indicates a special status. In younger generations in Japan, these customs are breaking down in informal situations, and close friends do use given names with each other, but in daily life and even more so in professional life, polite language is maintained.

Social Harmony

The appearance of social harmony must be maintained at all times. The rules of etiquette indicate a definite difference between *tatemae* (expected social relationships and their accompanying niceties) and *hone* (individual feelings and intentions) (Kodansha International 1999). The knowledge that what one says and what one feels may be at odds requires that formal interactions be deciphered on both a polite surface level as well as a concealed emotional level. The ingrained expectation is that individuals will learn and respect the order of etiquette, and that the emotional nature of the individual will be hidden so that politeness is maintained.

Insults and Slights with Honorifics

As all of these rules of honorifics indicate respect and politeness, using the wrong honorific for someone can be an insult, whether intentional or accidental. Using an honorific that is too familiar is considered rude; and while sometimes this may occur out of a misunderstanding, most often it is used deliberately by an antagonist to insult the addressee. In *Tsubasa: RESERVoir CHRoNICLE*, Sakura chides Syaoran for insisting on calling her by her title, princess, rather than by her given name. Given that they are childhood friends, their friendship is not in question, but Syaoran cannot quite get over the familiarity implied by calling Sakura by her name. In the same manga, Fai repeatedly teases Kurogane with cutesy nicknames, including Kuro-chan and other variations using the diminutive –chan honorific, much to Kurogane's annoyance. In watching anime, honorifics and prefixes are often left out of the dubbing as well as the subtitles, and it is only by listening to the original Japanese language track that you may decipher the honorifics and their potential significance in conversation.

When manga was first translated into English, honorifics were either left out entirely or replaced with a Miss or Mr. in front of the character's name. Unfortunately, Western forms of polite address do not match the Japanese customs and do not carry the same weight in conversation. These additions to the English translations sound awkward and old-fashioned instead of helping Western readers or listeners understand the implications of each address. Imagine calling your best friend Miss Elizabeth all the time, instead of Elizabeth—for Western audiences this would recall Victorian parlors rather than everyday courtesy. Fortunately, more companies are choosing to leave honorifics intact, providing an explanation at the front of each title, so that readers who are so inclined will not miss the connotations of these forms of address because they are omitted or unsuccessfully translated into English.

Format

When manga first began appearing translated into English, publishers were fearful that Western readers would not be willing or able to make the shift from reading in the traditional English format (left to right) to the Japanese format (right to left). Thus, in these first translations, manga pages were flipped so that they read from left to right. This process is fairly expensive because the art and sound effects must be altered or deleted and the translators must insert English sound effects in the manner of the original.

When it became apparent that fans preferred the unflipped format because it left the art and the sound effects intact, publishers began to print manga right to left in the United States. This original format is referred to as "traditional," "authentic," or "unflipped," depending on the publisher and context, but all these terms mean the same thing. Given the expense of flipping, leaving manga in the traditional format means not only that publishers can save money, but that they can release more titles with increasing frequency while also pleasing the fans.

Animating Manga

It is important to note that anime uses many if not all of the same symbols and storytelling tropes that manga does. In anime, of course, all of these symbols are set in motion. Blush lines turn red, anger signs pulse above characters' heads, and symbolic feathers and petals float across the screen. Anime and manga share an extended pacing created by the serial nature of the media through which they are published—magazines and television shows, respectively. All anime shares a common fine art heritage, but it is combined with the traditions of animation from Disney to Tezuka's first television shows to today's video games. Film inspirations, from the Hollywood films that still dominate the market to the 1940s noir that originally set Tezuka on his cinematic path, define anime on the screen as much as they define manga on the page.

All Together Now

All of manga's symbolic cues and traditions come together to create a text simultaneously similar to and distinct from its closest kin in the West, comics and graphic novels. The most apparent but least understood difference lies in visual differences in character design, layout, and symbols. Manga presents a more visual story than Western comics, and much of the depth and detail of the stories arises from visual signals. For a reader not in tune with the visual cues, manga can seem slow, flat, and lacking in detail or character development. For a visual learner, however, the slightest difference in expression and line will make all the difference to the story's depth. For readers who are strictly textual learners, manga may never be particularly appealing because of the relative paucity of language. Even for those who can read the visual language, the quality of the textual translation process may be off-putting. Aside from the more dramatic visual differences, the themes and unfamiliar, culturally significant histories, myths, and story arcs may also be barriers to understanding.

Ultimately, though, most readers are intrigued by these differences— enough of the story gets through to pique interest and the moments of confusion encourage readers to investigate the language and culture to deepen their understanding. The different levels of storytelling, from the visual to the cultural to the textual variations, attract readers who enjoy complex and multimedia presentations of stories. The language of sequential art demands active reading to provide the connections between panels, text bubbles, and art. Indeed, what happens between the panels is what provides all of the drama in comics and graphic novels. Manga pushes that sensibility even further to include interpreting foreign visual and textual languages, social cues, and ideas in the reading process. The challenge simply to understand is provocative for many readers, along with the feeling that they are learning something new and different from what is considered proper, canonical reading.

References

Brenner, Robin. "NFNT Teen Reader Survey." A report prepared by No Flying, No Tights, Arlington, MA. April 2006. http://www. noflyingnotights.com (accessed April 20, 2007).

Drazen, Patrick. *Anime Explosion: The What? Why? & Wow! of Japanese Animation*. Berkeley, CA: Stone Bridge Press, 2003.

Gravett, Paul. *Manga: Sixty Years of Japanese Comics*. London: Laurence King Publishing, 2004.

ICv2. "Shoujo Sales Soaring: Go! Comi Goes Back to Press." March 28, 2006. http://www.icv2.com/articles/news/8462.html (accessed April 4, 2006).

Kodansha International. *Japan: Profile of a Nation Revised Edition*. Tokyo: Kodansha International, 1999.

McCloud, Scott. *Understanding Comics: The Invisible Art*. Northampton, Massachusetts: Kitchen Sink Press, 1993.

Nimo, Toshitaka, and Alexander Besher. *You Are Your Blood Type*. New York: Pocket Books, 1988.

Poitras, Gilles. *The Anime Companion: What's Japanese in Japanese Animation?* Berkeley, CA: Stone Bridge Press, 1999.

Schodt, Frederik L. *Dreamland Japan: Writings on Modern Manga*. Berkeley, CA: Stone Bridge Press, 1996.

———. *Manga! Manga! The World of Japanese Comics*. Tokyo: Kodansha International, 1983.

Suzuki, Takao. *Words in Context: A Japanese Perspective on Language and Culture*. Tokyo: Kodansha International, 2001.

Thorn, Matt. "Girls and Women Getting Out of Hand: The Pleasure and Politics of Japan's Amateur Comics Community." In *Fanning the Flames: Fans and Consumer Culture in Contemporary Japan*. Albany: State University of New York Press, 2004.

Chapter Three

Culture Clash: East Meets West

Puzzled by a reference in a Japanese manga? Sometimes there's a simple explanation. By now you know that a nosebleed means a character is sexually aroused—and knowing that, manga makes much more sense. At other times, the cultural divide may be too wide to cross easily. For librarians trying to understand manga fully and catch up with the current generation devouring it at such a rapid rate, the cultural divide rears its head suddenly and without warning. In matters of humor, romance, nudity, and gender roles, manga diverges sharply from Western norms and thus befuddles and even shocks Western readers. As you start to evaluate manga titles for specific collections, acknowledging these wider gaps in understanding is vital.

The most easily identified enigmas are explained in Chapter Two, which discusses symbols in manga. Here I address more potentially troubling bumps in the road for Western readers.

Fantasy versus Reality

For the Japanese writers and readers of manga, fantasy is fantasy, reality is reality, and never the twain shall meet (Drazen 2003). The Japanese put few limits on the content of their fiction because fiction is fantasy and has no obligation to reflect real-life behavior and values. Because fiction occupies its own realm, Japanese audiences do not necessarily require strict realism even for stories set in realistic environments. A manga may take place in a Japanese high school or a historical setting lush with realistic details, but the addition of magical happenings, contrived coincidences, or outright goofball sight gags will not disrupt the story for the reader. The more remote the setting (nineteenth-century Europe, a distant planet), the greater the sense of fantasy. The fantasy is the point—the reader understands the idealization presented, and no one quibbles over historical or scientific details large or small. If one wants to write a history that presents Marie Antoinette as a heroine and her loyal captain of arms as a woman in disguise, all the better for the sake of a dramatic and exciting story. Add in witty repartee, tragic romance, and elaborate costumes and settings, and you've got a best-seller (see Ikeda Ryoko's *Rose of Versailles*).

Many novice manga readers become disturbed or annoyed by the unbelievable details and incredible acts, including sudden joking in the midst of an otherwise deadly serious drama or the distortion of characters into the stylized chibi form when they hit the extremes of emotion. As you read more manga, you'll grow accustomed to the conventions and visual conceits until you barely notice these shifts.

When manga takes on disturbing subjects, readers run smack into the fantasy-versus-reality divide in a very different way. Manga can and does portray feelings and behaviors that are forbidden or controversial while ignoring society's actual perception of those taboos. Depending on their story's needs and their desired level of realism, manga authors may depict incest, pedophilia, sadomasochism, or homosexuality as normal or accepted. They may acknowledge society's disapproval, but they are more concerned with the emotional world of the story. If it's a good story, it's a good story—taboo or not.

The Western world has its fair share of stories that push boundaries, including acknowledged classics such as Vladimir Nabokov's *Lolita*. At the same time, creators who cross these boundaries are greeted with suspicion, prurient curiosity, or outrage. Challenging tales provoke discussion of what the societal implications might be, or how susceptible audiences might react to or internalize messages in the work—especially when the topic is sex. True to our Puritan roots, U.S. readers can be more prudish and thus more easily scandalized when authors violate taboos in imaginary worlds. We may eventually accept such violations for the sake of art, as with Vladimir Nabokov's *Lolita*, but we are less likely to tolerate them in popular media.

In Japanese society, as seen in manga, controversial topics are fair game and appear without fanfare and are not halted by the odd knee-jerk reaction. Manga creators spend little time justifying their use of taboo themes to readers. For example, the popular shōjo manga, *Angel Sanctuary*, features an angelic hero who fully acknowledges that he is in love with his sister, and she with him. Within the first volume, they are struggling through obstacles to be together and consummate their love, and amid battles between heaven and earth with angels and demons on all sides, their relationship is the emotional center of the story. For many Western readers, the incest at the center of the story sours the pleasure of an otherwise appealing melodrama. Other readers are able to take the story on its own terms—as fantasy—and enjoy it.

Another shōjo manga, *Loveless*, contains elements that almost seem designed to unnerve the reader. The story takes place in a slightly skewed version of modern Japan in which people are born with cat ears and tails that are shed when they lose their virginity. *Loveless* revolves around a twelve-year-old student, Aoyagi Ritsuka. The shock of his older brother's murder drastically alters

Ritsuka's personality and steals two years' worth of his memories. The trauma-tized Ritsuka mistrusts himself and those around him. When a twenty-year-old art student named Soubi appears in his life, claiming to be a friend of his broth-ers', Ritsuka falls into an unexpectedly complex relationship with the older man. Soubi tells Ritsuka that he has inherited his brother's role as his partner in a mysterious battle, a role that necessitates an intense connection between them.

During battle, Soubi must connect physically to Ritsuka to draw on his strength, and this often involves kissing or caressing him. Ritsuka is both at-tracted to and unnerved by the contact and Soubi's repeated declarations of love and loyalty. Although not overtly sexual, a sadomasochistic element fur-ther complicates their relationship; a scene in which Soubi persuades Ritsuka to pierce his ears to mark him as Ritsuka's is rife with sensual overtones.

Identity, loyalty, revenge, and the growing affection between Soubi and Ritsuka tangle with an intricate mystery and science fiction plot to create a story both romantic and powerful. *Loveless* never allows the reader to forget the age difference between Soubi and Ritsuka, and characters within the story accuse Soubi of being a pedophile and a pervert. Although the two never express sex-ual desire for one another, the manga acknowledges the sexual potential in their relationship frankly enough to shock Western readers. The success of *Loveless* would also surprise them. Most Western publishers would run screaming from any story that smacked of condoning pedophilia. The fact that *Loveless* has a mainstream presence in manga and anime indicates just how far the Japanese imagination can roam without being perceived to condone the imagined behavior.

While Western audiences appear to distinguish between fantasy and reality—we know that books, film, and TV are not real and explore our own de-mons via these media—we examine and reexamine the effects of media on its audience. We fear that violent videogames or television programming may lead to acts of violence in real life. This kind of fear would never occur to the Japa-nese, and even if it did, they would dismiss it as too great a leap between cause and effect (Schodt 1996).

In the case of violence, statistical evidence bears out the Japanese point of view. Japan's rate of violent crime is extremely low compared with that of the United States, even considering the relative sizes of the two countries. A real-life Japanese teenager is far less likely to have access to guns than an American teen, despite the violent images in manga and anime (Schodt 1996). Fukushima Akira, a noted Japanese psychiatrist and writer, studied teens' ex-posure to "harmful" content in manga and argued that exposure to such content led Japanese teens to be less violent and less sexually precocious than their counterparts in other countries (Schodt 1996). Western readers flipping through manga aimed at teenagers and adults will find an eye-opening array of behavior, from boundary pushing to downright illegal, played for laughs or for drama. For readers used to the plethora of "issue" novels aimed at teens and the general tendency of Western stories to punish or reform deviants, this freedom of behavior is both refreshing and occasionally shocking or uncomfortable.

Content Confusion

Sense of Humor

Although shock and gross-out humor is a staple of Western media, the sexual joking and slapstick in manga can give even the most unflappable reader pause. Cultural differences in what we find funny explain some of this discomfort; the Japanese simply find things funny that we do not. Just like modern audiences viewing the comedies of Aristophanes, we may laugh at the broad humor but lack the cultural context and references to appreciate subtler jokes fully. What may have been funny to the ancient Greeks can seem odd at best, offensive at worst. In a more modern instance, British humor gets a lot of mileage out of naked bottoms. Although U.S. audiences will chuckle at them, bottoms are less of an American comedy staple.

Chidori foils panty exposure by wearing her gym shorts underneath her uniform (although admittedly, traditional girls' gym shorts are almost as revealing).

© Shoji Gatoh, Retsu Tateo KADOKAWA SHOTEN 2000.

In manga, panties are always a source of hilarity. Also extremely common in shōnen manga is the "oops, I fell and just happened to grope your breast" pratfall. Every culture makes sexual jokes that reflect whatever it finds embarrassing, but as a librarian, you may worry about content that crosses the line between funny and offensive. It is up to the reader, and to the selector, to decide whether cultural differences justify potentially controversial humor. *Dragon Ball* is a series marketed to, and immensely popular with, older boys and 'tweens, and many American parents and librarians purchased the series for children and children's collections sight unseen because the anime series was a morning cartoon hit. Unfortunately, buyers did not realize that the cartoon had been heavily edited. The manga series arrived with nudity, sexual jokes, and scatological humor intact. Although never truly explicit, many selectors were and still are surprised that a series aimed at boys would contain such humor.

What is the appeal of panty jokes and sexual pratfalls? The humor in accidental breast-groping is not hard to understand—as in many Western comics, embarrassing the hero provokes a chuckle, and this kind of stumble appears in everything from school dramas to science fiction space operas. Readers love the hero's expression of shock when he realizes his unintentional manhandling, and stammering and blushing entertainingly accompany his frantic backpedaling. Like any tale aimed at teens, the joke acknowledges their elevated hormone levels and profound sense of sexual awkwardness. It allows teens to giggle at something mortifying but understandable. Such jokes do not portray groping as socially acceptable—its very unacceptability, and the culprit's awareness of it, makes it funny.

Panty jokes are the equivalent of Western comics' gags involving a woman's bra strap, cup size, or derriere—intended as funny, occasionally offensive, and consciously over the top. Exemplified by Marilyn Monroe's skirt fluttering up in *The Seven Year Itch*, glimpses of legs, panties, and bras are just as much the stuff of teenage boys' fantasies. The ubiquitous schoolgirl characters, with their short skirts and hyper attitudes, are the most common objects of panty jokes, and anyone from preteen boys to lecherous old men may enjoy the view. The traditional pairing of teen girls with a lecherous old man character may make some readers uncomfortable with its offhand overtones of pedophilia. Japanese culture readily acknowledges a fetish for schoolgirls (Schodt 1996). The Japanese are fairly public about such kinks and are more inclined to laugh at them than to condemn them. Although the schoolgirl kink is certainly not unheard of in the United States (Britney Spears, anyone?), U.S. audiences are more sensitive about perceived pedophilia, and high-profile child pornography cases have added to their discomfort.

Sexually charged pratfalls and panty jokes appear more often in shōnen manga than in shōjo manga, but shōjo manga have sexual jokes all their own. Most often, a clumsy heroine ends up stretched intimately on top of her love interest, blushing furiously. Embarrassment—the more public the better—still reigns supreme as a source of laughter. Given Japan's strict notions of public propriety, this should come as no surprise. The gap between public behavior and unbridled fantasy underscores the fantasy versus reality divide.

Japan's more blasé attitude toward sexual humor contrasts sharply with the Western tendency to clothe our sexual fantasies in innuendo. We nervously poke fun at them but rarely admit them. In Japan, creators let their kinks and quirks roam free in all manner of comics aimed at all kinds of audiences. The simple fact that there is a popular subgenre of romantic comics aimed at teenage girls about gay relationships between boys and men boggles many Western readers' minds—how can the Japanese, who are no more accepting of homosexuality than Americans, have such a booming subgenre?

Western readers have the most trouble with this paradox when the humor crosses a line. Manga titles may contain jokes about absolutely everything, from the more benign sexual humor mentioned earlier to jokes about abortion, rape, incest, forced marriage, and sexual harassment. *Ouran High School Host Club* is a winning spoof of shōjo manga conventions and reverse harem manga. The story features an ordinary girl surrounded by a bevy of beautiful young men who run their own host club: they offer male companionship to the lonely young ladies at an elite high school. The series is comedy through and through, and part of the humor comes from acknowledging the romantic fantasies of teenage girls in Japan. There is the gorgeous dashing leader, the bookish, silent hottie with glasses, and the gruff bad boy—shōjo conventions all. The other members of the club are familiar to shōjo manga readers but may make new U.S. readers wonder: the romantic clinches of a pair of twins tantalize girls, and a high school senior who looks like he's about twelve cuddles teddy bears and acts like a child. These guys represent two separate kinks, incest between siblings and shota, or romance featuring prepubescent boys. Within the manga, it is understood that these relationships are all illusions—the twins are not lovers and the "child" is in fact a high school senior. Although strictly fantasies, such kinks are a visible enough part of the manga culture that readers recognize them in a send-up like *Ouran High School Host Club*.

As a reader, you can choose to ignore what you don't find funny or skip the rest of a story you find offensive. Each reader and community will have a different idea of where funny ends and insulting begins. You will need to be sensitive to the potential for controversy. Selectors for any collection should be aware of and familiar with the contents of their collections. Keeping community standards in mind, you can decide whether problematic themes will prevent you from selecting a particular title.

Consistency is the key—compare the content in a manga to content in films aimed at the same audience.

- In terms of content, is it better, worse, or the same?

- How many panels show jokes or situations that might cause controversy?

- How does the manga compare to films or books at the same level?
- What kind of rating might the manga have if it were a film?
- Who does the title appeal to most?

Be prepared to defend the presence of this kind of material in your collection by comparing the standards for other media collections in your library.

New readers are often startled when sensual or sexual humor appears in titles geared toward elementary and preteen readers. In the shōjo manga and anime *Princess Tutu*, an anthropomorphic cat teacher instructs the young ballerina heroine and her classmates. Mister Cat repeatedly threatens to force his students to marry him if they don't do their work. Each time, apparently aware that he crossed a line, he retreats and begins to groom his ears. The girls find his threats motivating: they are terrified and always comply with Mister Cat's demands as a teacher. Mister Cat's behavior is meant to be funny because of its ridiculousness, but for many Western readers, the joke is puzzling and a bit creepy. It brings a hint of predatory sexual behavior, not to mention abuse of power by a teacher, into an otherwise innocent and romantic tale. This kind of humor should not and does not negate the charm of the series as a whole, but be prepared for it to surface in unexpected places.

Devoted Friends, Romance, and Lust: Which Is Which?

In CLAMP's *X/1999*, a famous and popular shōjo work detailing an apocalyptic millennial battle through vignettes of each participant's life, high school teens Kamui and Fuma are best friends destined to fight on opposite sides. The two boys hold hands, embrace, gaze soulfully into each other's eyes, and tell each other without shame that they love each other. For Western readers, these boys seem a bit, well, intimate.

Western readers are used to clearly defined relationships. People fall into major relationship categories: friends, lovers, and family. Each of these labels indicates a level of intimacy and appropriate ways to demonstrate affection. Japanese tales allow for a bit more fluidity. Manga creators do not make every relationship clear—readers draw their own conclusions from facial expressions, body language, and sparse dialogue.

Most puzzling for Western readers are relationships like those in *X/1999*—sometimes the boys act like best friends, sometimes they act like boyfriends. Are they in love? Are they more like brothers? Are we even supposed to know for sure?

Japanese manga frequently uses signals we understand as romantic—holding hands, embraces, and even saying "I love you"—for nonromantic relationships. Manga stories value strong friendship and loyalty very highly. The intensity of a relationship matters more than its precise nature (Drazen 2003).

Most of the time, however, intense friendships are not romantic—fans may speculate that Kamui and Fuma are more than friends, but CLAMP does not intend them to be read as romantically involved.

Two opponents in *X/1999*, Seishirou on the left and Subaru on the right, push the boundaries of friendship, love, and hate.

Left: Volume 13 © 1998 CLAMP; right: Volume 12 © 1999 CLAMP.

The same comic illustrates the blurry lines between friendship and romance with another, more sexually charged relationship. For Sumeragi Subaru and Sakurazukamori Seishirou, another pair of destined enemies, affection has turned to hatred. Western readers will recognize this type of relationship—it's always the person you trust the most who betrays you in any great tragedy. In manga, creators allow love, lust, and hatred to mingle. Western authors, particularly when dealing with relationships between people of the same gender, tend to ignore or muffle such feelings with protestations of heterosexuality.

While Subaru and Seishirou fulfill their destinies, fighting on opposite sides, their combat is always cruelly personal, demonstrating that they cannot resist recalling their unfinished relationship. Their final battle ends with a tragic admission of love expressed too late, leaving paralyzing regret in its wake. Throughout their interactions, Subaru and Seishirou's body language and conversation has more sexual overtones than Kamui and Fuma's. These two previously starred in their own manga series, *Tokyo Babylon*, which explicitly acknowledged the romantic nature of their attraction. Readers of *X/1999* are expected to know of this past and carry those implications over into their final confrontations. When other characters comment on Seishirou and Subaru's relationship, the intimacy is acknowledged even though the romance is never fulfilled.

The tendency of manga to leave things undefined forces readers to interpret even Seishirou's final confession their own way: although he seems to be admitting his love, his words are lost to the wind and the reader never hears them. In *X/1999*, subtle differences in body language, invasion of personal space, and characters' past histories are all that indicate which relationships are romantic and which are platonic. These gray areas often leave Western readers wondering or drawing their own conclusions, which is what makes manga's storytelling patterns characteristic.

Sexual Intimidation

Another place where Western readers find unexpected sexual overtones is in the interactions between manga villains and their victims. In manga, bad guys of all kinds often threaten their opponents with sexual dominance or intimidation—the gender of their opponent scarcely matters. Part of being villainous seems to be using power and force in all ways, including threatening the rape or molestation of your enemy. In almost all of Watase Yu's series, for example, her heroines are threatened with violation or actually raped by the villain of the piece.

Male villains are not the only ones who employ sexual intimidation. An even more startling offshoot of this villain type comes in the form of women who prey on those weaker than themselves, often preteens or young teens of either gender. Their pedophilic actions make them all the more monstrous. In the manga, and more prominently in the anime *Here Is Greenwood*, one high school senior's older sister, Nagisa, is villainous not only because she lays elaborate traps for her younger brother but also because she picks up and sexually preys on underage girls and boys as a means to her nefarious ends. At heart a highly amusing high school comedy, all of this is played for humor in *Here Is Greenwood*, but Western readers and viewers may wonder how to react.

Violence in mainstream Western comics rarely has such a strong sexual component. You never see Batman threatened with rape, never mind the occasional comments by the Joker. There are examples, of course, of male villains who intimidate women sexually, but it is not par for the course, nor is the intimidation gender-blind it is in manga. For Japanese readers, a taste for sexual as well as physical violence seems to signal that a character is truly evil—force and misuse of power is always villainous, but taking it to a sexual level separates a true villain from someone who is just an opposing force.

Is It Romantic or Harassment?

Muddying the waters a bit more, however, is the fact that romance manga tend to convey a high tolerance for sexual harassment. Manga characters endure harassment without complaint, especially if they are protecting their beloved. In the wildly popular series *Mars*, the heroine Kira is frequently sexually harassed at her job at a fast-food joint. Rather than make trouble by complaining to her boss or telling her boyfriend Rei, a bad boy with a short fuse, she lets it slide, and her girlfriends advise her to keep quiet. Eventually Rei witnesses the harassment and puts the offenders in their place, but the "let it slide" attitude is common in shōjo manga.

The popular manga *Hot Gimmick* challenges Western ideas of sexual boundaries even more. Hatsumi is an uncertain teen girl desperate to keep her sister's possible pregnancy from shaming her family. When her upstairs neighbor Ryoki discovers the dangerous secret, he blackmails her into becoming his "slave." Hatsumi is bullied into increasingly intimate acts, and as the series goes through its twelve volumes, Ryoki never stops his constant barrage of insults and put-downs. For a man in love, he never seems to act like it, and despite the soap opera appeal of the story, the ultimate message is a troubling one. Two other suitors, one of whom goes so far as to try to rape Hatsumi before coming to his senses, complicate their relationship. Hatsumi ultimately chooses the guy who treats her the worst. When they head into the bedroom, Ryoki ignores Hatsumi's embarrassment and cries of "no" completely, again berating her for her timidity and physically and psychologically intimidating her. For a modern Western audience that believes "no means no," these allowances kill the romance.

This kind of romance begs the question: how much do these stories reflect or shape readers' expectations for their real-life relationships? The alpha male hero and the rape fantasies these comics portray were once staples of romance fiction here in the United States, and romances have also been accused of fostering unhealthy attitudes toward romance, but current romances have shifted to a more equal, consensual model. *Hot Gimmick* is extremely popular among teenage girls, its intended audience—its melodrama and who-will-she-choose plot fans feel outweigh the uncomfortable moments. For many readers, however, *Hot Gimmick* is romantic—and romance is another culturally defined ideal that you must wrangle with as you add manga and anime to your collection. In one sense, teens who experience coercion or pressure may appreciate seeing these realities addressed in comics. As someone who works with teens, you may well find it troubling to see such behavior treated as a natural part of romance.

Love and sexuality are bewildering territories for teens, and manga's willingness to bring it all out in the open—the good and the bad—resonates with Western and Japanese teens alike. Sometimes there are obvious differences between real-life and manga values; sometimes the differences are more subtle.

Teens vary in their awareness of how cultural differences affect the values that their favorite stories reflect, and adults can only benefit from initiating discussions of these topics with younger readers.

Nudity

As with sexuality, nudity is simply not the red flag in Japan that it is here in the United States (Drazen 2003). Essentially, the U.S. public is still prudish about naked bodies, especially if you can see any detail, and full frontal nudity will get a film rated NC-17. In Japan, nudity is a part of life and does not have much stigma attached to it. If you're getting dressed or taking a bath, then you're going to be naked, and there will be no convenient towels or palm fronds to hide that truth.

Baths and Bathing

Bathing among the family, not always segregated by gender, is a time-honored custom and is seen as a way to grab a little family time while still getting something practical done. Historically, community baths in towns were the place to hear the news, meet up with your neighbors, and simply hang out. Baths are not quite as common today as they were even up until the 1950s, but they are still a regular form of rest and relaxation, taken while on vacation or after a particularly hard day (Ueda 1994).

Part of the astonishment for U.S. readers concerning nudity also comes from the fact that, in manga, incidental nudity from bathing and dressing are just as common in children's manga as they are in manga for older readers. One example that has unnerved U.S. parents appeared in the internationally lauded children's anime *My Neighbor Totoro* by Miyazaki Hayao. The film is set in the 1950s, when it was common for families to bathe together as a way to relax and enjoy each other's company after the day's activities. In *My Neighbor Totoro*, the two young girls at the center of the story bathe with their father, and no one bats an eyelash. There are no explicit images in the film, but everyone is clearly naked. Most parents are more surprised than upset over such an obviously innocent scene. This kind of scene would not appear in a Disney film, however, because family bathing is not a U.S. custom and because it would require showing naked adults and children together.

As readers grow up, they are more likely to encounter nudity in manga. Most manga and anime nudity is incidental and not necessarily sexual. Although sexually charged nudity does exist in manga aimed at teens and adults, it is not as common as prejudice would have it. As mentioned in the humor section of this chapter, the Japanese are particularly intrigued with the humor potential of women's panties and accidental exposure. Titles aimed at teens depict some sexual situations, but these are usually in keeping with the tone of the story. Most nudity, sexuality, or sensuality in manga is on a level with Western young adult novels or films aimed at teens; evaluate these scenes as you would sensual scenes in other visual media. When considering humorous titles, think of recent raunchy film comedies like the *American Pie* series to measure their appeal and appropriateness.

Fan Service

Manga gets its reputation for raciness from the tradition known as fan service. Manga, especially shōnen manga, is famous for including fan service: scenes that exist only to gratify the wishes of fans. This often means a chance to ogle a female character in various states of undress or in a position displaying her charms. The most common type of fan service is the inclusion of "pinup" images of favorite characters: anything from slapstick "accidental exposure" to sexy maid outfits (Schodt 1996). The older the intended audience, the more explicit fan service will be. For example, manga for men will contain shots of breasts and crotches in skintight attire that leave very little to the imagination, and sexual nudity becomes much more common.

The objectification of women in comic art has long been a concern among female fans, as well as the general population, and not unwarrantedly so. Reading any recent volume of the U.S. comics starring strong but scantily clad female superheroes shows that similar fan service moments are par for the course in U.S. comics. Heroines wear just as many ludicrous costumes and often wander around in their underwear. One difference is that while fan service is part of U.S. comics, authors and artists are less likely to admit to creating a U.S. comic just for the pinups. In Japan, whole manga series are known and loved for fan service alone. Another difference is that girl's (or shōjo) manga provides just as much fan service for their readers as their shōnen counterparts, showing off their male heroes and often picturing them half naked and in enticing poses. Manga offers equal opportunity objectification, whereas you would have to flip through hundreds of issues of U.S. comics to see a male superhero as a pinup.

Harem Manga

There are many series that rely mostly on humor and fan service, as with Akamatsu Ken's *Negima* and *Love Hina*. A harem manga depicts an ordinary guy surrounded by a group of beautiful young women, and the bulk of the story will involve slapstick humor involving nudity, groping, "accidental" stripping, and sexual embarrassment. The best harem manga have a sweet side, usually focusing on our bumbling hero and the one girl who is right for him, while the less endearing simply maintain a parade of barely clad women with a bare-bones plot. Female creators are beginning to break into the subgenre with reverse harem manga, where lovely young men surround an ordinary girl vying for her attention. These are usually but not always spoofs, and include *Ouran High School Host Club* and *The Wallflower*.

This kind of fan service can be off-putting in shōnen manga, especially for a Western female reader. Teenage girls, while expecting a certain amount of such ogling in any media aimed at men, are startled by fan service's bluntness, and these scenes may deflate a young woman's enjoyment of an otherwise worthwhile story. This is also certainly true for male readers who may otherwise enjoy shōjo manga and may in fact be worse, given the stereotypical American male's nervousness about homoeroticism. You may hear cries of "I didn't need to see that!" from all kinds of manga readers.

Then again, many readers may be so accustomed to such images in U.S. media, from comics to television to movies, that they don't notice fan service. Sometimes the story and characters are compelling enough that readers can ignore it, and sometimes the fan service overwhelms the story. Every reader will have different limits. Some women have no problem with James Bond films, sexism and romps between the sheets included, and other women can't get past Pussy Galore; some men are perfectly happy watching "chick flicks," and others would feign illness rather than be dragged to the theater for the latest romantic comedy.

Every collection needs its own guidelines for balancing readers' demands and content standards. How much fan service can you tolerate in an otherwise high-quality series? Are the characters well developed and the story compelling? *Tenjo Tenge* is a series noted for its fan service, and it is certainly popular among male readers, but its quality as a story is arguable; you may also find it more suitable for an adult collection. *Cantarella* contains fan service for its female readers, but the milder content of the pinup shots and the high quality of the story should make it acceptable for teen collections. The fan service in Akamatsu Ken's *Love Hina* or Fujisawa Tohru's *Great Teacher Onizuka* is coy enough for most older teen collections, although when it is aimed at male readers, people are more likely to react negatively to fan service featuring female characters.

Explicit, full frontal nudity is still uncommon in most manga with the exception of hentai, ero, yaoi, and yuri manga intended for adult audiences. Erotic manga have a long history and the same freedom that other manga do in terms of content—it's a fantasy, so anything goes. Although erotic titles are not addressed within this text, it is important to recognize that they do exist and may attract curious teens. Some manga was never intended for teen readers and can be quite explicit, just as R- and X-rated films and romance novels here in the United States contain varying levels of explicitness.

For decades, showing genitalia was illegal in Japan; manga artists came up with creative ways to get around the rules, from substituting vegetables and other objects (eggplants, snakes, etc.) to simply leaving blank spaces where genitalia should appear (Schodt 1983). As with the filmmakers working under the U.S. film industry's Hayes Code in the 1940s, manga creators became masters of innuendo and implied, offscreen action. Most manga for teens or adults never approaches the level of explicitness found in ero manga. Be aware of the intended audience for a manga; manga truly intended for teens is unlikely to contain explicit content. As always, problems arise when one person's gentle love scene is another person's pornography—get to know your audience and consider titles accordingly.

Remember that although a manga series may start out at an appropriate content level for teens, the content may change as the series continues. Publishers try to anticipate the levels of content that a manga series will include, but the series may still be unfinished in Japan. When changes in the content of a series necessitate an 18+ or mature rating, publishers will go back and rerate the entire series. Unfortunately, you would have to police the publishers' Web sites constantly to track every ratings change. It often takes several volumes for mature content to surface; in Matoh Sanami's series *Fake*, about a pair of New York cops who fall for each other over the course of seven volumes of crime solving, the first six volumes are appropriate for teens. In the seventh, the lovers finally consummate their relationship in scenes explicit enough to warrant a mature content rating from the publisher. For this reason, although the series has teen appeal, it is better suited to adult collections.

Sexual Content

In manga aimed at teens, you will find nudity both incidentally and as part of the story; when teens make out or have sex, manga creators are more likely to show them undressed than their Western counterparts. In volume ten of Soryo Fuyumi's fifteen-volume romance *Mars*, lovers Rei and Kira have sex "onscreen," or in panel. The scene is gentle, sweet, and very much focused on the emotional impact of this progression in their relationship rather than on showing the mechanics of sex or titillating readers. Similar sequences appear in U.S. teen-oriented television series such as *Buffy the Vampire Slayer*, *Dawson's Creek*, and *Everwood*. Many teen novels and films have equally explicit scenes, but readers may not expect such explicitness in comics.

Manga Cover-Up

Fans expect and demand unedited content. When CMX, DC Comic's manga imprint, edited more than thirty images in *Tenjo Tenge*, a series beloved by fans for its wild combination of street brawls and fan service made up of panty shots and bare breasts, rather than keep the images intact and rate the series for mature audiences, CMX edited the images by covering up with panties and adding bras to previously topless torsos. Fans immediately attacked the company for eliminating what, for many readers, was a large part of the manga's appeal. Even with the uproar, the series remains a top seller, but the reaction has prompted publishers to watch how they alter manga (ICv2.com 2005).

Masamune Shirow's masterpiece *Ghost in the Shell* is a more extreme example of sexual content, one in which fan service plays a major role. The manga combines a complex and intelligent meditation on humanity, technology, and artificial intelligence. Elements of fan service exist throughout; the main character, Major Kusanagi Motoko, fits the pinup character design and wears an odd combination of armor and bustiers as her military uniform. Dark Horse comics recently published a new edition including a scene previously edited out of the English version. In it, Motoko engages in a virtual threesome with two other women. The scene has the surface intent of showing that adults can have sex virtually in the world of the story, but it is also a chance for the reader to see three pages of explicit lesbian action. Dark Horse restored the scene in an admirable mission to translate the art and story faithfully, but it does make things difficult for libraries. Although *Ghost in the Shell* is a classic, libraries that could have easily circulated the first edition may come under fire for purchasing the second.

Sexual content is something to watch for, but it should not automatically keep a manga title out of your collection. Each reader knows his or her limit for explicit content, and most selectors, be they parents or librarians, have a good sense of what is acceptable in their collection. Knowing that manga for teens may contain sexual content, you should be prepared for series that start out at a PG-13 level and progress to R. Maintaining an adult manga collection is one way to deal with a shift in content—you can simply move the entire series to the adult collection to acknowledge its changing appropriateness. If there is no possibility for an adult collection, then check reviews before collecting a series or, better yet, question manga readers and reviewers, including professionals, about the appropriateness and content of a particular series. Reviewers often use specific language to warn readers of explicit content but, given word limits, may not be able to list everything that happens in a title—if you are not sure, it's best either to question someone you know who has read it or to read the title yourself before purchasing it, either in a bookstore or comics store.

Gender Play

Of all the manga traditions that confound Western readers, the free play with gender and gender roles might top the list as most disorienting. In a society such as Japan in which gender roles seem so carefully defined, the number of manga characters that cross those barriers is relatively high compared with characters in the seemingly freer American society. Many see Japan as a culture in which women are decidedly second-class citizens, with men at the top of the food chain, whereas in the West, traditional male and female roles have ostensibly loosened.

These generalizations are both true and not true. In manga, gender and gender roles are far more complex than they would seem based on everyday interactions and Japan's long-held traditions. Challenges to conventional notions of gender appear all the time in Japanese popular media, while they rarely do in the United States. On the other hand, all of this freedom belongs to the imaginary world. The rift between imagination and reality appears once more. U.S. comics authors are beginning to play around with gender expectations; in Japan, where they are socially less tolerant of actual gender border crossing, comics are filled with characters who challenge gender roles: transvestites, drag queens, people with no gender or with more than one.

Gender roles in Japan were not always rigid. Just as attitudes toward sexuality shifted when Japan opened to the West in the 1860s, becoming a modern Western nation meant aligning gender roles with those of the West. Japan combined Western concepts of gender with their older Confucian teachings to confine women to expected roles and elevated men to the controllers of the business and governmental spheres. Women did not gain the right to vote until 1947, as a result of the U.S. occupation and their hand in the creation of Japan's new constitution (Kodansha International 1999).

Once again, however, the line between private and public life means that outside observers miss a great deal of how Japan's culture actually works. Women, for example, have traditionally controlled all of the finances of a household until about the last twenty years. Although men are undoubtedly the breadwinners of most households, they turn their salaries over to their wives who in turn give them an allowance and maintain all the accounts (Kodansha

International 1999). As with any culture where men remain in control legally and economically, women use their power behind the scenes. Japan's pop culture, including manga, reflects a much broader view of women's place in society, as well as cultural fears about how that place is changing as women move into the corporate world and gain independence.

While gender as performance has long been a part of Japanese culture, within Japanese manga it is most frequently a symbol, a performance or a joke. One of the most common traditions of gender play in Eastern and Western cultures is a plot device familiar from countless Western girls' chapter books as well as manga: a girl is determined to become a power within her community, whether as a knight or a magician or a player on the best basketball team, and because of society's restrictions she must dress as a boy to accomplish her goal. In what is often considered one of the first shōjo manga, Tezuka Osamu's *Princess Knight* (*Ribbon no kishi*), a girl born to the royal couple in a kingdom where only male children inherit is presented and brought up as a boy to ensure the kingdom is ruled fairly and does not fall into the hands of a scheming duke. The Princess Sapphire, now a prince, acts as a boy throughout the story, including fighting at night as a masked defender of the kingdom. While the manga follows a fairly traditional fantasy plot, it is notable that Sapphire is in fact a better swordsman than her many enemies and friends and wins the day in the end through the might of her sword, not the revelation of her true gender (Schodt 1996). In line with Shakespearean tradition, however, the gender roles are resolved in the finish by her revealing her actual gender and marrying a neighboring country's prince.

Gender bending in shōjo manga has clear origins in Japanese culture, most notably in the Takarazuka Revue. The Takarazuka theater started in the first decade of the twentieth century as an all female theater troupe. In Kabuki theater, men traditionally act all the roles. The Takarazuka is a female counterpart to the Kabuki tradition. Although the participants are trained in all the traditional female virtues offstage, from proper dress to making tea, the actresses play all the roles onstage, male and female. This freedom within their roles allows for stars to be revered as male impersonators, and as their entire lives are essentially a performance, even offstage, these women cultivate a romantic and fantastical allure as men. Within this culture, the actresses become pop idols, and many teen girls admire actresses known for their male roles to the point of fan clubs, fan magazines, and all the squeals and crushes that male pop idols attract (Robertson 1998). Takarazuka productions were and continue to be noted for their elaborateness and melodrama, and many of the current plots come from popular girls' manga as well as the legends and folktales of Japan. Tezuka grew up near Takarazuka and was a fan of their elaborate productions; *Princess Knight* reflects his admiration (Schodt 1996). The Takarazuka stars are also credited as one point of origin for the beauty of the young men in shōjo manga because they are in fact drawn more like women impersonating men.

From Tezuka's *Princess Knight* flowed a variety of stories involving gender play. Shōjo manga is especially full of stories in which characters present as the opposite gender, usually girls as boys but occasionally boys as girls. These switches happen for the flimsiest of reasons. The real point is the potential for both humor and drama in the situation. Many of these manga play out like modern versions of Shakespeare's gender bending plays from *As You Like It* to *Twelfth Night*. Although individual characters may experience the joys and burdens of being the other sex, in the end everyone returns to his or her assigned role and lives happily ever after in a socially acceptable way.

Girls as Boys, Boys as Girls

Girl Got Game follows the adventures of a girl basketball star sent to a special high school to join the famous Seisyu Academy basketball team. Her father, determined to have his daughter live out his dreams, conveniently forgets to tell her she'll have to pose as a male to join the prestigious boys squad. *Hana Kimi* has a similar plot, although this time our heroine is a track star.

In many manga tales of girls dressing as boys, the trouble starts when the girl meets her love interest, almost always a boy who may or may not have any idea he's meeting a girl in boy's clothing. It's a tried and true set up for romantic melodrama, and it works predictably in most manga. Even when girls are in masculine disguise, they often end up impressing their new compatriots with their innate leadership, good intentions, and spunky spirit. These are considered both female and heroic traits. In the fluffy comedy *Ouran High School Host Club*, gender swapping is both a joke and a convenient way to avoid other people's expectations. Our heroine Haruhi is a girl whose classmates at her new school take her for a boy because of her short hair and baggy boyish clothing —and she really doesn't care, being a bit asexual and confused by romance. She ends up, for complicated and screwball reasons, working as a "host" for her wealthy high school's Host Club. The Host Club is a group of attractive young men who run an escort service for the young ladies around campus as an after school job. Dressed as a boy, Haruhi becomes their clients' favorite—much to the dismay of their slightly batty leader, King, who holds the top spot among the Hosts. Of course, King also begins developing confusing feelings for Haruhi. Haruhi's inattention to her own attractiveness as either a boy or a girl leads to lots of jokes, while King's hidden feelings for her are complicated by the entire school's perception that she is male.

In *Tenshi Ja Nai!*, Hikaru discovers that her starlet roommate Izumi is in fact a beautiful young man who is willing to go to any length, including blackmailing Hikaru, to keep his secret. Hikaru objects to this secretive and obnoxious treatment, but Izumi's flashes of vulnerability and fear of being revealed convince her to keep the secret for the time being. The combination of a wild sense of humor, multilayered secrets, and increasingly complicated schemes to keep Izumi's gender undercover make the series frenetic, slightly off-kilter fun.

In *Tenshi Ja Nai!!,* Hikaru discovers her roommate is not precisely the idol of feminine beauty everyone thinks she is—in fact, she's a he.

Shōjo manga heroines, from Princess Sapphire on, let girls be the hero in their imaginations. Vicariously, they get to do everything that boys do in terms of position, power, and achievement. Since female authors took over shōjo manga in the 1970s, heroines have enjoyed this freedom more often. Shōnen manga has its share of strong, smart heroines, but they are still presented as women. In shōjo manga, girls get to play out their roles as boys and see what it's like to be on a boys' soccer team or part of a boys' academy—they gain secret access to what the boys do when no girls are around. In the end, though, these are fantasies; they are about what women pretend men are like rather than what men actually *are* like. When romance becomes a part of the plot, it usually means a return to the standard gender roles. Even if the spunky heroine, who does in fact act more like a boy than a girl, wins the heart of her chosen beau, she must return to being a girl for the relationship to be a success.

W Juliet flips this formula. Ito Miura, a tomboy who's suffered since the beginning of middle school from being the most dashing "guy" in her school, is determined to remind everyone that she's a girl. She wants to play Juliet in the school play but is instead cast as Romeo. She takes the part, with much grumbling, but then discovers that her Juliet may be the new transfer student Makoto Amano. Makoto is beautiful and an accomplished actress, which wins her friends and rivals, but Ito is the only one to discover her secret—Makoto is actually a boy in disguise. As it turns out, Makoto is desperate to become an actor while his traditionalist father demands that Makoto take over the family martial arts school. His father, in a moment of inspiration, gives Makoto a way out that he thinks his son would never accept—if Makoto can live for two years as a girl, with no one finding out his true sex, then he will be allowed to pursue his acting career. Makoto surprises everyone by accepting the challenge. Ito of course agrees to keep Makoto's secret, which proves to be harder than she would expect as their feelings for each other deepen. The story ends up as a sweet romantic comedy with a gentle critique of gender roles for both sexes at its center; Makoto admires Miura just the way she is, while other guys seem to insist that she conform to their womanly ideals.

The treatment of gender becomes even more complex in boy's love (BL) and yaoi manga, created as fantasies for girls and women by women. Taking the whole idea of infiltrating the boys' club even further, these stories do away with the pretense of having a girl present in the story. In these stories, two boys or young men fall in love and encounter a variety of barriers, from their own inability to admit their feelings to fear of society's condemnation. Some of these concerns are unique to Japanese society—often the characters worry less about the attraction they feel and more about the societal obligation to marry and produce heirs that will inevitably end their relationship. This obligation to the family group is overwhelming; personal happiness never takes precedence over familial ties.

Even within BL, titles are beginning to tread ever closer to reality. A recent title, *Only the Ring Finger Knows*, still has the trappings of a traditional BL story: the taller, more aggressive Kazuki pursues the innocent object of affection, Watari. Still, instead of falling into the expected dominant–submissive trope, in this title, Kazuki is more sure of himself only because he knows what he's feeling, whereas Watari is not as aware of his own heart. Once all is revealed, Kazuki turns out to be more vulnerable than expected, and although the two are worried about society's acceptance, they do not assume that their romance must inevitably end because of societal obligations.

Intriguingly, even though the characters in yaoi and boy's love manga are always two men, they assume the gender roles of a traditional relationship. One is the aggressive, arrogant pursuer, the other a more innocent and timid object of affection. Characters often worry about being perceived either within the relationship or by peers as the woman in the romance, and the dominant partner cannot accept being made to feel submissive in any way. Although the absence of gender inequalities allows for writers to experiment with love escaping gender expectations, the romantic tropes of BL manga often end up perpetuating gender stereotypes.

One of the most famous incarnations of gender play in shōnen manga is Takahashi Rumiko's *Ranma 1/2*, the enormously popular shōnen manga, which is rife with slapstick, parody, martial arts, and, yes, gender shenanigans. Because of an unfortunate incident at a cursed spring, any time the hero Ranma is splashed with cold water, he turns into a girl, and only when splashed with hot water will he return to his original gender. As the story begins, his father (who, because of the same kind of curse, changes back and forth from man to panda) explains that Ranma is engaged to the daughter of an old friend. Of course, once the daughter in question discovers the fluctuating gender of her fiancé, she is less inclined to agree to the whole arrangement. Wacky antics ensue, for everyone around Ranma is tangled up with either his male or his female persona. He himself is quite irritated by the whole situation, and readers know that Ranma does not switch genders by choice or by nature.

Manga has other, more ambiguous gender benders. In the long-running shōjo series *Fushigi Yugi*, one of the group of chosen warriors, Nuriko, cross-dresses as a woman. As with many fantasy plots, his reasons are complicated—when he first appears as a lady of Emperor Hotohori's court, it is revealed that he is driven to honor his dead sister by living the life she might have led in her place. Everyone believes he is a lady, and he fervently pursues Hotohori's love despite the general sentiment that Hotohori is too narcissistic to care for anyone but himself. Later, when Nuriko becomes one of the seven key warriors, he still chooses to dress as a woman. In the end, the author reveals him to be in love with the heroine, Miaka, and his proper sexuality is thus restored. For the bulk of the series, however, he presents as a woman for reasons other than comic relief.

Manly Women, Effeminate Men

Japanese history and legend have produced several examples of men who challenge Western notions of manliness. Effeminate men in Japanese stories are not automatically weak-willed wimps. In fact, they are most often the opposite. As Japanese legends and mythology idealize beauty and youth, so do they admire beautiful young men. One of their most famous military heroes is an eleventh-century general Minimoto no Yoshitsune, who was legendary as both an extraordinarily beautiful youth and as a brilliant strategist and warrior. He died for his ideals, committing *seppuku*, or ritual suicide, at age twenty and is revered as a great military figure (Buruma 1984).

Later, during the Meiji Era (1868–1912), Okita Soji was one member of the infamous Shisengumi, also known as Wolves of Kyoto. Another beautiful and effeminate young man, he was also counted as the most lethal fighter among this team of unequalled warriors. Okita is portrayed in fiction, including the manga series *Peacemaker Kurogane*, as a sweet-natured and gentle soul except in battle where he is precise, ruthless, and absolutely cold. In *Kaze Hikaru*, although still a cold warrior with feminine qualities, Okita is also the romantic lead. In this tradition, what Western readers see as effeminacy has nothing to do with weakness. A "feminine" young man is not acting like a woman so much as holding on to his youth and beauty, and no one can be condemned for wishing to linger in that state. The fact that Okita died from consumption at age twenty-five leaves him forever young, his legend untarnished and idealized.

Aside from physical appearance, "appropriate" behavior between members of the same sex is less rigidly defined in manga and anime. As with many cultures where there is a tradition of gender separation in both school and societal interaction, bonds between members of the same gender are highly valued in Japan. People are expected to form strong friendships with members of their own gender, and they are allowed to express this with open displays of love and affection (Drazen 2003).

While Western society allows women a variety of ways to show affection, from hugs to kisses to simple physical closeness, men are much more circumspect. In the United States, it's rare to see men walking arm in arm, sitting close together, or even hugging too much or too closely. Typical defense mechanisms include the "heterosexual male pat," or the back-slapping that often accompanies a hug between men to confirm to each other and everyone around them that it's a manly hug, not a romantic one. In Japan, men do not have to justify showing affection to one another. If you want to tell your best friend you love him, that's OK. You can even hug if you want, and no one will think you're gay.

Amusingly enough, both shōnen and shōjo manga use displays of male–male affection to titillate female readers and poke fun at the popularity of BL manga tropes. In the comedy *Here Is Greenwood*, upperclassmen Shinobu and Mitsuru unnerve their new classmate Hasukawa Kazuya by pretending to be more than friends and periodically flirt around him to see how much they can mess with his head. The entire short-lived CLAMP series *Legal Drug* was an affectionate parody of BL manga, complete with pretty bishōnen, increasingly ludicrous antics that forced the leads into compromising positions, and tension drawn out so long that it's a tease rather than a serious plot development.

In manga and anime, both genders show unrestrained love and affection, especially to close friends and siblings. Young male characters are much more likely to express their feelings, and to touch their friends in an affectionate manner, than we are used to seeing in the West. In the same way, young women are exuberant in their affection to the point of seeming to have romantic crushes on their best friends. As discussed earlier in this chapter, none of this indicates romantic intentions.

When sex enters the equation, manga characters lose their freedom from gender roles. In sexual relationships, a woman is submissive and a man is dominant. It is shameful for a man to be submissive, and if he acts so, he is being a woman. By the same token, a sexually aggressive woman is unnatural and often a villain.

Choosing Your Gender

As manga, especially shōjo manga, has diversified, gender play has become less idealized and more realistic. In *After School Nightmare*, Mashiro Ichijo is a boy on top and a girl on the bottom. He has passed as male his whole life, but when he gets his first period, he begins to struggle with how to keep his secret. Ichijo believes being male is better—he can do and be respected more as a boy and man. As he sees it, being a girl would mean being weak and without influence. The whole series balances on which gender Ichijo will ultimately choose to present and the forces that pull him toward each side.

The romantic drama *Paradise Kiss* by Yazawa Ai pushes gender roles subtly but surely beyond what is considered acceptable. The story focuses on Yukari, a girl who is adopted into a crowd of local arts high school students to be the model in their senior fashion show. Hidden within the series is one of the most realistic and accepting portrayals of a transgender character in manga. Drag queens and transsexuals are common in manga, perhaps because the history of gender as performance in Japan makes these characters less shocking than they might be in the United States. The outsider appeal of these characters makes them perfect comic relief and confidantes for main characters, usually in shōjo manga. Most often, however, they are not realistic or deep characters—they are there for the sight gag when people realize they're not the gender they claim to be, and they make everyone giggle at their outrageousness. Actual instances of transgender or even gay characters as they are understood in the West are rare.

In *Paradise Kiss*, however, we have Isabella, leading man George's best friend from childhood who, although born male, presents as a woman and is transgendered. Isabella has motherly qualities, acting as the confidante and caretaker of the ragtag band of students; she is not a wacky sidekick or comic relief. Within the series, when she explains how George was the first to realize her predicament and embrace her anyway—George was the first to present Isabella with a custom-made gown—it is a story of acceptance and love, not comedy. In the end, Isabella will not return to her biological gender or take on a masculine gender role—she is happy as she is, and no one would tell her differently.

Violence

One concern many readers may have with manga is the level of violence in some titles. Comedies depend on a fair amount of slapstick humor, which includes roughhousing and frequent smacks on the noggin. Exaggerated brawls between characters are never serious and the superhuman ability of characters to avoid blows or to take harsh blows and pop right back up again are indicators that a fight is not serious, nor should the reader be worried about any true damage to these elastic characters.

True violence does appear in manga, from fistfights to samurai duels; it is more or less explicit depending on the context of the fight as well as the intended audience for the title. Blood will be minimal in children's stories, but teen stories may display a bloodier side of violence. If it is comical violence, à la Wile E. Coyote, the ridiculousness of the situation and the resiliency of the victim clues in the reader that the violence is not realistic and is not intended to be.

The historical art traditions from which manga arose, most notably toba-e and ukiyo-e (see Chapter 1), commonly used dramatic splatters of blood and violent action. Many manga tales follow those same literary and artistic traditions. Titles aimed at boys and teens, including the ninja series *Naruto* and the pirate adventure *One Piece*, are not explicit in terms of violence. These titles concentrate on learning fighting skills and unarmed combat rather than on killing. *Naruto* is part comedy, part action series, and the famous ninja repertoire of skills are revered and mocked in the same breath. In fact, as with many of these series, sexual humor is more common and may be more surprising to Western readers than the physical action. One of Naruto's favorite tricks is the Sexy no Jutsu, an illusion in which he momentarily transforms into an almost naked buxom woman, and thus distracts his enemy (and gives them a powerful nosebleed that forces them out of the fight). In the same way, mecha stories usually contain robot violence or machine based battles and technological warfare, rather than person-to-person violence. Robot violence is still considerable, of course, but the sense of machines as disposable weapons is familiar from Western traditions.

Titles targeted to older readers, or those that want to make a point about the consequences of violence, may well show the bloody results of a fight. This is especially true of samurai or ninja series. In the anime *Peacemaker* and the sequel manga series *Peacemaker Kurogane*, for example, elite fighters engage in combat that is bloody, brutal, and vicious. Fifteen-year-old Tetsunosuke (nicknamed Tetsu), driven to avenge the murder of his parents, begs to join the ranks of the infamous Shinsengumi: the force of rōnin loyal to the Shogunate. The older members of the group, hoping to dissuade him, take him on missions specifically to make sure he understands what he is asking for in becoming one of them. The work is not all showmanship; being one of the Shinsengumi means ruthlessly killing people, and none of the men take that responsibility lightly. The series ends with Tetsu confronting his enemy but finding, in the end, that he cannot and will not kill. His fellows are killers, and their work is shown in fair amount of detail, but it is never frivolous or fun; instead, it is portrayed as a necessary evil and duty.

As mentioned earlier in the discussion of villains, truly cruel violence usually marks its perpetrator as a villain. Villainous violence may include battles and fights but may also veer into torture and painful experimentation, as with the evil Mikage corporation and scientists in *Ceres: Celestial Legend* or the inhumanly vicious queen Nakia in *Red River*. In teen titles, this kind of violence is implied offscreen or only witnessed in the aftermath rather than shown in panel. Adult titles might show such violence, assuming that their intended audience can handle it and that it is necessary to the telling of their tale.

A few titles teens enjoy include far more violence than most readers or viewers would find comfortable. *Hellsing* is extremely popular with older teens, with its combination of spy intrigue and gothic vampire lore, but the violent content of the manga is explicit and frequent enough to ensure a mature rating. The violence in the anime series is toned down for network television, but even so, it is most suitable for adults. *Battle Royale* is famous for a variety of reasons: it is an intense thriller and a harsh exploration of human nature, but it features a constant barrage of explicit violence paired with fan service. Fans cite the first two components as the major reason to read the title, but the third justifiably keeps many readers away. This series is well known, and teens are curious about it, but it is rightly marked mature for its explicit violence as well as its sexual content.

Religious Imagery

Japan is a country with a mixed religious history, from the nature-driven native religion of Shintō to the early import of Chinese Buddhism mingling with the social guidelines of Confucianism. Unlike many countries in which individual traditions remain strictly separate, in Japan all of these traditions are combined into a mishmash of ceremonies, ideals, and behavior. Christianity was a late arrival and is still very much a minority faith, but images from the Western Christian tradition have become part of the mix (Kodansha International 1999).

Mix and Match

Because many people practice more than one religion in Japan, ceremonies are held to suit the occasion rather than follow a particular faith. Weddings are often Shintō with Western touches creeping in (as white wedding dresses replace the traditional red gown), whereas funerals are Buddhist as Shintō has no ceremonies for death.

As with other cultural references in manga, uncovering the different religious traditions and ceremonies represented is part of the fun and learning process for non-Japanese readers. Christian traditions and imagery, on the other hand, are often used in unfamiliar and what some might consider blasphemous ways. Crucifixion, for example, is often used in manga as a type of execution. Most of the time, however, a crucifixion is not a specific reference to the story or death of Jesus Christ. In Japan, creators have taken the idea that crucifixion means a tragic and untimely death from Christian theology. They do not intend to imply a character has Christ-like qualities or to recall Christ's execution.

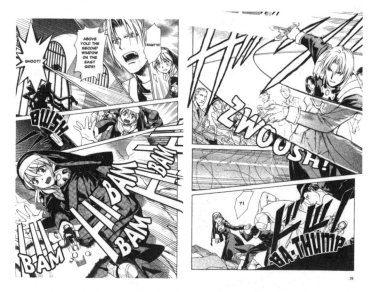

Sister Rosette and Father Remington battle demons in *Chrono Crusade*.
© Daisuke Moriyama KADOKAWA SHOTEN PUBLISHING, CO LTD.

Similarly, many manga characters are clad in outfits full of Christian paraphernalia, from crosses to crucifixes. Again, these are just interesting symbols and patterns and generally do not mean the character is any sort of Christian, unless expressly stated in the story. Christian characters do, of course, exist, especially in stories not set in Japan. Moriyama Daisuke's *Chrono Crusade*, for example, features Sister Rosette Christopher, a machine-gun-toting nun working for the Vatican as a special forces demon slayer. The popular horror manga *Hellsing*, a story of Alucard (or Dracula spelled in reverse) working as an agent against his own kind in Britain, features all sorts of Christian references. Christian objects serve as weapons for Dracula as well as being the driving force behind the Hellsing organization's power.

Stories that use religious imagery do not claim to offer realistic examples of a particular kind of worship. In Japan, strict adherence to the tenets of a particular faith is not expected or necessary; manga and anime feel free to represent religious traditions in a superficial, aesthetic way

Challenges and Concerns

This chapter has shown the variety of topics in manga that may lead readers to either avoid or embrace this unique body of literature. As a selector of graphic novels, there are a number of ways to identify and deal with inflammatory content while building your collection. It is fairly easy to flip through a manga volume and discover whether it contains objectionable content. Previewing can be helpful, because it will forewarn you about any content concerns. At the same time, it's very easy to flip through a manga and see disturbing content out of context. You may field questions about such content, or challenges, from browsers and staff members.

Maintaining separate collections of manga in children's, teen, and adult sections in libraries is vital to ensuring that both professionals and patrons understand the different audiences for graphic novel and manga titles. Although every section includes a wide range of maturity levels, especially teen collections that must serve readers from age thirteen to eighteen, separating titles into these three categories guides most library users well.

When evaluating a title, consider the following:

- How does the content causing concern compare to visual media—films, television, video games, and so on—for the same age range? Would you collect a film with the same content for your target audience, and if so, where would you place it in your collection?

- What is the publisher, production company, or distributor's recommended rating? How would that rating fit into your library collection?

- How does the content causing concern compare with all media, including books, for the same age range? If it were a film or television show, what kind of rating might it warrant, and for what reasons? Images of an action are more inflammatory than a textual description of the same action. Remember to consider the entire collection aimed at a particular audience to check your own standards against your audience's standards.

- What is the appeal of the title? Is the subject appealing to teens, adults, kids, or sections of all three? What are the ages of the main characters? For example, when a title has teen appeal but features adult characters and addresses adult concerns, it might be better placed in an adult collection.

- If there are panels or sections of a manga giving you pause, what is the context for those panels? How much of the title contains material that may not suit your audience? It may be best to err on the side of caution when there is material you as a selector feel is troublesome, but if the title is of exceptional quality for your audience, make sure to weigh its importance and appeal against content concerns.

In developing an appealing manga collection, it is vital that you be consistent about what is allowable within teens' media. If you purchase teen fiction or films with mature content, there's no reason to exclude similar manga just because the format is unfamiliar. On the other hand, you would be justified in placing a questionable manga or anime in an adult collection.

In my limited experience with patrons questioning graphic novel content, the objections often arise from a misunderstanding about the title's nature or intended audience. Adults may approach a librarian wondering about the content of an adult graphic novel, not quite realizing that the title is not intended for children. When concerns arise about unfamiliar representations of familiar icons, as with Christian imagery, consider explaining that these representations come from another culture where they have a different meaning. Not every conversation will end with the questioner feeling completely satisfied, but often discussing the nature and origin of a title helps a patron understand its value or point of view.

Once the titles are on the shelves, or even before, educate yourself, your readers and fellow staff on the media you are presenting. If you are starting a new manga or anime collection, or both, consider hosting a "Frequently Asked Question" night for parents and other curious patrons (see the Frequently Asked Question section in Appendix B). Offer definitions, information on the collection, articles related to the media, and a question and answer session with a librarian, and if possible a manga or anime expert or fan (see Appendix B for example questions and answers). If starting a teen collection, you may want to recruit an eloquent teen to help explain the appeal and fun of manga and anime to adults in their own words. Provide handouts at the event and make them available to the public on a regular basis, including print versions of frequently asked questions and recommended book lists by age.

Challenges: What to Do?

Be prepared to defend controversial material in your collection and do so by considering how the titles in question fit the standards developed for other library collections. In my discussions with colleagues across the country, no one has reported that graphic novels are challenged any more than any other type of book. If they are challenged, it is often a staff person who brings the challenge rather than a member of the public. Given manga and anime's rising popularity and visibility, we may be seeing more challenges in the future.

Like any other item in the collection, both manga and anime must be considered in accordance with your institution's collection development policy. In building a new collection, you might consider creating a graphic-novel-specific collection development policy. For most collections, this is not necessary because graphic novels and films are already covered in current collection development policies. You should apply these existing standards to manga and anime. If your library does not already have a reconsideration process clearly defined in your collection development policy or elsewhere within the governing rules of the organization, work to ensure one is implemented. Make sure the usual requirements for reconsideration are met, including asking the requester to read or view the entire work for context, provide specific objections, and fill out a formal reconsideration request form. Agree in advance as to who will respond to the reconsideration request and establish her or his authority to make a decision. Members of a reconsideration committee might include community members, librarians, and authority figures from local organizations and government.

Because manga and anime are visual media, consider some ways to define the amount of objectionable content in a particular work. Count the number of panels considered objectionable and compare that number to the total number of panels, as you might do with pages in a book. If your library has a policy in place for visual media, including films, computer games, or Internet sites, consider basing your graphic novel standards on standards for those media to ensure their visual nature is taken into account.

Librarians should only need these tools and warnings on rare occasions. This chapter is not meant to scare readers about potential challenges or unveil lurid content hidden in manga. Humor, friendship, romance, sexuality, and gender will always be much discussed issues in popular culture. Every population has its own boundaries between what's acceptable and what's objectionable, and communities may disagree more often than they suspect. This chapter's discussion is meant to inform you, so you can judge titles with some understanding of the cultural context and motivations behind their content. If you feel prepared to interpret manga and anime's unique aspects for your patrons and staff, you will feel more confident in your selections.

References

Buruma, Ian. *Behind the Mask: On Sexual Demons, Sacred Mothers, Transvestites, Gangsters, Drifters, and other Japanese Cultural Heroes*. New York: New American Library, 1984.

Drazen, Patrick. *Anime Explosion: The What? Why? & Wow! of Japanese Animation*. Berkeley, CA: Stone Bridge Press, 2003.

Kodansha International. *Japan: Profile of a Nation Revised Edition*. Tokyo: Kodansha International, 1999.

Robertson, Jennifer. *Takarazuka: Sexual Politics and Popular Culture in Modern Japan*. Berkeley: University of California Press, 1998.

Schodt, Frederik L. *Dreamland Japan: Writings on Modern Manga*. Berkeley, CA: Stone Bridge Press, 1996.

———. *Manga! Manga! The World of Japanese Comics*. Tokyo: Kodansha International, 1983.

Ueda, Atsushi, ed. *The Electronic Geisha: Exploring Japan's Popular Culture*. Translated by Miriam Eguchi. Tokyo: Kodansha International, 1994.

Chapter Four

Adventures with Ninjas and Schoolgirls: Humor and Realism

Manga titles cover a whole range of themes, from epic love and heroic journeys to the everyday concerns of academic achievement, bullying, romance, and athletic ambition. These themes are recognizable to readers across the world. The specifics, however, play out according to the culture from which they emerge. Universal themes such as group obligation, prejudice, and personal love are echoed across cultures and history, from Shakespeare's *Romeo and Juliet* to Brent Hartinger's *The Geography Club* or Stephenie Meyer's *Twilight*. How each theme appears in manga is distinctly Japanese in attitude, custom, and resolution.

Genres in the United States are fairly well defined—a mystery is a mystery and involves a dead body, a plot to be unraveled, and either a professional or amateur detective. Science fiction speculates on what might happen according to the laws of our universe, whereas fantasy speculates on what might happen if those laws were defined differently. Romances focus on romantic relationships between characters. Each genre has its crossover titles, as seen in supernatural romances, hard-boiled science fiction, and fantastical crime stories, but readers generally expect a genre to follow its major conventions as the pleasure of reading genres comes from satisfying those expectations.

Certain manga genres hold to the standard models—most notably mysteries and military science fiction—but frequently manga stories are a mishmash of different genres. Manga and anime blur the definitions of genres as we recognize them. Many martial arts dramas are crammed full of historical references, slapstick humor, and romance. A teen romance may feature bullying, harassment, school pressure, and screwball humor. A cyberpunk science fiction piece, full of violent action, genetically engineered people, and government conspiracies resolves into a meditation on love. Of course, the presumption that our own genres do not stretch as far does a disservice to genre writers, but in Japan the elements of genre are so regularly broken apart and recombined in new ways that it's rare to find a title that remains purely one genre. For new readers,

107

this shift from genre to genre, and attitude to attitude, feels uncomfortable and confusing; for manga readers it is all part of the appeal.

Genre Remix

Manga and anime mix and match genres. Here are a few famous examples:

Ranma 1/2: Martial arts/romance/comedy

Excel Saga: Science fiction/action/satire

Rurouni Kenshin: Historical/martial arts/romance/comedy/drama

Full Metal Panic!: Military/action/school drama/slapstick comedy

---

For all of the quicksilver shifts in tone, manga and anime are rooted in real life, exploring family life, school, and characters' fears and aspirations. Parental expectations, peer pressure, and academic careers add anxiety to the mix. Speculative settings and unusual powers allow creators to examine human problems on an exaggerated scale. Creators mine a rich, conflicted national history to bring the past to life, with irreverence or solemnity, seeking the roots of their current way of life. Popular culture, from the time period a manga is set in as well as when it is created, illustrates style, fashion, slang, and environment. Starting with everyday life, this chapter covers the genres and concerns manga and anime return to again and again.

List Annotations

For a complete explanation of the annotations for each title, please see the key at the beginning of Chapter Nine. These items are used in annotations in Chapters Four through Six.

Humor

Humor is everywhere. Even in the most serious manga, humor is used to lighten the mood, tease a character, or make fun of manga conventions. Many new manga readers are taken by surprise when they are in the middle of a serious moment and suddenly the characters appear in chibi form and play out a slapstick joke. Once the moment is over, the drama continues, but the abrupt appearance of jokes and bursts of laughter push readers out of the story. These short bursts of humor take some getting used to, but they also achieve their goal of making the reader laugh.

Many humor manga have the external trappings of other genres, from historical dramas to fantasy, but in essence they are humor titles. *One Piece* is an excellent example. The story is a mishmash of eighteenth-century European piracy and Japan's own traditions of pirate rogues but the characters bear only a passing resemblance to historical pirates. Luffy is determined to be king of all the pirates. He has, by virtue of blindly eating the magical fruit of the Gum Gum tree, a body that behaves like rubber. He meanders through the pirate world with little direction or plan except his final goal. The entire series' aim is humor. The hero's dimwitted but admirable perseverance, the elaborateness of the villains' schemes, and the sheer ridiculousness of, for example, a pirate ship made up entirely of clowns all contribute to the hilarity. The manic sense of humor in *One Piece* is present in almost all shōnen manga and in a fair number of shōjo manga.

Laugh Out Loud Titles

Azuma, Kyohiko. *Yotsuba&!* ADV Manga, 2003–2006 Japan (2005 U.S.). Publisher Age Rating: All Ages. Age Recommendation: M. Volumes: 1–3 [T]. Genres: Comedy, Slice of Life

 Yotsuba doesn't know what a doorbell is (but oh, does she catch on fast). With green hair and hints of a less-than-human origin, she's not your everyday five-year-old. A silly comedy great for all ages.

Fuji, Mihona. *GALS!* CMX Manga, 1998–2002 Japan (2005 U.S.) Publisher Age Rating: Teen. Age Recommendation: J. Volumes: 1–9+ [T]. Genres: Romance, School Drama, Comedy, Slice of Life. Related Anime: *GALS* (TV series)

 Diving right into the Harajuku district's Kogal culture, *GALS!* heroines are not fashion-obsessed airheads with questionable morals. They're defenders of the meek!

Gatou, Shoji. *Full Metal Panic!* ADV Manga, 2000 Japan (2003 U.S.). Publisher Age Rating: 13+. Age Recommendation: S. Volumes: 1–9 [T]. Genres: Action, Military, School Drama, Comedy. Related Manga: *Full Metal Panic Fumoffu!*, Related Anime: *Full Metal Panic!*, *Full Metal Panic Fumoffu!*

 High schooler Chidori, although spunky and full of sass, needs safeguarding. Sousuke is her secret military protector—but when he casually blows up her shoe locker or rappels down a wall, it's not so secret anymore.

Hatori, Bisco. *Ouran High School Host Club*. Tokyopop, 2003 Japan (2005 U.S.). Publisher Age Rating: Teen. Age Recommendation: S. Volumes: 1–9 [T]. Genres: Comedy, School Drama

After breaking a priceless vase, Haruhi must join her school's host club to pay for the damage. But what's a girl to do when she becomes the favorite host of all the girls in her class?

Hayakawa, Tomoko. *The Wallflower*. Del Rey Manga, 2000– Japan (2004 U.S.). Publisher Age Rating: Teen. Age Recommendation: S. Volumes: 1–13 [T]. Genres: Romance, Comedy, Slice of Life

Sunako is happy with her horror movies, her rubber duckies, and her own company. When four drop-dead gorgeous young men trade the task of taming Sunako into a "lady" for free rent to a fantastic house, they have no idea what they're up against.

Kishimoto, Masashi. *Naruto*. VIZ Manga, 1987–1991 Japan (2003 U.S.). Publisher Age Rating: Teen. Age Recommendation: J. Volumes: 1–13+ [T]. Genres: Action, Fantasy, Historical, Comedy. Related Anime: *Naruto* (TV series)

Naruto, an irrepressible apprentice ninja determined to prove his worth as a warrior, carries a magical burden—his body is the prison for the malicious spirit of a nine-tailed fox. A hilarious series with moments of real heart.

Nishimori, Hiroyuki. *Cheeky Angel*. VIZ Manga, 1999–2003 Japan (2004 U.S.). Publisher Age Rating: Teen. Age Recommendation: J. Volumes: 1–16+ [T]. Genres: Comedy, Romance, Action

Megumi wished to be the "manliest man on Earth" but, of course, through a misunderstanding, he ends up the "womanliest woman." A foxy girl with a boy's brash attitude—all the girls admire her, and all the boys want her. What's a girl to do?

Nishiyama, Yuriko. *Dragon Voice*. Tokyopop, 2001–2003 Japan (2004 U.S.). Publisher Age Rating: Teen. Age Recommendation: J. Volumes: 1–7+ [T]. Genres: Comedy, Slice of Life

Rin has a singing voice that sends audiences running, but he doggedly keeps trying. His voice becomes extraordinary when it blends with the harmonies of the latest boy band, the Beatmen. Together can they make a lasting impression in the fleeting world of pop stardom?

Nonaka, Eiji. *Cromartie High School*. ADV Manga, 2001 Japan (2004 U.S.). Publisher Age Rating: 13+. Age Recommendation: S. Volumes: 1–9+ [T]. Genres: Comedy, School. Related Anime: *Cromartie High School* (TV series)

Takashi has no idea what he's in for when he's transferred to the infamous Cromartie High—a high school populated entirely by thugs and misfits. He certainly didn't expect a robot, a guy who looks like Freddy Mercury.

Ohkami, Mineko. *Dragon Knights*. Tokyopop, 1991–2001 Japan (2002–2007 U.S.). Publisher Age Rating: Teen. Age Recommendation: J. Volumes: 1–25 [T]. Genres: Action, Comedy, Fantasy

Rune, Rath, and Thats are the greatest warriors in the kingdom. Slaying dragons and saving maidens are everyday chores, but getting some time to grab dinner would be nice. Parodying quest traditions with a joke a page, this series is a mockery of high fantasy epics.

Takahashi, Rumiko. *Ranma 1/2*. VIZ Manga, 1988–1996 Japan (2003 U.S., 2nd ed.). Publisher Age Rating: Older Teen. Age Recommendation: S. Volumes: 1–38 [T]. Genres: Action, Fantasy, Romance, School Drama, Comedy. Related Anime: *Ranma 1/2* (TV series)

After falling in a spring during martial arts training, Ranma is cursed: if he is hit with cold water, he becomes a girl. Hot water reverses the effect. His arranged fiancée is not so sure about the whole thing.

Toriyama, Akira. *Dragon Ball*. VIZ Manga, 1984–1995 Japan (2000 U.S.). Publisher Age Rating: Older Teen. Age Recommendation: S. Volumes: 16 of 16 [T]. Genres: Action, Fantasy, Comedy. Related Manga: *Dragon Ball GT*, *Dragon Ball Z*. Related Anime: *Dragon Ball* (TV series)

Son Goku is a wild child with a monkey tail and mad fighting skills. Bulma is a young woman seeking the legendary seven dragon balls, mystical orbs that can grant any wish when brought together. When these two collide, a grand adventure begins.

Yoshizumi, Wataru. *Ultra Maniac*. VIZ Manga, 2002–2004 Japan (2005–2006 U.S.). Publisher Age Rating: All Ages. Age Recommendation: M. Volumes: 1–5 [T]. Genres: Fantasy, School Drama, Magical Girl, Comedy. Related Anime: *Ultra Maniac* (TV series)

Nina's not a very good witch, but she's doing her best to observe the human world and learn while on exchange from her home school. With best friend Ayu in tow, she tackles romance and friendship.

When in Doubt, Embarrassment Is Funny

Extreme emotions are often mocked, especially when a reaction is far more violent than the situation warrants. Anger, puppy love, brutal honesty, and awkwardness are all played up for comic effect. Teasing and jokes may set off madcap chases and death threats from the prank's target. In *Peacemaker Kurogane*, the mischievous Okita steals his commander Hijikata's private haiku and reads them to the other warriors. Hijikata's embarrassment and explosive rage propel the episode into the realm of farce, with the entire unit involved in a screwball chase after the papers.

One of the most common emotions inspiring laughter is embarrassment. All of the nosebleeds that indicate inappropriate arousal, the shots of girls' panties, and the sudden loss of clothing are funny because of the acute embarrassment they cause characters. The frantic backpedaling and apologizing is the punch line of the joke, and readers feel grateful that it's not happening to them.

In "harem" manga, when an ordinary joe is surrounded by a bevy of beautiful ladies all vying for his attention, this kind of sexual embarrassment is key. Fan service abounds, as do nosebleeds and raging embarrassment. Akamatsu Ken's *Love Hina* and *Negima* are classic examples of the shōnen variety. This kind of setup is not as common in shōjo manga, although titles such as *Boys over Flowers* and *The Wallflower* make fun of harem plots by reversing the conventions. Embarrassment is played for laughs in more subtle ways when characters commit a social faux pas or misunderstand relationships, customs, or status (often indicated by the misuse of honorifics).

Comic timing and eloquent expressions are a vital part of manga humor. In no other genre is the chibi form so important. The manga that make readers laugh out loud use panels to extend a joke for perfect comic timing and punctuate it with facial expressions showing the reaction. School comedies are driven by side comments and reactions, from thunderclouds of anger to furious blushing, as seen in *Kare Kano* and *Here Is Greenwood*. *Antique Bakery*, which follows the customers and staff at a specialty pastry shop, depends almost entirely on reaction shots to sell the joke. *Yotsuba&!*, from the creator of the comical *Azumanga Daioh*, depends on Yotsuba's expressions and reactions to the world around her.

Slice of Life

This genre represents a large section of the manga market, in contrast with the U.S. comics industry. These dramas focus on school, that most dominant force in young people's lives, or on interpersonal relationships, either within a family or a romance. Other series locate the story in a particular setting, as with the many plots revolving around restaurants and cafes. Still more series infiltrate a specific trend or group, most often society's outsiders, as with the fashion design students in *Paradise Kiss* or the gangs in *Cromartie High School*.

Food Is Life

Food can be very important in relating stories and relationships. In *Whistle!*, an udon noodle stand is the setting for an unlikely friendship between soccer player Sho and the stand's elderly, grumpy owner. Onigiri—rice balls filled with a variety of ingredients—are key to the main metaphor used in *Fruits Basket*. Like onigiri, people can surprise you; they may appear the same on the surface, but what they hide inside their hearts and souls is what makes them different.

In *Antique Bakery*, creator Yoshinaga Fumi displays her great sense of comic art and timing in this exchange between the owner, a customer, and his wife.
© FUMI YOSHINAGA/SHINSHOKAN 2001.

These stories are not clear-cut realism—or more accurately, they employ an exaggerated sense of humor and contrivances more akin to melodrama than strict drama. The sheer number of traumatic situations and dramatically timed surprises border on laughable, but as always with manga, the point is a good story rather than a precise reflection of the world. These manga are the equivalent of teen dramas on television, such as *Dawson's Creek*, *The O.C.*, and *One Tree Hill*, followed and loved at their peak by their target audiences but ridiculed by adult critics.

Music: Pop Idols and Hipu Hopu

Japan has a booming industry devoted to churning out pop idols who enjoy their fifteen minutes of fame before the next star comes along to bump them down the ladder. *Dragon Voice* follows the rise and fall of a boy band, while in *Full Moon O Sagashite*, a terminally ill 'tween girl is transformed into a teen pop idol. The latest trend to influence manga and anime is hip-hop (or "hipu hopu," as it's translated). The most famous and imaginative example is the anime and manga *Samurai Champloo*.

The story takes place during the Meiji Era (1868–1912), but many of the minor characters' designs, dress, and activities draw heavily on hip-hop music, attitude, and fashion, from tagging to rap to beatbox tunes. The underground crime drama *Tokyo Tribes* shows a heavy hip-hop influence, from fashion to language to sensibility.

Family Life

Family life is a major source of both stability and consternation for many teens. Obligation and affection knit families together.

Family Snapshot

Since 1975, 60 percent of Japanese households are nuclear families.

Most households have three generations: grandparents, parents, and kids.

The husband and father is considered head of the household, although his wife is officially in charge of everything related to it from dispensing allowances (to everyone, including her husband) to child rearing.

As time passes and more women go to work, the family dynamic in Japan is changing, but depictions of family in manga tend to be traditional. In *Yostuba&!*, the daughters of the Ayase family teasingly react with shock and bewilderment when their father appears at breakfast one morning. In *Bleach*, some of the best jokes and most dramatic moments arise from family interactions, especially in the bickering between Ichigo and his father. The vicious attack on Ichigo's sisters and the family home sets the manga's dominant plot in motion. Grandparents' inclusion in the home often leads to jokes about overbearing mothers-in-law berating new wives as well as numerous stories about the children's relationship with their grandparents.

Sibling relationships, especially within the family as a whole, are crucial in characters' lives. Hokuto's fierce protection of her twin Subaru in *Tokyo Babylon* is just one example of sibling devotion. A rambunctious sister who nudges her shy brother toward friends and fun, Hokuto proves sharp and observant when their lives are threatened. Her determination to protect her brother leads to tragedy when she sacrifices herself to give her twin's heart and soul a chance at love and life.

On the flip side, in *Alice 19th* the rivalry between sisters leads to a mystical battle between good and evil. Older sister Mayura is smitten with fellow archery team member Kyo. When shy younger sister Alice realizes she's fallen for Kyo too, she's reluctant to express her feelings for fear of hurting Mayura. When she finds out, Mayura's rage leads her to become a pawn of evil forces.

Giri and Ninjō

Behavior surrounding obligation and personal feeling are among the strongest ideals to inform Japanese culture. *Giri* defines the conduct expected from society in relation to others and is driven by social expectations and thousands of years of tradition. The loyalty of a samurai to his lord, family members helping each other and coworkers offering advice to new and subordinate colleagues all exemplify giri. *Ninjō* are the personal feelings any person might express including love, sorrow, affection, and sympathy (Kodansha International 1999). Giri trumps ninjō in most situations. Strict enforcement of these ideals is considered outmoded, but lingering societal expectation still emphasizes the group over the individual in marked contrast to America's cultural ideal of individualism.

Historically, family obligations and the desire to save face were extremely important. In the anime series *Otogi Zoshi*, set during the end of the Heian era, Minamoto no Raiko is chosen to retrieve a magical artifact that will save the capital city. Raiko falls ill, and rather than allow the family to be disgraced, his younger sister Hikaru agrees to pose as Raiko and complete the mission in his stead.

Family obligation is not as powerful in modern settings, but saving face is still a big part of public conduct. Shaming the family is a concern for dutiful sons and daughters. In *W Juliet*, Makoto's whole problem springs from how desperate he is to avoid the family business. If he can live as a girl for two years and allow no one to discover his true gender, his father has promised to allow him to pursue his dreams of becoming an actor. The sense of duty Makoto feels toward his family, and the fear of losing that connection entirely, keeps him from simply running away without his family's blessing. He does not want to humiliate his father or family, nor does he wish to break all emotional and social ties with his traditional father.

National Holidays and Festivals

In manga and anime, one frequently sees characters heading out to celebrate festivals. Here is a list of holidays nationally celebrated (Poitras 1999).

New Year's Day (January 1)

Adult's Day (January 15)

National Foundation Day (February 11)

Vernal Equinox Day (March 21)

Greenery Day (April 29)

Constitution Memorial Day (May 3)

People's Holiday (May 4)

Children's Day (May 5)

Maritime Day or Ocean Day (July 20)

Respect-for-the-Aged Day (September 15)

Autumnal Equinox Day (September 23)

Health-Sports Day (October 10)

Culture Day (November 3)

Labor-Thanksgiving Day (November 23)

Emperor's Birthday (December 23)

On top of these national holidays, there are a few major celebrations that may also appear.

Bon Festival (July 13–15)

Annual Buddhist festival honoring ancestors' spirits

Doll Festival (March 3) Households with daughters exhibit a tiered display of dolls dressed as the imperial family

Feast days, or *ennichi,* are held on various special days according to Buddhist or Shintō traditions. During summertime, it is customary to don *yukata*, a lightweight cotton kimono, to attend a festival.

Where Are They? What Are They Eating?

For a compendium of all of the references in anime (and thus also in manga) from food to clothing to landmarks to slang, refer to Gilles Poitras's *The Anime Companion: What's Japanese in Japanese Animation?* and the updated volume, *The Anime Companion 2: More What's Japanese in Japanese Animation?*. Both are encyclopedias, providing short and witty explanations for everything you might run across in watching anime and reading manga.

School Stories

School is absolutely central to any Japanese teen's life. Schoolwork dominates life and, arguably more than in the United States, a Japanese student's entire future hinges on success in school. Although critics decrying the severity and inflexibility of the modern Japanese educational system have loosened up expectations, an enormous amount of activity and energy is focused on academic achievement and school life.

Life at School

Elementary school = ages 6–12

Middle school = ages 12–15

High school = ages 15–18

98 percent of students finish high school

50 percent of students attend college

Curriculum

Japanese language, social studies (including geography, history, and civics), arithmetic, science, arts, music, homemaking, health, physical education, and foreign language classes (most schools only offer English)

Physical education: includes judo, kendō, and sumo, as well as a variety of ball games, gymnastics, swimming, track and field, and dancing

Extracurricular: sports meets, dances and plays, club activities, class assemblies, excursions, and field trips. It is common for classes to take longer educational trips to visit a different part of Japan (Kodansha International 1999). In *Boys Be...*, two high school students, one from an all boys' school and one from an all girls' academy, meet and fall in love while visiting a historical shrine for the weekend. In *Eerie Queerie*, classmates bemoan their school trip fate of being stuck in a ramshackle, traditional Japanese inn.

Uniforms: Required from elementary through high school. The designs are recognizable enough so that everyone can tell who goes to what school by their uniform.

Sempai and Kōhai

The senior and junior, or the sempai and kōhai, relationship in schools, organizations, and companies is another way groups are defined by Japanese society. Any senior member of a school or organization is expected to be a mentor, advisor, and teacher to the junior members of the group. The juniors reciprocate with respect, gratitude, and, most valuably, personal loyalty (Kodansha International 1999). In school-centric manga such as *Here Is Greenwood* or *Azumanga Daioh*, these ties are important in understanding the characters' expectations and behavior around different members of their school.

Perfect Student versus Carefree Slacker

The incredible pressure on teens to make the grade appears in any school drama. Humor and camaraderie are how students deal with the constant sense of life's options narrowing down with their next test. Any traditional middle or high school comedy, including *Kare Kano, Here Is Greenwood*, and *Azumanga Daioh*, delight in needling the seriousness of the geekier students while acknowledging the importance of doing well and establishing a good reputation at school both academically and socially. *Kare Kano* mocks the drive to be a perfect student by showing a heroine who excels only for the praise of others, not a sense of accomplishment or desire to learn. *Here Is Greenwood* focuses more on dorm life than class life, but the importance of school loyalty, spirit, and achievement features throughout the series, especially in subplots that include major traditions like annual sports competitions.

Exams!

Japanese students take their first school exam at age six to determine where they will go to elementary school, and things only become more high pressure from there. Getting into the "right" school not only sets academic goals but also situates and restricts a student's career expectations. Students keep a carefully constructed study schedule and attend extra classes, *juku* ("cram school"), held after school, to make sure they can compete for the better schools. Because almost 98 percent of children go to high school, these exams do not decide whether students attend school but instead decide which high school they will attend. Exams are the ultimate measure of a student's worth.

The foils for these dutiful students, either as unanticipated romantic interests or true enemies, are students who scorn scholarly pursuits, the "cool" kids who skip class, disrespect teachers, and don't care about following the expected path. Reckless teens who ignore the academic routine are both admired and considered abnormal, as with *Paradise Kiss*'s Yukari and *Crazy Love Story*'s Shin Hae. The manga and anime *Cromartie High School* is a school made up entirely of misfits, generating hilarious, surreal episodes that speculate on just how a school full of renegade and delinquent teenagers would run.

In *Crossroad*, Natsu tries to comfort his stepbrother as the pressures of living up to expectations in school and at home push him toward self-destruction.

Crossroad © 2003 Shioko Mizuki/AKITASHOTEN. English text © 2005 Go! Media Entertainment LLC. Used by permission.

At the same time, the academic pressure and the social hierarchies of school are what haunt and drive many teens to endure bullying and are one factor in Japan's high suicide rate. The stress caused by school is laughed at in manga, as when students go to extreme lengths to retain information when studying for a particularly important test, but it is also shown as the source for desperate and often harmful behavior. *Life* by Suenobu Keiko follows two teens caught up in the pressure to succeed in their high school exams. Ayumu is devastated when her best friend fails and turns to cutting herself to deal with her pain and confusion. *Confidential Confessions* features a student who takes speed to help her get her schoolwork done, and for a while it works—she has enough energy finally to please her parents, but in the end her dependence on the drug and wild personality shifts cause her to lose everything: her friends, her family, and her self-respect. Even the traditional magical girl fantasy *Fushigi Yugi* starts off with its heroine Miaka desperate to avoid going to cram school but trapped by her mother's expectations that she apply to a high school she knows is far beyond her reach.

Tales Out of School

Azuma, Kyohiko. *Azumanga Daioh*. ADV Manga, 2000–2002 Japan (2003–2004 U.S.). Publisher Age Rating: 13+. Age Recommendation: S. Volumes: 1–4 [T]. Genres: School Drama, Comedy, Slice of Life. Related Anime: *Azumanga Daioh* (TV series)

    A series of vignettes about life in high school careens from silly to bizarre to sweet and back again, following ten slightly off-kilter teenage girls and their wacky teachers.

Fujisawa, Tohru. *Great Teacher Onizuka*. Tokyopop, 1997–2002 Japan (2002 U.S.). Publisher Age Rating: Older Teen. Age Recommendation: S, A. Volumes: 1–25 [T]. Genres: Action, School Drama, Comedy. Related Anime: *Great Teacher Onizuka* (GTO) (TV series)

    Onizuka is an ex-biker with attitude to spare, but he's decided to become a teacher. When he lands a job teaching a class the last few teachers have quit, he gains the students' trust through guts, moxie, and a refusal to give up.

Kamio, Yoko. *Boys over Flowers*. VIZ Manga, 1992–2004 Japan (2003 U.S.). Publisher Age Rating: Teen. Age Recommendation: S. Volumes: 1–21+ [T]. Genres: Romance, School Drama, Comedy. Related Anime: *Boys over Flowers* (TV series)

    Makino is tired of being hazed just for daring to take up space near the Flowery Four, her school's resident uber-clique of the hottest boys. When they come after her, she surprises everyone (including herself) by fighting back.

Nasu, Yukie. *Here Is Greenwood*. VIZ Manga, 1987–1991 Japan (2004–2006 U.S.). Publisher Age Rating: Older Teen. Age Recommendation: S. Volumes: 1–9 of 11 [T]. Genres: School Drama, Comedy, Slice of Life. Related Anime: *Here Is Greenwood* (OVA)

    Kazuya has a hopeless love for his brother's new wife. To escape his feelings, he decides to live on campus. He's sent to Greenwood, the dorms for the most bizarre (and hilarious) guys on campus.

Nonaka, Eiji. *Cromartie High School*. ADV Manga, 2001 Japan (2004 U.S.). Publisher Age Rating: 13+. Age Recommendation: S. Volumes: 1–9+ [T]. Genres: Comedy, School Drama. Related Anime: *Cromartie High School* (TV series)

Takashi has no idea what he's in for when he's transferred to the infamous Cromartie High—a high school populated entirely by thugs and misfits. He certainly didn't expect a robot, and a guy who looks like Freddy Mercury.

Suenobu, Keiko. *LIFE*. Tokyopop, 200 Japan (2006 U.S.). Publisher Age Rating: Older Teen. Age Recommendation: S, A. Volumes: 1–3+ [T]. Genres: School Drama, Slice of Life

Ayumu and her best friend Shii-chan are cramming for high school entrance exams. When Ayumu gets in and Shii-chan doesn't, their friendship shatters. Ayumu starts cutting herself to escape the loss, but will she get better or worse at her new school?

Tsuda, Masami. *Kare Kano*. Tokyopop, 1996–2005 Japan (2003–2006 U.S.). Publisher Age Rating: Teen. Age Recommendation: S. Volumes: 1–21 [T]. Genres: Romance, School Drama, Comedy. Related Anime: *His and Her Circumstances* (TV series)

Yukino and Soichiro are the same: brilliant students, kind friends, and humble in the face of praise. But for Yukino, it's an act—the only reason she acts so angelic is so that she can feed her need for others' praise. When Soichiro realizes her true nature, will their budding romance have a chance?

Sports and Competition

Like martial arts manga, sports stories focus on competition. The hero's stereotypical traits are perseverance, commitment, skill, and honorable sportsmanship. This kind of comic is almost nonexistent in the United States but is popular in Japan and finally making its way through the translation process. There are sports comics for both girls and boys, and many crossover readers for both types of series.

Sports manga focus on the ups and downs of competition to the point of having almost no other plot. Rivalry with other teams and between players, techniques and strategies, and team spirit are all key ingredients. Depending on the audience for a specific title, characteristic audience-pleasers will be included. For boys, there's stupendous achievement, humor, and a foxy woman to be ogled. For girls, there's a dreamy competitor on a boys' team queued up as a romantic interest and an emphasis on the emotional commitment to building a winning team. Most important, though, are the games—whatever the sport, the experience of going through a season or competition with each team or athlete is integral to the story. In the soccer drama *Whistle!* one of the first games starts in the second half of the second volume and finishes in very last panel of the third volume. Each point of the game is lovingly brought to life in the spirit of broadcast matches. These stories parallel the inspirational sports stories of our own culture, from movies to novels, complete with ramshackle teams that end up winning the championship by turning their flaws into strengths.

© 1998 by Daisuke Higuchi/SHUEISHA, Inc.

Best Sports and Competition Manga and Anime

CLAMP. *Angelic Layer*. Tokyopop Manga, 1999–2001 Japan (2002–2003 U.S.). Publisher Age Rating: All Ages. Age Recommendation: M. Volumes: 1–5 of 5 [T]. Genres: Action, Fantasy, Magical Girl. Related Anime: *Angelic Layer* (TV series).

The latest rage in Tokyo is Angels, or figurines controlled by an owner's will and voice on the game platform, and Misaki discovers that she is a natural player.

Hashiguchi, Takashi. *Yakitate!!* Japan. 2002– Japan (2006– U.S.). Publisher Age Rating: Older Teen. Age Recommendation: S. Volumes: 1–2+ [T]. Genres: Comedy

Azuma is a genius bread baker, and he wants to create a bread so good it will become the national bread of Japan. He transforms people into pandas with the tastiness of his baked goods (yes, pandas), and keeps his competition from getting too high and mighty.

Higuchi, Daisuke. *Whistle!* VIZ Manga, 1998– Japan (2004 U.S.). Publisher Age Rating: All Ages. Age Recommendation: M. Volumes: 1–15+ [T]. Genres: Action, Sports

In a welcome reversal of the genius prodigy plotline, Sho is just not a very good soccer player. But he won't give up. He won't dazzle the crowd with flashy moves or flawless plays, but he knows how to work on a team, and he won't ever let down his teammates.

Hotta, Yumi. *Hikaru no Go.* VIZ Manga, 1999–2003 Japan (2004 U.S.). Publisher Age Rating: All Ages. Age Recommendation: M. Volumes: 1–8+ [T]. Genres: Comedy, Sports, Slice of Life. Related Anime: *Hikaru no Go* (TV series)

Sixth-grader Hikaru never dreamed of playing the board game Go (if chess is a battle, Go is the war), but being possessed by the spirit of a feudal Go player desperate to make the "divine" move gives him little choice.

Inagaki, Riichiro. *Eyeshield 21.* VIZ Manga, 2002– Japan (2005 U.S.). Publisher Age Rating: Older Teen. Age Recommendation: M. Volumes: 1–11+ [T]. Genres: Action, Sports, Slice of Life

Sena, usually relegated to bullied peon, is handpicked by the team captain of the American Football Team to join. He proves to be a quick-footed running back, but can he lead the team to the country's championship game to win?

Konomi, Takeshi. *Prince of Tennis.* VIZ Manga, 2000– Japan (2004 U.S.). Publisher Age Rating: All Ages. Age Recommendation: J. Volumes: 1–16+ [T]. Genres: Action, Sports, Slice of Life. Related Anime: *Prince of Tennis* (TV series).

Twelve-year-old Ryoma is a tennis prodigy, but now he has to prove himself playing against guys older and bigger than he is to get on the team. His natural ability will help, but will it win him a place on the team—and will his teammates be impressed or hate him for it?

Nishiyama, Yuriko. *Rebound.* Tokyopop, 1997–2005 Japan (2003–2005 U.S.). Publisher Age Rating: Teen. Age Recommendation: S. Volumes: 1–16+ [T]. Genres: Action, Sports, Slice of Life. Related Manga: *Rebound* is a sequel to *Harlem Beat.*

Nate Torres and his team of basketball players use street ball know-how to get to the national competition, ready to prove their worth with every game. This series is a continuation of the out-of-print *Harlem Beat*, but new readers can start here.

Saijyo, Shinji. *Iron Wok Jan!* DrMaster Manga, 1995– Japan (2002 U.S.). Publisher Age Rating: NA. Age Recommendation: S. Volumes: 1–20+ [T]. Genres: Comedy

Jan is determined to defeat his grandfather's nemesis in the cooking arena. When he throws down the gauntlet, he's surprised to be met by his rival's granddaughter. Will this be a rivalry to continue the battle, or will a winner finally be declared?

Seino, Shizuru. *Girl Got Game*. Tokyopop, 2000–2001 Japan (2004–2005 U.S.). Publisher Age Rating: Teen. Age Recommendation: S. Volumes: 1–10 [T]. Genres: Sports, Romance, School Drama

Kyo is being forced to play out her father's dream of getting all the way to the NBA—on the best boys' high school basketball team in Japan. Of course, she's a girl, but that doesn't stop her father from enrolling her and packing her off to the team.

Takanashi, Mitsuba. *Crimson Hero*. VIZ Manga, 2003– Japan (2006– U.S.). Publisher Age Rating: Teen. Age Recommendation: J. Volumes: 1–4+ [T]. Genres: School Drama, Sports, Slice of Life

Nobara is willing to do anything to escape her destiny as a hotel hostess and pursue her dream of restarting the girls' volleyball team, including cooking and cleaning for a houseful of snooty fellow classmates.

The sports manga trope is so popular that it also appears in nonathletic stories. *Hikaru no Go* is an extremely popular manga about playing the game Go. It uses all of the dramatic build-up and tension found in sports manga to make a tale about a board game, with almost no physical action involved, into an intense competition drama. A long-time sports manga writer created *Dragon Voice* and it has many of the earmarks of that tradition as it relates to the rise of a young man in the competitive world of pop idol boy bands.

Teen Melodrama

The most common slice of life titles in manga follow the adventures of one teen or a group of teens coming of age. Many of these stories are about characters facing conflicts in their lives, either internal or external. In *Kare Kano*, for example, main character Yukino appears to be the most perfect high school girl—kind to all, an academic star, and cute besides. What her classmates don't know is that the driving force behind all of this perfection is Yukino's thirst for praise. When a rival for the school's attention, new boy Souchiro Arima, upstages her on all fronts, Yukino's perfect image is challenged. *Kare Kano* is an example of a great escape for teen girls—even as Yukino is the perfect student on the outside, she is flawed on the inside, and the conflict between ideal and reality resonates.

Aside from the many stories related to teens surviving families, school, and friendship, there are also stories about "good" teens being drawn into a group of outsiders, from social misfits to threatening thugs including gang members and organized crime. Yazawa Ai's manga, *Paradise Kiss*, is all about Yukari struggling to meet her family's expectations while they slowly suffocate her. At a vulnerable moment, Yukari is drawn into a circle of high school students studying to be fashion designers who are determined that she should be their model. Her true destiny just may be in this new world of misfits and artists, not to mention her first romance with head designer George. Unlike most shōjo romances or dramas, *Paradise Kiss*'s love story has no fairy-tale ending. George may be what Yukari wants, but he may not be what she needs.

You Are What You Wear

Outsiders and renegades are frequently identified by their choice of clothing. Punk characters with spiked hair, studded leather accessories, multiple piercings, and tattoos appear all over manga. Yazawa Ai's Arashi in *Paradise Kiss* and Osaki Nana in *Nana* are both excellent examples. *Paradise Kiss*, in both the manga and anime, is influenced by the glam rock homage film *Velvet Goldmine* and lovingly details both glam and GothLoli ("Gothic Lolita") fashion. *Ark Angels* shows obvious glam influences in the character's outfits. In *Kamikaze Girls*, a manga adapted from a hit live-action film, biker chick Ichigo and GothLoli devotee Momoke, two outsiders of different brands, form an unlikely friendship.

On the shōnen side of things, Shimoku Kio's *Genshiken* focuses on being a member of the anime and manga otaku crowd. Kanji, a young college student who is secretly a manga and video game fan, is trying to decide on a club to join. He is drawn to the Society for the Study of Modern Visual Culture, a deliberately academic name for the college's otaku haven. At first reluctant to admit his geekiness, he soon discovers these guys (and one girl) far surpass him in their obsession with manga, anime, and all related media. At its heart, *Genshiken* is about friendship and fandom and that it's okay to be an outcast, especially if you've got good company.

In manga there are also a number of titles that are the equivalent of what are called "issue novels" (or problem novels) in Western teen literature. These novels reveal teen specific problems or issues, including eating disorders, prejudice, sexual or physical abuse, rape, bullying, gang violence, teen pregnancy, and racial tension. These books aim to reflect life in fiction and provide a way for teens to talk about problems, peer pressure, and expectations. The most direct correlation between this type of tale and manga is the series *Confidential Confessions*. Despite the lurid title, the series is an anthology of short stories dealing with everything from teen prostitution to sexual and physical harassment to drug abuse. The teen girls who devour titles such as Dave Pelzer's *A Child Called It* and Laurie Halse Anderson's *Speak* are the same girls who zoom through *Confidential Confessions*.

Confidential Confessions was written for a Japanese audience, and the stories highlight specifically Japanese concerns and problems. High school girls dating and sleeping with older men who take on the role of sugar daddies is a more visible problem in Japan than it is in the United States. This kind of companionship has been such a commonly understood part of culture that teen girls know and use the power their uniforms hold over middle-aged businessmen. When the issues turn to abuse of drugs, and specifically speed, a girl begins using the drug not as a result of peer pressure but instead despite peers' objections so that she can compete academically and get into the university of her parents' dreams.

Sugar Daddies and Harajuku Girls

The dark side of the geisha tradition has led to the understanding that older men can buy favors from younger women, usually teenage girls, by acting as sugar daddies. Cautionary tales and joking abound in manga about this trend—for example, showing teen girls who manipulate older men by granting them glimpses of their panties. The more infamous teens seen in *GALS!* and *Confidential Confessions* are the Harajuku girls, named after the district they frequent, who reportedly provide sexual favors to men in return for money to buy designer accessories. Such behavior is perceived as a desperate and unsavory route for keeping up with fashion.

Bullying

A constant in any school, bullying has been a problem in the United States for decades. Recent high-profile consequences of bullying, from school shootings to suicide, have made parents and students more aware of the warning signs. Unfortunately, informal tolerance of bullying continues to be all too common in middle and high schools. Japanese students suffer from ill treatment by their peers and teachers, including the willful blindness of adults concerning bullying. Bullying usually happens in or around school but out of the line of sight of adults. This kind of violence and pressure is a reflection of what teens are familiar with in their own lives, and aggressors are as likely to be girls as boys, whether the bullying is physical or psychological. In the school romance *Mars*, Sae and her posse physically and emotionally bully shy Kira for attracting the attention of bad boy Rei.

Bullying is commonplace in manga stories, but adults are almost never called in unless they discover the bullying by accident or are the perpetrators. Students do not want to make a fuss, or do not feel they can count on adult support. *Confidential Confessions* features a disturbing view of a high school teacher allowed too much power. When his abuse of authority leads to a girl's suicide, another student decides she can no longer remain silent. She challenges everyone complicit in his behavior, from her silent peers to other faculty to parents, but she finds little support in her exposé.

Of course, the same trope is seen is U.S. teen fiction, especially when peers pressure others not to depend on adults or to inform on other students. In Japanese manga, characters hide incidents to avoid bringing shame on their families. The need to maintain the family's reputation is still a very strong force in any young person's life, and other teens and adults may prey on that desire. In *Hot Gimmick*, heroine Hatsumi discovers her younger sister Akane may be pregnant. While purchasing a pregnancy test on the sly, she runs into her obnoxious upstairs neighbor Ryoki, son of her apartment building's most influential family. To save her sister and her family's reputation, Hatsumi is blackmailed into becoming Ryoki's slave. The driving force behind the plot is Hatsumi's need to save face, and the "slavery" she endures to cover for her family borders on abuse.

Bullying is not confined to school, of course, and intimidation by gangs or local thugs is also a common trope in both shōnen and shōjo manga. From the delinquent reputation Megumi struggles to uphold in *Cheeky Angel* to the confrontations between a variety of gangs that punctuate *Kill Me, Kiss Me*, group fighting and confrontation is an acknowledged part of life. The most elevated level of thuggery is found in the organizations of the Japanese mafia, or yakuza, who are convenient bad guys in many stories (they provide the threat of mercenary violence in *Confidential Confessions*).

Suicide

The rising suicide rate is of growing concern in Japan. In comparison to the United States, which has seen a slight drop in the number of suicides in recent years, Japan's suicide rate has doubled since 1990.

Suicide Rates

United States: 11 suicides per 100,000 people (level for more than 50 years)

Japan: 24 suicides per 100,000 people (doubled since 1990)

Fastest growing segment of the population committing suicide: seniors

Source: World Health Organization 2005, Japan; World Health Organization 2005, United States.

Historically suicide was considered the honorable way out of a bad situation and even today is not considered a sin, as it is in many Western countries. The samurai example of ritual suicide, or *seppuku*, is part of their romantic image, and the desire to die well and without becoming a burden to one's family or peers echoes the samurai's commitment to die for the good of others. In samurai stories written today suicide may be seen as necessary and honorable, but it is never easy. *Peacemaker Kurogane*, follows the real-life history of local samurai enforcing peace in Kyoto just before the Meiji Restoration. When one of their founding members, Yamanami Keisuke, is accused of desertion, he is expected to commit *seppuku* according to their strict code of honor. His compassionate fellows give him multiple opportunities to clear his name or to escape, but his own honor will not allow him to take advantage. In the end he forces his own friends to attack him, counting on them to finish the job when his pain becomes too great. His oldest friends are horrified and openly weeping, and the ripples of grief and anger that result from his death push the manga from action-comedy towards tragedy.

Manga also take an unflinching look at the motivations of modern suicide. Teens in desperate situations who consider suicide the only way out are common in school and teen dramas. *X-Day* addresses the combination of suicidal tendencies and the desire for revenge against bullies that lead four students to plan to blow up their school. A stand-alone volume, *Line*, is both a thriller and an examination of suicide. A girl discovers a cell phone on a train, and when she answers it, she is told she has mere minutes to stop someone from dying. She is skeptical until she arrives at the address given and witnesses a death. The sadistic stranger has taken advantage of a suicide hotline, convincing callers to leap to their deaths unless someone arrives to save them.

Most of manga's suicide stories end with unsuccessful attempts, emphasizing the idea that suicide does not solve any problems and only wastes a character's potential to heal and recover. There are some exceptions. One of *Tokyo Babylon*'s gentler story lines follows Subaru's friendship with a local senior citizen who eventually kills himself so as not to burden his daughter and her family. The family is shown to regret their uncharitable and impatient attitudes, but they are also shown to be free of the responsibility of taking care of him, while his ghostly form smiles down on them.

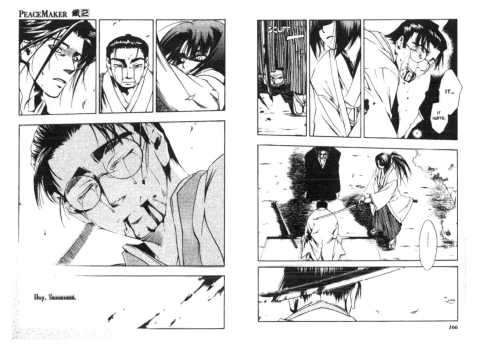

In *Peacemaker Kurogane*, Yamanami Keisuke commits *seppuku* as punishment for desertion while his heartbroken comrades assist.
© Nanae Chrono 2003 KODANSHA.

An episode of the anime miniseries *Paranoia Agent* shows that suicide attempts are common enough to be parodied. A young man, a senior citizen, and a preteen girl meet on the Internet and make a suicide pact. The two men are dubious about the girl's seriousness, and they attempt to lose her before they all go through with their plan. The episode becomes an increasingly dark comic adventure as the three are foiled by twists of fate in a variety of suicide attempts.

Arranged Marriage?

In Japan marriage was traditionally seen as an alliance of families not overly concerned with romance. Although the custom of introducing a suitable couple is still practiced, it is more like a dating service (Kodansha International 1999). Romantic stories are born out of star-crossed lovers, but most young people hope for a match that both meets their family's expectations and blooms into true love.

Romance

It's impossible to talk about manga without talking about romance. Although there have been romance comics in the West, the genre dwindled at the end of the 1970s. In Japan, romances are one of the top genres, especially shōjo romances. As with romance novels here, manga romances are defined by the focus of the story on romantic relationships, but these stories often cross genres.

For the Girls

A typical shōjo manga romance revolves around a central romantic relationship, and though the tension may originally come from the buildup to a confession of love, stories usually concentrate on the work required to keep a relationship going. There are too many popular shōjo romances to list them all, but *Mars*, *Peach Girl*, *Kare Kano*, and *Boys over Flowers* all fall under the romance label. Almost all of these series have made the transition to anime series that are faithful to the original series in spirit, if not to the letter.

For the Boys

There are shōnen romances as well, although many manga readers aren't quite aware that's what they're reading when they pick up these titles. The most famous shōnen romance is Takahashi Rumiko's long-running series *Maison Ikkoku*. More recent additions include the romantic anthology *Boys Be...*, puzzling out the unfathomable behavior of teen girls, and *Love Roma*'s sweet and awkward romance between a no nonsense girl and a too honest guy.

Confession

Confession is an identifiable and codified custom in Japan. Confession may include the presentation of a letter, if the confessor is too shy to have a face-to-face conversation, but may also simply be blurting out, "I like you. Do you want to go out with me?" The confessee is expected to behave sympathetically, especially if the confessor's affection is not reciprocated. In *Only the Ring Finger Knows*, Kazuki is admired for the polite way he turns girls down. In *Love Roma,* Hoshino, although often oblivious, tries his best not to hurt a girl who's just confessed to him although she knows he's unavailable.

Romantic Bentō

Another dating custom that appears in a lot of manga is the tradition of one half of a couple, traditionally the girl, making a box lunch, or *bentō*. A hopeful girl might declare her affection by making a bentō lunch for a crush. In *Love Roma*, the tradition is gently mocked.

Valentine's Day and White Day

Valentine's Day is the day when girls traditionally confess their love by gifting the boys they like with chocolate. Girls do not get chocolate on Valentine's Day but are instead given gifts of white chocolate one month later on White Day, March 14. This tradition has become so powerful that it has also become a chore, with duty or *giri* chocolate exchanged between coworkers and friends as a matter of courtesy rather than true affection (Poitras 1999). Some girls give chocolate just to get sweets back on White Day, as Yuko does in *XXXholic,* and less popular guys often bemoan their lack of chocolate gifts on Valentine's, as in *Here Is Greenwood* and *Boys Be ....*

Romance is central to many manga and anime that might not appear to belong to the genre. *Clover* is a perfect example of a series that has all of the trappings of science fiction—genetic engineering, cybernetic implants, and dramatic action sequences—but is at heart a romantic reflection on love and loss. *Clover* crosses over between shōnen and shōjo readers, although the prettiness of the characters makes it more identifiable as shōjo. The short but powerful anime

Voices from a Distant Star is a romance and a tragedy despite a plot that includes the theory of relativity and vast alien battles.

Gender Roles, Stereotypes, and Romance

Manga romances tend to reinforce Japanese gender stereotypes. Those stereotypes are not so different from our own culture's concepts of what makes a proper girl or a desirable gentleman. These are fantasies, despite their realistic settings, and most romances do not challenge the romantic ideal of the gentle and withdrawn heroine and the persuasive, domineering alpha male hero. These types are familiar to Western romance readers, especially fans of romances from the 1970s and 1980s, but can send negative messages about romance, sex, permission, and force. A frequent message is that doing anything for love is an acceptable and expected sacrifice.

Other romances play with stereotypes, as with *Never Give Up*, a romance following a gangly girl who has inherited her father's male model looks while the object of her affection is a boy so pretty he is nicknamed Princess. Both characters are determined to become what they are not naturally to win their love's heart—girly and manly, respectively. Both refuse to see they are already a perfect match. *W Juliet* puts forth a similar premise, with the tomboy of the school falling for a new exchange student who, although at first appearing as a girl, is in fact a guy in disguise. The fiddling with gender in shōjo romances is almost Shakespearean, although, as with Shakespeare's works, everyone assumes their correct and desired gender by the end of the tale.

Best Romances and Melodrama

Akamatsu, Ken. *Love Hina*. VIZ Manga, 1998–2001 Japan (2006 U.S.). Publisher Age Rating: Older Teen. Age Recommendation: S, A. Volumes: 1–2+ [T] 2nd ed. Genres: Romance, School Drama, Comedy. Related Anime: *Love Hina* (TV series)

As a child, Keitaro promised a girl he would meet her at Tokyo University, but he fails the entrance exam twice. Desperate for a place to stay, he ends up as the dorm manager of an all-girls dorm, where pratfalls and fan service may be constant, but will he find true love?

Asakura, George. *A Perfect Day for Love Letters*. Del Rey Manga, 2001 Japan (2005 U.S.). Publisher Age Rating: 13+. Age Recommendation: S. Volumes: 1-2 [T]. Genres: Romance, Comedy, Slice of Life

Awkward, exhilarating, quirky, intense, and sweet, the short stories in Asakura's anthologies cover a wide range of love stories. The series highlights finding love in unexpected places and with the person you'd least expect.

Emura. *W Juliet*. VIZ Manga, 1999–2003 Japan (2004 U.S.). Publisher Age Rating: Teen. Age Recommendation: J. Volumes: 1–14 [T]. Genres: Romance, Comedy, School Drama

> Tomboy Miura and beauty Makoto are destined to be lovers—on stage, that is, in the all girls' high school performance of *Romeo and Juliet*. Then Miura discovers Makoto's secret—she's a he in disguise. Will their onstage relationship spark offstage romance?

Kamio, Yoko. *Boys over Flowers*. VIZ Manga, 1992–2004 Japan (2003 U.S.). Publisher Age Rating: Teen. Age Recommendation: S. Volumes: 1–22+ [T]. Genres: Romance, School Drama, Comedy. Related Anime: *Boys over Flowers* (TV series)

> Middle-class Makino is smart. Because she actually prefers books to beauty magazines, she catches the attention of the "flowery four," the boys clique that rules the school, and she surprises them by not backing down.

Kannagi, Satoru. *Only the Ring Finger Knows*. Digital Manga, 2002 Japan (2004 U.S.). Publisher Age Rating: 16+. Age Recommendation: S. Volumes: 1 [T]. Genres: Romance: BL/Yaoi, School Drama. Related Manga: *The Lonely Ring Finger* (novel sequel), *The Ring Finger Falls Silent* (novel sequel)

> Wataru tracks the trend of students using rings as cues: couples wear matched rings, singles wear unique rings. Then Wataru discovers he and admired senior Kazuki wear matching rings.

Miyasaka, Kaho. *Kare First Love*. VIZ Manga, 2002–2004 Japan (2004 U.S.). Publisher Age Rating: Teen. Age Recommendation: S. Volumes: 1–10 [T]. Genres: Romance, Slice of Life

> Karin seems an ugly duckling with thick glasses and a shy manner, but when Kiriya approaches her, she manages to take the plunge and agrees to a date. Can Karin date the first boy to ask her out and keep her best friend when they both like the same guy?

Nakajo, Hisaya. *Hana Kimi*. VIZ Manga, 1997–2004 Japan (2004– U.S.). Publisher Age Rating: Older Teen. Age Recommendation: J. Volumes: 1–16+ [T]. Genres: Romance, School Drama, Sports, Slice of Life

> Mizuki transfers schools so she can admire her favorite track star, high-jumper Izumi Sano, in action. Never mind that she's a girl at an all-boys school, and her idol is having doubts about his life's direction.

Reiko, Momochi. *Confidential Confessions*. Tokyopop, 2000–2002 Japan (2003–2005 U.S.). Publisher Age Rating: Older Teen. Age Recommendation: S. Volumes: 1–6 [T]. Genres: School Drama, Slice of Life

> Quick cash lures a teen into becoming a hostess, and worse, at a sleazy club. A girl who watched her friend commit suicide rather than deal

with abuse stands up to her offending teacher and her entire school. Melodramatic, but the impulses and dangers are real.

Soryo, Fuyumi. *Mars*. Tokyopop, 1996–2000 Japan (2002–2003 U.S.). Publisher Age Rating: 13+. Age Recommendation: S. Volumes: 1–15 [T]. Genres: Romance, School Drama. Related Manga: *Mars: A Horse with No Name* (prequel)

> After seeing "good girl" Kira's beautiful, Klimt-inspired drawings, "bad boy" Rei offers himself as a model. This romance literally has it all: romance, motorcycle races, bullying, haunted pasts, child abuse, friendly transvestites, murder, sociopaths, and more romance.

Takahashi, Rumiko. *Maison Ikkoku*. VIZ Media. 1980–1987 Japan (2003–2006 U.S.). Publisher Age Rating: Older Teen. Age Recommendation: S, A. Volumes: 1–15 [T] 2nd ed. Genres: Romance, Comedy, Slice of Life. Related Anime: *Maison Ikkoku* (TV series)

> Godai has failed the college entrance exams three times. He's reduced to living in a ramshackle apartment building with a pack of interfering neighbors. Now he's falling for his cute new landlady—but although she's smitten, she's a recent widow.

Toyoda, Minoru. *Love Roma*. Del Rey Manga, 2003– Japan (2005– U.S.). Publisher Age Rating: 16+. Age Recommendation: S. Volumes: 1–5 [T]. Genres: Romance, School Drama, Comedy

> Blunt, honest, and awkward Hoshino confesses his love for Negishi. She reacts by stuttering, feeling flattered but not quite sure whether this guy is really the guy she wants to try out this whole dating thing with.

Tsuda, Masami. *Kare Kano*. Tokyopop, 1996–2005 Japan (2003–2006 U.S.). Publisher Age Rating: Teen. Age Recommendation: S. Volumes: 1–21 [T]. Genres: Romance, School Drama, Comedy, Slice of Life. Related Anime: *His and Her Circumstances* (Publisher Age Rating: Teen. Age Recommendation: J. Volumes: 1–8 [T]. Genres: Romance, School Drama, Slice of Life. Related Manga: *Peach Girl: Change of Heart* (sequel), *Anime: Peach Girl* (TV series)

> Students tease Momo for her blond hair and tan, calling her a beach bunny and a slut. Her "friend" Sae, is actually her back-stabbing rival. Will Momo get the object of her affection, the quiet Toji, or will Sae win the day?

Various Authors. *Boys Be...* Tokyopop, 1992–1997 Japan (2004 U.S.). Publisher Age Rating: Older Teen. Age Recommendation: S. Volumes: 1–11+ [T]. Genres: Romance, Slice of Life

Romance from the guy's point of view can be all about babes, scores, and lots and lots of fan service. *Boys Be...* has a little bit of these, but the short stories are more about heart than jiggle.

Voices of a Distant Star. ADV Films, 2003, Short Film (25 minutes running time), 1 DVD. Publisher Age Rating: 13+. Age Recommendation: J. Genres: Action, Science Fiction, Romance, Military, Mecha. Related Manga: *Voices of a Distant Star* (alternate version)

When Mikako leaves to become the pilot of a giant robot, fighting the good fight, she leaves her boyfriend Noboru behind. Can you stay in love when the very laws of science are forcing you apart?

BL/Boy's Love/Yaoi

One of the fastest-growing subgenres of romance is boy's love romances (originally *shōnen-ai*, now more often referred to by the English acronym BL), a trend that is either puzzling or predictable depending on your point of view. BL stories present a romantic relationship between two male characters. Women almost exclusively write the genre. Started in the 1970s by the first female manga creators, the genre's intended audiences are teen girls and women. The appeal of gay romances for teenage girls may puzzle and even offend some readers, but at a very basic level, these stories are romances. If the story is told well and according to romance convention, romance fans' hearts will pitter pat the same way they do for straight romances.

What's in a Name?

Japanese and American fans use a variety of terms to identify romances between two male leads. *Shōnen-ai*, the original term, indicates an overtly romantic tale, typically not very explicit. Boy's Love, the literal translation of shōnen-ai, now known by the acronym BL, is the most common and inclusive term, covering all levels of romance and explicitness. In Japan yaoi, which literally means "no plot, no point, no climax," refers to same-sex romance dōjinshi, but in the United States it has come to identify the more explicit stories. Muddling the terms even more are the varying uses by publishers and fans alike. Digital Manga originally launched its BL line as the Yaoi line, but their titles were less explicit than the U.S. fans had expected from the label. Fans recognize all the terms but continue to discuss their proper use.

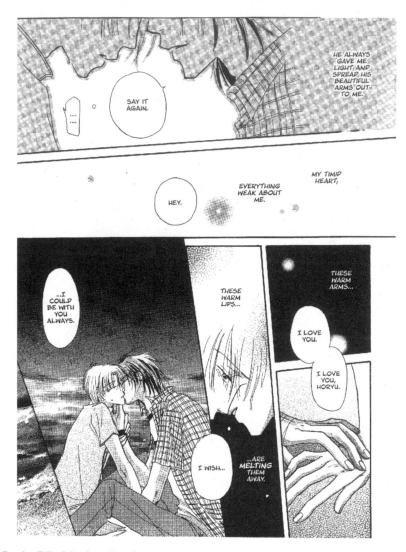

In the BL title *Our Everlasting*, surfer Horyu and classmate Shouin confess their love.

© Toko Kawai 2000.

Written by women for teen girls and women, these stories deal in the same romantic fantasies as other manga romances, from the pained confessions to the fumbling first attempts at intimacy. When I did a survey of teen BL/yaoi readers, I asked why they liked the subgenre, and patterns emerged in their answers. On a purely aesthetic level, looking at two pretty boys is better than looking at just one. Many readers claimed they hated the typical romantic heroine in shōjo romances, rejecting the bumbling, meek, and dim-witted girls they were expected to identify with. When both members of the couple are male, they are ostensibly free of the inequalities in traditional relationships. Many readers cite this equality as part of the appeal, but BL couples often play out stereotypical relationship dynamics with the more effeminate, weaker, and reluctant guy standing in for the heroine. The prejudice and societal pressure against gay relationships, although not quite the same as in the West and commonly ignored as a serious obstacle in many BL stories, heightens the romantic drama.

Not Just for Girls

About a quarter of survey responses were from male readers. A few self-identified as straight but most were bisexual or gay. The guys love these stories for their romance and sexiness just as female fans do. A number of male respondents expressed delight at seeing gay romances at all. The titles' very fluffiness gave them hope that romantic life may not be as hard as teen fiction leads them to believe it can be when you're gay. In teen fiction, David Levithan's *Boy Meets Boy* hit a similar audience of optimistic gay teens and teen girls who embraced the story for the very fact that it wasn't an "issue" novel and had a happy, if fairy tale, ending.

Teen BL/Yaoi Titles

CLAMP. *Tokyo Babylon*. Tokyopop, 1991–1994 Japan (2004–2005 U.S.). Publisher Age Rating: Teen. Age Recommendation: S. Volumes: 1–7 [T]. Genres: Fantasy, Romance; BL/Yaoi, Mystery. Related Manga: *X/1999* by CLAMP. Related Anime: *Tokyo Babylon* (OVA), *X* (TV series), *X* (film)

    Subaru and Seishiro are enemies according to fate and family history. As neighbors, though, they form a friendship while Subaru solves mystical mysteries performing his onmyoji (or yin-yang magician) duties. Still, Seishiro has hidden a lot from him, and Subaru is in for a shock.

Gotoh, Shinobu. *Time Lag*. Digital Manga, 2000 Japan (2006 U.S.). Publisher Age Rating: 16+. Age Recommendation: J. Volumes: 1 of 1 [T]. Genres: Romance: BL/Yaoi, School Drama

    Satoru's decided the third time's the charm: he'll confess his love to one-time best friend Shiro one last time, even though Shiro's already rejected him twice. A new player on the field, Seiichi, who's determined to win Satoru for himself, tests his dedication.

Kannagi, Satoru. *Only the Ring Finger Knows*. Digital Manga, 2002– Japan (2004 U.S.). Publisher Age Rating: 16+. Age Recommendation: S. Volumes: 1 of 1 [T]. Genres: Romance: BL/Yaoi, School Drama. Related Manga: *The Lonely Ring Finger* (novel sequel), *The Ring Finger Falls Silent* (novel sequel)

Wataru tracks the trend of students using rings as cues: couples wear matched rings, singles wear unique rings. Then Wataru discovers he and admired senior Kazuki wear matching rings.

Kawai, Chigusa. *La Esperanca.* Digital Manga, 2000–2006 Japan (2005–2006 U.S.). Publisher Age Rating: 13+. Age Recommendation: J. Volumes: 1–5 [T]. Genres: Romance: BL/Yaoi, School Drama, Slice of Life

Georges is the ideal student and friend to the point of being saintly. Robert is the brash new student determined to knock George down a few pegs. Robert's attitude exposes Georges' secrets and weaknesses, but Robert has a few secrets of his own.

Kouga, Yun. *Earthian.* Tokyopop Blu Imprint, 1988–1994 Japan (2005–2006 U.S.). Publisher Age Rating: Older Teen. Age Recommendation: S. Volumes: 1–4 [T]. Genres: Science Fiction, Romance, Romance: BL/Yaoi. Related Anime: *Earthian* (OVA)

Angels exist, as an alien race surveying Earth from the Moon, and they have reached a point of decision: is humanity benevolent enough to be allowed to survive, or do they deserve extermination for their evil deeds?

Murakami, Maki. *Gravitation.* Tokyopop, 1996–2002 Japan (2003–2005 U.S.). Publisher Age Rating: Older Teen. Age Recommendation: S. Volumes: 1–12 [T]. Genres: Romance: BL/Yaoi, Comedy. Related Manga: *Gravitation: Voice of Temptation* (novel), Anime: *Gravitation* (TV series), *Gravitation: Lyrics of Love* (OVA)

Fleeing writer's block, exuberant Shuichi, an aspiring pop singer-songwriter, meets novelist Eiri Yuki in a park. Shuichi is crushed when Yuki judges his writing. He can't get Yuki out of his mind, so he decides to prove himself by inviting the author to his next concert.

Sumomo, Yumeka. Same Cell Organism. Digital Manga, 200-Japan (2006 U.S.). Publisher Age Rating: 16+. Age Recommendation: S. Volumes: 1 [T]. Genres: Romance: BL/Yaoi, Slice of Life

A pair of friends takes awkward steps toward deepening their relationship. A solitary teen remembers why love is important when an angel descends to keep him company. The art makes these gentle snapshots of love indelible.

Ratings: These titles are suitable for teens and teen collections, but many teens will pursue the more explicit titles aimed at older audiences, including the following mature titles.

Kawai, Toko. *Our Everlasting*. Digital Manga, Japan (2005-2006 U.S.). Publisher Age Rating: 18+. Age Recommendation: A. Volumes: 1–2 [T]. Genres: Romance: BL/Yaoi, Slice of Life

Horyu was always a ladies' man, while Shouin watched from the wings, but a secret confession pushes Horyu to realize Shouin is more than just a friend to him.

Matoh, Sanami. *FAKE*. Tokyopop, 1994 Japan (2003–2004 U.S.). Publisher Age Rating: Older Teen. Age Recommendation: A. Volumes: 1–7 [T]. Genres: Action, Romance: BL/Yaoi, Mystery

New partners Dee and Ryo are opposites. Where Dee is blunt, impulsive, and arrogant, Ryo is calm, politic, and accommodating. As cops, they balance each other in their investigations. After work ... well, you know what they say about opposites.

Tateno, Makoto. *Yellow*. Digital Manga, 2002–2004 Japan (2006 U.S.). Publisher Age Rating: 18+. Age Recommendation: A. Volumes: 1–4 [T]. Genres: Action, Romance: BL/Yaoi, Mystery

Taki and Goh work for the police stealing back drugs. Taki is straight while Goh's gay, and there's never been anything but a game of sensual chicken between them. When his past comes back to haunt him, Taki begins to rethink the definitions of friend or lover.

Yoshinaga, Fumi. *The Moon and the Sandals*. Digital Manga, 1996 Japan (2007 U.S.). Publisher Age Rating: Mature 18+. Age Recommendation: A. Volumes: 1–2 [T]. Genres: Romance: BL/Yaoi, School Drama, Comedy

Kobayashi has a crush on his teacher, Mr. Oda. Best gal pal Rikuko loves Kobayashi. The steps to romance are never clear. By turns sweet and bittersweet, this title is an engaging meditation on how crushes are wonderful but oh, how they can hurt.

References

Kodansha International. *Japan: Profile of a Nation Revised Edition*. Tokyo: Kodansha International, 1999.

Poitras, Gilles. *The Anime Companion: What's Japanese in Japanese Animation?* Berkeley, CA: Stone Bridge Press, 1999.

World Health Organization (WHO). *Suicide Prevention: Country Report: Japan*. Geneva, 2005. http://www.who.int/mental_health/media/japa.pdf (accessed April 28, 2006).

World Health Organization (WHO). *Suicide Prevention: Country Report: United States*. Geneva, 2005. http://www.who.int/mental_health/media/usa.pdf (accessed April 28, 2006).

Chapter Five

Samurai and Shogun: Action, War, and Historical Fiction

Titles such as *Naruto* exemplify action and adventure manga.

© 1999 by MASASHI KISHIMOTO/SHUEISHA Inc.

Action and Adventure

Action and adventure manga are a large part of the boys' or shōnen manga market, although shōjo manga also has its share of swashbuckling, fighting, and competition stories. Shōnen manga's concentration on action over character development means many of the titles aimed at this market fall into this genre. If you flip through *Shōnen Jump*, most of the titles present in the anthology are action-oriented. The sheer amount of witty banter, comical asides, slapstick, and sight gags link action almost inseparably to humor—and because both are standard fare that appeals to guys, this comes as no surprise. From the famous martial arts comedy *Ranma 1/2* to the gleeful *Naruto*, a ninja-in-training tale, to *Full Metal Panic!*, a kinetic spoof of both military action and school stories, action is the focus of the manga. Pure action in the form of police dramas, spy stories, and fighters of all kinds is more common in titles aimed at older audiences. Examples include the sniper assassin tale *Golgo 13* and the rōnin samurai epic *Lone Wolf and Cub*. Of course, action is also a key element in many other manga titles that could be considered fantasy (*Saiyuki*), science fiction (*Mobile Suit Gundam*), or historical (*Rurouni Kenshin*).

In adventure stories, where the action takes place doesn't matter. The setting may be the past, outer space, or a fantasy world. Action can also be divided between fights that are physical, as in *Ranma 1/2* and *Rurouni Kenshin*, or magical or supernatural fights as seen in *GetBackers* and *Inuyasha*. Most of the time, the framework of the story is an excuse for elaborate and inventive action sequences, from fighter pilots zooming through space to the elegant, lethal dance of samurai duels.

The common visual language of action includes a variety of distinct conventions. Hand-to-hand combat is often accompanied by a narration of each side's tactics. Fight scenes may take anywhere from a few panels to an entire volume to complete. Action lines (lines of varying weight that angle across the background of a panel) replace the background and focus the reader's attention on movement. Sound effects for weapons, hits, and injuries are specific and break through the panel structure in a violent swipe across the page. The pace of the story is drawn out, full of visual pauses to prolong as long as possible the dramatic conclusion of the confrontation. In anime, fights show the same visual flair and dramatic tension. In *Samurai X*, one of the many interrelated *Rurouni Kenshin* anime, the fights are extended and the blows carefully deployed and lightning fast. To increase the tension, when two samurai collide, the animation slows down or even freezes, pausing for a beat. When the action restarts, the blows have made contact and the results, from spattering blood to a grunt of pain, flash across the screen.

War and Apocalypse

War will likely be a universal theme for as long as humans fight. In Japan, however, the attitude toward battle and war has shifted dramatically from one honoring warriors and conflicts to a modern society that is antiwar. Reverence for warriors, idealized in the historical samurai and the more recent yakuza (members of Japanese organized crime), is still a strong part of Japanese culture, and competition remains a galvanizing force for innovation and success. War, on the other hand, has been forced out of modern society and is now considered incredibly dangerous and rarely justified (Drazen 2003).

The nuclear bombings of Hiroshima and Nagasaki that ended World War II in Asia were a turning point in Japanese history. Part of the result of Japan rapidly becoming a modern nation in the early twentieth century was the adoption of a policy of expansion and military conquest, attacking neighboring countries including China and Korea. Nationalist tendencies, propagated and exploited by the government, led to an ultra-nationalist belief that Japan was a liberator, not a conqueror. During World War II, the image of the heroic warrior was used to inspire and drive the war effort. The infamous kamikaze pilots were mirroring the samurai of legend in their willingness to sacrifice themselves for the greater cause. The obliteration caused by the nuclear bombings and their impact on civilians not only ended the war but also irrevocably altered the Japanese point of view on militarism.

The postwar constitution, carefully written by the U.S. occupying forces, included Article 9, which reads, "the Japanese people shall forever renounce war as a sovereign right and the threat or use of force as means of settling international disputes" (Kodansha International 1999). The Japanese periodically consider repealing Article 9; however, the near apocalyptic destruction of World War II has had such a lasting impact on the national consciousness that pacifism has become the dominant feeling in a once warlike society.

The Future of Article 9

An article in the *Boston Globe* (December 18, 2005), titled "Japanese Factions Clash over Resurgence of Military—Nationalists Warn of China's Power," reported that Prime Minister Koizumi Junichiro proposed the Japanese abolish Article 9 and return to equal footing with their neighboring nations in their right to maintain armed forces. At this point, the discussion among both politicians and the public are heated—some believe the change is a long time coming, while others fear the renewal of a sense of national entitlement and aggression.

The conclusion that war is futile is common in Japanese manga, even in stories that are all about war. Wars are separated from our reality by time, distance, or setting. Historical Japanese conflicts are presented, but more and more common are conflicts set in fantastical worlds that parallel our own. Military epics like the *Gundam* series and *Fullmetal Alchemist* explore the causes and consequences of war. *Madlax* and *Ghost in the Shell: Stand Alone Complex* examine genocide and terrorism. Studio Ghibli's recent film, *Howl's Moving Castle*, altered the novel it was based on to emphasize the perils of war, giving the story a distinctly Japanese twist. The wizard Howl participates in war because of a sense of national duty, transforming himself into a flying creature reminiscent of a fighter plane. Each time he fights, however, it is harder and harder for him to regain his human form. The message is clear: the horrors of war will eventually obliterate Howl's humanity, no matter how just the cause.

As with any piece of good speculative fiction, war stories reflect the current world's conflicts and prejudices in a skewed mirror. This distance allows a more impassive point of view. Manga and anime rarely portray war as an effective solution, but as demonstrated by the recurring challenges to Article 9, the role of war is still being actively debated in Japanese society. Japanese pop culture critic Murakami Takashi points out that Japan entered the conflict in Iraq with its Self-Defense Forces and thus is not above participating in conflict. Japan is not as at ease with its pacifist identity as it would like to believe (Murakami 2005).

Many contemporary war stories focus on the entire scope of a war, from foot soldiers to military leaders to the politics that propel and resolve conflicts. Because both manga and anime tend to progress at a leisurely pace, war stories have the time to build the political landscape and to display the motivations and misunderstandings that often lead to war.

Wars are part of a historical drama. The anime *Otogi Zoshi* highlights the rise of the warrior class during the Heian period, while *Samurai X* takes place during the bloody conflicts between shogunate and emperor during the Meiji Restoration. The one war that is rarely directly considered is World War II. *Barefoot Gen* is the major manga departure from this trend. It is a partially autobiographical tale of a young man and his younger sister attempting to survive in the aftermath of the bombing of Hiroshima. Although it obliquely criticizes Japanese militarism, *Barefoot Gen* concentrates on the predicament of surviving the bombings and aftermath. In anime, the most famous film to address World War II is the piercing antiwar film *Grave of the Fireflies*, which follows two children attempting to survive after the fire bombings of Kobe. Neither of these tales directly addresses the aggressive side of the Japanese war.

Nonfiction Manga?

Although there are many realistic and historical manga currently in print in the United States, there are far fewer nonfiction titles. This growing subsection, however, is worth noting, especially the engaging Project X series from Digital Manga, highlighting invention and enterprise. Katoh Tadashi's *Project X: Nissin Cup Noodle* is excellent for all collections—who doesn't want to know the ingenuity that led to the food of generations of broke college students?

This deliberate avoidance of World War II as a subject has not stopped the impact of the war itself. Japanese civilians of the era are the only group in recent memory to have endured an apocalyptic event of such scale. The bombings were arguably the single most formative event in the creation of the modern Japanese state. Although the bombs were dropped more than fifty years ago, the shockwaves created by their detonation are still echoing through Japanese pop culture. Anyone who's seen Godzilla knows the monsters were created by nuclear explosions; however hokey, Godzilla remains one of the first symbols of atom bombs in the pop culture landscape. Apocalyptic devastation is the reason for current storylines in titles as diverse as *Akira*, *Neon Genesis Evangelion*, and *Nausicaä of the Valley of the Wind*. In other tales, the plot is a fight to prevent the apocalypse, as with *X/1999*, *Revolutionary Girl Utena*, and countless mecha series from *Gundam* to *Gravion Zwei*.

The almost subliminal appearances of nuclear imagery—an explosion will form the distinctive mushroom cloud of a nuclear detonation, although the pointed image is neither noted nor explained in the context of the story—is an oblique reminder of World War II. The image needs no explanation, although its meaning can be unclear. Starting with scenes in the short film *Daicon IV*, shown at the 1983 Japan SF Convention and created by men who would become the modern masters of Japanese animation, nuclear detonation has become a symbol for war, arrogance, and both an ending and a chance to restart civilization (Murakami 2005). In the credit sequence of Kon Satoshi's spooky miniseries, *Paranoia Agent*, a man is presented, arms raised in victory, as a nuclear explosion blossoms behind him, and in one of the final scenes, an old man is seen perched on the moon with the Earth behind him showing multiple detonations all over the surface of the planet.

Apocalyptic Pop Art

For more information on the current pop culture and art reflecting war, Murakami Takashi's excellent book of essays and artistic examples *Little Boy: The Arts of Japan's Exploding Subculture* is not to be missed.

Martial Arts

Most manga series focus on martial arts as a way of life in a historical setting or as a sport in the modern world. *Lone Wolf and Cub*, *Rurouni Kenshin*, and *Samurai Deeper Kyo* are all examples of traditional historical dramas centered on warriors and thus martial arts. The multiple *Dragon Ball* series are excellent examples of modern-day competition tales aimed at boys and teens. There are also many science fiction crossover series that involve fighting via an avatar or controlling a robot. Examples include CLAMP's *Angelic Layer* in which girls fight with foot-high dolls in a game field, or layer.

The traditional Japanese martial arts are as follows:

- Archery
- Horsemanship
- Spearmanship
- Fencing (kendō)
- Swimming
- *Iai* (sword drawing)
- The short sword
- The truncheon
- Dagger throwing
- Needle spitting
- The halberd
- Gunnery
- Roping
- *Yawara* (present-day judo)
- *Ninjutsu* (spying)
- The staff
- The chained sickle

Modern Martial Arts include:

- Judo (unarmed combat)
- Jujitsu (unarmed combat)
- Karate (unarmed combat, originally from China)
- Kendō (fencing)
- Kyūdō (archery)
- Sumo (wrestling)

Kendō, sumo, and judo are all taught as part of physical education in schools, and kyūdō is a common after-school club. In *Alice 19th*, a typical shōjo magical girl fantasy, Alice's sister Mayura and love interest Kyo are both members of the archery club and are seen practicing wearing traditional kyūdō garb.

Ninjutsu refers to the specific training needed for spying, hence the many ninja characters in manga from *Naruto* to *Ninja Nonsense*. Karate is not considered one of the traditional Japanese martial arts because it originated in China, but it certainly plays its part in martial arts dramas (Kodansha International 1999). Almost all of these disciplines involve a spiritual or mental aspect vital to the mastery of the art. While in the United States we rarely consider fencing or wrestling to be a top sport or one relevant to personal defense today, in Japan prowess in any martial art is valued and admired. For a police officer to advance his career, for example, he must show skill in either kendō or judo before he can be considered for a promotion (Schodt 1995).

Most traditions are taught in *dōjo*, or schools, and each provides a particular skill set unique to the dōjo and the master or sensei. Historically, fighters mastered a particular style or school of techniques and self-identified as a member of that school. Trademark stances or moves are given specific names to identify them as they are being taught or observed. In the anime *Samurai Champloo*, for example, members of a school of swordsmanship recognize Jin by his fighting style, and others can identify his master on the basis of his master's reputation and Jin's observed moves.

Fight Scene Callouts!

One of the quirks of fighting stories is that opponents shout the name of the move they are about to execute. Even if the combatant does not, an audience member often will. This does not happen in real competition, but it has become a convention of manga and anime tales both to identify the move and to draw out the tension. In *One Piece*, Luffy repeatedly shouts out his moves including "gum gum pistol," a reference to his magically rubbery limbs and the power of his punch.

Manga and anime can go elaborately over the top with fighting, both in terms of impossible feats of skill and the endurance of the fighter. As with everything in manga, the point is the competition and the drama of the story, and the more exaggerated the sequence of events, the greater the high of winning and the more crushing the defeat. Martial arts heroes exemplify certain qualities—skill, persistence, honor, and sportsmanship—whereas the villains are cheaters who enjoy violence and are driven by their vendettas rather than their love of the art itself.

Top Action Titles

Aida, Yu. *Gunslinger Girl*. ADV Manga, 2002 Japan (2003–2004 U.S.). Publisher Age Rating: 15+. Age Recommendation: A. Volumes: 1–3+ [T]. Genres: Action, Crime, Suspense. Related Anime: *Gunslinger Girl* (TV series)

> Fatally wounded young girls are remade into soulless assassins by a secret government agency. This eerie, suspenseful series is as much about psychological distortion as it is violent action, but the presence of both make it best for mature teens and adults.

Akimine Kamijyo. *Samurai Deeper Kyo*. Tokyopop, 1999–2006 Japan (2003 U.S.). Publisher Age Rating: Older Teen. Age Recommendation: S. Volumes: 1–23+ [T]. Genres: Action, Historical, Military. Related Anime: *Samurai Deeper Kyo* (TV series)

> Mibu Kyoshiro is a mild-mannered medicine peddler—or is he? Four years after the most violent battle of the civil wars, Kyo struggles to contain the infamous Demon Eyes Kyo, a warrior known for his bloodlust. Who will win out in the end?

Aoki, Yuya. *GetBackers*. Tokyopop, 1999 Japan (2004 U.S.). Publisher Age Rating: Older Teen. Age Recommendation: S, A. Volumes: 1–17+ [T]. Genres: Action, Fantasy, Mystery. Related Anime: GetBackers (TV series)

> Ban and Ginji will get back anything you've lost—as long as you pay. Jobs are either scarce or go haywire in the middle. Old enemies come back to haunt them. Their loyalty and one-of-a-kind powers get them through.

Kishimoto, Masahi. *Naruto*. VIZ Manga, 2000-Japan (2003 U.S.). Publisher Age Rating: Teen. Age Recommendation: J. Volumes: 1–12+ [T]. Genres: Action, Fantasy, Comedy. Related Anime: *Naruto* (TV series)

> Naruto, an irrepressible apprentice ninja determined to prove his worth as a warrior, carries a magical burden—his body is the prison for the malicious spirit of a nine-tailed fox. A hilarious series with moments of real heart.

Koike, Kazuo. *Lone Wolf and Cub*. Dark Horse Manga, 1970–1976 Japan (2000–2002 U.S.). Publisher Age Rating: 16+. Age Recommendation: A. Volumes: 1–28 [T]. Genres: Action, Historical, Military, Slice of Life. Related Manga: *Lone Wolf and Cub 2100*

> A rōnin bent on avenging the murder of his wife and restoring his family to honor travels through Feudal Japan working as an assassin for pay with his toddler son in tow. The hard decisions, brutal action, and moments of quiet tragedy defined seinen manga.

Kubo Tite. *Bleach*. VIZ Manga, 2002 Japan (2004 U.S.). Publisher Age Rating: Teen. Age Recommendation: S. Volumes: 1–17+ [T]. Genres: Action, Fantasy. Related Anime: *Bleach* (TV series), *Bleach* (movie), *Bleach: Memories of Rain* (OVA)

When Ichigo becomes a Soul Reaper, or shinigami, balancing high school and supernatural duties test his limits. Humor, pathos, and compelling action make this one of the best recent shōnen action titles, with a slew of crossover readers.

Madlax. ADV Films, 2003, TV series (26 episodes, 24 minutes running time), 7 DVDs. Publisher Age Rating: 13+. Age Recommendation: S. Genres: Action, Military, Mystery

A preoccupied schoolgirl and an assassin with scruples live across the globe from each other, but a conspiracy and linked memories bind them together. This atmospheric but suspenseful series tackles genocide, political ethics, and secret societies with aplomb.

Minekura Kazuya. Saiyuki. Tokyopop, 1997–2002 Japan (2004–2005 U.S.). Publisher Age Rating: Older Teen. Age Recommendation: S, A. Volumes: 1–9 [T]. Genres: Action, Fantasy, Historical, Comedy. Related Manga: *Saiyuki Reload*. Related Anime: *Saiyuki* (TV series), *Saiyuki Reload* (TV series), *Saiyuki Requiem* (film)

A grumpy monk, a starving brat, a sly ladies man, and a bespectacled mechanic walk into a bar ... and defeat all the demons hiding out there. Welcome to the foul-mouthed, quick on the draw, irreverent world of Saiyuki.

Noir. ADV Films, 2003, TV series (26 episodes, 24 minutes running time), 7 DVDs. Publisher Age Rating. 15+. Age Recommendation: S. Genres: Action, Mystery

A mercenary gun for hire and a broken but ruthless 'tween assassin make a pact—the fragments of their past seem to lead to each other, and as long as they're piecing together the puzzle, they can each live. In the end, though, one must die to keep their secrets.

Samurai Champloo. Geneon, 2004, TV series (26 episodes, 24 minutes running time), 7 DVDs. Publisher Age Rating: 16+. Age Recommendation: S, A. Genres: Action, Historical, Comedy. Related Manga: *Samurai Champloo* (adaptation)

Mugen, a brash but lethal fighter, and Jin, an impeccable samurai, are conned into helping Fuu, a waitress with an enormous appetite, find the "samurai who smells of sunflowers." Hip-hop and samurai traditions combine, with exhilarating results.

Watsuki, Nobuhiro. *Rurouni Kenshin*. VIZ Manga, 1994–1999 Japan (2003–2006 U.S.). Publisher Age Rating: Older Teen. Age Recommendation: S. Volumes: 1–28 [T]. Genres: Action, Fantasy, Historical, Military, Comedy. Related Anime: *Rurouni Kenshin* (TV series), *Samurai X* (OVA)

Rōnin samurai Kenshin appears to be a happy-go-lucky fellow living life to help those around him. His extraordinary fencing skills and past as a vicious killer jar with this image, but he will do everything he can to make peace with his history.

Yasuhiro, Nightow. *Trigun and Trigun Maximum*. Dark Horse/Digital Manga, 1997–2004 Japan (2003 U.S.). Publisher Age Rating: 13+. Age Recommendation: S. Volumes: 1–12+ [T]. Genres: Action, Science Fiction, Comedy. Related Anime: *Trigun* (TV series)

Vash the Stampede, the quickest draw on the planet, has a 60 billion double dollar bounty on his head. Vash is also a gentle, pacifist, donut-loving goof. Or is he?

The *Samurai X* anime, left, and the related manga *Rurouni Kenshin*, right, are both popular and enduring series following a wandering or rōnin samurai during the Meiji Era (1868–1912).

Left: © N. Watsuki/Shueisha * Fuji-TV * SME Visual Works. Right: © 1994 by Nobuhiro Watsuki/SHUEISHA, Inc.

Samurai

Samurai exist in the Japanese imagination much like cowboys do in the United States—as icons of an admired, fading past and an instantly recognizable character type. Unequalled masters of the sword, honorable to a fault, and loyal even unto death, samurai are revered. The image of the samurai has penetrated into the West: an elegant, silent figure carrying two swords wearing a subdued combination of kimono and coat or *haori*. Samurai are most famous for being loyal to the point of disregarding their personal obligations and their own lives. Only the wishes of their *daimyō*, or lord, matter, and if he decrees it, they are willing to commit *seppuku*, or ritual suicide. Rōnin, or masterless samurai who have lost their lords through death or dishonorable behavior, are dramatic favorites because they live on the edge of what is accepted but are nonetheless admirable for their adherence to the strict way of life they have adopted.

Samurai in Manga and Anime

Heian Era (794–1185)
Otogi Zoshi
Sengoku Era (1467–1615)
Lone Wolf and Cub
InuYasha
Tokugawa Era (1600–1867)
Samurai Champloo
Samurai Deeper Kyo

Meiji Era (1868–1912)
Kaze Hikaru
Peacemaker
Rurouni Kenshin

Samurai as Characters

Because of their legendary reputation, the samurai ideal has never truly left Japanese stories or mythology. Many of the ideals of the samurai appear today in stories of the yakuza, or Japanese organized crime, where loyalty to one leader and lethal skill are still the tradition. Samurai and yakuza stories both involve the conflict between group loyalty and personal feelings in the most dramatic of circumstances (Drazen 2003). Samurai are stock characters in manga; they may be heroes or louts, historically accurate or intentionally anachronistic. In fact, they have become such classic characters that they are the most mocked, reinvented, and tweaked types. A recent example of such reinvention is the anime *Samurai Champloo*, an exhilarating if unexpected collision of samurai tropes with modern hip-hop culture.

Outsiders and Renegades

In a society where there is much more conformity than rule breaking and the people themselves are more homogenous than diverse, those who ignore society's rules are both admired and feared. Japanese stories are almost gleeful about those who dare to cross boundaries. At the same time, an outsider is still an outsider and not to be emulated. The illicit thrill of otherness reinforces the sentiment that an ordinary, unremarkable life is preferable (Drazen 2003). The classic rōnin samurai tales are the most iconic examples of outsiders in manga and anime. Their masterless state means they have no rank or official place and thus can be equally cast as renegade heroes, hoodlums, or villains. *Lone Wolf and Cub*, Kazuo Koike's masterpiece, places a samurai, framed by political enemies and thus dishonored and exiled, as the hero of his story. No longer bound to a lord, he now travels the countryside with his infant son and survives as an assassin for hire.

Historical Fiction

Japanese History

Historical fiction titles are still a minority in U.S. comics, but Japan's rich past provides fertile ground for manga creators. Japanese storytellers treat their history with the same creativity, respect, and irreverence as their folktales, religion, and authority figures. With more than 1,200 years of recorded history, filled with numerous shifts in politics, internal conflict, and external influences, manga creators often head to the past for inspiration.

Japanese Eras

Jomon (10,000–300 B.C.)

Yayoi (300 B.C.–250 A.D.)

Yamato (250–710)

Nara Era (710–794)

Heian Era (794–1185)

Kamakura Era (1185–1333)

Muromachi Era (1333–1568)

Sengoku Era (1467–1615), also known as the Warring States period

Azuchi-Momoyama Era (1568–1600)

Tokugawa (or Edo) Era (1600–1867)

Meiji Era (1868-1912)

Taisho Era (1912–1926)

Showa Era (1926–1987)

Heisei Era (1989–present)

In most manga, historical accuracy is not uppermost in the creators' minds—the story must be dramatic, well-told, and highlight the spirit of the era, but it need not be exacting in every detail. The key seems to be to research as much as possible but, once you've filled up on records, memoirs, and images, to create a living history that will grab readers. Many creators do extensive research when setting their tale in the past, and copious end and side notes often detail their adventures in research, but they are always aiming for fiction, not fact.

In historical manga, readers are expected to know the history behind the story and thus how the story begins and ends according to the timeline. In one of the newest shōjo manga from VIZ, *Kaze Hikaru*, an orphaned young woman disguises herself as a boy in order to join the ranks of the Shinsengumi, a group also depicted in *Peacemaker Kurogane* and *Rurouni Kenshin*. The Shinsengumi, from their names to their legends to their ultimate fates, are all recognized in Japan. These figures might be compared to generals and soldiers in the U.S. Civil War—their names and general accomplishments are part of our cultural memory and hold particular weight in our own historical fiction. Because most Western readers have no background for the era in general or the Shinsengumi legacy, *Kaze Hikaru* requires a wealth of historical background and notes in translation.

Best Historical Titles

Buddha

Cantarella

Emma

Godchild

Grave of the Fireflies

Kaze Hikaru

Lone Wolf and Cub

Otogi Zoshi

Princess Mononoke

Rurouni Kenshin

Samurai Champloo

Historical Fantasy: The West That Exists Only in Dreams

Historical manga are not limited to Japan's own history. Some of the most entertaining and occasionally puzzling manga are those set in other countries and eras. Many manga exist in an idealized and relatively vague European past, more noted for its elaborate costumes and gothic touches than any adherence to historical fact.

Shōjo manga were the original titles that selected a far-off and fabulous setting. Hagio Moto's legendary *Rose of Versailles* follows the story of Oscar, a young woman raised as a young man and now head of Queen Marie Antoinette's bodyguard. Higuri You's deliciously wicked *Cantarella* depicts the exploits and conquests of the infamous Borgia siblings, Cesare and Lucrezia, in Renaissance Italy. Both provide complex political and romantic stories, inspired by history but not tied to recorded details, and both feature fantastical touches, as in *Cantarella* where Cesare Borgia's evil side is explained by demonic possession. A number of the BL (boy's love) subgenre titles are set in European private boarding schools, giving their forbidden romances an even more exotic flavor. Higuri You's older title *Gorgeous Carat* features turn of the century Vienna, and within her author notes she acknowledges that she did little research, begs forgiveness from her readers, and notes that the period is full of such romance that she's always wanted to set a story during the time (Higuri 2006–present). European or American settings are most often used to give the tale an air of exoticism and romance. Exotic historical settings are certainly not limited to shōjo manga, however—fantasy action titles such as *Chrono Crusade*, set in 1920s New York, display just as much interest in historical details from the design of buildings and cars to costume design.

In *Cantarella*, flowing costumes and melodrama make for a rich and satisfying mix.

Best Historical Series

Grave of the Fireflies. Central Park Media, 1988, feature film (88 minutes running time), 1 DVD. Publisher Age Rating: NR. Age Recommendation: S. Genres: Historical, Military, Slice of Life

One of the few films set during World War II, Seita and Setsuko are orphaned during an air raid on Kobe. With diminishing food and no one to turn to, they struggle to stay alive in a devastated landscape. A heartbreaking look at civilians caught on the losing side of a war.

Higuri, You. *Cantarella.* Go Comi! Manga, 2001–2005 Japan (2005 U.S.). Publisher Age Rating: Older Teen. Age Recommendation: S, A. Volumes: 1–6+ [T]. Genres: Action, Fantasy, Historical, Military, Horror

Power, politics, wealth, and legacy are an explosive mix. Lucrezia Borgia had a devious, lethal sweetness, and Cesare was her ambitious, bloody older brother. History, though, is written by the conquerors—what if the Borgias were not what they seemed?

Koike, Kazuo. *Lone Wolf and Cub.* Dark Horse Manga, 1970–1976 Japan (2000–2002 U.S.). Publisher Age Rating: 16+. Age Recommendation: A. Volumes: 1–28 [F]. Genres: Action, Historical, Military, Slice of Life. Related Manga: *Lone Wolf and Cub 2100*

A rōnin bent on avenging the murder of his wife and restoring his family to honor travels through feudal Japan working as an assassin for pay with his toddler son in tow. The hard decisions, brutal action, and moments of quiet tragedy defined seinen manga.

Mori, Kaoru. *Emma.* CMX, 2002–2006 Japan (2006 U.S.). Publisher Age Rating: Teen+. Age Recommendation: S. Volumes: 1–4+ [T]. Genres: Historical, Romance, Slice of Life.

When William, a member of the upper crust in Victorian London, meets Emma, his former nanny's shy but lovely maid, he knows he's found love. Can they break away from society's disapproval and find happiness?

Otogi Zoshi. Anime Works, 2004, TV series (26 episodes, 24 minutes running time), 6 DVDs. Publisher Age Rating: NR. Age Recommendation: S. Production Company: Anime Works. Genres: Action, Fantasy, Historical, Military. Related Manga: *Otogi Zoshi* (prequel)

Minamoto no Raiko is sent to recover a gem destined to save the country, but when he falls deathly ill, his younger sister Hikaru must go in his place. A realistic manga rich with the pageantry, politics, and strife of the end of the Heian Era.

Princess Mononoke. Buena Vista/Disney, 1997, feature film (133 minutes running time), 1 DVD. Publisher Age Rating: PG-13. Age Recommendation: J. Genres: Action, Fantasy, Historical

The conflict between technology and nature becomes an all-out war. Cursed by a demon, young prince Ashitaka seeks a cure. Along with a fierce wild girl, Sand, he ends up negotiating peace between the forest gods and the ambitious and greedy Lady Eboshi.

Samurai Champloo. Geneon, 2004, TV series (26 episodes, 24 minutes running time), 7 DVDs. Publisher Age Rating: 16+. Age Recommendation: S, A. Genres: Action, Historical, Comedy. Related Manga: *Samurai Champloo* (adaptation)

Mugen, a brash but lethal fighter, and Jin, an impeccable samurai, are conned into helping Fuu, a waitress with an enormous appetite, find the "samurai who smells of sunflowers." Hip-hop and samurai traditions combine, with exhilarating results.

Tezuka, Osamu. *Buddha*. Vertical, 1974–1984 Japan (2003–2005 U.S.). Publisher Age Rating: NA. Age Recommendation: S, A. Volumes: 1–8 [T]. Genres: Historical, Slice of Life

An ultimately breathtaking work, Tekuza's biography of Siddhartha Buddha demonstrates all of his mastery of the manga format in one epic work.

Watanabe, Tacko. *Kaze Hikaru*. VIZ Manga, 1997– Japan (2006 U.S.). Publisher Age Rating: Older Teen. Age Recommendation: S. Volumes: 1–3+ [T]. Genres: Action, Romance, Historical, Military

When her family is murdered in front of her, Sei cannot leave them unavenged. Passing as a young man, she joins the Shinsengumi, Kyoto's warriors loyal to the Shogunate, to learn to defeat her enemies, and she might just fall in love along the way.

Watsuki, Nobuhiro. *Rurouni Kenshin*. VIZ Manga, 1994–1999 Japan (2003–2006 U.S). Publisher Age Rating: Older Teen. Age Recommendation: S. Volumes: 1–28 [T]. Genres: Action, Historical, Military, Slice of Life. Related Anime: *Rurouni Kenshin* (TV series), *Samurai X* (OVA)

Rōnin samurai Kenshin appears to be a happy-go-lucky fellow living life to help those around him. His extraordinary fencing skills and past as a vicious killer jar with this image, but he will do everything he can to make peace with his history.

Yuki, Kaori. *Godchild*. VIZ Manga, 2001–2004 Japan (2006 U.S.). Publisher Age Rating: Older Teens. Age Recommendation: S, A. Volumes: 1–5+ [T]. Genres: Action, Historical, Horror. Related Manga: *The Cain Saga* (prequel)

Cain Hargreaves is a gentleman detective who has witnessed the worst in people. The only people he cares about are his sweet sister, Marie Weather, and his devoted manservant Rafe. As he unravels clever, gruesome mysteries, his past enemies threaten his fragile peace.

References

Kodansha International. *Japan: Profile of a Nation Revised Edition*. Tokyo: Kodansha International, 1999.

Chapter Six

Giant Robots and Nature Spirits: Science Fiction, Fantasy, and Legends

Science Fiction

A lot of science fiction in Japan has one goal in mind: to sell toys—specifically, toy robots. From these consumerist beginnings, however, many tales have evolved that examine the depths of the connections between man, machine, technology, and nature.

Science fiction's innovation and exploratory mission reflects a society's fears, hopes, and dreams. Japanese science fiction touches on myriad concerns about technology and its increasing presence in our lives and in the world. At the same time, these stories glorify the genius of invention and human adaptability. Science fiction becomes a tool for investigating emotional and cultural ideas including the definitions of identity, the soul, morality, and life itself.

Apocalypse

Science fiction in Japan cannot escape the idea of apocalypse. An uneasy balance between the desire to explore and create and the twisting of those ideals toward destruction is reflected in many titles. From *Neon Genesis Evangelion* to *Ghost in the Shell* to *Nausicaä of the Valley of the Wind*, many tales begin in a world already destroyed by a holocaust. Countless tales pit nature against technological advances, a powerful commentary from a society with rapidly diminishing space and natural resources.

The most common themes in science fiction are space exploration, utopian and dystopian societies, artificial intelligence, and genetic engineering and manipulation. We frequently ask the question of what it means to be human by postulating a world in which we could manipulate the human genome (as in Marvel's *X-Men* franchise, the film *Gattaca*, and Nancy Werlin's teen novel

159

Double Helix). The Japanese tend to look at that same question through the lens of artificial intelligence. As technology becomes smaller and smaller and more integrated into daily life, from ubiquitous cell phones to digital music players to wireless Internet access, many manga speculate on how far the integration of man and machine might go.

Mecha: A Boy and His Robot

Toys were, and still are, a major inspiration for stories revolving around robots, artificial intelligence, and combinations of man and machine. Tezuka himself fired the starting gun for this genre with his creation of *Astro Boy*, the tale of a robot boy aiding his human creator and society. *Astro Boy* is not just an automaton: he questions his makeup, purpose, and soul much like the child he seems to be. After *Astro Boy*, whether the impulse was to merchandise a collectible toy or not, manga and anime were filled with robots.

Most of the time mecha stories are stories of war and conflict. The numerous *Gundam*, *Patlabor*, *Robotech*, and *Neon Genesis Evangelion* series follow the same model. The heroes are usually teenage fighters brought in as the last hope in an ongoing battle with enemy, often alien, forces. The hero or heroine is a new recruit, acting as a stand-in for the reader. As they are inducted into the ranks with copious explanations of the forces they are joining, the conflict they are fighting, and the machines they will be using, the reader learns the rules of the world. More often than not, humans are piloting giant human-shaped robots or giant exoskeletons that the human pilot controls from a cockpit, much like a fighter plane. Traditional mecha include stories of teams of paired pilots and vehicles, all built with the ability to combine and form one giant robot as in the cartoon series *Transformers*.

Many tales unfold on an operatic scale, barreling into outer space, down into the oceans, and through urban landscapes. Other mecha focus more narrowly on the day-to-day relationship between a fighter and a machine or police procedure, as in the anime *Gad Guard*. Mecha is also marked by two kinds of fan service—the scantily clad, well-endowed women on display, and the extended coverage of the robots, their transformations, and their technical specifications. At one time in anime, the transformation sequences became so elaborate that the journey from the pilot setting out to board his craft to finally entering the battle could take more than ten minutes of choreographed, detail-laden shots.

The best of these tales ask complex and often unanswerable questions.

- What is the relationship between pilot and vehicle?
- When does artificial intelligence become self-awareness?
- Can machines gain souls, and if so, what does that make us?

- What would the logic and loyalty of robots be like?

- What is our obligation to our own creations?

Not Just Giant Robots, but Robots with Souls

When creators want to take a mecha story to a level beyond straight action and conflict, they introduce hints that the robots are gaining self-awareness through their symbiotic relationship with an individual pilot. These may remain merely hints, keeping the focus on the pilots' internal and external struggle with their mission. Confronting the fact that the weapon they are piloting may also harbor a separate intelligence adds another layer to the story.

Saikano explores the consequences when Shuji discovers his new girlfriend Chise is a weapon of mass destruction employed by the government.

Today the most traditional manga and anime series involving giant fighting robots are undoubtedly the *Gundam* series, consisting of more than fifty manga titles and almost thirty anime titles. All of the *Gundam* series feature the same basic setup—pairing pilots with the enormous Gundam, fighter robots warring in the space surrounding Earth. A common mecha reference in the United States for younger generations of fans has been the anime and manga adaptation of *Neon Genesis Evangelion*, often referred to as simply Eva, adopted from the names the characters give their piloted vehicles. The basic plot is traditional: in Tokyo 3, the third reconstructed Tokyo after a series of attacks on Earth by alien forces, the survivors of humanity are trying to destroy their enemies, called angels, once and for all. A young pilot, thirteen-year-old Shinji, is recruited to pilot an Eva. The series develops into a slow exploration of duty, love, loyalty, spirituality, and, above all, humanity.

Neon Genesis Evangelion © GAINAX / Project Eva. • TV Tokyo

One of the giant Eva battle robots in *Neon Genesis Evangelion*.
© GAINAX/Project Eva * TV Tokyo.

Neon Genesis Evangelion is more of a meditation on the human soul than a traditional science fiction action piece. The dynamic animation and the spectacular Eva and angel designs catch viewers' attention. There is no lack of action and robotic fan service, but the mecha aspect of the story is a cover for exploring the psychology of Shinji and the other pilots.

More recent incarnations of the combination and /fighting robot series include *Gravion* and *Gravion Zwei*. The *Gravion* series hits all the right notes: spectacular robot action sequences, the importance of teamwork above the squabbling and slapstick rivalry among the pilots, and more than enough fan service to entertain teenage guys. *RahXephon* has broader appeal. The series imagines an apocalyptic attack that leaves two high schoolers just starting their relationship stranded on either side of an impenetrable barrier with time running at different speeds within and without the barrier. One becomes a soldier and one remains a high school student until destiny forces them into battle (aboard the necessary giant exoskeletons). A much more serious drama than *Gravion*, *RahXephon* turns the mecha story into an examination of invasion, occupation, genocide, and the relationship between two very human lovers.

Man, Machine, and Cyborg

Mecha is not just about giant robots. The relationship between man and machine also appears in subtler incarnations. An excellent example is *Ghost in the Shell*, a manga that has been transformed into two films and a TV series. In this world, the robot is no longer outside the body but inside it. All three versions of the story follow the stealth government organization Section 9, a group of trained operatives specializing in containing threats to national security involving technological abuse. The original manga is justly reputed to be one of the most intelligent and complex explorations of the blurred line between technology and its creators. *Ghost in the Shell* presents a world where cyborg technology and artificial intelligence have advanced so far that few people have not tinkered with their own bodies. People inhabit entirely artificial bodies or incorporate robotic implants into their own flesh. The heroine, Major Kusanagi Motoko, is human, but her soul (or "ghost") inhabits an artificial cyborg body that is faster, stronger, and more durable than a human body could ever be. She and her fellows have the equivalent of superpowers, but so do the villains. Her immortality comes with a price, however, as her body is in fact government property, provided only while she works as their agent. She is literally owned by the state.

Tanks with Hearts

Section 9 employs robots about the size of cars, collectively called *tachikoma*, that are essentially advanced tanks. Each has its own artificial intelligence and a growing sense of consciousness. When a tachikoma becomes too self-aware, its memories must be obliterated: a weapon that can feel is useless.

The series shows an imaginative variety of *cyberization* as it explores the various crimes and manipulations possible in this world. In this universe, one politician has given up his human form entirely and now resides inside a two-foot-square robot on wheels with only a small mechanical arm. People are able to switch bodies with relative ease, leading to all manner of illegal swaps and an inability to trust anyone's presented persona. People can also be hacked and their memories can be altered or erased without their knowledge or consent. Cyber crime is rampant and difficult to trace, and much of the genius of the series revolves around speculating on how society could and would change in integrating so completely with machines. Due to explicit content, the film and manga are decidedly adult, but the television series *Ghost in the Shell: Stand Alone Complex* is a fascinating speculative work wrapped up in a police procedural that older teens will enjoy.

A Girl and Her Robot

Although mecha and cyborg stories are traditionally aimed at guys, girls now have their share of artificial characters and plots. In *Absolute Boyfriend,* Watase Yu explores how having a programmable and drop-dead gorgeous boyfriend turns one girl's world upside down.

In between *Neon Genesis Evangelion*'s robots and *Ghost in the Shell*'s cyborgs are numerous tales about humans' partnerships with machines. The less science-based, more relationship-driven series such as *Gad Guard* will appeal to readers and viewers less inclined toward science fiction, while titles like *Ghost in the Shell* require a lot of wading through technological jargon to reach the essential plot.

Although the partnership between man and machine is the more common theme in science fiction titles, genetic manipulation and experimentation is becoming equally popular. Even though genetic tinkering may well produce creatures more inhuman than human, creators of science fiction manga are concerned with what happens to the soul and individuality of humanity once people can be created or changed so fundamentally.

CLAMP's *Clover* explores a world where certain people have been genetically manipulated by the government to manifest extraordinary talents intended for government use. The question posed is simple—what would happen if we decided to create people as weapons? How would we treat them, and how would we deploy them? How would they feel, and how would we maintain control? CLAMP's series *Chobits* explores a different kind of relationship in a world where personal computers are built to look and act like young women.

The series asks the question: When a computer looks like a person and seems able to learn, is she still a machine?

The series *Doll* explores the dark side of the human creators. In this manga's world, people with enough money can purchase human-sized dolls built to detailed specifications. Each doll is loyal to his or her master and will perform any duty the owner requires. In one story, a lonely woman gets a doll for company to escape the emptiness of her life as a wife and mother. In another installment, an emotionally closed-off man ends up falling in love with his doll, only to have his coworkers mock the relationship. He pays for her to be remade so that she will be as human as possible, forgetting that human frailty can lead to tragedy as well as happiness. The responsibility and consequences for creating or manipulating life through genetics, whatever the original intention, is the crux of the question.

Space Travel

Space travel and exploration is a favorite topic of all science fiction. Manga set in space cover themes that range from speculation on the progression of space exploration, as in the excellent series about space garbage collectors *Planetes*, to epic conflicts involving alien forces, such as *RahXephon*. Space stories frequently combine with mecha stories: given that humans cannot travel through space without vessels, using giant piloted robots instead of spaceships is not an uncommon leap.

Space is used as a setting to discuss human ambitions, weaknesses, and relationships. *Planetes* is a great example of a series set in local space about three space garbage collectors charged with gathering the obsolete satellites that now clutter the sky. Each has his or her own ambition, from finally making it as an astronaut to trying to forget a past tragedy, and their simple interaction and struggles with their lot in life are the heart of the story. Space is still wondrous for them, as it is for us, and is not just a backdrop but another character.

In the fifty-minute anime *Voices from a Distant Star*, two high school sweethearts are separated when one stays on Earth to lead an ordinary life, while his girlfriend travels into space as a pilot and ultimately is sent to the edge of our Solar System to help defend Earth from alien attack. As she travels farther and farther away at near–light speed no time passes for her while an ever increasing number of years passes for her love. The time in between messages grows from weeks to years, and each must come to terms with the fact that the gulf between them has ended their relationship against their will. It is, in essence, a tragedy that takes a simple scientific fact, the theory of relativity, and turns the consequences of the true distance of space into a heartbreaking story of love and hope.

Games and Gaming

Gaming, whether in the form of video games, virtual reality, or Massive Multiplayer Online Role-Playing Games (MMORPGs), is a frequent subject or setting for manga. Japanese and Asian games still dominate game production worldwide and are part of the reason today's teens embrace manga and anime so readily—the design conventions of manga and anime shows in Asian game design.

Some manga embrace the gaming world wholeheartedly, as in the many incarnations of the *.hack* (or dot Hack) series in anime, manga, and video games. In *.hack*, the characters are players in a MMORPG, the dominant game in a future world where billions of people play in a virtual environment called The World. You rarely see the players outside of the game, in the real world, and when you do, their faces are obscured or unclear. The series acknowledges the wide variety of players online, from teenagers to businesspeople, and mines the odd-couple partnerships for drama inside the overarching mystery and adventure plots that drive each installment in the series. *.hack* is constructed such that you need to explore all the titles and formats to fully understand the world. When it was released in Japan, it was released as an anime series, a manga series, and two video games, each illuminating a different facet of one larger story.

Most manga are not so completely integrated into the gaming world, but many reference the activity and characteristics of gamers. One of the many alternate worlds the heroes visit in *Tsubasa: RESERVoir CHRoNICLE* seems like a land of demons and warriors until the crew figures out that in fact they are all inside a virtual MMORPG. Once they leave the game, everything seems explained, until the demons from the game start attacking in the real world. *Genshiken* and *Welcome to the NHK*, titles portraying otaku culture, wouldn't be complete without showing the games and gaming addictions, from ties-ins to favorite pornographic relationship games popular among otaku.

On top of all the manga featuring gamers or games, increasingly more manga are appearing that are inspired by games and gaming. *Ragnarok* is a Korean *manhwa* that spins off from a favorite Korean (and worldwide) MMORPG of the same title. *Sakura Taisen* and *Suikoden III* both spin tales from the worlds of video games, whereas *Kingdom Hearts* and *Warcraft* are manga-style comics that take their inspiration from a Disney video game and an online role-playing game, respectively. Many manga have their own video games, from fighting games based on *Naruto* and *Rurouni Kenshin* to role-playing and story-based games similar to *The SIMs*. As games and manga both permeate more of U.S. culture, crossovers and integrated packages will multiply.

Dystopias

Among these many speculations on the destiny of mankind, you will notice very few rosy pictures of our future. The science fiction landscape contains few utopias, and when they do exist, they exist on very shaky ground.

In the *Wolf's Rain* manga and anime, wolves are reputed in legend to be the only creatures that can find and lead the world to Paradise. The problem is that wolves have been extinct for decades. The current culture is surviving on the ashes of previous cultures decimated by apocalyptic wars that created vast wastelands. The one safe place on the planet is a city ruled ruthlessly by Lady Jagara, one of many elite nobles who fight bitterly over obsolete territories. Her iron control over her domain is what gives her people the illusion of safety and control, but the price for their blissful existence is far greater than any of them know. The pristine walls and lucrative jobs all hide a corrupt and sadistic ruling class.

Shirow Masamune's *Appleseed* presents a similar landscape but with less maliciousness at its core. Once again the landscape of the world has been mutilated by conflict; pockets of soldiers are still fighting wars that are long over. Briareos, a cyborg soldier, and his human partner and lover, Deunan, are brought into the haven of Utopia, a peaceful city equally populated by humans and artificially intelligent robots. The city, however, is far from perfect, and the city's rulers have less benevolent intentions toward humanity than they confide to their guests.

Many science fiction titles take a dim view of humanity's ability to abstain from warmongering. At the same time, they tend to portray any society blinded by greed, jealousy, or divine right as a dangerous and ultimately evil force even if individuals are redeemable. Some of this may be in reaction to the dark consequences of Japan's ultra-nationalism in World War II and the desire to mute that impulse in their own society. In many manga and anime, but especially in science fiction, creators choose to pose questions without providing any definite answers.

Environmentalism

Concern for the environment is seen everywhere in manga and anime, from the gentle natural spirits in *My Neighbor Totoro* to the magical journey to save extinct species in *Ark Angels*. Numerous manga feature environmental concerns both as occasional plot points and major motivations within the story.

Concern over pollution in the twentieth century has provoked a renewed awareness of the environment, and in particular to preserving and saving natural resources. Since the industrialization of Japan in the late 1860s, pollution has been a problem; and the rapid post–World War II economic boom also did its part to deteriorate the environment. Japan currently has a number of government laws and policies in place to deal with water and air pollution, as well as natural preserves and parks. The sheer lack of space and land plus the increasing population has led the Japanese to be more aware of their own waste and the environment around them (Kodansha International 1999).

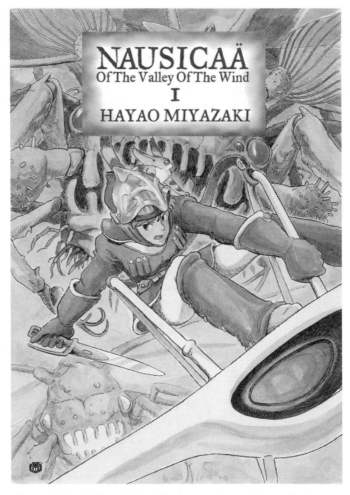

Nausicaä of the Valley of the Wind **remains a science fiction classic.**
© 1983 Nibariki Co., Ltd.

In both the manga and anime *Nausicaä of the Valley of the Wind*, the world has been nearly obliterated by human wars and destruction, leaving only pockets of arable land and stable countryside where the remnants of the race can survive. The poisonous results of warfare have created large sections of the planet covered by jungles of noxious plants and insects fatal to humans, and these areas are spreading. Nausicaä, a princess of an idyllic woodland community living in relative peace with their natural surroundings, is unafraid of the changing nature around her and curious about its potential to help her people survive. When her fellow humans decide to wipe out the jungles once and for all and in doing so resurrect the previous generations' most vile weapon, Nausicaä is the only one who realizes that the very nature they're trying to destroy is the key to humanity's survival. At once a science fiction epic and a powerful fable about respect for nature, Nausicaä's environmental questions are clear and pointed.

Nature Spirits

A concept of nature as an inextricable part of life derives from the Shintō and Buddhist beliefs ingrained in Japanese culture. In Shintōism, it is believed that spirits inhabit natural phenomena from mountains to rivers to trees; in Buddhism, there is an understanding that the divine lives among nature, not somewhere above us. In one of the major Shintō myths of the origins of mankind, the parents of man, Inanagi and Izanami, were islands and land rather than either gods or human. Thus, there is a strong sense that humans are not superior to land, but instead a kind of relation to it (Kodansha International 1999).

Science Fiction Titles for Your Collection

Aki, Shimizu. *Suikoden III*. Tokyopop, 2002–2005 Japan (2004–2006 U.S.). Publisher Age Rating: Teen (13+). Age Recommendation: S. Volumes: 1–11 [T]. Genre: Action, Fantasy, Military, Video Game

Suikoden III satisfies fans of the original and draws in new readers. A young woman loses her father but becomes the leader of a band of knights. Across the land, a chief's son and his best friend, a griffin, prepare for war, setting into motion a fantasy epic.

Amano, Shiro. *Kingdom Hearts*. Tokyopop, 2005–2006 U.S. Publisher Age Rating: All Ages. Age Recommendation: J. Volumes: 1–4 [T]. Genre: Action, Fantasy, Video Game

Inspired by the wildly popular Disney videogame cited in the title, this is a stand-alone story of hero Sora keeping the Disney-themed worlds safe. The manga covers the same territory as the game, but this best-seller and demonstrates the power of game–manga crossovers.

Eureka 7. Bandai, 2001–2003, TV series (50+ episodes, 24 minutes running time), 4+ DVDs. Publisher Age Rating: 13+. Age Recommendation: J. Genres: Science Fiction, Military, Mecha

Renton wants nothing more than to be a "lifter"—to pilot a mecha that can also transform into an air board—to join a renegade force. When a pilot crashes into his grandfather's shop, he gets the chance, but life as a rebel is less glamorous than he thought.

Gad Guard. Geneon, 2004–2005, TV series (26 episodes, 24 minutes running time), 7 DVDs. Publisher Age Rating: 13+. Age Recommendation: J. Genres: Action, Science Fiction, Mecha

The simple style and different take on mecha make *Gad Guard* a nice addition to collections, especially for younger viewers. Instead of hiding inside their giant companions, these pilots ride atop their shoulders, telling stories more personal than epic.

Gravion. ADV Films, 2004, TV series (13 episodes, 24 minutes running time), 3 DVDs. Publisher Age Rating: 13+. Age Recommendation: S. Genres: Action, Science Fiction, Mecha, Comedy. Related Anime: *Gravion Zwei* (TV series)

The melodramatic, tongue-in-cheek mecha series Gravion boasts a mad genius, female pilots in maid outfits (unabashed fan service), a bumbling hero, and, of course, a giant robot built out of each individual pilot's ship (complete with a giant robot sword).

.hack//SIGN. Bandai, 2003–2005, TV series (26 episodes, 24 minutes running time), 6 DVDs. Publisher Age Rating: 15+. Age Recommendation: J. Genres: Fantasy, Science Fiction, Mystery, Video Game

Subaru, an avid player in The World, cannot logout. The break from reality provides a much needed escape, but as he is drawn into a puzzle that threatens the very core of the game, allies and enemies refuse to leave him serenely stranded.

Kishiro Yukito. *Battle Angel Alita.* VIZ Manga, 1991–1995 Japan (2003-2005 U.S.). Publisher Age Rating: Older Teen. Age Recommendation: S. Volumes: 1–9 [T]. Genre: Action, Science Fiction, Mecha. Related Anime: *Battle Angel Alita* (OVA)

Alita was built for one thing: battle. With an artificial fighting body and reawakened human soul, she struggles to balance what she was born to do with a conscience that keeps her from becoming merely a human weapon. A classic of the genre.

Mobile Police Patlabor. Geneon, 2001–2005, TV series (47 episodes, 24 minutes running time), 11 DVDs. Publisher Age Rating: 13+. Age Recommendation: S. Genres: Action, Mecha, Mystery

Avoiding the epic plot, Patlabor is a police procedural with robots. Patlabors aid the police in fighting criminals who have their own "labors," each outfoxing the other. Police hierarchies and political pressure add realism, while the labors provide satisfying action.

Mobile Suit Gundam. Bandai, 2001–2002, TV series (43 episodes, 30 minutes running time), 10 DVDs. Publisher Age Rating: 13+. Age Recommendation: S. Genre: Action, Science Fiction, Military, Mecha. Related Anime: *Mobile Suit Gundam 0080, Mobile Suit Gundam 0083, Mobile Suit Gundam 08th MS Team, Mobile Suit Gundam F91, Mobile Suit Gundam SEED, Mobile Suit Gundam SEED Destiny, Mobile Suit Gundam Wing, Mobile Suit Gundam: Char's Counterattack, Mobile Suit Zeta Gundam Manga: Mobile Suit Gundam: The Origin, Mobile Suit Gundam 0079, Mobile Suit Gundam SEED, Mobile Suit Gundam Wing*

The many Gundam series set the mold for many of today's mecha stories. Teen recruits pilot giant robots, or Gundams, in wars taking place in the space surrounding Earth. Political, pacifist, and personal conflicts all come into play in monumental battles.

Neon Genesis Evangelion. ADV Films, 2004–2005 (Platinum edition), TV series (26 episodes, 24 minutes running time), 7 DVDs. Publisher Age Rating: 14+. Age Recommendation: S. Genres: Action, Science Fiction, Military, Mecha. Related Manga: *Neon Genesis Evangelion* (adaptation)

Shinji is recruited by his obsessed father to pilot an Eva, a giant exoskeleton built as humanity's last hope of defeating the invading force represented by alien, adaptive Angels. The tale becomes a complicated exploration of psychology and the human soul.

Otomo Katsuhiro. *Akira.* Dark Horse, 1982–2000 Japan (2000–2002 U.S.). Publisher Age Rating: 14+. Age Recommendation: S, A. Volumes: 1–6 [F]. Genres: Action, Science Fiction, Military, Apocalypse. Related Anime: *Akira* (feature film)

In post-apocalyptic Tokyo, biker gang member Kaneda runs afoul of the government when he encounters a wizened child with strange powers. He and his best friend try to decipher the meaning of Akira and are swept into government and military conspiracies.

RahXephon. ADV Films, 2003, TV series (26 episodes, 24 minutes running time), 7 DVDs. Publisher Age Rating: 15+. Age Recommendation: S. Genres: Action, Science Fiction, Romance, Military, Mecha

In an instant, teenage sweethearts are divided by the apparent destruction of everything outside Tokyo. Then the Mu arrive, and everyday life covers dangerous conspiracies. Giant robots play a substantial part, but the character development makes the series shine.

Shirow Masamune. *Appleseed*. Dark Horse, 1985–1989 Japan (1995 U.S.). Publisher Age Rating: 16+. Age Recommendation: S, A. Volumes: 1–4 [F]. Genres: Science Fiction, Mecha, Military. Related Anime: *Appleseed* (feature film)

    Deunan and robot lover Briareos have been unwittingly fighting a war that ended years ago. Brought out of the war zone, they are invited to stay in an idyllic city inhabited by humans and cyborgs together … but is all as harmonious as it seems?

Shirow, Masamune. *Ghost in the Shell*. Dark Horse, 1991, Japan (1995, 2004 U.S.). Publisher Age Rating: 18+. Age Recommendation: A. Volume: 1 [T] 2nd ed. Genres: Mecha, Science Fiction. Related Manga: *Ghost in the Shell: Man-Machine Interface, Related Anime: Ghost in the Shell* (feature film), *Ghost in the Shell: Innocence, Ghost in the Shell: Stand Alone Complex* (TV series)

    Man, machine, and networks in the future are not only inseparable but indistinguishable—and in global intelligence agencies, everyone and everything is dangerous. What makes you human is the belief that you started out human—but how can you know for sure?

Takahashi, Shin. *Saikano*. VIZ Manga, 2000–2001 Japan (2004–2006 U.S.). Publisher Age Rating: M. Age Recommendation: A. Volumes: 1–7 [T]. Genres: Action, Science Fiction, Romance, Military, Mecha. Related Anime: *Saikano* (TV series)

    Having your first girlfriend is awkward but exciting. Having your first girlfriend also be a weapon of mass destruction—literally—changes a lot. Military missions, weighty responsibility, and guilt are all thrown into the mix.

Fantasy

Fantasy is one of the largest and broadest categories of manga, encompassing everything from magical fairy tales inspired by legends to epic adventure to urban fantasy. Fantasy can include wizards but may be as simple as a girl discovering a benevolent spirit of the forest, as in Miyazaki's *My Neighbor Totoro*. The subjects for fantasy are myriad and too numerous to list in one section alone, but there are subgenres that appear only in manga and anime.

    The most traditional fantasies take their cue from the epics of the Western fantasy and Japanese folklore. Reluctant heroes and heroines are swept into a quest, whether to fulfill personal goals or a destined role, and as they gain the companions, skills, and tools necessary to win out in the end, they uncover wells of courage, confidence, and heart. Hero quests are most common and may be combined with uniquely Japanese themes and traditions including their own myths and legends as well as concerns about the environment, community responsibility, and the desire for peace.

Like science fiction, fantasy explores the relationship between man and machine, but fantasies feature creations that never existed. They have a particular fondness for giant airships and dirigibles as seen in the manga and anime *Escaflowne*, the anime TV series *Last Exile*, and many of Miyazaki's films, from *Castle in the Sky* to *Howl's Moving Castle*. The combination of alchemy and mechanics that fills the world of *Fullmetal Alchemist* is an inventive marriage of cyborg technology and the long and gothic history of the alchemic search for the Philosopher's Stone. These fantasies are closely aligned with the Western concept of steampunk: speculative inventions inspired by obsolete technology that extrapolate an alternate world based on their use. Although these creations seem to veer toward science fiction, magical elements are what power the machines, the characters, and the story.

Fullmetal Alchemist combines steampunk fantasy with alchemy to create a vivid world.
© Hiromu Arakawa/SQUARE ENIX.

Manga creators draw inspiration for their fantasy universes from cultures, history, and legends across the globe, as well as tales of Japanese origin. CLAMP's excellent series *Tsubasa: RESERVoir CHRoNICLE* is part hero quest and part ride through alternate versions of CLAMP's previous worlds, stories, and characters mixed with Japanese legends. A group of four travelers, including a princess, her best friend (an archeologist), a warrior, and a magician, are bound together on a quest to recover the princess's lost memories. Guided by the advice of a mercenary yet wise witch, the mismatched band travels from one universe to another to collect the missing pieces of the princess's past. They journey through versions of CLAMP's previous series, like *Cardcaptor Sakura*, *Clover*, and *The Legend of Chun-Yang*. They also visit alternate versions of the their own world such as a baseball-obsessed Hanshin Republic (a whole universe that mocks Osaka's sport obsession) and a gothic fairy-tale town straight out of the Brothers Grimm. The setup of the series allows the creators free reign to draw on any and all inspirations—after all, they need only send their characters to a new world to visit another trope.

Fantasy also has its share of humorous tales. In these titles, fantastical circumstances involving curses, genies, or some other magical twist wreak havoc on a character's once-normal life, causing embarrassing, awkward, and guffaw-inducing escapades. The premises of these titles rely on fantasy, as with *Cheeky Angel*, in which a boy is transformed through a misunderstanding with a magical spirit into "the womanliest woman in the world" rather than the "manliest man in the world." Most of the story and the laughs in this manga deal with the impact of this change on Megumi's everyday life. *D.N.Angel* has an equally fantastic character predicament as the ordinary Daisuke fulfills his family's genetic legacy: when he thinks of the one he loves, he transforms into the legendary art thief Dark, an older, arrogant, and sexier guy who tangles up Daisuke's love life so much that neither will be able to find happiness any time soon. Other favorites in this trope include *Ranma 1/2*, a brilliant hybrid of humor, fantasy, and martial arts action.

Daisuke from *D.N.Angel* turns into Dark, on the right, when he thinks of the girl he loves.

© YUKIRU SUGISAKI - KADOKAWA SHOTEN PUBLISHING CO. LTD. PROJECT DNA.

Curses!

Ito Junji. *Uzumaki*. VIZ Manga, 1998–1999 Japan (2001–2002 U.S.). Publisher Age Rating: M. Age Recommendation: S, A. Volumes: 1–3 [F]. Genres: Horror, Mystery

A seaside town is slowly overtaken not by spirits but by a shape, the spiral. As people, objects, and thoughts conform to the shape, one teenager witnesses the horrifying results.

Katsumoto, Kasane. *Hands Off!* Tokyopop, 1998–2001 Japan (2004–2007 U.S.). Publisher Age Rating: Teen (13+). Age Recommendation: S. Volumes: 1–8 [T]. Genres: Action, Fantasy, Comedy

Kotarou isn't quite aware that when he touches someone, he has visions of that person's future. His cousin Tatsuki can sense people's pasts. As they grow up, Tatsuki's natural reticence turns to hostility, but the two reluctantly pair up to crack confounding mysteries.

Nishimori, Hiroyuki. *Cheeky Angel*. VIZ Manga, 1999–2003 Japan (2004– U.S.). Publisher Age Rating: Teen. Age Recommendation: S. Volumes: 1–15+ [T]. Genres: Action, Fantasy, School Drama, Comedy

Megumi wished to be the "manliest man on Earth," but, of course, through a misunderstanding he ends up the "womanliest woman." A foxy girl with a boy's brash attitude—all the girls' admire her, and all the boys want her. What's a girl to do?

Princess Tutu. ADV Films, 2005–2006, TV series (26 episodes, 24 minutes running time), 7 DVDs. Publisher Age Rating: 14+. Age Recommendation: M. Genres: Fantasy, Romance, Magical Girl, Comedy. Related Manga: *Princess Tutu*

A duck who turns into a girl who turns into a superheroine ballerina. Add in a splash of romance, a mission to find a prince's lost heart, and classical ballet references left and right, and you've got one dramatic and charming show.

Sugisaki, Yukiru. *D.N.Angel*. Tokyopop, 1997–2003 Japan (2004 U.S.). Publisher Age Rating: Teen. Age Recommendation: J. Volumes: 1–11 [T]. Genres: Action, Fantasy, Romance, Mystery. Related Anime: *D.N.Angel*

Daisuke is cursed: when he thinks of Risa, the girl he likes, he becomes Dark, a legendary thief. If his love is returned, he'll keep his form. Daisuke likes Risa, but Risa likes Dark, and Riku, Risa's twin, likes Daisuke. At this rate, no one's going to find love!

Takahashi, Rumiko. *Ranma 1/2*. VIZ Manga, 1987–1996 Japan (2003 U.S.). Publisher Age Rating: Older Teen. Age Recommendation: S. Volumes: 1–38 [T]. Genres: Action, Fantasy, Comedy. Related Anime: *Ranma 1/2* (TV series), *Ranma 1/2* (OVA), *Ranma 1/2: Big Trouble in Nekonron, China* (movie sequel), *Ranma 1/2: Nihao My Concubine* (movie sequel), *Ranma 1/2: One Flew Over the Kuno's Nest* (movie sequel)

After falling into a spring during martial arts training, Ranma is cursed: if he is hit with cold water he becomes a girl. Hot water reverses the effect. His arranged fiancée is not so sure about the whole thing.

Watase, Wu. *Ceres: Celestial Legend*. VIZ, 1996–2000 Japan (2003– U.S., 2nd ed.). Publisher Age Rating: Older Teen. Age Recommendation: S, A. Volumes: 1–14 [T]. Genres: Action, Fantasy, Romance, Magical Girl. Related Anime: *Ceres: Celestial Legend*

Aya is your ordinary karaoke loving girl, but she's about to discover her family's secret. Her destiny is one of vengeance and violence, and her own family will do anything, even kill her, to stop the inevitable.

Magical Girl: Schoolgirls with Powers

Alice 19th.
© 2001 Yuu Watase/Shogakukan, Inc.

Magical girl fantasies are the bread and butter of shōjo fantasy manga. Just as *Astro Boy* launched a thousand mecha plotlines, Tezuka's *Princess Knight* inspired countless stories of swashbuckling yet girlish heroines. The elements that distinguish magical girl stories are clear: an ordinary girl, usually a student dealing with the mundane troubles of school, family, and boys, discovers she is not just an ordinary teenager. Through a magical transformation, she becomes a super-powered heroine who must now fight to save herself, her friends, and her world. Frequently a team of fellows and a cute animal sidekick aid her. The most well-known series in this genre include *Sailor Moon*, *Cardcaptor Sakura*, *Magic Knight Rayearth,* and *Revolutionary Girl Utena.* Alternately, a magical girl from another world might come to Earth to perform a mission or learn about humans, as in the recent manga and anime series *Ultra Maniac* or the Korean manhwa *Ark Angels.*

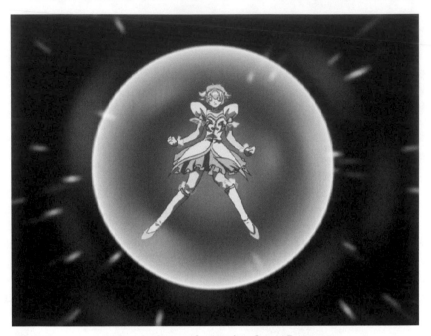

A magical transformation from *Pretear*.
© 2001 Junichi Sato * Kaori Naruse/Project Pretear.

Transformations in magical girl manga have become as legendary as the spectacular robot combinations mecha exhibits. Magical girls go through an elaborate sequence of activation, mystical levitating and twirling (often appearing nude to indicate their purity), and reemerge in a new and fabulous costume indicating their superhero status. Much like Clark Kent and Superman, the girl's two incarnations may not be recognized as the same person, and the story deals with the strain of being both an ordinary girl and a savior of mankind. Transformations not only provide a key moment of spectacle but also signal externally the character's ability to access newfound strengths. In the charming magical girl manga and anime series *Princess Tutu*, a duck periodically transforms into a girl named Duck who also transforms into Princess Tutu, a spirit of dance who can lead troubled souls in dances that heal their pain while on her personal mission to collect the pieces of her prince's shattered heart.

Magical girl manga are intentionally fluffy. These titles are for escaping the pressures of school, family, and self-doubt—what better way to escape a crowded subway or take a break from cramming for exams than to imagine life as a beautiful, unbeatable heroine? The lighter-weight titles fill the same needs that series fiction does, providing entertainment and escape without expecting too much work from the reader. The magical fantasy hero element allows girls in Japan, who in life are still relegated to the background, to escape the constraints of expectations and become the traditionally male heroes and the fighters. Most of the time magical girls do not fight alone. The friendships and relationships formed by gaining allies, as well as making enemies, are what propel the story forward. The possibilities for heroine and team combinations are endless, and true to shōjo form, the star is often surrounded by a bevy of beautiful young men who are her loyal knights or seductive enemies, depending on the twist of the tale. *Pretear* features a heroine who can magically meld with each of seven Pretear Knights, gaining a specific element-based power with each combination, not to mention a brand new outfit befitting each power. These traditions have become so familiar that they are often parodied in anime such as *Nurse Witch Komugi* and *Magical Play*.

Authors spin tales far darker than the genre's stereotypical wish fulfillment daydreams. Some of the best magical girl stories deal with meaningful issues, using the genre to address sensitive or challenging topics within a comfortable context. *Ark Angels* features admonitions concerning the rapid extinction of rare animals. *Ceres: Celestial Legend*, one of manga creator Watase Yu's many similar series, features a spunky heroine with a magical destiny just like any other magical girl drama. In a brutal family ritual gone wrong, Aya discovers her powers and confronts dangers as diverse as rape, incest, genetic testing, and apocalyptic power before the tale is over. The lengthy story provokes Watase's readers to think about the inequality of women in Japan, both historically and in the present. Using a magical girl story to present these concerns is akin to U.S. comics publishers framing messages about drugs, video game violence, and hate crimes in superhero comics and provokes readers to confront subjects they would not normally seek out in their entertainment.

Best of Magical Girls

CLAMP. *Cardcaptor Sakura*. Tokyopop, 1996–1998 Japan (2004 U.S., 2nd ed.). Publisher Age Rating: All Ages. Age Recommendation: M. Volumes: 1–6 [T]. Genres: Action, Fantasy, Romance, Magical Girl. Related Manga: *Tsubasa: RESERVoir CHRoNICLE*. Related Anime: *Cardcaptor Sakura* (TV series), *Tsubasa: RESERVoir CHRoNICLE*. Related Anime: *RESERVoir CHRoNIClE* (TV series)

Long ago, a powerful sorcerer created a set of cards to contain the spirits of magical beings. Now, fourth-grader Sakura must recapture them before they destroy the world. Luckily, she's got hidden powers and faithful friends, both human and otherwise.

Fujishima, Kosuke. *Oh My Goddess!* VIZ Manga, 1989–1999 Japan (2005 U.S.). Publisher Age Rating: 8+. Age Recommendation: S. Volumes: 1–5+ [T] 2nd ed. Genres: Fantasy, Romance, Comedy. Related Anime: *Oh My Goddess!* (TV series)

A wrong number usually leads to an apology and a hang-up, but when Keiichi misdials, he gets a live-in goddess for his trouble. The setup could lead to ridiculous shōnen fan service fare, but instead it's a sweet romantic comedy from the guy's point of view.

Pretear. ADV Films, 2001–2005, TV series (13 episodes, 24 minutes running time), 4 DVDs. Publisher Age Rating: 15+. Age Recommendation: J. Genres: Action, Fantasy, Magical Girl

Himeno's father moons over her stepmother, and her stepsisters are cold and distant. Family tension provokes transformation, however, when Himeno discovers powers by partnering with seven magical knights while her isolated stepsister becomes her nemesis.

Princess Tutu. ADV Films, 2005–2006, TV series (26 episodes, 24 minutes running time), 7 DVDs. Publisher Age Rating: 14+. Age Recommendation: M. Genres: Fantasy, Romance, Magical Girl, Comedy. Related Manga: *Princess Tutu*

A duck who turns into a girl who turns into a superheroine ballerina. Add in a splash of romance, a mission to find a prince's lost heart, and classical ballet references left and right and you've got one dramatic and charming show.

Saito, Chiho. *Revolutionary Girl Utena*. VIZ Media, 1997–1998 Japan (2003–2004 U.S., 2nd ed.). Publisher Age Rating: Older Teen. Age Recommendation: S. Volumes: 1–5 [T] 2nd ed. Genres: Action, Fantasy, Romance, School Drama, Magical Girl. Related Manga: *Revolutionary Girl Utena; The Adolescence of Utena*. Related Anime: *Revolutionary Girl Utena* (TV series), *Revolutionary Girl Utena*.

Utena has dreamed of being a prince. At her elite new school, Utena clashes with the fencing team that rules the school, uncovering secrets and upsetting control. Can she save herself and her friends from the vicious and strict rule of her classmates?

Takahashi, Rumiko. *Inuyasha: A Feudal Fairy Tale*. VIZ Media, 1996 Japan (2003 U.S.). Publisher Age Rating: 16+. Age Recommendation: S. Volumes: 1–26+ [T] 2nd ed. Genres: Action, Fantasy, Romance, Historical, Magical Girl. Related Anime: *Inuyasha* (TV series), *Inuyasha The Movie: Affections Touching across Time* (film), *Inuyasha: The Castle beyond the Looking Glass* (film), *Inuyasha: Swords of an Honorable Ruler* (film), *Inuyasha: Fire on the Mystic Island* (film)

Kagome falls down a well at her family's shrine and drops into Feudal Era Japan, complete with demons and magic. After a hair-raising escape from a centipede demon, Kagome is told she's a reincarnated heroine destined to save the town—but can she do it?

Tsukuba, Sakura. *Land of the Blindfolded*. CMX, 2000–2004 Japan (2004 U.S.). Publisher Age Rating: All ages. Age Recommendation: J. Volumes: 1–9 [T]. Genres: Fantasy, Romance

Kanade can see glimpses of people's futures when she touches them, and new boy Arou can see their pasts. The question is—should they do something to help people with their paths through life, or should they just allow destiny to take its course?

Watase, Yu. *Alice 19th*. VIZ Media, 2001–2003 Japan (2003–2004 U.S.). Publisher Age Rating: Older Teens. Age Recommendation: S. Volumes: 1–7 [T]. Genres: Fantasy, Romance, Magical Girl

Sisters Alice and Mayura both like Kyo, but Alice remains silent. When Mayura uncovers Alice's true feelings, jealousy overwhelms her, unleashing the siblings' magical destiny. Alice must become a Lotis master to save her sister from her own dark side.

Watase, Yu. *Ceres: Celestial Legend*. VIZ Media, 1996–2000 Japan (2003 U.S.). Publisher Age Rating: Older Teens. Age Recommendation: S, A. Volumes: 1–14 [T] 2nd ed. Genres: Action, Fantasy, Science Fiction, Romance, Magical Girl. Related Anime: *Ceres: Celestial Legend* (TV series)

Aya is your ordinary karaoke-loving girl, but she's about to discover her family's secret. Her destiny is one of vengeance and violence, and her own family will do anything, even kill her, to stop the inevitable.

Watase, Yu. *Fushigi Yugi*. VIZ Media, 1992–1995 Japan (1999 U.S.). Publisher Age Rating: Older Teens. Age Recommendation: S. Volumes: 1–18 [T]. Genres: Action, Fantasy, Romance, Historical, Magical Girl. Related Manga: *Fushigi Yugi: Genbu Kaiden*. Related Anime: *Fushigi Yugi* (TV series)

Miaka wishes she could get away, but she gets more than she bargained for by falling into a library book. Magically transported to The Universe of the Four Gods, everyone insists she's the prophesied Priestess of Suzaku and must gather celestial warriors to save the world.

Yoshizumi, Wataru. *Ultra Maniac*. VIZ Media, 2002–2004 Japan (2005–2006 U.S.). Publisher Age Rating: All Ages. Age Recommendation: M. Volumes: 1–5 [T]. Genres: Fantasy, Magical Girl, Comedy. Related Anime: *Ultra Maniac* (TV series)

Nina's not a very good witch, but she's doing her best to observe the human world and learn while on exchange from her home school. With best friend Ayu in tow, she tackles romance and friendship. Her spells often go awry, but her heart is always in the right place.

Paranormal and Horror

Japanese legends and myths are filled with ghosts, spirits, gods, and demons, so it should come as no surprise that their manga often focus on supernatural happenings. The spirits of Shintō tradition, the ghosts and demons of Buddhist tales, and fantastical or supernatural events are all elements used to enhance the escape manga provides.

Onmyoji

Not to be confused with Buddhist or Shintō priests, *onmyoji*, or yin-yang magicians, are not quite religious figures, despite their rituals, traditional clothing, and mysticism. Onmyoji were the court diviners in the capital during the Heian era (Kodansha International 1999), and they combined cosmology with occult sciences to guide courtiers' lives, protect them from evil spirits, and advise the Buddhist priests and government. In *Tokyo Babylon* and *X/1999* Sumeragi Subaru descends from a long line of powerful onmyoji, while in *Otogi Zoshi* court politics and intrigues are observed by the powerful onmyoji at the center of court.

Ghosts

The importance of ancestors' spirits in Buddhist and Shintō tradition mean ghosts are regular characters. Ghost stories are traditionally told in summertime to distract from the sweltering temperatures, as seen in *XXXholic*.

Revering the Dead

The annual Bon Festival, July 13–15, is the time when ancestors return to Earth to visit their living relatives, and families visit with each other and light welcome fires (Poitras 1999). When someone dies, death day anniversaries are observed for up to fifty years to honor the deceased (Kodansha International 1999).

XXXholic, one of CLAMP's latest series, follows the career of Watanuki, a young man who sees ghosts and has been trying to shake them his entire life. Yuko, a shady but persuasive witch who grants clients' wishes in her own roundabout way, promises to help Watanuki stop seeing spirits in exchange for his working as her housekeeper. He agrees, not guessing at the adventures, cleaning, cooking, and ego massaging that lie in his future. In *Bleach*, Ichigo puts spirits to rest as part of his shinigami duties. *Ghost Hunt*, part school comedy, part horror tale, follows the missions of a wide variety of ghost hunters, from a Shintō priestess to a self-proclaimed spiritual expert to a reluctant schoolgirl, as they try to exorcise a school. Titles such as *Bleach*, *Tokyo Babylon*, and *Legal Drug* all weave ghosts into already supernatural storylines, from laying murdered spirits to rest to discovering love after death.

Horror

Manga creators have a great flair for atmospheric horror, full of suspense and an impeccable sense of timing chills and thrills. Many hint at a horrific idea rather than shock with a gruesome act—the psychological damage is more unsettling and moves at a slower, less predictable pace. Just as science fiction can be more about human responsibility than gadgets, horror manga and anime often ask questions about violence, psychosis, and morality. A masterpiece of horror manga, *Uzumaki*, tells the story of a seaside town haunted not by a vengeful ghost but by a shape, an *uzumaki* or spiral. As people's minds and bodies are twisted to conform to the shape, the townspeople witness the slow dissolution of their world and sanity. Kon Satoshi's anime *Perfect Blue* and the miniseries *Paranoia Agent* show how our own selfish desires and ignorance lead to grisly ends. *Boogiepop Phantom* remains one of creepiest, although relatively bloodless, anime created mainly because of an extraordinarily manipulative and subtle soundtrack and a slowly unwinding plot that jumps back and forth in time, never letting the viewer feel at ease.

Ofuda

Ofuda are spells or talismans used in both the Shintō and Buddhist traditions. Most ofuda are either wood or paper with the name of a deity written or stamped on the surface. Traditionally ofuda are placed on home shrines and are intended to bring good fortune (Poitras 1999). In more mystical anime and manga, ofuda are used to cast spells and defend against demons as used by Subaru in *Tokyo Babylon* and *X/1999*, Hasunama in *Eerie Queerie*, and Chiaki in *The Demon Ororon*.

This is not to say that manga creators avoid splatter—far from it. As with samurai tales, blood splatter is a tradition and can be used sparingly to chilling effect or effusively to disgust the reader. In Akino Matsuri's *Pet Shop of Horrors*, new pet owners get not only a pet but also a brutal and occasionally fatal lesson highlighting their personal weaknesses. Their comeuppances feature a fair amount of blood, slashing, and brutality. *The Kindaichi Case Files* creator Yozaburo Kanari is not one to shy away from showing a particularly nasty murder, but neither does he dwell on the scene. Titles aimed at older teens and twenty-somethings, like *Hellsing*, let loose with gouts of blood, gore, and creative violence—the entire sixth volume of *Hellsing* is devoted to an explicitly violent duel between heroine and enemy that would merit at least an R rating by the Motion Picture Association of America. Some of the impact of these bloody scenes is softened because it is rendered in black and white and the scenes are executed with an eye toward drama and aesthetics, rather than shock and splatter. In the world of underground manga, aimed mainly at adult men, horror is a frequent topic, and creators such as Ito Junji and Hino Hideshi are masters of sexual, grotesque, and unnerving images.

Legends and History

Along with human ghosts, spirits and gods populate many series. Sometimes references are as brief as a character name or costume. Both main and side characters can embody or reference common legendary figures as a joke, an aside, or an homage to source material.

Kami

According to Shintō beliefs, natural elements like the wind, moon, sun, mountains, and trees are all kami, as are the variety of spirits and gods believed to have created the world. Animal spirits of all kinds can be kami, as shown in the film *Princess Mononoke*.

Animal Spirits

One of the most common legendary references in manga is to *kitsune*, or fox spirits. Foxes are tricksters and shape-shifters, and they can transform into people to play tricks on unsuspecting humans whom the foxes deem worthy targets for mischief. They are also the messengers of Inari, the *kami* of cereal crops. There are a variety of traditional stories about fox wives enchanting husbands only to leave them behind to return to the wild, much like the *selkie* legends of Celtic tradition and the faerie changeling stories told across Europe. In *Naruto* and *XXXholic*, the legendary nine-tailed fox appears. In *XXXholic*, Watanuki bumps into a fox-owned udon noodle stand in the course of shopping for his mistress. The side story is at once a mellow moment of magical companionship and a pointed comment on the kind of company his boss keeps.

Examples of Kami and Kami-Inspired Spirits in Manga and Anime

In *XXXholic*, Watanuki is given Valentine's Day chocolate by a zashiki-warashi, or a benevolent, protective spirit of a house or place, portrayed as a young girl.

CLAMP's one-shot manga *Shirahime-Syo: Snow Goddess Tales* speculates on a number of incidents involving the Snow Maiden kami.

In *Pet Shop of Horrors*, Count D's pet shop is stocked with numerous examples of creatures inspired by kami, from cats, dogs, birds, and lizards who all shift between human to animal shape. The Pet Shop also includes legendary creatures from around the globe, including mermaids, basilisks, and one powerful creature from Chinese legend, the Kirin.

In *Her Majesty's Dog*, a demon dog protector accompanies powerful medium Amane—but there's competition for the position. Note the quick visual shifts and symbols common in manga illustration.

In *Her Majesty's Dog*, Amane is a medium who by sensing spirits helps them find peace. Her companion Hyoue seems like her boyfriend to everyone else, given how much they are caught smooching at school. Hyoue, as it turns out, is a guardian dog spirit who, while they are away from their home village, hides himself in human form to protect his mistress. All that kissing is how he feeds—Amane struck a deal with Hyoue that he would be her protector and aid if she allowed him to feed off her life force. Of course, as in any shōjo manga worth its salt, romantic tension builds between the pair as they are challenged by the traditions of their home village as well as the everyday work of settling restless spirits. The series uses ghost stories and folklore in each installment, providing another view into the rich mythological history mined by manga creators.

Tanuki are another animal believed to possess supernatural trickster powers. They are mammals native to Japan that look like a cross between a dog and a raccoon and who, in legend, are also shape-shifters and tricksters. The Studio Ghibli film *Pom Poko* features a group of tanuki trying to use their powers to save their forest home from the encroachment of the modern human world. Tanuki also appear in *Inuyasha*, *Naruto*, and *Shaman King*.

Never Cross a Black Cat

Black cats are believed to be able to cure disease, and cats who have been killed are reputed to come back and haunt their killers for seven lifetimes.

Oni

Oni are evil spirits or demons similar to Western demons or ogres. They are usually humanoid in appearance but may have grotesque features including extra eyes, limbs, or appendages. Oni were once recognized as benevolent spirits, but in current mythology, they are depicted as brutes intent on destruction. In *Tactics*, Kantaro exorcises demons and renegade spirits as well as communing with friendly spirits and sprites known as *youkai*. Kantaro mainly deals with *tengu*, or minor demons that can be controlled once a person names them. Among his company is Youko, a *kistune youkai*, or fox spirit, now forced to obey Kantaro.

CLAMP vividly reimagines the Yuki-onna, or snow woman, in *Shirahime-syo: Show Goddess Tales*. This mythical woman, with pure skin and floor-length hair, haunts the mountains, her tears reputedly creating snowfall. The trio of original melancholy stories in this collection mimics the magical realism and iconography of myths.

Shinigami

Another common and variously interpreted legend is that of the *shinigami*, supernatural beings responsible for recording, cataloging, and escorting departed souls. In some stories they are like angels of death, present to record deaths, exorcise lost souls, and fight against demons, as Ichigo and Rukia do in *Bleach*. In *Death Note*, the shinigami are shown to be humanoid but monstrous, having lost interest in a fair reckoning of death and instead killing at whim. *Descendants of Darkness* puts yet another spin on their role by making the shinigami the investigators of the afterlife, responsible for tracking down the souls that slip through the cracks of the Ministry of Hades' bureaucracy. These three manga show how easily manga creators can take one idea and run with it in entirely different directions without any qualms about remaining true to the "original" idea or myth.

Celestial Maidens

Ceres: Celestial Legend reinterprets an old legend of the *tennyo*, otherwise known as celestial maidens, nymphs, or angels. Tennyo are magical women with a special winged coat, or pair of wings, that enable them to fly. Men who glimpse them frolicking or bathing by the seaside steal their coats to keep them nearby, exacting the price of anything from a dance to a marriage (Poitras 1999). Like the Celtic selkie legends, these stories are doomed to end unhappily; after years of seemingly happy marriage, the maiden discovers the secret hiding place of the coat and, unable to resist her nature, immediately disappears back to wherever she came from. *Ceres: Celestial Legend* follows both the original legend and strays from it, endowing the tennyo with superpowers, a vendetta passed through genetic material to her many female descendants, and a coat that is less a garment than an alien transporter.

Mythology outside Japan

Once manga make the leap into legends and literature outside of Japan, any figure or story is fair game. *RG Veda* draws its inspiration from Sanskrit mythology. *Saiyuki* and *Dragon Ball* are two vastly different manga inspired by China's favorite traditional heroic tale *The Journey to the West*. The only common ground in the two stories is a character named and inspired by the original hero, the monkey king Son Goku, but these nods to source material are evident to Japanese readers. Watase Yu's *Fushigi Yugi* is based on Chinese legends about the Three Kingdoms. The enormously popular series *Fruits Basket* depicts a family who, when hugged by a member of the opposite sex, turn into the animals from the Chinese Zodiac. Christian traditions and imagery are used in unfamiliar and what might be considered blasphemous ways. Many manga characters are clad in outfits full of Christian paraphernalia, from crosses to crucifixes. These are more interesting symbols and patterns than objects of faith in Japan where Christians represent a small minority and religious observance is a mix-and-match affair.

Inspiration

Not only do manga and anime creators draw inspiration from Western myths and literature, they also constantly reference each other's work. In *Here Is Greenwood,* the students vacation in an old-fashioned inn and discover a forbidden, darkened hallway. As they peer into the darkness, they wonder why it's so dark, and one of them suggests it is the soot spirits featured in Miyazaki's *My Neighbor Totoro,* and a second student starts singing the infectious *Totoro* theme song.

Legend, Myth, and Literature

Dragon Ball, Saiyuki (Journey to the West)

Fruits Basket (Chinese Zodiac)

Pom Poko (tanuki)

RG Veda (Rig Veda)

Alice 19th, Godchild, Miyuki-chan in Wonderland (Alice in Wonderland by Lewis Carroll)

Gankutsuou: The Count of Monte Cristo (The Count of Monte Cristo by Alexandre Dumas)

Howl's Moving Castle (Baba Yaga, original fantasy by Diana Wynne Jones)

Spirited Away (multiple legends)

Tactics

Like superheroes and cowboys, Japan has contributed its own cast of characters and genres to storytelling. Deciphering each new element engages non-Japanese readers while the familiar trappings of standard genres support their reading and watching. Some aspects take getting used to, like the sudden bursts of slapstick or the lengthy transformation sequences in mecha and magical girl tales, but as you immerse yourself, the imaginative world of manga and anime becomes a rich new world to explore.

Best of Horror and Suspense for Teens

Akino, Matsuri. *Pet Shop of Horrors.* Tokyopop, 1996–1998 Japan (2003–2005 U.S.). Publisher Age Rating: Older Teen. Age Recommendation: S. Volumes: 1–10 [T]. Genres: Fantasy, Comedy, Horror, Mystery. Related Anime: *Pet Shop of Horrors* (TV series)

Count D and his pet shop are connected to an inordinate number of unsolved murders and mysteries, and hotheaded Detective Leon Orcot is convinced that Count D is providing something a little more dangerous, and probably illegal, to his clients than mere pets.

Boogiepop Phantom. Right Stuf, 2000, TV series (12 episodes, 24 minutes running time), 3 DVDs. Publisher Age Rating: NA. Age Recommendation: S. Genres: Fantasy, School Drama, Horror, Mystery. Related Anime: *Boogiepop and Others* (live action film). Related Manga: *Boogiepop Never Laughs*; *Boogiepop Phantom*

Five years ago, a serial killer stalked the streets, and now … no one's sure. Boogiepop may be a protector or the killer, but each student lives through his or her own private horror. Deliciously spooky with unforgettable multilayered sound and images.

CLAMP. *XXXholic.* Del Rey Manga, 2003 Japan (2004 U.S.). Publisher Age Rating: 13+. Age Recommendation: J. Volumes: 1–8+ [T]. Genres: Fantasy, Comedy, Horror. Related Manga: *Tsubasa: RESERVoir CHRoNICLE*. Related Anime: *XXXholic* (TV series), *Tsubasa: RESERVoir CHRoNICLE*

Spirits no one else can see have plagued Watanuki as long as he can remember. Magically pulled into a mysterious shop, he meets Yuuko, a witch who promises to make the spirits vanish ... for a price!

Hakase, Mizuki. *The Demon Ororon.* Tokyopop, 1998–2001 Japan (2004 U.S.). Publisher Age Rating: 13+. Age Recommendation: S. Volumes: 1–4 [T]. Genres: Action, Fantasy, Romance, Horror

Chiaki is the orphaned daughter of an Archangel and a human woman. Ororon is the King of Hell. When Ororon decides to go AWOL to stay with Chiaki, all of the forces of hell come after them both.

Matsushita, Yoko. *Descendants of Darkness.* VIZ Manga, 1997 Japan (2004–2006 U.S.). Publisher Age Rating: Older Teen. Age Recommendation: S, A. Volumes: 1–11 [T]. Genres: Action, Fantasy, Comedy, Horror, Mystery. Related Anime: *Descendants of Darkness* (TV series)

Seventy years of collecting wayward souls is no picnic, especially when there's no hope of promotion. Tsuzuki and his rookie partner guide souls and battle the sadistic Dr. Muraki; zany humor lightens the horror. Note the final volume moves into adult territory.

Mihara, Mitsukazu. *Doll.* Tokyopop, 2004–2005 Japan (2004–2006 U.S.). Publisher Age Rating: Older Teen. Age Recommendation: S. Volumes: 1–6 [T]. Genres: Science Fiction, Romance, Mecha

Mihara examines feelings of ownership, lust, and loneliness in this anthology about realistic androids and their human owners. The stories run the gamut from romantic to horrifying. The people are GothLoli visions, but the interactions are all too human.

Moriyama, Daisuke. *Chrono Crusade*. VIZ Manga, 1999–2004 Japan (2004–2006 U.S.). Publisher Age Rating: 13+. Age Recommendation: S. Volumes: 1–8 [T]. Genres: Action, Fantasy, Historical, Military, Comedy. Related Anime: *Chrono Crusade* (TV series)

Sister Rosette is not an ordinary nun. She and her fellows of the Magdalene Order tote high-powered, blessed machine guns that exorcise demons and purify the world. Rosette and Chrono, a demon loyal to her, are determined to rescue her fallen brother Joshua.

Paranoia Agent. Geneon, 2005, TV series (13 episodes, 24 minutes running time), 4 DVDs. Publisher Age Rating: 16+. Age Recommendation: S, A. Genres: Fantasy, Horror, Mystery

A youngster known only as Li'l Slugger viciously attacks pedestrians with a golden baseball bat. The police are stumped and rumors are flying. *Paranoia Agent* is a compelling examination of the power of rumor, fear, and willful ignorance.

Park, Sang-sun. *Tarot Cafe*. Tokyopop, NA Korea (2005 U.S.). Publisher Age Rating: Teen. Age Recommendation: S. Volumes: 1–4 [K]. Genres: Fantasy, Horror, Mystery

Pamela is a tarot card reader, but her clients are not ordinary people: she is particular help to those supernatural beings in need of a bit of guidance. Werewolves, vampires, and dragons all come to her, but she will have to face her own dark past to find peace.

Perfect Blue. Manga Video, 2000, feature film (81 minutes running time), 1 DVD. Publisher Age Rating: R. Age Recommendation: A. Genres: Mystery

Mima is the current favorite pop idol: cute, sweet, and bubbly on demand. When she quits to pursue acting, one fan starts stalking her. As Mima is menaced, she starts losing any sense of what's real and what, or who, is a figment.

Witch Hunter Robin. Bandai, 2002–2004, TV series (26 episodes, 24 minutes running time), 6 DVDs. Publisher Age Rating: 13+. Age Recommendation: S. Genres: Action, Fantasy, Mystery

Witches, or craft users, are a real threat. The special STN-J division tracks and captures witches to try to harness and understand them. Robin is a novice agent, but unlike her peers, she uses her own craft against what she is beginning to realize are her own kind.

Yuki Kaori. *Godchild*. VIZ Manga, 2001–2004 Japan (2006 U.S.). Publisher Age Rating: Older Teens. Age Recommendation: S, A. Volumes: 1–3+ [T] Genres: Historical, Horror, Mystery. Related Manga: *Count Cain* (prequel)

Cain Hargreaves is a gentleman detective who has witnessed the worst in people. The only people he cares about are his sweet sister Marie Weather and devoted manservant Rafe. As he unravels clever, gruesome mysteries, his past enemies threaten his fragile peace.

References

Kodansha International. *Japan: Profile of a Nation Revised Edition*. Tokyo: Kodansha International, 1999.

Poitras, Gilles. *The Anime Companion: What's Japanese in Japanese Animation?* Berkeley: Stone Bridge Press, 1999.

Chapter Seven

Understanding Fans and Fan Culture

Being an Otaku

Manga and anime appeals to its fans for a variety of reasons that have been discussed throughout this book, but the major reasons bear repeating to give perspective on U.S. fans.

- They appeal to teens acclimated to a multimedia world, full of visual, textual, and auditory components to stories.

- Readers discover unfamiliar and challenging customs, ideas, and traditions.

- Readers feel they are within an imaginary world far from what most adults read and understand.

At its center, being a fan of manga and anime requires a love of the medium, but increasingly being a manga and anime fan leads to a wide variety of expressions of fan identity, including meeting other fans at conventions, communicating and creating fan fiction and fan art online, and becoming a manga creator oneself. Today more and more fans identify themselves as manga and anime fans, or *otaku*, with pride.

The Title *Otaku*

In Japan, the word otaku is a very formal way of saying "you." Literally translated, o-taku means "house" or "your house" and is used to address another person in an especially formal conversation. Rabid manga and anime fans, those unwashed and socially inept figures akin to what we in the U.S. refer to as "fanboys" or "comic book guys," were observed to refer to each other using otaku in conversation. Given the fact that most of these young men were more than acquaintances, just why they adopted the habit is unknown. A commentator on popular culture and the manga scene, Nakamori Akio, cemented the slang nickname when he began referring to all rabid manga and anime fans as otaku, and although he may not have intended it, the name stuck. As Japanese slang shifted over time, otaku began to be used to refer to any obsessive fan. Whether the obsession of choice is toy trains or manga makes no difference (Macias 2004).

As a name, otaku has gone through a variety of associations and connotations in a short amount of time. It was and still is used as a formal way of saying "you" in very polite conversation. Most notoriously, however, otaku was linked with the darkest side of manga and anime fandom when Miyazaki Tsutomu, a violent serial killer who murdered four prepubescent girls, was discovered to have been an obsessive fan of the child pornography subgenre of manga, known as *loli-con*, and a dōjinshi creator. In a country where the crime rate is almost nonexistent, the public was horrified to discover such gruesome activity in its backyard. Otaku suddenly took on a horrible connotation as reporters began to label anything otaku as deranged, dangerous, and sadistic. This association understandably upset manga and anime fans. Eventually, as the furor died down and Miyazaki's actions were understood to be the act of one man rather than a community, associations stabilized so that otaku, although not the most flattering term, is still the most common label for obsessive fans (Schodt 1996).

In *Beyond My Touch*, Mikuo picks up a favorite manga magazine on the way home.
© TOMO MAEDA/SHINSHOKAN 2003.

In the United States more than Japan, the term otaku has been reclaimed with pride by manga and anime fans. Among fans there is still some stigma attached to being an otaku—and peers will gently mock their friends who display obsessive tendencies by calling them "true otaku"—but at this point, the term has lost its bite in the United States. The title lost many of its negative associations through its addition to fan vocabulary and, although it still indicates a more than cursory interest, many fans wear T-shirts and other gear proclaiming their otaku status.

A Day in the Life of an Otaku

These titles are manga and anime otaku hold near and dear to their hearts. Some are about the otaku lifestyle, and some are so full of in-jokes that only otaku really understand them.

FLCL. *Geneon,* 2005–. OVA series (6 episodes, 24 minutes running time), 3 DVDs. Publisher Age Rating: 13+. Age Recommendation: S. Genres: Comedy, Science Fiction, Fantasy
  Sixth-grader Naota is an ordinary kid, except for the alien girl, hired as a housekeeper, who may or may not be trying to kill him. Then there's the robots. A solid story hides underneath all the insanity, but what enjoyable insanity it is!

Inui, Sekihiko. *Comic Party.* Tokyopop, Japan (2004–2006 U.S.). Publisher Age Rating: Teen. Age Recommendation: S. Volumes: 1–5 [T]. Genres: Comedy, Slice of Life. Total Volumes: 5+ (of 9+)
  Kazuki's otaku friends wrangle him into going to a comic convention and then convince him to start creating his own work. Get ready for a goofy but sweet journey through comics convention craziness, from exuberant cosplayers (short for "costume players") to competitive artists.

Magical Play. ADV Films, 2004. TV miniseries (23 episodes, 7 minutes running time). Publisher Age Rating: 15+. Age Recommendation: S. Genres: Fantasy, Magical Girl, Comedy
  Padadu has fallen from the sky to compete to become the most magical magical girl in the kingdom of Sweetland. Rife with in-jokes about anime and manga conventions, this series may puzzle the wider audience, but fans will find it hilariously bizarre.

Shimoku, Kio. *Genshiken*. Del Rey Manga, 2002–2005 Japan (2005– U.S.). Publisher Age Rating: 16+. Age Recommendation: S, A. Volumes 1–7+ [T]. Genres: School Drama, Comedy, Slice of Life

Kanji joins the Society for the Study of Modern Visual Culture, an academic name for his college's otaku haven. Timid at first, he discovers the best company are people who are just as weird as he is. Frequent references to adult games and anime keep the series interesting for older teens and adults.

Tatsuhiko, Takimoto. *Welcome to the NHK*. Tokyopop, 2004– Japan (2006– U.S.). Publisher Age Rating: Mature. Age Recommendation: A. Total Volumes 1+ [T]. Genres: Comedy, Slice of Life

Sato is a hikkomori, or an anime-obsessed recluse. Will he shape up and get the cute girl studying hikkomori, or will he indulge his fantasies by creating the best ero game ever? The title is a direct feed from otaku culture, but the erotic images make it adult.

The Fan Community

Where to Find Your Local Otaku

As mentioned in the introduction to this book, U.S. manga and anime fans can both be seen in one common venue: bookstores. As bookstores have become the main supplier for manga, many fans can be observed reading, browsing, trading, and discussing the titles available with fellow fans in the aisles devoted to the format. Although fans used to have to troll comic book and specialty stores, the bulk of manga fans today can purchase (or just read) their favorite manga series in the larger bookstore chains (Griepp 2006). Anime fans often haunt the anime sections of video stores, especially those stores that cater specifically to anime fans by providing a wide array of titles, gear, and paraphernalia for sale. Many such goods are inspired by anime rather than manga, and much of what can be purchased is related to watching rather than reading.

Fandom on Display

More often than not, the clues that lead fans to recognize each other take the form of merchandise: from buttons and pins to cell phone charms and cosplay caps—hats designed to represent a particular series or character. Every fan can afford at least a button, and each purchase can be specifically chosen to focus on a favorite character or story arc. Almost every popular series has some sort of product associated with it, from wearable items including T-shirts, jackets, pins, buttons, messenger bags, and cell phone cases to collectibles such as character models, action figures, plush toys (or plushies), wall scrolls (a poster design printed on fabric), chopsticks, key chains, and notebooks. Cross-marketing is a way of life in Japanese industry, and almost every manga has something else associated with it, from anime to video games to toy robots to cologne. Most of these items can be found online, at fan conventions, or in video and bookstores that cater to the otaku crowd. Ambitious fans will troll online auction sites for merchandise direct from Japan, including many items not available in the United States, then show off their collections with a running commentary of how they got it, how much it cost, and why it's especially notable. Those who visit Japan hit the jackpot, heading to the Mecca of otaku shopping, the Akihabara district in Tokyo, to purchase as many items of memorabilia they can pack away for the trip home, becoming the envy of their fellow fans.

Aside from these noticeable clues however, manga and anime fans can be hard to spot. They are truly of every type, age, inclination, and identity. Being a fan is expressed in all kinds of ways. Fans move from reading and discussing titles to creating fiction, art, and other works based on a favorite series. Many join online forums and participate in fan conventions. Most fans start participating in fan culture on a small, low-key scale, and for many that means going online. Once they gain more confidence and discover the larger fan community, they are more likely to head out to face-to-face events such as clubs, local screenings of anime, and nearby fan conventions.

Fandom Online

Anyone who works with teens can observe how wired they all are. Teens are the most technologically savvy generation interacting today, and they spend a great deal of time discussing, rehashing, recreating, and processing their lives online. Teens are some of the top users of online communication, whether it be instant messaging, blogs, e-mail, listservs, or bulletin boards. They are also almost instinctively aware of how to use said technology, knowing, for example, to e-mail "old people," or adults, while instant messaging and text messaging their friends, understanding each generation's comfort zones. Teens' familiarity with, and love for, gaming, from Nintendo to online role-playing games such as *Runescape*, make them adept at using online tools with an ease that eludes many adults. Reading e-mail, instant messaging, playing a game, and listening to a podcast all at the same time is not difficult—it is the standard state of play (Pew Internet and American Life Project 2005).

Due to the Internet's ability to allow like-minded individuals to find each other, an enormous amount of manga and anime fandom takes place online. In the United States, there are nine magazines in print focusing on these formats—two that are anthology collections of manga series, two that are anthropologies of U.S. manga-style comics, and five that combine excerpts, reviews, and industry news. In contrast, there are at least 15,000 Web sites devoted to manga and anime listed on Google. As is often true with fan pursuits in this age, most of the fan-driven information is available online rather than in print. Of all the encyclopedias in print or online, the only resource to explain, correctly and thoroughly, anime is Wikipedia, the online encyclopedia maintained and edited entirely by Internet users (Wikipedia 2006).

Manga and Anime Magazines

Shōnen Jump
> Manga Anthology (shōnen focus)
> $29.95 annual subscription (12 issues)
> http://www.shōnenjump.com

Shōjo Beat
> Manga Anthology (shōjo focus)
> http://www.shōjobeat.com
> $34.95 annual subscription (12 issues)

NewType USA
> Articles, reviews, and news
> http://www.newtype-usa.com/
> $9.95 per issue; $80.95 annual subscription (12 issues)

Protoculture Addicts
> Articles, reviews, and news
> http://www.protoculture.ca
> $30.00 annual subscription (6 issues)

Anime Insider
> Articles, reviews, and news
> http://www.wizarduniverse.com/magazines/anime.cfm
> $28.00 annual subscription (12 issues)

Manga Magazine
> Preview anthology (Tokyopop titles)
> http://www.tokyopop.com/mangaonline/
> Free

Animerica
> Anthology and articles (VIZ titles)
> http://www.animerica.com/
> Free

Rumble Pak
> Original English Language
> Manga Anthology (shōnen focus)
> http://rumblepak.com/

Sakura Pak
> Original English Language
> Manga Anthology (shōjo focus)
> http://sakurapakk.com

Although the most visible manga and anime fans may be those who attend fan conventions, the amount of discussion, reconstruction, criticism, summary, and creative work that can be found online is staggering. Communities devoted to anime and manga are everywhere—the common community blogging tool Livejournal hosts 425 communities focusing on anime and 395 focusing on manga. Google's Directory service, a hierarchical listing of Web sites by subject, lists 91 sites under general manga fandom with 1,377 sites devoted to individual series. Under anime, there are 2,115 sites in general anime fandom with 8,556 sites devoted to individual series. More and more, today's teens create creative playgrounds around their favorite literature and express their fandom both in person and online—manga fandom is no exception.

A perusal through the listings of any of these sites shows the variety of activities in which fans are involved:

- creating fan work, from fan fiction and fan art to anime music videos (AMVs)

- reviewing, translating, and writing essays about favorite series or characters

- translating, scanlating (a combination of scanning and translating manga), and fansubbing (fans subtitling anime television and films before their official U.S. release)

- downloading manga and anime

- joining communities and forums for the discussion and dissection of favorite series, genres, characters, and creators

The Gamer Connection

Online manga and anime fan communities themselves have taken on aspects of gaming, blogging, cosplaying (or manga and anime costume creation), and creative pursuits, whether it's in how fans write or in their Web design. In this way especially, the link between video games, the gamer generation and the manga and anime community is strong. A new kind of literacy is necessary for both: active participation in creating the story and the translation of visual, auditory, and textual clues into a complete tale are a few of the intersecting skills. Gamers are predisposed to enjoy and immediately understand manga and anime's visual language given the practice they've had over years of playing games, many of which are of Japanese origin from companies such as Nintendo. There are numerous games based on manga or anime series, and many fans are first introduced to the characters and premise by games, leading them to seek out the series in other forms. Shōnen series especially inspire action and fighting games, such as *Naruto*, *One Piece*, *Dragon Ball Z*, and the *.hack* series.

Gaia Online, a community repeatedly mentioned to me by teen fans, is just one example of an online community where games and manga collide. The site acts more like a game than a community Web site. Once you arrive, you create a manga-style avatar for yourself, complete with choice of hairstyle, eye color, and eye shape. As you travel through the online world, participating in discussions, playing online games, posting fan art and fan fiction, creating your own Gaia journal, homepage, and identity, you gain "gold," or points that are used to purchase clothes for your avatar, furnishings for your online home, and tokens that will allow you special items or access. This virtual economic world may seem bizarre to nongamers, but teens find the setup familiar from games and devote time to collecting outfits and tools for their online selves as well as, of course, posting and reading in communities.

Fan Creativity

Undoubtedly the most impressive examples of manga and anime fandom that exist online are the fan creations. Many librarians, teachers, and parents are aware of fan fiction only peripherally, mostly from recent articles discussing the phenomenon related to the *Harry Potter* series ("Harry Potter and the Copyright Lawyer," *Washington Post,* June 18, 2003). Most reports tend to focus on the potential infringement of copyright represented by the trend. Teens, aside from being relatively unconcerned with the idea that they may be breaking the law, are avid consumers and creators of fan fiction and fan art. Some 57 percent of the teens online create content online, which amounts to 50 percent of all 12 million U.S. teens, while 30 percent, or two of five, share self-authored content like blog entries, Web sites, fan fiction, and fan art (Pew Internet and American Life Project November 2005).

Wallpapers, Avatars, and Web Design. Some of the simplest but most visually stunning examples of fan creation are the works of art fans create for the decoration and personalization of their computers or other devices, from cell phones to mp3 players. The sheer number of wallpapers, or image files designed to fit each variety of computer screen to beautify each user's machine, is impressive; and the artwork presented requires skill to produce. Wallpapers may simply be a favorite image from a manga or anime, scanned and cropped to suit the standard size of computer screens and perhaps emblazoned with the series title or character name, or they may be full of creative work as they get more complex. Creators make collages, use illustration and design programs to edit, add effects, and adjust images to particular color schemes or themes, and image editing programs give fans free reign to manipulate the images in whatever way they desire, from adding effects to manipulating scenes so that, for example, characters from different shows appear in the same scene. The more adventurous manipulate characters, often romantically pairing together couples, whether it is a part of the original story "canon" or not. Images are also often linked together to create screensavers for fans to download, although this requires a bit more finesse with programming.

A similar impulse, as more and more teens participate in social networking communities, is the creation of user pictures or avatars related to manga and anime. Livejournal communities and AOL Instant Messenger (AIM), which both allow users a certain number of small images that personalize their communication, are full of users who use manga and anime to represent themselves online. The clear visual examples of emotions from manga and anime are particularly appealing as they can be easily and humorously used to denote the user's emotional state when posting or chatting. Many teens add quotes or short snippets of text to the icons to indicate a joke, comment, or reflect the icon's fandom. Some fans use these icons only for fan communities, knowing that their online fellows will get the joke, while maintaining a separate pile of icons for conversations with nonfans. Creating and trading icons has become a specialty, and many users with the tools and the talent will create hundreds of icons for friends and fellow fans to suit their attitudes, requests, and favorite series.

A bit more ambitious but no less prevalent is the amazing amount of skilled Web design on display on various fan Web sites. Although there are, as with any area of the Internet, varying levels of expertise and attention to Web design, many manga and anime fans take care to present Web sites that communicate the visual style of manga as well as their favorite series. Blogs, online journals that are all about personal expression, are equally vibrant examples of how fans express their fandom. These sites are not only examples of creativity but also a kind of record of the individual or group's tastes—when fans discover a new series to revel in, they change their blog or site to reflect their new pursuit. For example, the extremely popular networking site Myspace allows users to shift their profiles' designs to reflect their interests, and the visual inventiveness is only limited by the fans' creativity.

Anime Music Videos. The anime music video (AMV) is an expression of fandom that could only exist so widely in today's online world, where recycling and reimagining content is a key part to how every teen reads, watches, and imagines. Fans of a particular anime series will create an original music video using clips from their favorite anime series edited together in a new order and setting the progression to a favorite song. By editing together footage in new ways, these creators can and do create any kind of impression, including pairing characters who may never have interacted in the original series or spoofing the original by using a ridiculous or alternate soundtrack to the images. In the past, AMVs were customarily presented at manga and anime fan conventions as part of contests or as part of the customary parade of anime screenings. With the arrival of the Internet, fans no longer have to wait for conventions but can now post their AMVs online for other fans to download, comment on, and critique on sites like Anime Music Video (http://www.animemusicvideos.org) and Youtube (http://www.youtube.com).

**At Deviantart.com, a popular fan art Web site, artist asuka111
posts her fan art of *Fullmetal Alchemist*.**

© A. Patipat (asuka111).

Fan Fiction and Fan Art. Fan fiction is creative writing based on or inspired by an original source from within the media world, most often books, movies, and television shows. Many adults know about fan fiction from the recent spate of articles concerning the question of copyright infringement posed by these creations as well as a few notably large and visible fandoms, including fan fiction inspired by the *Harry Potter* series and *The Lord of the Rings* films and novels. For teens, however, fan fiction is an integral part of how they read, why they read, and how they process their imaginary worlds. Almost any teen on the Internet nowadays knows of fan fiction, and most read it at some point in their Internet wanderings. Fan fiction among the manga community is global; many fans from non-English speaking countries try out their English skills by writing fan fiction. In turn, if they are from or near Japan, they are treated as experts in the culture and traditions that inform manga and anime and thus highly valued by other online fans (Black 2004).

Fan fiction includes a vast array of creative output. One particular trait of fan fiction is that what is written usually fills in the gaps in the original work—stories are set in between, before, or after the original works, filling in moments that were not fully explained or creating backgrounds for characters that catch the author's interest. Stories are also written as wish fulfillment in that fans use fan fiction to rewrite the canonical stories to suit what they wish would or think should happen. This can mean anything from linking two characters together romantically to reviving a character killed off in the canon source. The stories may bear only a passing resemblance to the original work, changing characters' worlds, environments, occupations, ages, and sexualities in whatever ways inspire the author. Fan fiction stories consist of a variety of unique genre categories denoted by acronyms and notations from alternate universes (AU), hurt/comfort (h/c), slash (homoerotic stories similar to BL or yaoi), and the infamous Mary Sue stories, or stories in which the author places a thinly disguised, idealized version of themselves into the story to be romanced by a favorite character (Moore 2005).

Although books dominate, by sheer number of stories based on literature on the popular fan fiction site Fanfiction.net (http://www.fanfiction.net), anime and manga fandom take second place. The top categories in anime, by number of stories published, are *Yu-Gi-Oh!* with 38,038 stories and *Dragon Ball Z* with 26,946 stories (Fanfiction.net 2006). In manga and anime fandom, there are added categories and rules: most couples' names are connected by a small "x," such as KaorixInuyasha, and sexual content is indicated by a "lime" story, or the equivalent of an R rating, or a "lemon" story, the equivalent of NC-17 These stories are almost entirely about playing around with both writing and the creators' imaginations—none of it is intended to replace the original work.

Fan Fiction Vocabulary and Terms

Scanlation: manga that has been scanned and translated by replacing the Japanese text with English text by fans for fans

Fansub: anime that has been translated and subtitled by adding English subtitles by fans for fans

NamexName: implies a romantic pairing in the story, for example, SakuraxSyaoran

Lime: the equivalent of an R rating in terms of sexual content

Lemon: the equivalent of an NC-17 rating in terms of sexual content

When starting my manga and anime club, I was a bit taken aback that one of the first questions I was asked, by both a parent and a teen, was where to find good fan fiction. I knew of the phenomenon, but I hadn't yet realized what a substantial part of manga and anime fandom it is. In Japan, manga especially has a long tradition devoted to fan creation. Dōjinshi, or fan comics, are essentially sanctioned fan fiction, and because of looser copyright enforcement in Japan, dōjinshi have created a precedent for embellishing and reinventing previously published work. Many of the industries' superstars, from Takahashi Rumiko to CLAMP, came from dōjinshi work, and manga and anime creators and companies do not look upon fan creations with concern. Instead, wary of alienating the giant fan base, the industry encourages fans to continue creating work and some even troll dōjinshi conventions in search of up-and-coming talents (Thorn 2004).

Fan fiction and its artistic counterpart, fan art, are not unusual in any aspect of teen interaction with their favorite media, from books to films to manga. Teens still read to read. However, in the course of their reading, many are on the lookout for something new to write about. Fan fiction and fan art are modern parallels to the retellings of fairy tales and folk tales that have happened through the centuries. In the United States, however, our current laws surrounding original works have made such activity less than legal and the fear of legal retribution keeps many fan fiction and fan art creators from revealing their true identities. They instead go by online personae, building up reputations and fan bases of their own through Web sites, blogs, and activity within online communities. These communities have sped up the storytelling process and added their own unique bells and whistles to the proceedings. By posting their creations online, teen authors gain instantaneous feedback and give free reign to the desire to create something new from something old (Black 2004).

Fan art is very similar to fan fiction and is a natural offshoot of both the impulses that create fan fiction as well as the manga and anime formats. As fans begin creating visual art, they usually stick with character studies, character design, and posed compositions. However, as they begin to master the basics of creating manga, seeking out the numerous "how to draw manga" titles in the process, they often grow more creative and start their own original comics. Fan art often fulfills the same desires as fan fiction and wallpaper by allowing the artist to create moods, relationships, and character shifts according to what they desire from a story rather than necessarily what was present in the original work. Fan art is also often linked to fan fiction as illustrations or cover designs for particular fan-created stories.

The skill level apparent in fan art is across the board, from amateurs doodling in their school notebooks to artists using computer art programs with a professional level of skill. Much like fan fiction, part of the appeal of fan art comes from the community surrounding its creation, where creators get the instant gratification of immediately sharing their finished work with fellow enthusiasts and seeking their comments. The comments surrounding a particular piece of fan art or a fan art gallery is simply another way of processing the story, both for the artist and for the fans.

Translations, Scanlations, and Fansubs

Copyright Concerns

As we get further into the territory of fandom that verges on copyright infringement, it is important to distinguish one key difference between U.S. and Japanese copyright. Japanese law is not particularly less strict than U.S. law, but it is less strictly enforced. In the United States, copyright holders have to defend their trademark, or it becomes public domain. In Japan, this is not the case, so creators are more inclined to allow fan creations rather than alienate their core audience (Schodt 1996).

Translations

Because of copyright loopholes, an atmosphere of freedom surrounds fan participation in getting the word out about series that are not yet available in the United States. One of the first ways this happens is simple translation. As U.S. fans get their hands on manga in the original Japanese, they translate the dialogue and type up a text document translation formatted like a screenplay or comic book script, indicating panels and speakers. Once finished, they will post these translations online, and any other fan who buys the original Japanese manga will have access to a ready-made translation.

Scanlations

One step up from translation is the more recent phenomenon of *scanlation*. Scanlation, a combination of scan and translation, involves the scanlator translating the dialogue and sound effects, scanning in each page from an original Japanese manga into a computer, and replacing the Japanese text with the translated English words using an image editing program. The availability of cheap scanners has allowed this trend to take over the fan releases of manga—there are many more scanlations than translations at this point. It is not an easy or quick process, but fans put their knowledge of Japanese and desire for fast translations of personal favorites to use by creating scanlations. Most often it is not one person doing all the work but a group of fans working together to release translations for other fans. Usually, scanlations are released chapter by chapter, and fans wait anxiously for the next installment in their favorite manga storyline. Scanlation also provides access to titles by a favorite artist whose work may not ever be translated into English because the creator is less popular in the United States, or the subject of the manga makes it unlikely to get translated. One of the few ways fans can access the dōjinshi market is through scanlations because very few dōjinshi are officially translated into English.

Scanlations were originally not easy to find. Fans had to leap through a number of hoops to gain access to scanlated files. Most were distributed through online scanlation groups via Internet Relay Chat (IRC), a basic, free chat program that allows fans to sign on and share files with each other. Because of the unreliability of who had what file, how big the files were, and the speed of both the provider and downloader's connection, a download could take hours or days. With the arrival of fast file downloading software like BitTorrent, in which the more participants you have, the faster the download goes, fans can now download scanlations within a matter of minutes instead of hours or days.

Scanlation also provides an interesting comparison to those titles that are eventually translated into English. Most scanlators and translators recognize the potential copyright issues surrounding their activities and make it a general courtesy to stop distributing their work once a title is published in English. The difference between fan translations and the official English release are important to fans, and many find the fan scanlation superior to the released version. The comparison gives insight into just how tricky a process translation can be. Manga publishers, including ADVs, have admitted they pay attention to scanlations to predict what will be popular in the marketplace. If hundreds of fans are clamoring for a particular manga scanlation, companies know to pursue the rights to translate that manga (Roth 2005). Intriguingly, the system of scanlation does not appear to have a negative impact on sales—if anything, the buzz surrounding scanlated titles usually means more fans will purchase the title once it is published, simply because they are already fans.

Fansubs

Akin to scanlation, but requiring even more work, fansubbing is essentially the same process, except done for anime instead of manga. Of course, due to the more complex process of translating the dialogue, creating the subtitle track, timing the track to follow the dialogue and video, and putting it all together in a downloadable format, fansubbing is a longer process requiring a larger number of people to perform the different tasks.

Fansubbing started as an underground process using VHS in the 1980s. Fans made fansubbed titles available at conventions, and for many years, these productions were the only way to see a wide variety of anime (Schodt 1983). Today, however, the Internet has amped up the proceedings. Many fansub groups now get digital copies of Japanese anime television programs the day they air in Japan. Due to demand, and with enough fans willing to help, these groups release the just-aired anime for English-speaking fans within days. As with scanlation, the process seems to increase fan attention as well as sales, because the awareness of a series means more fans want to own the official, higher quality DVD release. Fansubbing, as with scanlation, is also a way to get titles that will rarely or never be released stateside. In addition to fansubbing and scanlation, many fans trade original soundtracks only available in Japan via BitTorrent the same way they exchange anime and manga.

Anime companies have struck very much the same balance with fansubs that manga publishers have, allowing fans to do their work and help advertise the medium as a whole. On the other hand, it is expected within the industry that once an anime is officially released in English, fansubbers will no longer provide that series for fans. When the releases were on VHS, this simply meant that fansubbers destroyed the tapes and no longer distributed that series. In the online world, it is a bit trickier—fansubbers will take down the links to the series' downloadable files, but they cannot prevent fans who are adept at sharing files from continuing to trade episode files among themselves. Thus far, this exchange has not brought down the anime companies' wrath, but if the process continues, it may spell the end of fansubbing as we know it. The rise of Youtube has taken downloading out of the equation entirely as fans can now watch entire series through the popular Web site.

Major Fan Web Sites

Fan Fiction
Fanfiction.net (Anime and Manga Fan fiction): http://www.fanfiction.net/cat/201/

Fan Art
Deviant Art: http://browse.deviantart.com/traditional/drawings/fanart/anime/

Scanlation
Manganews.net: http://www.manganews.net
Stop Tazmo: http://www.stoptazmo.com/
Manga Viewer: http://mangaviewer.com/
Manga Updates: http://www.mangaupdates.com
Naruto Fan: http://www.Narutofan.com/

Downloading and Watching
Anime Suki: http://www.animesuki.com
Torrent Spy: http://www.torrentspy.com/
Mininova: http://www.mininova.org/
Youtube: http://www.youtube.com

The Ethics of Fandom

All of these processes are enough to make anyone sensitive to copyright concerns more than a bit nervous. According to the July 2005 Pew Internet Life Survey, one in five teens goes online to remix, recycle, and recreate content found online. This culture of recycling content is undoubtedly creative and is akin to the use of sampling in music as well as the retelling of classic tales from fairy tales to Sherlock Holmes. The crux of the problem lies in teen understanding of copyright. Fan fiction and fan art are allowable in their minds—why should they have to ask or pay for permission when they are not claiming to be the original author or making any money from the created work? Most of them seem to feel that copyright law is archaic and should not apply to fan creation. As programming like Napster and BitTorrent continue to challenge copyright law, it is anybody's guess as to how all of these activities will eventually change the nature of copyright.

What Do Lawyers Think?

To check out how legal professionals are considering fan work, check out this paper presented at Berkeley by two professors of law at the University of California, Davis: "The Right to Mary Sue" by Anupam Chander and Madhavi Sunder, forthcoming in the *California Law Review,* 2007, v. 95. The current link is located at the Intellectual Property Scholars Conference Web site for their 2006 meeting:

http://www.law.berkeley.edu/institutes/bclt/ipsc/papers2/ChanderSunder.pdf).

Whatever the debate, however, under international copyright law, it is still illegal to distribute or screen any anime or manga title without permission from the copyright holders. Thus far, no company has actually brought a case against fans: threats of legal action are often enough to end distribution of fan-created media, but it can also lead fans to boycott the challenging company's materials. For most companies, the drop in business is not worth the legal wrangling yet, but if the fan distribution starts harming business, the copyright holders might well launch challenges. Intriguingly, there are conventions within the community that allow both industry members and fans to offer an example of how the newest technology and fan enthusiasm does not automatically mean the end of business. Most anime companies embrace their fans' activities as a way to help predict and consult with their fans (Roth 2005).

At the same time, anime distributors have been some of the first companies to make use of new technology such as BitTorrent to promote their releases. ADV Films provides a variety of downloads via BitTorrent, including extended trailers, screensavers, wallpapers, and exclusive interviews and commentary from performers involved in the production. Central Park Media has a variety of first episodes available for download for the video iPod. These companies are aware of the behavior of their fans, and instead of ignoring their desires for immediate access, they figure out a way to give it to them.

Downloaded Material: To Show or Not to Show?

One of the first hurdles librarians and teachers may encounter is teen fans asking to screen downloaded anime or share scanlated manga with fellow fans in the institution. Certain anime and manga clubs have decided to air fansubbed anime—one example being the longstanding MIT Anime Club, although they abide by the rules of not showing a fan-created title once the official DVD has been released. One benefit of showing fansubbed anime is the novelty—seeing a show just aired in Japan allows fans to see immediately what the new trends are and enjoy advancements in each media at the same time as their counterparts in Japan.

No company has yet enforced copyright law to shut such viewings down, but legal danger definitely still exists. At this point, you should make your own decisions regarding sharing downloaded anime and manga with clubs or fans, but be sure to investigate the law carefully and use the opportunity to discuss copyright with teen fans. For many librarians, the answer will have to be no to fansubbed or downloaded screenings. In the end, there is no lack of anime or manga being licensed at this point that would necessitate allowing fan-created work into the library or school sphere; no one should feel pressured to include it in their programming. Teens may well share it among themselves and will certainly continue to download such copies, but taking the step to include material in an event should be entirely up to the institution.

Conventions

Conventions are one of the few times anime and manga fans can get together and not feel like the odd ones out. Like any gathering of fans, manga and anime conventions provide the sense of community that fans crave—the exhilarating feeling that they are not alone in their enthusiasm and that there are, in fact, other people out there who want to discuss *Naruto* as much as they do. A lot of that sense of community comes from online discussion today, but nothing quite beats the overwhelming feeling of acceptance that comes from walking into an anime convention and seeing people laughing, debating, and parading by dressed as characters from this year's hottest series.

Manga and Anime Conventions in the United States

West

Anizona
Phoenix, Arizona
http://www.anizona.org/

Anime Expo
Anaheim, CA
http://www.anime-expo.org/

Anime Overdose
San Francisco, CA
http://www.aodsf.org/

Anime LA
Los Angeles, CA
http://www.animelosangeles.org/

Anime Vegas
Las Vegas, NV
http://www.animevegas.com/

Sakura Con
Seattle, WA
http://www.sakuracon.org/

North

AnimeNEXT
Secaucus, NJ
http://www.animenext.org/

Genericon
Troy, NY
http://genericon.union.rpi.edu/

Tekkoshocon
Monroeville, PA
http://www.tekkoshocon.com/

Anime Boston
Boston, MA
http://www.animeboston.com/

Bakuretsu Con
Colchester, VT
http://www.bakuretsucon.org/

Central

Anime Central
Rosemont, IL
http://www.acen.org/

Youmacon
Troy, MI
strighthttp://www.youmacon.com/

Animaritime
Sackville, New Brunswick, Canada
http://animaritime.mtaanime.org/

Ohayo Con
Columbus, OH
http://www.ohayocon.com/

MatsuriCon
Worthington, OH
http://www.matsuricon.org/

South

Metrocon
Tampa, FL
http://www.animemetro.com/metroconventions/control.cfm

Momocon
Atlanta, GA
http://www.momocon.com/

Numa Rei No Con
New Orleans, LA
http://www.numareinocon.com/

Otakon
Baltimore, MD
http://www.otakon.com/

Middle Tennessee Anime Convention 6th Period
Nashville, TN
http://www.mtac.net/

Project A-Kon
Dallas, TX
http://www.a-kon.com/

Oni-Con
Houston, TX
http://www.oni-con.com

Shiokazecon
Houston, TX
http://www.shiokazecon.com/

Ushi Con
Austin, TX
http://www.ushicon.com/

Katsucon
Arlington, VA
http://www.katsucon.com/

Further Afield

Kawaii Kon
Honolulu, HI
http://www.kawaii-kon.org/

Anime North
Toronto, Ontario, Canada
http://www.animenorth.com/

There are a number of manga and anime conventions, large and small, across the United States every year. Most conventions provide a standard slate of programming:

- guest speakers from the manga and anime industry in Japan

- guest speakers from the U.S. industry, most often voice actors

- anime and manga company panels highlighting new and future releases

- fan-hosted panels on a variety of subjects

- cosplay events

- fan art, music video, and comic presentations and galleries

- Japanese pop and rock (or j-pop and j-rock) dances

- manga reading rooms and daylong anime screenings

- an exhibit floor for anime and manga consumers

Together all of these activities provide attendees access to both the official community represented by the industry guest, as well as the fan community of peers. At this point in the manga and anime boom, there is a lot of crossover between the two—more and more old school manga and anime fans are now in the ranks of the U.S. manga and anime production and publishing companies. Voice actors are often fans themselves, and their appearances are the highlights of many conventions. Not only can voice actors discuss their own roles in depth, they can provide a window into the industry, the translation process, interactions with their Japanese counterparts, and their upcoming work. Many voice actors are celebrities in their own right, and their anecdotes, humorous asides, and speeches in character are always entertaining. The graciousness with which voice actors and company representatives answer fans' questions on minutiae, a hazard with any fan convention, is laudable and comes from a sense that the crowd is truly a community. Fan behavior is most exceptional when interacting with Japanese creators—everyone is on their best behavior, leaving their tendency toward outbursts and running commentary at the door, treating the visiting creators as honored guests.

The Exhibit Hall is where fans can purchase all the merchandise they want, from U.S.-produced items to paraphernalia direct from the Japanese market to every possible manga or DVD they might wish to collect. This is also where anime distributors and manga publishers set up shop to show off their latest acquisitions and interact directly with their fan base. Most industry reps are adept at balancing the obvious sales focus with the questions, criticisms, encouragement, and commentary that fans stop by to discuss. Many companies set aside special times for fans to present original work, especially those manga artists aspiring to join the ranks of manga creators.

Fan panels show a broad range of interest and expertise, from screenings of some of the most laughable and ridiculous moments in anime to in-depth discussions of the mythology in anime to chances for fans to try out for the voice-acting world. When attendees need a break from the hustle and bustle of the panels and exhibits, they can relax by going to read the hundreds of volumes of manga available in the manga reading room or taking in a few favorite anime episodes at the numerous anime screening rooms. The atmosphere at any convention is like a carnival, and the parade of cosplayers makes the festival atmosphere complete, often stopping and posing for fellow fans to take their photographs.

Cosplay

All from Anime Boston 2006, these participants in the competitive Cosplay Masquerade exemplify the creativity, hard work, and commitment that go into creating and presenting cosplay outfits.

Regan Cerate as Fai Floweright from
Tsubasa: RESERVoir CHRoNICLE.

Ginger Anne Roy as Riku from
Kingdom Hearts.

Chloe Metcalf as Kaoru from *Dir en Grey.*

Carly Bradt as Sue from *Clover.*

**Mere Doyle as the Forest Spirit from *Princess Mononoke*,
which transformed into the Nightwalker on the right.**

Costume play, better known as *cosplay*, is not unique to manga and anime fandom, but the high level of participation has made *cosplay* one of the standout activities for fans. *Cosplay* is similar to the dressing up seen at all manner of conventions although it is most often recognized as part of science fiction, fantasy, and comic conventions where fans wander the halls dressed as Klingons, Storm Troopers, and members of the Justice League. In manga and anime fandom, *cosplay* dominates convention activity both in terms of sheer visibility and as one of the most complicated programs to join. *Cosplay* contests, often called masquerades, are colorful, hilarious, and require planning, rehearsal, and anywhere from hours to months of work on costumes. Other variations on masquerades include special events such as *Cosplay* Chess, where individuals dressed as characters represent the pieces on a chessboard. As other fans play the game, each *cosplayer* acts out the chess moves in character.

A *Cosplay* masquerade is an event devoted to participants arriving in full costume, often acting in character and presenting their creations for judgment by other fans. Masquerades provide great opportunities for fans to act, to show off their creativity and fandom or character of choice, and to have fun with a group of peers. Many masquerades have different levels of participants, from novices to advanced competitors, to ensure that everyone is competing at the same level of experience and expertise. Much of the fun of the masquerades comes from the skits that competitors perform to show off their acting, scriptwriting, and costume design all together. Spoofs and parodies are common, as are skits that combine characters from different series in madcap adventures.

The rules of masquerade are very strict—for example, every participant has to have a handmade rather than a professionally made costume, every costume will be judged by how accurate the garment is to the manga or anime source, and skits are limited in length. At Anime Boston, New England's largest anime convention, the rules for masquerade are divided into twelve parts. The list of rules includes requirements for costumes, deadlines for registration as a competitor, and all types of rules about participation from parents accompanying younger contestants to the fact that electrical sockets will not be available for costumes that need to be plugged in. These rules have been cemented through the years of masquerade experience, and despite the draconian complexity, the framework allows fans to feel confident in the contest's judgment.

Cosplay requires specialized skills—few teen pastimes require them to become expert tailors—and the amount of time and effort each individual puts into cosplay is incredible. The results are a spectacle to behold. The online component of cosplay activity is mainly that of support—cosplayers share photo galleries of their creations with other fans, and exchange advice on sewing, supplies, ideas, and problem solving. Some fans also turn cosplay into a business —one long-time cosplayer makes wigs for fans, and given the complexity of the hairstyles for many characters, her wigs will sell anywhere from $50 to $300 (Katie Bair's Petting Zoo Wig Design 2006).

Global Awareness

One of the most fascinating aspects of being a manga and anime fan is a fairly simple concept: in becoming a fan of products from another culture, manga and anime fans necessarily have a broader understanding of global culture. All of the activity previously discussed—learning Japanese, researching Japanese folklore and mythology, investigating Japanese history—lead manga and anime fans to a complex view of the world rather than the immediate view of their town, their school, and their family. Questions such as why the Japanese sense of humor is noticeably different from ours leads to grander questions about what traits are culturally defined, how much members of a culture are aware of the impact society has on their individual and collective behavior, and which cultural bridges can be crossed. When teens start to realize that all the of the comics they are reading do not have the same origin—that some of it is Korean manhwa, for example, and expresses a worldview different from Japanese manga—they begin to question our own pop culture output in a similar way. They try to reconcile the outrageous sense of humor and sexual innuendo with the stereotypical image of the Japanese as a reserved, polite people, and when they discover they cannot, they investigate to find out why there are gaps in the images they see. In seeing how Western characters are presented in Japan, they begin to reflect on what the image of the United States and its citizens is around the world, investigating how much is stereotype and how much is fantasy.

References

Black, R.W. "Access and Affiliation: The Literacy and Composition Practices of English Language Learners in an Online Fan Fiction Community." *Journal of Adolescent and Adult Literacy* 49, no. 2 (2005): 118–28.

Fanfiction.net. http://www.fanfiction.net (accessed April 28, 2006).

Griepp, Milton, ed. *ICv2 Retailers' Guide to Graphic Novels* 7 (2006).

Lenhard, Amanda, and Mary Madden. "Pew Internet Life Survey: Teen Content Creators and Consumers." November 2005. Washington, DC: Pew Internet and American Life Project. Available at http://www.pewinternet.org.

Macias, Patrick, and Tomohiro Machiyama. *Cruising the Anime City: An Otaku Guide to Neo Tokyo*. Berkeley, CA: Stone Bridge Press, 2004.

Moore, Rebecca C. "All Shapes of Hunger: Teenagers and Fan Fiction." *Voice of Youth Advocates* (April 2005).

Roth, Daniel. "It's... Profitmon! From *Pokémon* to *Full Metal Panic*, the Anime Industry Is Doing Everything the Rest of Show Biz Isn't: Embracing Technology, Coddling Fans—and Making a Killing." *Fortune* 152, no. 12 (2005): 100.

Schodt, Frederik L. *Dreamland Japan: Writings on Modern Manga*. Berkeley, CA: Stone Bridge Press, 1996.

———. *Manga! Manga! The World of Japanese Comics*. Tokyo: Kodansha International, 1983.

Thorn, Matt. "Girls and Women Getting Out of Hand: The Pleasure and Politics of Japan's Amateur Comics Community." In *Fanning the Flames: Fans and Consumer Culture in Contemporary Japan*. Albany: State University of New York Press, 2004.

Wikipedia. http://www.wikipedia.org (accessed April 27, 2006).

Chapter Eight

Draw in a Crowd: Promotion and Programs

Creating Fan Interest

Fan Collecting

Most fans start to build a collection of favorite titles, although due to manga's serial nature, it can be an expensive collection to maintain. Given that most anime titles cost around $30 per DVD, and manga average $10 per volume, most teens start collections by buying manga. Although $10 seems affordable and some teens are willing to buy titles in a favorite series as new volumes are released, often they do not have the expendable income to purchase all of the titles in a series unless the series is short. Popular manga series run anywhere from fifteen to more than one hundred volumes, making it impossible for teens with limited resources to buy everything they want. Part of the dilemma comes from the issue that most manga are not something teens want to read over and over again—they just want the whole of the story. In Japan, most readers solve this problem by purchasing one of the many inexpensive manga magazines. These magazines contain chapters from several different manga, allowing the reader to follow several stories at once, then dispose of the magazine once that month's or week's issue has been read. In the United States, only two such manga anthology magazines exist for teens: VIZ Media's *Shōnen Jump* and the more recent addition *Shōjo Beat*. Both magazines are successes, but they only cover a tiny fraction of the manga available in book form.

Anime is even more expensive, averaging $30 per volume, and fewer fans commit to purchasing a series unless it is one they will watch over and over again. Many depend on renting videos and DVDs, especially now that online rental stores carry a wide selection of titles. Viewers also rely on the television networks such as Cartoon Network to provide their weekly anime fixes.

The cumulative price combined with a desire to finish a series is what leads many teens to treat bookstores like libraries—they see little reason to buy a manga if they can read it in an hour sitting on the floor of the bookstore. This is, of course, the gap that libraries are already expanding into by building strong collections within individual libraries as well as in larger networks. Until libraries can collect the wide array of titles available, however, meeting teen expectations for the variety and newness of titles is still a struggle. To work within a budget, consider buying manga and anime with a network collection in mind. Individual libraries could commit to purchasing certain series in their entirety and on standing order. Once teens realize the collections are there, an awareness brought about by advertising interlibrary loan services and network-wide collections, they will use the library to read the entire series.

Appealing to Fans and Creating New Ones

Once the teens know there's manga in the library, they will learn exactly where to go to find the latest additions to the collection. The problem is, how do you let them know it's in the library in the first place?

First, start in the library itself. Rather than just adding manga to your graphic novel collection, show off the new additions by displaying them or shelving them together with your newest titles. Make sure to complete the advertising with signs identifying the collection and fliers with a short explanation of the format and a purchase request form that teens can hand in to the selectors to let them know their favorite titles will be considered for the library. Consider going a step further by adding posters or manga and anime merchandise to the display. Manga and anime wall scrolls sell for about $15 each at any manga and anime store or at conventions and will add a great splash to any wall (and are easier to take up and down than paper posters). Many publishers, including VIZ, Tokyopop, GoComi!, and Central Park Media will send out advertising posters, bookmarks, and postcards to manga and anime clubs as well as libraries, so make sure to keep a few of these freebies around to add color to your displays.

In order to inform and appeal to fans and nonfans alike, it is important to advertise your new collection with a flyer or brochure introducing the format and the new collection. If possible, combine the information with a request form that fans can use to suggest new titles for acquisition. A succinct and informative flyer is great for curious patrons and will help staff who feel less confident talking about the collection. See the samples on pages 233, 238, and 239.

Go Outside the Library

Getting the word outside the library is key: many manga and anime fans may not frequent the library already, being unaware that the library carries their medium of choice, and attracting their attention outside the library is vital. Creating word of mouth is important, especially because teens are much more likely to listen to the recommendations of their friends and family than read a poster. Contact your local schools to see if they have manga, anime, or gaming clubs (often all three interests intersect) and ask if you can contact either the student leader or the faculty advisor for the clubs. Send over fliers for your collections and special events, and, if possible, either arrange to meet the group on their turf or invite them to hold a meeting at the library so you can show them what you've started. Treat it as a collaboration—many clubs will have an established identity, and whether they join in library activities may depend on whether they view your activities as competition or complementary. School club members can help you create word of mouth with their fellow fans as well as lend your activities credibility among their peers.

Partnering with Local Businesses

If you have local bookstores and comics stores that stock manga, contact the owners and staff to see whether you could advertise library events in their store. Ask if they might be interested in collaboration on events, including the annual Free Comic Book Day every May, but also partnering on comic book swaps or creator visits. Most comics stores are still slanted toward Western comics rather than manga, but combination events are encouraged and will draw fans of all comics. Consider locating a U.S. manga creator in your area or another member of the U.S. manga industry, such as an editor or translator, and suggest cosponsoring a visit.

Bookstores, on the other hand, have embraced manga as the current moneymaker that it is and may have extra displays or posters that they might be willing to donate to the library for event giveaways and prizes. My local Waldenbooks, for example, stocks a wide variety of manga, and the store manager is generous with cardboard cutouts and the sturdy floor-to-ceiling posters the stores have used to advertise their manga sales. Once these items had served their purpose in the store, the library could use them for prizes, and the teens were deliriously happy to compete for a wall-sized portrait of Rurouni Kenshin. We were also able to advertise our continuing manga and anime club by posting small posters near the manga shelving. Partnering with local businesses is always a balance between the library's needs and the business's goals, but both sides can benefit from the simplest of crossover advertising.

Outside of comics stores, however, the key is to get advertising where the teens are. If you have a local coffee shop that's crammed with teens after school, make sure to put up fliers and posters advertising events in their designated displays. The same goes for any local hangout, from ice cream shops to music stores. If the high school and middle schools have their own newspapers, contact them about placing ads for library events within their pages. Similarly, getting the word out to parents via school and parent-run newsletters, e-mail lists, and in the local newspapers will provoke parents to suggest these events to their teens, especially if they know of their interest but recognize their own teens may not read the local paper. If you have a Teen Advisory Group, or even a few friendly manga fans, ask them where to advertise and for their help in spreading the word. These teens will know how to get out the word, from texting their friends to hanging posters in their schools' halls. Make sure both you and your teens abide by whatever posting rules each establishment has, and, if possible, strike up a relationship with local businesses that may lead to further collaboration in library events.

Speaking the Language

A teen manga reader doesn't usually expect a librarian or teacher to know about manga. When he or she discovers a librarian who understands, the reaction is enthusiastic and excited. All of this leads back to the need for librarians to read at least a few manga and watch a few anime, to be familiar with the conventions, style, and current favorites. On top of that, though, the key is being able to speak the language—to know what a samurai or magical girl is, to understand the significance of a giant sweat drop, and to recognize the manic humor exemplified in chibi forms.

When you are booktalking, at your local school or just off the cuff to patrons, don't be afraid to throw in a manga title or two—not only will it show the library's acceptance of manga as a format to read and collect, but it will also show that you the librarian know what manga is, why it's fun, and that it's something your audience is interested in.

Sample Booktalks

Death Note by Ohba Tsugumi

What if you had the power to control who lived and who died with the written word? What would you do? Light decides to rid the world of evil, one criminal at a time. When the police notice killers dropping like flies, the hunt for the assassin is on. Light realizes he has to get rid of his pursuers to continue his righteous work—but is it right to kill, even for the good of mankind?

One Piece by Oda Eiichiro

Luffy is going to be the leader of all of the pirates—he knows this is his destiny. But that's about all he knows. He cannot navigate, has zero skills in piracy, and has neither a ship nor a crew. But never mind—he's got a magically rubber body, determination, and more luck than any hero deserves. Plus, pirate clowns! Who can resist pirate clowns?

Nana by Yazawa Ai

Nana K needs to get to art school on her own steam to prove that, this time, she can make it on her own. She needs to prove to herself and her new boyfriend that she's more than just a hopeless romantic who only lives for her man. Nana O is determined to leave behind her broken heart and become the great punk rock star she knows she was always meant to be. When the two Nanas meet in Tokyo, they'll discover that life never quite works out according to plan.

I've spoken with teens from all over Massachusetts about manga and anime history, and the excitement generated in those group and one-on-one discussions testifies that these teens are starving for adults who support their enthusiasm for the format. They are happy to listen to a librarian advising them on what to read in manga and beyond, once they sense a kindred spirit. Most of these teens do not read only manga, and many are likely to pick up a book if it has something in common with the manga they love reading—from a screwball sense of humor to a romantic drama. A teen who loves Stephanie Meyer's *Twilight* loves the goth romances of *Model* and *The Antique Gift Shop*. Fans of Miyazaki's *Howl's Moving Castle* film have all read the Diana Wynne Jones source novel and debate the latest installment of the *Harry Potter* series with all the precision and fervor of other Rowling fans.

Booklists and Displays

Manga contain every category of literature. It's important to remember that although manga is a different format, genre booklists and displays can and should include manga titles as well as traditional prose, films, and books on tape. Stories defined by their humor, fantastical elements, or historical setting appeal to a wide range of readers, not just manga readers. Creating cross-format displays is a fine way to promote similar stories in prose to those readers who are reluctant to pick up anything but manga. When discussing favorites, think of ways to integrate different titles into a genre list, including manga but also including prose, film, and books on tape or CD of similar style and attitude.

First, of course, are the genre display lists we all do as librarians to highlight the best of a particular type of story. In many ways, these are the easiest displays to add manga to—just remember your manga titles when you put together a list or display. For example, if you are concentrating on fantasy titles with strong female heroes, including *The Song of the Lioness Quartet* by Tamora Pierce and retold fairy tales like Margaret Haddix Pierce's *Just Ella*, remember to include magical girl manga like CLAMP's *Cardcaptor Sakura*, Watase Yu's *Ceres: Celestial Legend*, Itoh Ikuko's *Princes Tutu*, and Kaori Naruse's *Pretear*. Don't forget the related anime series—multimedia displays not only acknowledge the crossover between mediums but also lead many viewers to the source books they might not have picked up otherwise.

If you've decided on a more thematic display, manga and anime titles are just as suitable to include as any prose title. For example, the Young Adult Library Services Association's Popular Paperbacks for Young Adults Committee put out an excellent list in 2003 called "I've Got a Secret." There are many manga and anime tales that revolve around secrets kept or revealed, including Alice's unspoken love in Watase Yu's *Alice 19th*, Kurosaki Ichigo's double life as a high school student and Soul Reaper in Kubo Tite's *Bleach*, and the obscure missions of both Light and L in Ohba Tsugumi's *Death Note*.

Aside from just including manga and anime titles in displays, however, there are also many starting points from within manga and anime that could easily include titles outside the formats. The advantage of displays that start from manga comes from cashing in on manga's appeal and directing manga fans toward other works that they might never consider because they do not fall into the coveted format. Create displays on Japanese pop culture by pairing manga with titles such as Patrick Macias's *Cruising the Anime City* mapping out the fan city inside Tokyo, Aoki Shoichi's *Fruits* and *Fresh Fruits* photo essays of Shinjuku fashion culture, and Murakami Takashi's *Little Boy: The Arts of Japan's Exploding Subculture*. Such combinations will give manga and anime fans a window into the culture their favorite stories come from, although keep in mind these books cover the full range of pop culture including adult culture. Similarly, a display on the history and culture of Japan related to manga will give readers a sense of the format's growth and history, from the ukiyo-e prints of the seventeenth and eighteenth century to the galvanizing force of Tezuka Osamu. Food plays a large part in many manga titles, from *Antique Bakery* to *Iron Wok Jan!!* Take advantage of the theme by providing displays pairing manga with cookbooks and histories of cuisine that derive from the manga work, from pastry creation to sushi.

Outside of texts related specifically to anime, manga, or pop culture, a number of excellent teen novels and nonfiction related to Japanese culture and history will draw in manga and anime fans. Because many teens don't often realize the difference between Japanese manga, Korean manhwa, and even U.S.-created original English-language manga, consider doing a display showing the similarities and differences between Japanese culture, Korean culture, and the U.S. trend toward all things Asian from inventions such as Nintendo to fashion like the Shinjuku fashion culture adopted by pop star Gwen Stefani.

Comics and Pop Culture Titles for Display

Consider adding these nonfiction titles for the curious manga and anime fans in your library who want to know a bit more about the cultures that surround their favorite reading. Most of the titles do contain adult content and thus are best collected in an adult collection.

Comic Artists—Asia: Manga Manhwa Manhua edited by Comickers Magazine
Both volumes show the crossover between manga artists and illustrators. The first volume concentrates on Japan, and the second looks into comics all over Asia.

Cruising the Anime City: An Otaku's Guide to Neo Tokyo by Patrick Macias
A glimpse into the intricate world of otaku culture.

Fruits and *Fresh Fruits* by Shoichi Aoki
A parade of Harajuku fashion captured in candid photos.

Japan Comcikers: Draw Anime and Manga Like Japan's Hottest Artists edited by Comickers Magazine

Japan Edge: The Insider's Guide to Japanese Pop Culture by Mason Jones
Manga, anime, and games are all addressed as inextricable facets of Japanese pop culture in essays.

Little Boy: The Art of Japan's Exploding Subcultures by Takashi Murakami
Popular culture and fine art combine with academic critiques of creation since the second World War.

Programs and Events

Anyone interested in providing programs that will appeal to the manga and anime fans has a wide array of programs to consider. Some require a minimum of effort from the coordinators, such as simply providing space for a manga club to meet and discuss favorite titles; others, like hosting a fan convention, require months of planning and piles of resources. This section gives you starting points and basic outlines for the variety of programs to consider for any organization.

As with all programming, the basic questions are the following:

- What audience do you want to attract with your program?

- What resources do you already have?

- What kind of commitments, in terms of time, money, and effort, will you have to make to bring about the program?

- What resources will you have to seek out?

- Are there partners that might be useful or necessary to present the program?

- What, if any, restrictions are necessary to run the program? Will content or participants be limited?

If your institution already has a manga or anime collection, you may see simply from rising circulation statistics that there is an audience for a manga or anime event in your area. However, it is also important to remember that just because manga and anime fans are not immediately obvious does not mean they are not there. Most teens are still not aware that libraries or schools would even carry manga or anime in their collections and thus do not expect librarians to provide any services for this medium. The popularity is obvious in market statistics, but if you host an event or club, advertising outside of the library will likely be necessary to gain fan attention. By the same token, one of the best aspects of starting a manga and anime club, or hosting a stand-alone event, is that many teens who never step foot into the library will be drawn in and realize just what the library can offer them. Many teens, for example, are now the top users of interlibrary loan services as they cycle through reading manga series volume by volume, and they are noticeably gleeful that they no longer have to buy a series to read it. The habit of passing manga around among family and friends is certainly part of fan culture here. Many teens go to the bookstores, sit on the floor in front of the manga stacks, and read whole series by passing volumes around the circle of readers. Sadly for the bookstores, they are less likely to buy manga, but if libraries provide similar collections for just this purpose, just imagine how many teens would be drawn to hang out at the library.

An Easy Treat to Make: Candy Sushi

Ingredients:

    Crispy rice cereal treats (marshmallows, butter, and crisped rice cereal)

    Fruit roll-ups

    Gummy candies

Press the rice treat flat onto cookie sheet. Using a sharp knife, cut a rectangular section of treat, about 3 by 7 inches or the length of a fruit roll-up. Place a variety of gummy candies horizontally along the center. Using the fruit roll-up plastic wrapper, roll the rice treat around the gummy center, as with real sushi. Once the treat is shaped into a roll, wrap the fruit-roll up around the roll, mimicking sushi's seaweed wrapping. Slice the sushi into 1-inch rounds.

Be creative! Invent innovative sushi with squares and using gummy fish on top, à la real sushi. Get as many gummy candies as possible, with a variety of shapes and flavors, including sour gummy peaches, gummy sharks, gummy fish, gummy worms, gummy octopi, and spice drops.

The following special events can be held independently or in conjunction with a manga and anime club. All address a particular aspect of manga and anime fandom, and the combinations of these events make the possibilities for programming numerous and available for every budget of staff time and expense.

Manga Café

Popular in Japan, manga cafes, or *manga kissa,* are establishments where readers pay a small fee to sit and read from a vast library of manga titles at their leisure while consuming the usual café fare, from coffee to light snacks. Many are open twenty-four hours a day and provide free Internet service; in some, readers can even stay overnight in tiny podlike compartments to sleep (Macias 2004). Libraries and schools, if they have a reasonably large manga collection, could very easily set up a similar experience for their readers. The appeal of reading while drinking your favorite beverage has certainly been demonstrated by Barnes and Noble and Starbucks combinations across the country, and because many teens simply want a place to hang out rather than structured time, manga cafes could both show off the collection and, without taking up too much time or resources, be a low-key program acknowledging the fans' tastes and interests. Comic book and manga stores may also agree to participate and provide manga for reading as long as their store is advertised, as with the comic book swaps that are traditional in the U.S. comics market.

A How to Draw Manga and Anime Program at Your Library!

The folks behind the excellent Manga University are now offering to host "How to Draw Manga" workshops at libraries. Contact them at http://www.howtodrawmanga.com.

How to Draw Manga and Anime

Many teens express their love for manga and anime through art, whether creating fan art or their own manga-style comic strip or ongoing story in sequential art. Although manga art seems simple on the surface, it requires a lot of practice and a good eye to master. The simplicity of the art encourages many teens, who may be intimidated by the draftsmanship necessary to produce Western comic art, to give the manga style a try. Of course, the best manga features exceptional art, but mastering the basic visual language is attainable for many teen artists (Lehmann 2005).

Many teens spend a good deal of time and effort working on their art in this style, often in a notebook, a sketchbook, or even on professional-grade drawing paper. A "How to Draw Manga and Anime" event is a natural one-shot event for aspiring artists and writers. The simplest program could simply be providing interested participants with the many series of "How to Draw Manga" books, paper, pencils, and the space to draw. Many kids and teens would take advantage of the offering, but this kind of program also requires that the teens have the inspiration, confidence, and drive to give it a go.

A step up from this requires a leader or mentor for the group willing to demonstrate technique, style, and advise the participants in their own work, possibly over a set period of time. Obviously, this requires an artist willing to offer his or her services. Some communities may well have a professional manga-style artist local to them willing to help present a program, usually for a fee. Local comic book stores are a good place to start the search for local creators who may be willing to provide programs at local libraries because most comic stores host signing events and keep lists and contact information for local talent. Many institutions may also have luck asking around the local colleges, either art or liberal arts, to see whether there are any aspiring manga-style artists who are willing and able to host such an event. Many illustrators starting out enjoy sharing their passion and training for a low fee or even for free, although they may not be as practiced in teaching their technique to others.

Manga Creator Resources

Anime Mania series by Christopher Hart

How to Draw Manga series by the Society for the Study of Manga Techniques
These books are the choice for the artists looking for traditional manga techniques direct from Japan. The one catch is that there are more than thirty volumes, each demonstrating a certain style or aspect—start with the Getting Started volume and try a few others, like mecha robots or shōjo characters. From there you can slowly add what teens request or is particularly popular in your area.

Japanese Comickers: Draw Manga and Anime Like Japan's Hottest Artists edited by Comickers Magazine
These art books showcase artists who work both in manga and in general art and particularly focus on lesser-known artists inspired by Japan's vivid popular culture. The content heads into adult territory, making these best for an adult collection, but they are excellent windows into the variety of art styles we have yet to see in the United States.

Manga Mania series by Christopher Hart
Christopher Hart's books are library favorites, although some more traditional fans find them "too American" and not quite fitting the Japanese standard they want to achieve. They are great beginner books, though, and circulate heavily.

Manga: Masters of the Art by Timothy Lehmann
Lehmann collects interviews with manga artists both famous and obscure in the U.S., but all the discussions are an in-depth look at what makes a manga artist. The focus is mostly toward the art—the materials, the schedule, and the inspiration. As the artists work for audiences from kids to adults, this title will suit an adult collection best.

Mangaka America by Various Artists
This new collection includes interviews, advice, instructional features, and lush art from today's top American creators in the manga style.

Shojo Beat's Manga Artist Academy by Various Artists
This manga art book is one of the few that includes authors well known in the manga world: Watase Yu and Takada Rie both contribute advice.

Manga Series for Aspiring Artists

Theses series are notable for their art, style, layout, and innovative design. Check out the variety of manga art and get inspired.

Hakase Mizuki. *The Demon Ororon*. Tokyopop, 1998–2001 Japan (2004 U.S.). Publisher Age Rating: 13+. Age Recommendation: S. Volumes: 4 [T]. Genres: Action, Fantasy, Romance, Horror
> Experimental layout, stylized design, and less "cute" characters can contribute so much to a story. Ororon wouldn't be nearly as suave without lounging in the panels so carefully, proving that more doesn't always mean better.

Nihei, Tsutomu. *Blame!*. Tokyopop, 1998–2003 Japan (2005– U.S.). Publisher Age Rating: Older Teen. Age Recommendation: S. Volumes: 1–6+ [T]. Genres: Action, Science Fiction, Military, Apocalypse, Horror
> *Blame!* has very few words. The pictures have to tell everything, from character personality to the action to advancing the plot. The style is grittier and less slick than a lot of current manga series and expertly indicates the decaying, hopeless atmosphere of the tale.

Ninomiya, Tomoko. *Nodame Cantabile*. Del Rey Manga, 2002–2005 Japan (2005– U.S.). Publisher Age Rating: Teen. Age Recommendation: S, A. Volumes: 1–4+ [T]. Genres: School Drama, Comedy, Slice of Life, Music
> Another shift from the slick art of many manga, this series represents a loose, almost impressionistic style. The quick lines focus your attention on the movement and lend the story a sweet, childlike quality not unlike the heroine Nodame herself.

Mizushiro, Setona. *After School Nightmare*. Go Comi, 2000– Japan (2006– U.S.). Publisher Age Rating: Older Teen. Age Recommendation: S. Volumes: 1–6+ [T]. Genres: Fantasy, Horror, Romance, School Drama. Related Anime: *Death Note* (live action movie), *Death Note* (TV series)
> Mizushiro's gorgeous, stylized artwork is like another character in this series. By turns sinuously creepy and seductive, her lines capture and keep any reader's attention.

Tezuka, Osamu. *Buddha*. Vertical, 1974–1984 Japan (2003–2005 U.S.). Publisher Age Rating: NR. Age Recommendation: S, A Volumes: 8 [F]. Genres: Historical, Slice of Life
> Tezuka's artwork is rounded, stylized, and, to today's manga readers, verging on old-fashioned. This title should educate readers to Tezuka's brilliance, showing off his superior use of layout and cinematic techniques.

Yazawa, Ai. *NANA*. VIZ Media, 2000– Japan (2005– U.S.). Publisher Age Rating: Older Teen. Age Recommendation: S, A. Volumes: 3+ [T]. Genres: Romance, Slice of Life. Related Anime: *NANA* (TV series), *NANA* (live action film)

> The tendency toward tall, slender beauties is followed to an extreme in Yazawa's work, but she makes it work with detailed costumes, dramatic layout, and never forgetting that the real story is not just the glamour but also the hearts of the characters.

Check out the competition: manga-style titles show how U.S. artists have adopted manga's language and melded it with their own:

Chmakova, Svetlana. *Dramacon*. Tokyopop, 2005–. Publisher Age Rating: Teen. Age Recommendation: S. Volumes: 2+. Genres: Slice of Life, Romance

> Christie's exhilarated to go to her first anime and manga convention and show off her comic art. When her boyfriend makes eyes at every cute cosplayer that walks by, she gets fed up—and meets a new potential love. Will the romance last once the con is over?

Cloonan, Becky. *East Coast Rising*. Tokyopop, 2006– Japan (2003–2004 U.S.). Publisher Age Rating: Teen. Age Recommendation: J. Volumes: 1–3. Genres: Action, Science Fiction

> Pirates in New Jersey? This swashbuckling tale is set after the United States has been all but destroyed by disreputable pirates roaming the coasts of New York. Abandoned after a pirate attack, young Archer joins Cannonball Joe and his crew on the trail of lost treasure.

Clugston, Chynna. *Blue Monday*. Oni Press, 2002– Japan (2003–2004 U.S.). Publisher Age Rating: 13+. Age Recommendation: S. Volumes: 4+. Genres: Slice of Life, Comedy, Romance

> *Blue Monday* is one of the earlier titles adopting manga-style art. Major's sassy series recounts the adventures of teen Mod girl Bleu, her brash friend Clover, and their crushes and romantic foibles.

Espinosa, Rod. *Rod Espinosa's Alice in Wonderland*. Antarctic Press, 2002– Japan (2003–2004 U.S.). Publisher Age Rating: NR. Age Recommendation: M. Volumes 1+. Genre(s): Fantasy

> We all know the story: Alice, rabbit hole, queens, tea, and the Jabberwocky. This is a faithful and imaginative adaptation, lively with bright art. Espinosa is behind top manga-style comics, but this adaptation is a labor of love not to be missed.

Gallagher, Fred. *Megatokyo*. CMX/DC Comics, 2002– Japan (2003–2004 U.S.). Publisher Age Rating: NR. Age Recommendation: S. Volumes: 4+. Genres: Romance, Comedy, Slice of Life

    Largo and Piro blow all their money buying games and figures in Tokyo, and now have no way to get home to the U.S. As they settle in to live, gaming and anime references are everywhere, but the series appeals to readers who don't catch all the lingo.

O'Malley, Brian Lee. <u>Scott Pilgrim</u>. Oni Press, 2003–2004. Publisher Age Rating: 13+. Age Recommendation: S. Volumes: 1–3+ Genres: Romance, Comedy, Slice of Life

    While still dating his high-schooler girlfriend, Scott Pilgrim is hit by love at first sight when he sees Ramona. Little does he know that to win her, he'll have to triumph over every single one of her evil ex-boyfriends. And by evil, she means *supervillian* evil.

Quick, Jen Lee. *Off*beat*. Tokyopop, 2005–. Publisher Age Rating: Teen. Age Recommendation: S. Volumes: 1–2+. Genres: Romance: BL/Yaoi, School Drama, Slice of Life

    Tory can't seem to stop paying attention to his new neighbor Colin. He's frequently absent from school, his house hides secrets, and he never seems to talk to anyone. But is it just boredom and curiosity that makes Tory pay attention?

Rising Stars of Manga

The annual competition is a great chance for accomplished amateur artists to try to break into the business. Tokyopop runs a solid competition, and the judges are encouraging to everyone who enters, giving pointers and recommending that young artists try again if they don't quite make it. Check out everything you need to know at Tokyopop's Web site: http://www.tokyopop.com.

Manga Art Supplies and Suppliers

Except where noted, these supplies are available at any art supply store.

- An assortment of pen nibs
- Copic Markers and screentone sets (http://www.copicmarker.com)
- India ink
- Mechanical pencils

- Nibbed ink pens

- Paper

- Screentones (http://www.bluelinepro.com)

- Manga art computer programs (http://www.e-frontier.com/)

- Manga Studio
  - Beginner level Manga Studio
  - Manga Studio EX
  - Professional level Manga Studio

The kind of art supplies specific to manga and anime can be accentuated by providing supplies especially prevalent in the field, from illustration paper to ink pens to the shaded and patterned Screen Tones used to create shadows, clothing, and backgrounds in manga. These supplies are not prohibitively expensive, nor are they cheap, but a few examples would certainly help artists understand the process for creating manga. Keep in mind, as well, that most manga creators still work predominantly by hand, rather than via computer or other technological equipment. So long as you can provide paper, pencils, pens, and photocopier, you've got most of the supplies the professionals use.

Depending on how much time can be devoted to the event, from an hour to a whole week, the event can be divided into sessions. A creative workshop for fans could aim for teens to group together, each taking on the roles of writer, artist, layout designer, or even editor to create their own manga style comic. Many teens will want to try for a longer story, but give them an achievable goal by setting a page limit to create a sequential art short story.

Divide meetings into brainstorming among the creators with the following considerations:

- Establishing the world and characters

- Deciding on character design

- Outlining a plot

- Creating storyboards of each scene

Each meeting can teach the participants all of the elements necessary to create a comic from beginning to end. Individual sessions can be dedicated to a component necessary to the creation of a part of a complete manga. If, for example, the session is about character design, the leader of the group can first ask participants to brainstorm the usual characters, including heroes, villains, sidekicks, and romantic interests.

Example Session: Character Design

List what makes each character visually identifiable, including clothing, expressions, hairstyle, and body type.

If stumped, refer to favorite manga or anime series:

Who is the villain? How is he or she noticeably the villain? How does the villain differ from the hero: In words? In appearance?

How do you identify sidekicks? How does the sidekick differ from the hero? The villain?

Do you, as creators, want to follow conventions or break them?

What will your villain sound like? How does he or she speak?

Do you know who the villain is at the beginning, or will it be revealed later?

Writers could focus on exercises on writing dialogue, script structure, character development, and the creation of individual voices for each character. The following books will help writers get off on the right foot in terms of comics writing in particular:

- *Writing for Comics with Peter David* by Peter David
- *Making Comics: Storytelling Secrets of Comics, Manga, and Graphic Novels* by Scott McCloud
- *Alan Moore's Writing for Comics* by Alan Moore
- *The DC Guide to Writing Comics* by Dennis O'Neill

This kind of activity will not only help the artists and writers move toward creating a solid work but also provoke them into addressing how manga works as a storytelling form. This kind of awareness of method, especially in terms of literary devices such as point of view and flashback, often leads teens to be more aware of such devices in everything they consume, from films to books.

Manga and Anime Clubs

As manga and anime have become popular, fans and professionals hoping to jumpstart programming dedicated to these media have started clubs in venues all over the country, from comics stores to schools to universities to libraries. Starting a manga and anime club is easier than ever. With the variety of resources available for starting clubs, the instigators no longer have to be fans, just inspired to give it a try.

**An example of a flyer for a club-run anime marathon—
it's easier than you may guess to run one!**

© Robin Brenner 2005.

Most manga and anime clubs start from the simple premise of providing time and space for fans of these media to get together, discuss favorites, and read manga or watch anime. This may be as simple as encouraging a fan at your institution, be it a library or a school, to bring his or her fandom to another level by starting a club. In schools, of course, there are procedures for establishing any new club, and any teacher or school librarian could act as a guide for students to form their own club as well as help establish guidelines, ideas, resources, and support. In public libraries, the rules may be less clear, and so the librarian may need to take on a more active role in initially setting up a manga club with a plan to allow the instigator to take over the club once it is established and stable. It's also often true that no matter how dedicated teen fans are, they may not be quite organized enough to start their own club and thus may need a librarian or teacher's support to get started.

Clubs may focus on either manga or anime, or they may encompass both forms. If the group leader is someone already familiar with one or the other, their area of interest may be a good place to start, keeping in mind that the focus should not be so narrow that there will not be enough of an audience for the program. Combining clubs to focus on both anime and manga is natural because the media are so intertwined; if members are more inclined to screen anime in a group rather than the more active participation in a manga discussion, however, anime may be the best focus. If the group leader is entirely new to the subject, the prepackaged selections offered by anime distributors and production companies are a fast way to get a club off the ground. These will necessarily focus the clubs on anime viewing at first, but as the club finds its feet, the members will stretch the club's domain to include their interests.

Prepackaged Anime Clubs

More and more anime production companies are providing special services for clubs, whether the clubs are hosted in libraries, schools, or another institution. The following are the currently active clubs.

ADV Advocates

> Company: ADV Films
>
> Contact: animeclubs@advfilms.com
>
> Web site: http://www.advfilms.com/advocatesnew

Description: ADV provides monthly mailings including anime screener DVDs (usually 3–4 full episodes from 1–3 series, subbed and dubbed, and 15–20 trailers of upcoming ADV titles), copies of the ADV *Advocates* newsletter, special offers for club members including discounts on subscriptions to ADV's *NewType USA* magazine, and their catalog of titles. Club membership also allows for screening of any ADV title, provided the club leader requests permission in advance.

Restrictions: Club members must fill out a monthly survey about the screener DVD's contents.

Pros: Exceptional customer service; response to screening requests arrives within hours to a few days. Newest releases on screener DVDs have high appeal for club members.

Cons: Because of the variety of clubs involved, screener DVDs may not be appropriate for a club's audience.

Good for: Any beginning anime club—the monthly packages are very much anime clubs in an envelope and are especially good for institutions with limited resources or collections of their own.

Operation Anime

> Company: FUNimation, Inc.
>
> Contact: sophie.mcnutt@Funimation.com
>
> Website: http://www.operationanime.com

Description: FUNimation provides a selection of popular anime DVDs to club members and special offers for club members including discounts on FUNimation's catalog of titles. Club membership also allows for screening of any FUNimation title, provided the club leader requests permission in advance.

Restrictions: Club members must fill out a survey accompanying title. Club must have at least twenty members to be eligible for participation. Screenings must be limited to club members and must be free of charge.

Pros: Club may keep DVD either for club use or to add to the library or school's collection. Great customer service; response to screening requests arrives in a few days to a week. New titles are added to club offerings promptly and periodically.

Cons: Not a monthly program—club leader must request titles for each event

Good for: Occasional events or in combination with other sources for anime to view.

As of this writing, Bandai's Anime Addict program and CPM's Anime University program are both missing in action—their Web sites are in evidence, but participating clubs have not had any communications for over a year.

VIZ Media offers a form from *Shōnen Jump* (http://www.shōnenjump. com/mangaanimeclub/) for clubs to sign up for information and free giveaways. VIZ Media, for example, supplies manga and anime merchandise for special events. Tokyopop will send out copies of their free *Manga Magazine* for club events as well.

Audience Age Ranges

The simplest considerations can be the most important in forming a club. For example, the age range of members—there are manga and anime fans of all ages, and each club will have to decide how exclusive it will be. Teen librarians, for example, will likely limit club members to the population they serve. However, if an event or club would like to reach a wider audience, planners might consider opening the program up to adult fans. The interaction between old school anime and manga fans and the next generation can have great value for both sides of the discussion. It is harder to combine children and teens—children are usually interested in manga and anime at their maturity level, and although they can stretch up into the 'tween range in terms of interest, most will not enjoy older fare. On the other side, teens may well enjoy the occasional title intended for younger audiences, but in general they are inclined to explore more mature subject matter than many children will want to see or read.

The most obvious age ranges for clubs at this point seem to fall into three categories: older children from age nine to thirteen, teens from thirteen to eighteen, and adults eighteen and up. The least served group is the youngest age range, partially because they are the newest fans. Although professionals working with children may be aware of manga and anime from their charges, few feel comfortable enough with the media to start a club or host an event. Many of the stereotypes, specifically regarding more mature content in all titles, are still believed by both parents and professionals working with this age range. This gap is something parents and other professionals may well want to start filling because many of these younger readers are frustrated by their inability to join teen groups and the lack of clubs for fans at their level. Keep in mind that many of the anime kids watch today are edited for television because they were originally intended for a teen audience. The subsequent DVD releases are unedited and contain content fine for teens but questionable for younger viewers. Programs for younger viewers are currently limited to films including Miyazaki's works and activities such as drawing characters and folding origami.

Teen clubs have been formed everywhere, by fans as well as by librarians, teachers, and parents. The range of content appropriate for teens aged thirteen to eighteen is a bit limited at the younger end of that scale, but there are so many titles currently available that no group is going to run out of quality titles any time soon. As an example, many library clubs limit the anime they watch to that in keeping with a PG to PG-13 rating or, with titles that are not rated by the Motion Picture Association of America, have a top age-range limit of 13+ rated titles. Many of the teens participating may well have seen fare aimed at older audiences, but in a public group, no club leader can be guaranteed that what is watched will sit well with everyone in the group. Many librarians and teachers preview any anime screened for their club to ensure that they are aware of and comfortable with the title's content.

In the adult range, of course, the choice of titles is vast, and manga and anime clubs at universities show all manner of anime for their members. For example, the Massachusetts Institute of Technology Anime Club opens up its screenings to anyone who wants to make the trek to the university, from local teens to adult fans, and it shows a wide variety of titles from seven o'clock at night through midnight every Friday.

Advertise Guidelines

No matter what the age range of your club, it is important to be clear both to participants and, in the case of children and teens, to their parents or guardians, just what will be shown and what behavior is expected as an active member of the club. Short "Frequently Asked Questions" sheets will be helpful to patrons who have questions about the format, the event or the club (see the samples that follow). Many librarians, for example, insist on a combination permission form and club member contract for their teens. The first part of the document is for parents or guardians. It covers the basic setup of the club, definitions of manga and anime, what being a member entails, and explains the guidelines of what will be read or screened within the club. The second part of the document explains the rules of being a club member, including rules of behavior for participating in meetings including, for example, not talking during anime screenings and not making personal attacks during discussions. This kind of document ensures that the teens' parents know precisely what the club will entail and also provides the librarian backup if a member of the club causes problems that lead to discipline or a ban from participating. Most likely, group leaders will never have to enforce such extreme measures, but it's good to be clear from the start.

If possible, host an information night about the formats, the event or club, and the institution's reasons for hosting such events—this is helpful to many parents, teachers, and adults. Not only will such a program help reassure patrons, it will also ensure that the leaders of the club—whether it be librarians, teachers, or students—are able to explain, advertise, and defend the event or club. Often a meeting of this type makes club leaders aware of concerns they may not have considered and allows patrons a chance to ask questions directly. If the club is just beginning, collect the names and addresses of parents as teens sign up to join the club so that postcards can be sent home advertising the information night.

Aside from simple book discussions, many groups can help create a collection. If a group is part of a larger institution like a library or school, the group can advise the librarians or teachers on what titles to purchase for their collection or what kinds of titles might work for particular units of study. Clubs can produce newsletters, full of reviews, member-created art, top-ten lists, and feature articles on creators, fan conventions, or personal essays on their own experiences as manga and anime fans.

JAPANESE MANGA AND ANIME AT YOUR LIBRARY

Check out the library's new additions to the graphic novel section, Japanese manga and Korean manhwa!

What is manga?
Manga (pronounced mahn-guh with a hard "g") is the general term for Japanese print comics, the equivalent of comic books and graphic novels in the U.S. You may also hear the related term, *manhwa* (mahn-hwah), which refers to Korean print comics.

What is anime?
Anime (pronounced ah-nee-may) is the general term for Japanese animated work, including television shows, movies, and direct-to-video releases.

Why does the library have them?
Both *anime* and *manga* have a rich, distinct visual storytelling style. *Anime* is often related to *manga* — the two industries inspire each other and often create related titles together. Both are also much more common in Japan than their counterparts in the U.S and are a dominant part of Japanese pop culture. *Manga* is used for everything from titles on how to do your job to biographies of famous figures to bestselling fiction. Both formats are great fun — not to mention fascinating in terms of looking at different cultures, translation methods, history, and language.

Where can I find out more?
Please consult our Frequently Asked Questions flier about manga and anime. Our librarians will also be happy to help you find resources on the subject.

Have some suggestions?
Fill out this form and
drop it off at the Reference Desk!

Title:

_____

Author:

_____

Is it a series? ___ yes ___no

Title:

_____

Author:

_____

Is it a series? ___ yes ___no

Title:

_____

Author:

_____

Is it a series? ___ yes ___no

Title:

_____

Author:

_____

Is it a series? ___ yes ___no

Title:

_____

Author:

_____

Is it a series? ___ yes ___no

A template for an Information and Recommendations Flier.
© Robin Brenner 2005.

Club Otaku
FAQ for Parents

Everything you ever wanted to know about Club Otaku at Your Library!

What in the world is Club Otaku?

Club Otaku is a club for Anytown's teen patrons to gather and discuss two popular media: manga, or Japanese print comics, and anime, or Japanese animation. Each meeting will focus on specific titles. The aim of the club is both to create a forum for teens to discuss these increasingly popular formats as well as encourage discussion about the sequential art format: cultural variations, mythology, and history as represented in these media.

What is Otaku?

Otaku (oh-tah-koo) is a Japanese word that means "geek." This word has been adopted by Western fans of manga and anime to identify themselves.

What is sequential art?

Sequential art is the term for stories presented in the traditional comic art format — so, anything from the newspaper comic strips to comic books to graphic novels use sequential art to tell their tales. Sequential art is most often marked by the use of panels and text bubbles.

What is manga?

Manga (pronounced mahn-gah with a hard "g") is the general term for Japanese print comics, the equivalent of comic books and graphic novels in the U.S. You may also hear the related term, manhwa (mahn-hwah), which refers to Korean print comics.

What is anime?

Anime (pronounced ah-nee-may) is the general term for Japanese animated work, including television shows, movies, and direct-to-video releases.

Who are Club Otaku's members?

Club Otaku is for teens from age 13-18.

> Please don't hesitate to contact the club moderator Robin Brenner. She'll be happy to answer all questions about the club.

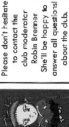

Who is Club Otaku's moderator?

The club is moderated by staff member Robin Brenner. She has been working at Your Library for almost three years. During that time, she has become a graphic novel expert and enthusiast. No Flying, No Tights (http://www.noflyingnotights.com), her website reviewing graphic novels for teens, kids, and adults has been highlighted in Booklist and School Library Journal. She is currently a member of the Young Adult Library Services Association's Great Graphic Novels for Teens Committee for the American Library Association. She has written a guide to manga and anime for librarians and parents and has been quoted in the New York Times Book Review on the topic. On top of all of those official crocodilians, she is certainly an otaku herself.

Why would my teen want to join Club Otaku?

Club Otaku is the place for teens to meet and discuss manga and anime with other teens who share their interests. Members include teens curious about graphic novels, Japan, animation, art, or those just looking for a way to spend an afternoon. All are welcome to join the club. Discussions range from the titles themselves to visual literacy, Japan and Western history, culture, and pop culture.

Why a club about anime and manga?

Both anime and manga have a rich, distinct visual storytelling style. Anime is often related to manga – the two industries inspire each other and often create related titles. Manga, too, are also much more common in Japan than their counterparts in the U.S and are a constant part of Japanese pop culture. Manga is used for everything from titles on how to do your job to biographies of famous figures to bestselling fiction. Both formats are great fun – not to mention fascinating in terms of looking at different cultures, translation methods, history, and language.

What would my teen gain from joining Club Otaku?

As with other media, graphic novels embody a different kind of literacy than traditional text, and in this world where TV, the Internet, and multimedia are increasingly the mode by which information is distributed, visual literacy is a vital tool for teens to master.

More specifically, manga presents not only a different way of telling a story, but also a window into a different and rich culture. Reading manga and watching anime frequently inspires fans to read Japanese mythology, learn to speak Japanese, and investigate the country's history.

Members of the club will also be invited to share their enthusiasm and expertise with the library community by producing recommended title lists as well as producing their own newsletter featuring member articles, reviews, and artwork.

What kinds of anime and manga will you be showing and reading?

As all genres are represented, we will be reading and watching a variety of titles, featuring realistic dramas, science fiction epics, historical fiction, and fantasy adventure, just to name a few common genres. The aim is to experience the breadth and depth of the media as well as discover the kinds of stories told, both familiar and unique, in Japan.

How do you decide what to read and show?

In terms of anime, the moderator will choose titles for each month in keeping with suggestions from the group. All anime shown will be at the PG to PG-13 level, as ranked by the production company as well as a number of other resources including The Parent's Guide to Anime (see web resources below). The moderator will preview each title to ensure it's age appropriateness.

Manga titles will be chosen with the same eye for popularity, requests from the group, and age appropriateness.

Why is the club limited to only 13-18 year olds?

This club is for teens, and the manga and anime chosen are interesting to and appropriate for teenagers (rated PG or PG-13). Thus, these titles may not be appropriate for younger participants, and as the club is intended to be for our teen patrons, older patrons are also not allowed to join.

I've heard that anime and manga are full of schoolgirls, revealing outfits, and swordfights—is this true?

While schoolgirls and samurai are common characters, the way they are represented depends on the intended audience. Unlike in the U.S. where many comics and animated films are aimed at and are appropriate for younger readers and viewers, both manga and anime are produced for a variety of audiences and age ranges, from girls to boys, toddlers to adults. In fact, a much wider variety of titles are produced than in the U.S. as these two media. The variety of titles can be compared to the productions on U.S. television or films: yes, there are titles produced which contain sensuality and violence, but these are intended for an adult audience. By no means do all or even most anime and manga titles fall into this category.

How can I find out more about anime and manga?

There are a number of great resources both in print and on the web. Here are a few titles and websites to get you started, all available either at Cary Library or within our network.

Print Resources:

Anime Explosion: The What? Why? And Wow! Of Japanese Animation
by Patrick Drazen
An enlightening book which covers the trends and common stories in anime, explaining in detail the links between anime and Japanese culture.

Manga: 60 Years of Japanese Comics
by Paul Gravett
A visually engrossing book on the variety and history of Japanese manga. The breadth of the topic means that this book includes some adult content, but definitely not to be missed if you want to see visual examples of manga.

Anime Essentials: Everything a Fan Needs to Know
by Gilles Poitras
A short guide to all of the ins and outs of anime, from the films themselves to the fan communities.

The Anime Companion: What's Japanese in Japanese Animation?
By Gilles Poitras
A dictionary of anything and everything you might see in anime, from gestures to food — a whole lot of fun to browse through, not to mention informative.

Manga! Manga! The World of Japanese Comics
By Frederick L. Schodt
One of the first books to thoroughly explore manga, covering everything from its history to current motifs — again, there is some adult content as Mr. Schodt addresses manga for all age ranges including adults.

Web Resources:

The Librarian's Guide to Anime and Manga
http://www.koyagi.com/Libguide.html
A great place to start, full of vocabulary, definitions, frequently asked questions, and recommended titles.

No Flying, No Tights
http://www.noflyingnotights.com/
Moderator Robin Brenner's site — to find out a bit more about graphic novels in general as well as reviews of new manga series.

The Parent's Guide to Anime
http://www.abcb.com/parents/
A useful list of titles with short reviews, commentary, and ratings according to the MPAA standards.

The Anime Companion Online Supplement
http://www.koyagi.com/ACPages/ACmain.html
The supplement to Mr. Poitras' above book.

A template for a Frequently Asked Questions Flier

Club Otaku Contract and Photo Permission Form

I WANT TO BE A MEMBER OF CLUB OTAKU!

To sign up, please complete this contract!

In Joining Club Otaku, I agree to:

- Attend at least four of twelve meetings per year
- Participate in creating the Club Newsletter for the library
- Allow everyone to watch screenings in peace — no talking, please!
- Respect other members' opinions during discussion — no personal attacks

Date: _____

Name: _____ Grade: _____ Age: _____

Address: _____

Telephone: _____ E-Mail: _____

Parents Permission: _____ **permission to**
I/We grant our son/daughter
participate in the Your Library Anime and Manga Club.
Parent/Guardian

Signature: _____

Date: _____

I/We can be contacted at Home: _____

Work: _____

In case of emergency/alternate please contact:

Name: _____

Relationship: _____

Telephone: _____

Club Otaku Contract and Photo Permission Form

PHOTO PUBLICATION RELEASE FORM

Dear Library Patron,

Periodically, our library staff members or representatives of the media (especially the local newspaper) wish to photograph, videotape, or record library users engaged in library activities, for the purposes of publicizing or reporting on programs and services at Your Library.

In addition, patrons' photographs, writing or artwork may be published on the Your Library website (www.yourlibrary.org) or displayed at the library.

In order that we may follow your wishes, please complete this release form and return it to the library as soon as possible.

Thank you.

Betsy Library

Library Director

Date: _____

Your name: _____

Your signature: _____

In connection with the programs and activities of Your Library, I give permission for the following:

YES   NO

_____ My photograph, videotape, recording, writing or artwork (identified by name) may be submitted to a newspaper, posted on the Your Library website, or displayed in the library.

_____ My photograph, videotape, recording, writing or artwork (with no name) may be submitted to a newspaper, posted on the Your Library website, or displayed in the library.

A sample anime club information, contract, and photo permission form—it's best to get it done all at once.

© Robin Brenner 2005.

Given the prevalence of online fandom, the club can certainly create all manner of Web sites, from group blogs to online review collections to galleries of fan art, given that they probably have the expertise and Web space available to them. Many manga and anime clubs host any or all of these activities, and special events are often imagined, proposed, and presented by manga and anime clubs in concert with adult or official support from schools, libraries, and other institutions.

Cosplay

Cosplay (or costume play) events provide two kinds of opportunities: a cosplay masquerade, and a preparatory cosplay costume-making workshop. Any smaller masquerade can be as simple or as complex as the club leader and the fans would like. Participants should be involved in deciding the rules, from the creation of the costume to the accomplishments the judges will consider. The clearer the rules, the better, but they should also allow for creativity, fun, and the possibility that everyone has a chance to win.

For these very reasons, a cosplay costume creation program is welcome, focusing on the skills needed to create a costume from sewing to design to creativity with found objects. This kind of event is especially useful if an experienced tailor or costume maker can provide advice and teach skills to the cosplayers. Timing such an event so that it aids cosplayers heading out to conventions is ideal, although a sewing event at any time of year would appeal to cosplayers if the advertising promoted the skills necessary to create costumes.

Cosplay Inspiration and Instruction

- Angelic Star: The Costuming Art of Yaya Han

  http://www.angelicstar.net/index2.html

  An inspirational site for any cosplayer, featuring one the masters of convention cosplay.

- Cosplay.com

  http://www.cosplay.com

  Cosplay central for photo galleries, community advice, and recommendations for supplies.

- *Cosplay: Catgirls and Other Critters* by Gerry Poulos (Stone Bridge Press)

- *Cosplay: Schoolgirls and Uniforms* by Gerry Poulos (Stone Bridge Press)

Cosplay Supplies

- Cosworx

  http://www.cosworx.com
  Every kind of cosplay supplies can be found here, from wigs to
  Wonderflex, material that can be formed when heated and then
  cools into a solid shape.

Mini-Conventions

Of course, many of these smaller programs can be combined into a
mini-convention for manga and anime fans. The format of conventions is easily
adjusted to fit whatever time and space is provided, although at least a daylong
schedule is preferable simply to bring the convention experience to life. A simple schedule could include an anime marathon running all day, an area devoted
to manga reading, a how-to-draw event, and a cosplay masquerade to finish off
the day. Depending on the resources available, the mini-convention can be adjusted to the talents of the staff available as well as the events most desired by
the potential audience. If none of your participants are cosplayers, there may be
no need for a masquerade, but if there are a number of aspiring artists, a visit
and presentation from an artist in the field could provide an excellent end to the
festivities.

Building Your Audience

Now it's up to you! By this point, you've gained some insight into the
world of Japanese manga and anime. Start small by building a core collection
with the help of the following lists, and draw out local fans. If you already know
you've got a crowd of otaku, consider ways to draw them in to events at the library or entreat their help in building a better and broader collection.

Manga/Anime Club Discussion Topics

Art and Symbols

What are the different symbols you can pick out from manga and anime? Use
examples from Western comics, including speech bubble, thought bubble, stars
circling around the head, a light bulb above the head. Compare these with Japanese
symbols: nosebleeds, sweat drops, anger symbols, chibi forms, and so on.

Investigate a specific manga layout together. Consider the following:

Why does this look different from a Western comic?

How do you know where to look? What leads you through the page?

What is the story on this page? Give specifics about what leads you to understanding each panel.

What symbols do you all recognize? (Examples: cherry trees/blossoms, an anger symbol, torii in a scene, a chibi figure.) What do they mean to a Japanese reader? What do they mean to you? Did you have to learn the Japanese meaning, and if so, how did you figure it out?

Collecting

How do you decide what to collect?

Do you have to own certain titles/series? Why or why not?

Where do you get your manga and/or anime?

Do you use the library to read manga? To watch anime? Why or why not?

What can the library provide that it doesn't already?

Fan Art/Fan Fiction/AMVs

Creation, consumption, and communities:

Do you look at fan art? Read fan fiction? Watch fan videos (anime music videos—AMVs)?

What do you like about it?

What gets on your nerves?

How important is it that it be close to the original? In terms of art? In terms of character and world depiction?

What makes the best fan work?

Do you create any fan work?

How did you get started?

How do you do it?

What inspires you?

Do you know about the questions of copyright raised by creating these fan works? Do you understand it?

Do you think fan fiction (fan art, fan videos) should be legal? Illegal? Why or why not?

Should there be any restrictions? Who should set the rules or restrictions?

Fansubbing/Scanlation

Fansub: An anime title, usually just aired in Japan, which is subtitled for fans by fans and distributed by computer file over the Internet to fellow fans to download to their own computers.

Scanlation: A manga title, usually just released or an older title unlikely to be translated, that is scanned, translated, and distributed by fans for fans by computer files over the Internet.

At present, it is common practice to stop distributing any anime or manga once it has been licensed in the United States to protect the original creators and distributors' sales as well as to keep on the right side of the law.

Do you download either fansubbed anime or scanlated manga?

What do you think about the trend?

Do any of you participate as translators or in other ways?

Do you understand the copyright questions raised by these practices?

Should fansubbing and scanlation be allowed? Should there be any restrictions?

What do you think about how fans' demands contribute to the industry? Is it a good thing? A bad thing?

Historical Topics

Ask members of the club to read manga or watch anime set in a particular era. Provide a list of historically significant events and dates for the club members to compare with the manga and anime set during that period.

Examples: For the era surrounding the Meiji Era (1868–1912), have members read or watch *Rurouni Kenshin*, *Peacemaker* or *Peacemaker Kurogane*, and *Kaze Hikaru*.

Following is some information for reference.

Key Players in the Meiji Restoration:

- Choshu and Satsuma clans: These two samurai *han* led the outbreak to restore the emperor to rule and abolish the shogunate

- Emperor Meiji (given name Mutsuhito): The emperor was restored to power at the age of fourteen in 1867.

- U.S. Commodore Matthew Perry: The naval officer who began the opening of Japan to the West by landing near Edo.

- Saigo Takamori: Samurai leader of the Satsuma Rebellion.

Important dates of the Meiji Era:

- November 8, 1867: Tokugawa Yoshinobu relinquished government control to the emperor.

- 1868: The Meiji Restoration moved toward democratic participation in government and restored the emperor to divine status and head of the government.

- 1877: Satsuma rebellion, considered the last stand of the samurai, occurred.

- 1885: Intellectual Fuuzawa Yuchiki wrote, "Leaving Asia," an essay that encouraged Japan to emulate the West and leave behind "backward" Asian neighbors, namely, Korea and China.

- 1888: The Meiji Constitution (also known as the Imperial Constitution) established the law of the land until 1947.

- 1894–1895: In the Sino-Japanese War; Japan defeated China in Korea.

- 1904–1905: Russo-Japanese War took place, an event that further established Japan as an international power in the region.

Important events in the Meiji Era:

- Japan was opened to Western trade after two hundred years of isolation.

- Restoration of the emperor.

- Creation of the Shinsengumi (stars of both *Kaze Hikaru* and *Peacemaker*, enemies in *Rurouni Kenshin*).

- The emperor declared the samurai outdated and stripped them of their status and weapons.

- Samurai uprisings occurred (see Satsuma Rebellion).

- The beginning of the industrialization of Japan.

Virtues associated with *bushidō*

Bushidō is the way of the warrior that defined the samurai class and was refined and formalized during the Tokugawa Era (1600–1867), preceding the Meiji Restoration. These virtues include rectitude, benevolence, courage, respect, honesty, honor, loyalty, filial piety, and wisdom. As an example is the strict Shinsengumi code:

A Shinsengumi could not:

- Deviate from the samurai code

- Desert the Shinsengumi

- Raise money privately

- Get involved in others' legal matters
- Be involved in private fights

Breaking any of these rules required *seppuku*, or ritual suicide.

Questions to consider:

What are significant aspects of this era in manga and anime—how do you recognize its setting?

What questions did you have as you read or watched?

How accurate was what you read or saw to what you know of the period?

Did anything strike you as entirely wrong or anachronistic to the period? Did it bother you?

What were you expected to know as an audience? What would a Japanese audience know? An American audience?

How much could you pick up as you go?

Did you learn anything you didn't know about before?

Japanese Language

Bring in samples of the many "learn Japanese from manga" texts, including *Kanji de Manga* and *Kane de Manga* from Anime University.

What language have you picked up watching anime? Reading manga?

How is it for you to sound out? Does anime and manga help you understand the language?

Have any of you tried learning to read, write, or speak Japanese? How did you start?

What did you think of the language?

Share what you've learned!

What's the easiest way for you to learn: take a class? Listen to an audio language course? Study Japanese textbooks?

Have group members look through the textbooks, learn at least one word, and report it back to the group.

Sense of Humor

What do the Japanese find funny that we don't, and vice versa?

What is up with all the panty jokes? Can you think of something similar that we find funny that other nationalities or cultures don't?

What do you think makes something funny? Is it the thing itself? The reaction to someone or an event? The sense of familiarity and embarrassment —as in "I'm glad that's not happening to me!"?

What kind of jokes have you seen in manga that weren't funny to you? What about those that were?

How about translated jokes? Do you think it's better to preserve the original joke, even if it's not funny to us? Are explanatory notes enough to explain a joke in context? Or would you rather translators picked a similar joke or pun that *is* funny to us?

Shōnen/Shōjo

Can you tell when a manga or anime is a shōnen manga? How about a shōjo manga?

Raise your hands: how many of you read *Shōnen Jump*? *Shōjo Beat*? Both?

Raise your hands: how many of you read shōnen manga? Shōjo manga? Both?

Shōnen and shōjo divisions are about intended audience, but obviously people don't always read along the gender lines. They're also divided according to the Japanese idea of what girls and boys want to read. Do you think that Japanese ideas of these two audiences—guys and girls—are the same as the U.S. ideas of guys' and girls' stories?

Have you ever picked up a manga and started to read it, only to put it down once you realized it was either "too girly" or "too guy" for you? What tipped you off (the cover, the story, the drawing)? When did you stop reading? Why did you stop reading?

Title- or Topic-Specific Discussion Questions

Manga

Death Note by Tsugumi Ohba

- *Death Note* deals with some fairly heavy questions about life, death, power, and responsibility. Let's start with some basic questions to think about:

- Is killing ever OK? Are there situations in which killing another person is justified, as in self-defense? How do you know if it's justified or not? How should someone decide who should die and who should live? Should one person decide this? Should many?

- Who is the good guy in *Death Note*? Who is the bad guy? Why? How would Light answer this question?

- Does Light think he's doing the right thing? If not the right thing, the necessary thing? Does L?

- How does each character justify his actions?

- Who are you rooting for to win in the end? Why?

Anime

Fullmetal Alchemist

- What is the stated goal of the Elric brothers' quest? Are there other goals? Identify as many as you can.

- Do their goals change throughout the story?

- Why did they try to bring their mother back to life, even when they knew it was forbidden to try?

- Do you think their punishment or loss when things went wrong was fair? Why or why not?

- Why did Edward join the military? What does he think of the military? What about other characters: Winrie? Al? Fury?

- How are Ed and Al similar to each other? The same?

- Who are the villains so far? What makes them villains?

- The idea of equivalent exchange is vital to both alchemy and the whole story. To get something, you must be willing to give up something of equal value. What do you think of this idea? What does it mean in alchemy? What does it mean in general? Is this a code to live by?

- What happens when you ignore equivalent exchange?

- How do you judge something's value? Someone's value? Is it possible? How would Ed answer this question? How about Al?

The variety of clubs means that all manner of activities can be included in club meetings. Most manga and anime fans need little encouragement to start talking about their favorite anime and manga. A good moderator, whether an adult or a member of the group, is always a guide, especially in encouraging the less confident members of the group to share their ideas and comments. Ardent fans may get passionate about defending their favorites, and everyone needs to bring both their sense of humor and their willingness to disagree without mockery or mean-spirited comments to the meetings.

A good way to focus discussions can be to limit them by genre. If, for example, you want everyone to read in the science fiction mecha subgenre, give them a list of titles that are considered mecha and have everyone come back and discuss what they read, why they chose the title they did from the list, and whether that genre engaged them. Also remember that book discussions do not necessarily have to happen at the meeting—if a club has the option of creating an online community, whether a listserv, group blog, or wiki (a resource collectively edited by users), for their club, the discussion of manga titles can be ongoing and the meetings devoted to screening anime.

Genre Discussions: Magical Girl Manga

Have everyone in the club read at least one of the following examples of magical girl manga:

Ceres: Celestial Legend

Alice 19th

Cardcaptor Sakura

Princess Tutu

Pretear

Ultra Maniac

- What do you consider magical girl manga? What are the necessary elements of a magical girl story?

- Who do magical girls stories appeal to? Why?

- What did you choose to read? Did you like what you read? Why or why not?

- Do you see any ideas or themes repeating in magical girl stories? What are they?

- Can you think of stories—books, movies, TV—created here in the United States that could be considered magical girl stories? Which titles? Why?

- Why do you think that Japanese creators started this genre? Where does it come from?

- We have superheroes, but the Japanese don't have quite the same tradition. Magical girls are sometimes considered the closest to that tradition. What do you think about that? How are magical girls similar to superheroes? Different?

References

Cha, Ariana Eunjun. "Harry Potter and the Copyright Lawyer: Use of Popular Characters Puts 'Fan Fiction' Writers in Gray Area." *The Washington Post*, Wednesday, 18 June 2003, sec. A, p. 1.

Drazen, Patrick. *Anime Explosion: The What? Why? & Wow! of Japanese Animation*. Berkeley, CA: Stone Bridge Press, 2003.

ICv2. "CMX Bowlderizes Tenjho Tenge Manga." http://www.icv2.com/articles/news/6528.html. March 07, 2005 (accessed September 30, 2006).

Katie Bair's Petting Zoo Wig Design. http://www.katiebair.com/wigs.html (accessed April 28, 1996).

Kodansha International. *Japan: Profile of a Nation,* rev. ed. Tokyo: Kodansha International, 1999.

Lehmann, Timothy. *Manga: Masters of the Art*. Scranton, PA: Collins Design, 2005.

Macias, Patrick, and Tomohiro Machiyama. *Cruising the Anime City: An Otaku Guide to Neo Tokyo*. Berkeley, CA: Stone Bridge Press, 2004.

Chapter Nine

Collection Development

Collection Building

To build a great collection, there are few basic starting steps. Following are the top five things to do when starting a manga collection:

1. Read manga! Read at least three of the following types: shōnen manga, shōjo manga, seinen manga, josei manga, and nonfiction or educational manga. Choose a manga based on the genres you enjoy reading in prose. These are the staples of manga, and to get a feel for what manga is all about, these are a good place to start.

2. Watch anime! It's the same as with manga—it's hard to collect wisely what you haven't watched. Pick a title that seems of interest from the recommend anime list at the end of this chapter. Ask patrons who check out anime what they like, and what they recommend for new anime watchers.

3. Read reviews! Of course, not every librarian has the time to read the piles of manga (or watch the piles of anime) that come out every month. Rely on your colleagues' help in providing helpful and timely reviews. Although professional review sources are great for knowing what you're getting from the library point of view, also try to check in with the industry and fan reviews (listed later in the chapter) to see where the fans are coming from for comparison.

4. Talk to local experts! Whether you just chat with your local comics or manga and anime store manager or take a trip to an anime or manga convention, hearing from the established local experts gives anyone a crash course on manga and anime reading, watching, and fandom. Conventions are not for the faint of heart, but local comics store staff are helpful and knowledgeable. They provide a supportive perspective on their readers and maintaining collections.

5. Elicit your manga fans' help! Once the manga and anime fans know you are willing to listen, they will be a treasure trove of information about what to buy, what to avoid, what the latest trends are, and how to attract fans' attention.

Print Reviews

Japanese manga and anime are now being reviewed in almost all of the professional journals. A few journals devote columns or periodic special sections to graphic novels (including manga) or even specifically to manga, exemplified by Kat Kan's excellent monthly "Graphically Speaking" column in Voice of Youth Advocates. Most currently review manga titles alongside other titles, grouping them with fiction, nonfiction, or graphic novels as their publication requires.

Professional Reviews

Booklist

The Graphic Novel Spotlight special issue is published annually every February.

Graphic novel and manga reviews are interspersed throughout the review section.

The Horn Book

Graphic novel and manga reviews are interspersed throughout the review section.

Library Journal

"Graphic Novel Reviews" is a bimonthly review column by Steve Raiteri and Martha Cornog. At the Library Journal Web site (http://www.libraryjournal.com), they also provide Web-only weekly Graphic Novel Xpress reviews.

Publishers Weekly

Regularly covers manga and anime trends in short feature articles.

Graphic novel and manga reviews are interspersed throughout the review section.

School Library Journal

Graphic novel and manga reviews are interspersed throughout the review section.

Video Librarian

Japanese anime reviews are included in their own section in every bi-monthly issue.

Voice of Youth Advocates

"Graphically Speaking" is a bimonthly review column by Kat Kan.

Graphic novel and manga reviews are interspersed throughout the review section, marked with an oval red "g" symbol indicating the graphic format.

Industry Reviews

Outside of the professional journals, there are a variety of industry magazines and journals that present reviews from the fan point of view.

NewType U.S.A.

This glossy magazine is expensive to collect, but it does provide competent reviews of manga, anime, Japanese pop and rock music, and related video games.

Anime Insider

Linked to superhero central magazine, *Wizard*, *Anime Insider* provides the same tongue-in-cheek feature articles and reviews for manga and anime fans.

Protoculture Addicts

A more in-depth magazine aimed at adult fans, the quarterly *Protoculture Addicts* contains lengthy features and in-depth reviews.

The Comics Journal

The most academic of the comics-related journals out there, the *Comics Journal* is generally more focused on Western comics, but its periodic detailed articles and interviews featuring Japanese manga creators are great for readers seeking an investigative approach to the ins and outs of manga creation and appeal.

ICv2 Guide

A new incarnation of what was once the *ICv2 Retailer's Guide*, these guides come out eleven times a year, alternating their focus on games, graphic novels, and anime/manga. Statistics and features on the market are enhanced by professional author reviews. A useful and concise periodical.

Online Reviews

Anime News Network
http://www.animenewsnetwork.com

Aside from providing an extensive encyclopedia of manga and anime titles, the folks at Anime News Network regularly provide in-depth reviews of the latest manga and anime titles. Particularly of interest in terms of anticipating titles, Anime News Network also provides reviews of fansubbed anime, giving fans a preview of titles likely to be released later on DVD for collections.

Manga4kids
http://manga4kids.com/

A regularly updated Web site devoted to manga reviews with parents in mind, this excellent site features substantial reviews of all manner of titles that will appeal to and are appropriate for younger readers.

No Flying, No Tights
http://www.noflyingnotights.com

My own graphic novel review site, which covers all graphic novels, provides periodic manga reviews. No Flying, No Tights reviews are also cohosted on Teenreads.com in their Manga Reviews section.

Sequential Tart
http://www.sequentialtart.com

A graphic novel review site run entirely by women, this site provides a change in perspective on many of the titles. These reviews are a good resource for age ranges and the more obscure titles that mainstream magazines and reviewers may not touch on. The site is also particularly helpful because more than one person reviews many titles, providing different impressions of the same title.

Teenreads
http://www.teenreads.com. *See* No Flying, No Tights

Online Resources

Aside from reviews, there are numerous online resources that provide further information of interest to collectors of manga and anime.

ICv2
http://www.icv2.com
    This pop culture industry Web site is the place to go for news concerning both the manga and anime industries, especially when you are looking for statistics and market information. The site periodically produces the excellent *Retailers' Guide to Anime and Manga*, an up-to-date look at the state of the industry, the best-selling titles, and the latest trends.

Graphic Novels in Libraries Listserv
http://www.angelfire.com/comics/gnlib/
    This e-mail listserv is the place to be for any librarian working with graphic novels, whether you are just beginning a collection or are trying to decide between the two latest shōnen titles. The list is made up of interested professionals including librarians, teachers, publishers, reviewers, columnists, and library staff. It covers a wide range of topics, from answering the usual "where does X title belong in my library?" to "What's the best shōnen manga?" to "Help! I've got a challenge to defend!" In short, this is the speediest and most informative support network a librarian can hope for in working with graphic novels.

Anime Discussion Community sponsored by YALSA/ALA
http://communitics.ala.org/
    Recently started, the YALSA/ALA Anime Discussion group promises to be a great forum for librarians to exchange ideas, advice, and recommendations on Japanese anime. You must create a username and password to join the community.

AnimeonDVD Comparison Charts
http://www.animeondvd.com/specials/manga/compcharts.php
    A handy reference when you're trying to figure out how many volumes to expect in Japanese manga, Korean manhwa, and Chinese manhua. These charts handily collect together all the basic information about any manga title: how many volumes are in print in the United States, how many volumes are in print in the country of origin, whether the title is currently continuing, and how many volumes are appearing or projected in the U.S. run.

> **Anime News Network Popular Lists**
>
> Top Ten Manga: http://www.animenewsnetwork.com/encyclo-pedia/ratings-manga.php
>
> Top Ten Anime: http://www.animenewsnetwork.com/encyclo-pedia/ratings-anime.php
>
> These lists help anyone keep their finger on the pulse of each media's popularity and offer category lists, including the best, worst, and most popular of each.

Manga Awards

You may have noticed certain manga titles sporting quotes exclaiming that they have won the Kodansha Award in 2003 (as *Antique Bakery* did). Publishers give manga awards in Japan to their own creators—so the Kodansha awards, for example, go to the best titles within that publisher's collection.

Awards

Manga Awards—Japan

Kodansha Award (1960–present)

Awarded annually, only titles published by Kodansha are eligible for the four categories of children's, shōnen, shōjo, and general/adult manga awards.

Past winners include *Sailor Moon* by Takeuchi Naoko, *Great Teacher Onizuka* by Fujisawa Toru, *One Piece* by Oda Eiichiro, *Peach Girl* by Ueda Miwa, *Nodame Cantabile* by Ninomiya Tomoko, and *Antique Bakery* by Yoshinaga Fumi.

Osamu Tezuka Culture Award (1997–present)

Awarded annually, this award recognizes a manga creator who excels in following in the tradition of Tezuka Osamu.

Past winners include Inoue Takehiko for *Vagabond*, Urusawa Naoki for *Monster.*

Shogakukan Award (1955–present)

Awarded annually, only titles published by Shogakukan are eligible for the four categories of children's, shōnen, shōjo, and general/adult manga awards.

Past winners include *Doraemon* by Fujio Fujika, *Patlabor* by Masami Yuki, *Yu Yu Hashuko* by Yoshihiro Togashi, *Hikaru no Go* by Hotta Yumi, *Nana* by Yazawa Ai, and *Fullmetal Alchemist* by Arakawa Hiromu.

Tezuka Award (1971–present)

Awarded semiannually by the publisher Shueisha under the auspices of their weekly Shōnen Jump, this prize recognizes new talent in the manga industry.

Anime Awards—Japan

Manaichi Film Awards

Awarded annually, these awards recognize excellence in animation in Japan, from cell animation to stop-motion animation. The Animation Grand Award recognizes long, large-scale animation pieces, and the Ofuji Noburo Award focuses on shorts.

Tokyo Anime Award

Presented annually at the Tokyo International Anime Fair, these awards are divided into professional and amateur categories. More than 180 industry professionals nominate titles created commercially for Animation of the Year, Notable Animations, and Individual of the Year (a person connected with a particular production). The Open nominations are also judged by professionals and include recognition for the best student films, the best general films, the best company films, and a grand prize for the top of the heap.

Manga Awards—United States

The Eisner Awards

The Eisners are the Oscars of the comics world, and although they predominantly focus on Western-created comics, the award has recognized numerous manga titles over the years with both nominations and awards.

ICv2.com Manga Awards

This industry site's editors define the year's happenings by annually awarding recognition for the following categories: Publisher, New Publisher, Manga Release, Marketing Campaign, Phenomenon, Deal, and Controversy of the Year.

Anime Awards—United States

Academy Awards

Anime films have started to become regular contenders for the Academy Awards Best Animated Feature category. Miyazaki Hayao's *Spirited Away* won the award in 2002.

ICv2.com Anime Awards

This industry site's editors define the year's happenings by annually awarding recognition for the following categories: Company, Product Release, Marketing Campaign, Phenomenon, Deal, and Controversy of the Year.

American Anime Awards

These awards, first given in 2006 at the New York Comic-Con, are designed to honor the best anime as voted by fans. Titles are nominated by industry professionals and companies and must be available during the calendar year. The event is cosponsored by ADV Films' Anime Network and the New York Comic-Con.

Trendspotting: Daily and Weekly Updates

Keeping up with the pop culture trends in manga and anime can be daunting. You can count on your teen fans letting you know their latest favorites, but moving beyond local fans' interests is important to maintaining a diverse collection. A great way to keep up with the latest news in the manga and anime industry is to visit the best blogs and podcasts devoted to keeping the world informed about manga and anime trends. Here are a few of the most consistent and entertaining manga and anime-related blog sites to consider visiting daily.

Manga and Anime Blogs and Podcasts

- Librarian and Industry News:

Irresponsible Pictures

http://irresponsible.patachu.com/

Pata, a regular columnist on Anime News Network, reflects once or twice a week on manga, anime, and Japanese pop culture. Much less of a news site than the others, but the commentary is entertaining and spot-on.

- **Mangablog**

http://www.mangablog.net

Brigid Alverson's site highlights the discussions and news items for any manga fan, acting as a touchstone site connecting all of the other online chatters together.

- **Precocious Curmudgeon**

http://precur.blogspot.com/

David Welsh, a columnist for *Comics News Weekly*, writes with humor and insight on the world of manga, comics, and fandom.

- **Publisher sites**

Tokyopop

http://www.tokyopop.com

Tokyopop's site is an experiment in creating a site that's part fan portal, part publisher site. The fan community aspects are fascinating and already booming: the site, once you register, allows you to post fan fiction, fan art, fan manga, and blog the night away. The publisher side of the site, while still providing the basic book and series information, also presents a wide variety of commentators and columnists discussing everything, including manga trends, cons, and productions.

Now that you've waded your way through everything from the history of both media to the visual cues to watch out for, it's time to read! The following lists are titles any reader can use to become acquainted with manga. They can also be used to start or develop collections, as well as for consulting in starting or running a manga and anime club or other related event.

Treat manga like any other media. If you like memoirs and biography, try Nakazawa Keiji's *Barefoot Gen* or Tezuka Osamu's *Buddha*. If you like historical drama, try Watsuki Nobuhiro's *Rurouni Kenshin* or Higuri You's *Cantarella*. I've drawn these lists from my experiences in reading and discussing manga, watching anime with local teens, as well as my own judgments as a reviewer, so the selections are somewhat subjective and slanted toward recent titles.

Recommended Title Lists

Key to Bibliography Annotations

Total Volumes: Indicates the total number of volumes published in the series in the United States. If the series has been completed in Japan, then this number is indicated in parentheses, to indicate how many final volumes are anticipated. If the series is still being continued in Japan, a plus sign indicates that there are more volumes to come.

Publisher: The U.S. publisher.

ISBN: The International Standard Book Number for each volume.

[T] This symbol indicates that the ISBNs listed indicate the books published in the traditional Japanese format, which reads from right to left.

[F] This symbol indicates that the ISBNs listed indicate the books published "flipped" or in the Western format which reads from left to right.

[K] This symbol indicates that the title listed is a Korean title, and thus read right to left.

Date of Publication

(Japan) The years during which the manga books, or tankoban, were published in Japan.

(U.S.) The years during which the manga titles have been, or are being, published in the U.S. If volumes are continuing to be published, a plus sign indicates more volumes to come.

Genres: Action, Fantasy, Science Fiction, Romance, Romance: BL/Yaoi, Historical, Military, School Drama, Mecha, Magical Girl, Apocalypse, Comedy, Horror, Mystery, Sports, Slice of Life

Publisher Age Rating: The age rating given by the publisher, if provided.

Age Recommendation: Indicates interest level as well as potential content concerns: M (middle, grades 6–8), J (junior, grades 7–9), S (senior, grades 9–12), A (adult).

Related Manga: Any related manga series listed by title.

Related Anime: Any related anime television series, movies, or OVA (original video anime) releases listed by title.

For more reviews, please consult my own Web site, *No Flying, No Tights* (http://www.noflyingnotights.com), which provides manga reviews, updated every other month.

Top Younger Reader Titles

These titles are specifically for younger readers, from older kids to 'tweens to younger teens. Most of these titles will appeal to older readers as well.

Azuma, Kiyohiko. *Yotsuba&!*. ADV Manga, 2003 Japan (2005 U.S.). Volumes 1–4 [T]. Publisher Age Rating: All Ages. Age Recommendation: M. Genres: Comedy, Slice of Life.

    This is the all-ages title that readers have been waiting for. The plot is simple: join Yotsuba in her adventures around the neighborhood, from visiting her neighbors to summer festivals to playing out gangster movie clichés. Knowing, hilarious, and sweet, the clear art and excellent sense of comic timing makes the whole series a treat.

CLAMP. *Cardcaptor Sakura*. Tokyopop Manga, 1996–2000 Japan (2004 U.S.). Publisher Age Rating: All Ages. Age Recommendation: M. Volumes: 1–6 [T]. Genres: Action, Fantasy, Magical Girl. Related Manga: *Cardcaptor Sakura: Master of the Clow*, *Tsubasa: RESERVoir, CHRoNI-CLE* (alternate retelling). Related Anime: *Cardcaptor Sakura* (TV series), *Cardcaptor Sakura* (movie), *Cardcaptor Sakura*: *The Sealed Card* (movie)

    An essential magical girl title. Fourth-grader Sakura is the destined Clow Master and must collect all of the magical Clow cards to master her magic and save the world. On top of that, she has to maneuver through a crush on her brother's best friend. Energetic and full of enough laughs, adventure, and magic to fulfill any schoolgirl's daydreams.

CLAMP. *Tsubasa: RESERVoir CHRoNICLE*. Del Rey Manga, 2003– Japan (2004 U.S.). Publisher Age Rating: 13+. Age Recommendation: M. Volumes: 1–10+ [T]. Genres: Action, Fantasy. Related Manga: *XXXholic* (crossover), *Cardcaptor Sakura* (alternate retelling). Related Anime: *Tsubasa: RESERVoir CHRoNICLE* (TV series), *Tsubasa: The Princess of the Land of the Birdcage* (movie), *XXXholic* (TV series)

    Basically, a fantasy *Quantum Leap* with CLAMP's universe. What do you get if you mix five strangers on a quest to recover a princess's lost memories? The answer is world famous manga creators CLAMP's engaging, inventive fantasy. CLAMP's art and design has only gotten better over the years, refined to almost an art nouveau sensibility. Although there are nods to previous series and in-jokes aplenty, the main story is comprehensible for new readers.

Higuchi, Daisuke. *Whistle!*. VIZ Manga, 1998 Japan (2004 U.S.). Publisher Age Rating: All Ages. Age Recommendation: M. Volumes: 1–12+ of 24+ [T]. Genres: Action, Sports, Slice of Life.

> Mistakenly reputed to be a top player from one of the best high school soccer teams in the country, novice Sho plays along with expectations to get onto the soccer team. All too quickly, he is proved to be the beginner he is, and his teammates' adulation and hope sours, provoking resentment instead. These guys have another thing coming. One of the newer sports manga released in the United States, *Whistle!*'s never-say-die attitude is unflagging, the team is admirable, and the soccer games quick and exciting. This title is especially appealing for readers looking for inspiration, heart, and the spirit of fair competition.

Hiiragi, Aoi. *Baron, the Cat Returns*. VIZ Manga, 2002 Japan (2005 U.S.). Publisher Age Rating: All Ages. Age Recommendation: M. Volumes: 1 [T]. Genre: Fantasy. Related Anime: *The Cat Returns* (movie)

> When Haru saves a cat from being road kill, she didn't expect a marriage proposal, but that's exactly what she gets: from the prince of cats, no less. An utterly charming adventure into the parallel land of cats, this recently released single volume is the basis for the classic Studio Ghibli film. If you've ever wondered just what your cats are thinking and whether they really do have a royal origin, give this a try.

Hikaru no Go by Hotta Yumi.

© 1998 by YUMI HOTTA, TAKESHI OBATA/SHUEISHA, Inc.

Hotta, Yumi. *Hikaru no Go*. VIZ Manga, 1999–2003 Japan (2004 U.S.). Publisher Age Rating: Ages 9–12. Age Recommendation: M. Volumes: 1–9+ [T]. Genres: Action, Historical, Comedy, Slice of Life. Related Anime: *Hikaru no Go* (TV series)

Sixth-grader Hikaru never dreamed of playing the board game Go (if chess is a battle, Go is the war), but being possessed by the spirit of a feudal Go player desperate to make the "divine" move gives him little choice. A traditional, endearing competition manga with sweeping art and enough dramatic suspense to propel any reader, this manga inspired a record number of young people in both Japan and in the United States to rediscover their grandfather's favorite game.

Hung-Lee, Jee. *Demon Diary*. Tokyopop, Unknown—Korea (2003–2004 U.S.). Publisher Age Rating: 13+. Age Recommendation: M. Volumes: 1–7 [K]. Genres: Action, Fantasy, Comedy.

Demon Lord Ranaef has a problem. He's too nice. Expected to take over the reins on evildoing from his predecessor, he can't seem to do anything right. His teacher, Eclipse, alternately scolds and comforts him, but in the end, Ranaef must decide his own fate. This Korean title stands out with flowing art and a wacky sense of humor. Despite the demonic premise, evil goings-on are presented as something to avoid rather than embrace.

Miyazaki, Hayao. *Nausicaä of the Valley of the Wind*. VIZ Manga, 1982–1994 Japan (2004 U.S.). Publisher Age Rating: Teen. Age Recommendation: J. Volumes: 1–7 [T]. Genres: Action, Fantasy, Science Fiction, Military. Related Anime: *Nausicaä of the Valley of the Wind* (movie)

Although most famous in its recently rereleased and restored anime film form, the story of *Nausicaä of the Valley of the Wind* was expanded into this seven-volume manga series over ten years. Both a study of prejudice and a cautionary tale about science and belligerence silencing human empathy and hope, the manga is a masterpiece. With a slower pace and a deeper storyline, the manga may not catch all readers, but the action and message are vivid and heart wrenching.

Tatsuya, Hamazaki. *.hack//Legend of the Twilight*. ADV Manga, 2002–2004 Japan (2003–2004 U.S.). Publisher Age Rating: 13+. Age Recommendation: J. Volumes: 1–3 [T]. Genres: Action, Fantasy, Comedy, Mystery. Related Anime: *.hack//Legend of the Twilight* (TV series), *.hack//SIGN* (TV series)

Two newbies to "The World," the most popular online role-playing game played by billions worldwide, luck out by being given the original character designs and tools of two legendary "World" heroes, the dot Hackers. When a rogue artificial intelligence threatens to disrupt everything in its search for the experience of true death, these two siblings will have to live up to their characters' legends. The *.hack* multimedia series is an impressive example of cross-marketing, but the concentration on identity, loyalty, intelligence, and fair play makes the whole experience worthwhile.

Yugisaki, Yukiru. *D.N.Angel*. Tokyopop, 1997–2004 Japan (2004–2005 U.S.). Publisher Age Rating: 13+. Age Recommendation: J. Volumes: 1–10 of 10 [T]. Genres: Action, Fantasy, Mystery. Related Anime: *D.N.Angel* (TV series)

>Daisuke doesn't just stutter and stammer when he thinks about the girl he likes; instead, he turns into an entirely different person. Literally. Daisuke becomes the current incarnation of Dark, a master art thief, and while his entire family is set on continuing the tradition at all costs, Daisuke just wants to get the girl. This dual-personality tale is, dare I say it, cute at the same time as being full of action and contemplating just what love means. Romance and daring escapes are the order of the day, but tussles and a few kisses are as explicit as it gets.

Top Shōnen Titles

These are the top titles that fall into the general shōnen, or boys manga, category. The gendering of the lists does not mean these titles do not have broad appeal—many are top sellers with all audiences.

Arakawa, Hiromu. *Fullmetal Alchemist*. VIZ Manga, 2002–Japan (2005 U.S.). Publisher Age Rating: Teen. Age Recommendation: S. Volumes: 1–9+ [T]. Genres: Action, Fantasy, Military. Related Anime: *Fullmetal Alchemist* (TV series), *Fullmetal Alchemist: The Conqueror of Shambala* (movie sequel)

>Alchemy starts with a basic principle: equivalent exchange. If you want something, you have to give up something else of equal value. Judging value, of course, is the sticky part of that equation. Edward and Alphonse Elric broke the rules and paid dearly. Now they are trying to find a way to mend what, perhaps, can never be fixed. This tale has its share of serious undertones, from discussions of souls to military corruption, but sibling bickering, snappy action, and a fascinating world make all the elements hang together nicely. The anime adaptation remains one of the most popular in recent years.

Eiji, Nonaka. *Cromartie High School*. ADV Manga, 2001 Japan (2005 U.S.). Publisher Age Rating: 13+. Age Recommendation: S. Volumes: 1–5+ [T]. Genres: School Drama, Comedy. Related Anime: *Cromartie High* (TV series)

When Takashi transfers to Cromartie High, he's more than a bit nervous about landing in a school notorious for a student body made up entirely of bad-ass misfits. Little does he know that these guys are not as cool as they think they are. When your new classmates include a robot (who no one seems to realize is a robot), all kinds of punks and thugs, and an ape, your weirdness threshold increases pretty quickly. *Cromartie High* is a bit of an acquired taste—the rapid-fire and eclectic mix of jokes, visual puns, spoofs of shōnen manga traditions, and ridiculous to farcical situations make the series a bit much to swallow. If it's funny to you, though, it's uproarious, and the whacked-out brand of humor appeals to more teens than you might expect.

Kazuya, Minekura. *Saiyuki*. Tokyopop, 1997–2002 Japan (2004–2005 U.S.). Publisher Age Rating: Older Teen. Age Recommendation: S. Volumes: 1–9 [T]. Genres: Action, Fantasy, Comedy. Related Anime: *Saiyuki* (TV series), *Saiyuki: Requiem* (movie), *Saiyuki Reload* (TV series), *Saiyuki Gunload* (TV series)

A monk, three demons, and a dragon (that can change into a Jeep) walk into a bar.... *Saiyuki* is loosely based on the Chinese epic *Journey to the West*. By loosely, I mean very loosely—the cast may be vaguely familiar, but with all the shooting, drinking, and talking smack—this is not classical literature. The basic plot is familiar: a Buddhist priest, Genjo Sanzo, must quell attacks across the countryside and is sent to India by his superiors to discover the source of the problems. In this version, however, demons pose the threat, Sanzo is more Dirty Harry than a holy man, and his crew of controlled demons make unlikely allies. Colorful language, smoking, bloody action, and general rowdiness make this a series intended for older teens and adults. The banter and honor among thieves message make it more than just a popcorn action piece.

Kishimoto, Masashi. *Naruto*. VIZ Manga, 2000 Japan (2003– U.S.). Publisher Age Rating: Teen. Age Recommendation: S. Volumes: 1–34+ [T]. Genres: Action, Comedy, Fantasy. Related Anime: *Naruto* (TV series), *Naruto* (OVA)

Shunned since childhood, the rambunctious and mischievous Naruto gains attention the only way he can: through pranks. What he doesn't know is that there's a reason everyone is wary of him. An extraordinarily powerful nine-tailed fox threatened his hometown until the creature was magically sealed into a newborn's body—Naruto's. While now all Naruto wants is to succeed as a ninja, the magic inside him will bring a much more complicated destiny. Crammed full of action and comedy, this wildly popular series also zeroes in on the coming of age of Naruto and his fellow ninjas, creating a counterbalance of serious drama.

Bleach by Kubo Tite.
© 2001 by TITE KUBO/SHUEISHA Inc.

Kubo, Tite. *Bleach*. VIZ Manga, 2002 Japan (2004 U.S.). Publisher Age Rating: Teen. Age Recommendation: S. Volumes: 1–13+ [T]. Genres: Action, Fantasy. Related Anime: *Bleach* (TV series)

Ichigo wasn't really looking to become a soul reaper—seeing ghosts was problem enough—but when hollows, or evil spirits, attack his family, he takes on the job to save them. Now he must balance school, family life, and soul reaper duties, all while hiding his supernatural guide and supervisor Rukia in his closet (yes, his closet). A smash hit both in Japan and in the United States, spawning one of the best recent anime series, *Bleach* does an excellent job of alternating between serious and silly subjects. The violence is mostly human–hollow, although it can be violent, and Ichigo's sense of what is honorable and right shines.

Masahiro, Itabashi. *Boys Be...*. Tokyopop, 1992–1997 Japan (2004 U.S.). Publisher Age Rating: 16+. Age Recommendation: S. Volumes: 1–9+ [T]. Genres: Romance, School Drama, Slice of Life. Related Anime: *Boys Be...* (TV series)

Romance is not often portrayed from the guy's point of view, and when it is, it's all about babes, scores, and lots and lots of fan service. *Boys Be...* has a little bit of all these elements, but the interconnected short stories are actually more about heart than jiggle. There are moments that verge on fantasy, although no worse than many shōjo romances, and the tales of nervous, unsure, and, yes, hormone-filled guys finding their girls are true to life. In keeping with the spirit of the series, the flashes of near nudity or panty shots are coy, keeping the emphasis on the emotional content.

Moriyama, Daisuke. *Chrono Crusade*. ADV Manga, 1999–2004 Japan (2004 U.S.). Publisher Age Rating: 13+. Age Recommendation: S. Volumes: 1–8 [T]. Genres: Action, Fantasy, Historical, Comedy. Related Anime: *Chrono Crusade* (TV series)

   Throw all your expectations about nuns, priests, and demons out the window. Sister Rosette may wear a habit, but she also carries a gun specially created to exorcise demons. Her order, the Magdalene, are all specialists fighting the good fight against demons and the forces of evil. Rosette and her companion, a demon called Chrono, are rambunctious, dysfunctional, and destined to play key roles in the battles between Heaven and Hell. Christian imagery mixes freely with more traditional Japanese ideals of balance while the setting of an alternate 1920s New York lends events a familiar but exotic flavor. The shower and panty-shot fan service, along with a lecherous older priest always trying for a glimpse, signal this is a shōnen manga, but these moments are few in an overall dramedy full of faith, affection, and epic struggles.

Nobuhiro, Watsuki. *Rurouni Kenshin*. VIZ Manga, 1994–1999 Japan (2003–2006 U.S.). Publisher Age Rating: Older Teen. Age Recommendation: S. Volumes: 1–28 [T]. Genres: Action, Historical, Comedy. Related Anime: *Rurouni Kenshin* (TV series), *Samurai X: Reflection* (OVA), *Samurai X: The Motion Picture* (OVA), *Samurai X: Trust and Betrayal* (OVA)

   No list would be complete without a samurai story, and *Rurouni Kenshin* remains a lasting favorite. An action-filled period piece set after the Meiji Restoration, the series follows the title character as, having vowed to never kill again, he attempts to shed his dark past as an assassin. Coming to the aid of the mistress of a dōjo and collecting allies, Kenshin is sadly plagued by warriors who, recognizing his past occupation, insist on challenging him. A cheerful and polite man naturally but lethally trained, can Kenshin ever find peace? The Meiji Era (1868–1912) is idealized but full of historical backdrop, and the pacifist message is powerfully presented in comparison to our hero's bloody past. Most, but not all, teens will be fine with the level of violence.

Oda, Eiichiro. *One Piece*. VIZ Manga, 1997–Japan (2003 U.S.). Publisher Age Rating: Teen. Age Recommendation: J. Volumes: 1–11+ [T]. Genres: Action, Fantasy, Comedy. Related Anime: *One Piece* (TV series)

   Pirates! You can't go wrong with pirates. Plus, there is a hero with a rubber body, clowns, legendary treasure, a long lost mentor, and more slapstick than you can shake a stick at. *One Piece* is so silly that it's almost a guilty pleasure. Determined pirate-to-be Luffy is a manic, peculiarly loyal, increasingly stubborn, and amusingly dim-witted hero. More outrageously cartoony in terms of art than many shōnen manga, the trip around the page is quick, easy to follow, and always funny.

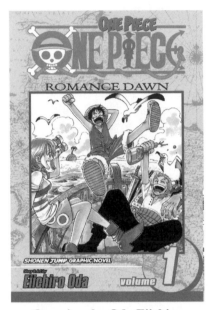

One piece by Oda Eiichiro.
© Takeshi Obata, Tsugumi Ohba SHUEISHA 2004.

Ohba, Tsugumi. *Death Note*. VIZ Manga, 2004– Japan (2005– U.S.). Publisher Age Rating: Older Teen. Age Recommendation: S. Volumes: 1–8+ [T]. Genres: Action, Fantasy, Horror, Mystery Related to Film: *Death Note* (live action movie)

A dark venture into questions of responsibility, passing judgment, and power's insidious ability to corrupt, *Death Note* is a title that both teens and colleagues insisted I read. Light, a teen boy from an upstanding family, discovers an abandoned *Death Note*, a book used by the legendary shinigami (soul reapers) to mete out death. Filled with righteous inspiration, Light starts to use the Death Note to wipe out all criminals and force a better world. As convicted criminals start dropping like flies, the mysterious and xenophobic investigator known only as "L" is brought in to stop the killing. A cunning game of cat and mouse begins—but who is the cat and who is the mouse? Not for the faint of heart, but remarkably free of gore, *Death Note* is entirely about the horror in the idea. These dark questions make it most appropriate for mature teens and adults.

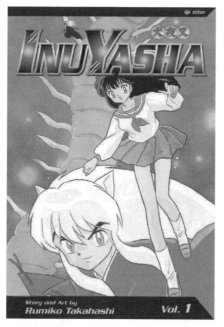

Inuyasha by **Takahashi Rumiko.**
© Rumiko Takahashi SHOGAKUKAN 1997.

Takahashi, Rumiko. *Inuyasha: A Feudal Fairy Tale.* VIZ Media, 1996– Japan (2003 U.S.). Publisher Age Rating: 16+. Age Recommendation: S. Volumes: 1–26+ [F] 2nd ed. Genres: Action, Fantasy, Romance, Historical, Magical Girl. Related Anime: *Inuyasha* (TV series), *Inuyasha The Movie: Affections Touching across Time* (movie), *Inuyasha: The Castle beyond the Looking Glass* (movie), *Inuyasha: Swords of an Honorable Ruler* (movie), *Inuyasha: Fire on the Mystic Island* (movie)

Kagome is your typical schoolgirl until she falls down a well at her family's shrine only to arrive in the past—the feudal era to be exact. After a hair-raising escape from a centipede demon, she discovers she's the reincarnation of a heroic priestess and must now take up her past quest anew. The shattered pieces of the Shikon jewel must not be allowed to fall into enemy hands, and with half-dog-demon Inuyasha as her reluctant companion, she agrees to the quest. One of the longest running and wildly popular series in both manga and anime, this magical schoolgirl adventure rises above the rest with snappy humor, complex character-driven plotlines, and the unfailing sense of escape into another world that the best fantasy novels evoke.

Takahashi, Rumiko. *Ranma 1/2.* VIZ Manga, 1987–1996 Japan (2003 U.S.). Publisher Age Rating: Older Teen. Age Recommendation: S. Volumes: 1–34+ [T]. Genres: Action, Fantasy, Comedy. Related Anime: *Ranma 1/2*

(TV series), *Ranma 1/2* (OVA), *Ranma 1/2: Big Trouble in Nekonron, China* (movie sequel), *Ranma 1/2: Nihao My Concubine* (movie sequel), *Ranma 1/2: One Flew Over the Kuno's Nest* (movie sequel)

    Ranma 1/2 has rightly come to represent the comic and romantic genius of Takahashi Rumiko and is beloved worldwide. The setup is classic manga: after falling in a cursed spring during martial arts training, Ranma is cursed so that if he is hit with cold water, he becomes a girl. Hot water reverses the effect. His arranged fiancée is not so sure about the whole thing. This premise is ripe for all kinds of comic shenanigans, and Takahashi is an expert at showing them all with heart. This series is popular with teens, although the nudity, an easy visual reminder of Ranma's current gender, may keep it from collections aimed at younger audiences.

Yasuhiro, Nightow. *Trigun* and *Trigun Maximum*. Dark Horse/Digital Manga, 1997–2004 Japan (2003 U.S.). Publisher Age Rating: 13+. Age Recommendation: S. Volumes: 1–12+ [T]. Genres: Action, Science Fiction, Comedy. Related Anime: *Trigun* (TV series)

    Vash the Stampede has a 60 billion double dollar bounty on his head. Reputed to be a fast draw, he is also the most pursued man on the planet. Wherever he goes, bounty hunters and a pair of cheeky insurance agents follow, inevitably bringing destruction (but miraculously no death) in their wake. Vash is also a gentle, pacifist, donut-loving goof. Or is he? This beloved manga and anime science fiction western speeds through action, jokes, and plot with expert aplomb, keeping all the different balls in the air to create an entertaining and memorable ride. A teen favorite in both media, the violence is restricted to pursuit fallout.

Yozaburo, Kanari. *Kindaichi Case Files, The*. Tokyopop, 1993–1997 Japan (2003 U.S.). Publisher Age Rating: 13+. Age Recommendation: S. Volumes: 1–11+ [T]. Genres: Horror, Mystery

    Kindaichi has always been a bit of a slacker, but whether he wanted to or not, he's inherited his legendary grandfather's detecting skills. Like any investigator of note, crimes and murders crop up wherever her goes. Kindaichi handles each case with humor and intelligence, and the character development throughout the series brings a solid emotional core to the surface investigations providing plot. Akin to Agatha Christie mysteries with a teen protagonist, these case files will appeal to mystery fans keen for a new format as well as provide a break from manga's more traditional genres. The crimes do get a bit gruesome, but the art errs on the side of necessary rather than gratuitous.

Yukimura, Makoto. *Planetes*. Tokyopop, 2001–2004 Japan (2003–2005 U.S.). Publisher Age Rating: 13+. Age Recommendation: S. Volumes: 1–4 [T]. Genres: Action, Science Fiction, Slice of Life. Related Anime: *Planetes* (TV series)

When most stories focus on space, they highlight the exploration, the final frontier, and the derring-do of those who venture into the unknown. In *Planetes* our heroes are space garbage collectors. Not a glamorous job, but necessary in a near future that is clogged with the remnants of old spaceflights spinning in our orbit. The trio at the center of the stories are admirable and definitely human rather than space-walking heroes. Space itself often takes center stage, creating a quiet wonder and awe that imbues the whole series. The anime is equally powerful, and both recall with fondness the potential for achievement witnessed at the beginnings of the space program. The measured pace makes this series most appealing for older teens, but younger teens ready to be absorbed in a rich story will be rewarded.

Top Shōjo Titles

As with the shōnen titles, many of these titles cross over into broader audience categories. I met one young man at a workshop who was desperate to read *Gals!*

W *Juliet* by Emura.
© Emura (1997)/HUKESEHSHA, Inc.

Emura. *W Juliet*. VIZ Media, 1999–2003 Japan (2004 U.S.). Publisher Age Rating: Teen. Age Recommendation: S. Volumes: 1–11+ [T]. Genres: Romance, School Drama.

You have to include at least one gender-bender when discussing shōjo manga, and *W Juliet* is one of the most endearing. The gender bending isn't all for gags. Tomboy Miura and beauty Makoto are destined to be lovers—on stage, that is, in the all girls' high school performance of *Romeo and Juliet*. Miura, admired for her boyish cuteness, reluctantly takes on the role of Romeo while fetching and talented transfer student, Makoto, jumps at Juliet. Then Miura discovers Makoto's secret—she's a he in disguise (and for good reason). In some ways, the reasons don't matter—the most important thing is whether the couple will keep undercover through scheming rivals and nosy school reporters. You can bet they fall in love in the process.

Hayakawa, Tomoko. *The Wallflower*. Del Rey Manga, 2000 Japan (2004 U.S.). Publisher Age Rating: Older Teen. Age Recommendation: S. Volumes: 1–7+ [T]. Genres: Comedy, Romance, Slice of Life. Related Anime: *The Wallflower* (TV series)

Sunako couldn't care less whether she's pretty, girly, or likeable. She has her horror movies, her rubber duckies, and her own company. When four drop-dead gorgeous young men trade the task of turning Sunako into a "lady" for free rent to a fantastic house, they have no idea what they're up against. Then again, Sunako shouldn't underestimate these lovely four either. Hayakawa uses her hilariously unkempt and kick-butt heroine, stubborn bishōnen, and sly sense of humor to tackle questions about physical perfection and self-esteem with witty flair.

Only the Ring Finger Knows by **Kannagi Satoru.**
© 2002 by Satoru Kannagi & Hotaru Odagiri.

Kannagi, Satoru. *Only the Ring Finger Knows*. Digital Manga, 2002 Japan (2004 U.S.). Publisher Age Rating: 16+. Age Recommendation: J. Volumes: 1 [T]. Genres: Romance: BL/Yaoi, School Drama. Related Manga:

The Lonely Ring Finger (novel sequel), *The Ring Finger Falls Silent* (novel sequel)

Wataru Fujii, a relatively ordinary junior, passes the time tracking the new trend of students using rings as cues: couples wear matched rings on their left ring finger, singles wear rings on their right middle finger. Wataru couldn't much care either way until, when he runs into admired senior Kazuki, the two boys discover they wear matching rings. Both are shocked, and defensive spats ensue. Of course, everyone knows they're so prickly because of attraction, not repulsion. These characters act like teenagers, full of awkwardness and confused by their own hormones. Some steamy sexual tension and a few good kisses are all you get, but it's just the right amount for the story. This title, based on a prose novel, is one of the best to introduce the romantic subgenre of shōnen-ai/yaoi.

Mihona, Fuji. *GALS!*. CMX/DC Comics, 1998–2002 Japan (2005 U.S.). Publisher Age Rating: Teen. Age Recommendation: S. Volumes: 1–6+ [T]. Genres: School Drama, Comedy, Slice of Life. Related Anime: *Super GALS* (TV series)

Kogal Ran may win out as the shōjo heroine with the cutest clothes and the biggest eyes, but she also has the gumption to keep troublemakers in the famous (and infamous) Mecca of shopping, Shibuya, at bay. With a smart mouth, a willing fist, and a fair heart, Ran takes it upon herself to protect the meek, the clueless, and the fashion challenged. Surrounded by loyal girlfriends and battling the negative kogal image, Ran still wouldn't be caught dead aspiring to her family's profession—cops—or so she keeps insisting. A good talking to and a sassy tussle win the day in *GALS* every time, even when tackling teen prostitution, stealing, or bitter rivals.

Here Is Greenwood by Nasu Yukie.
© Yukie Nasu 1986/HAKUSENSHA, Inc.

Nasu, Yukie. *Here Is Greenwood*. VIZ Media, 1987–1991 Japan (2004 U.S.).
Publisher Age Rating: Older Teen. Age Recommendation: S. Volumes:
1–9+ [T]. Genres: School Drama, Comedy, Slice of Life. Related Anime:
Here Is Greenwood (OVA)

Hasukawa Hazuya has a big crush ... on his brother's new wife. To
escape the painful home situation, he enrolls in a new high school only to
land in the oddest dorm in the place, Greenwood. The guys in Greenwood
are all likeable, they're all just a bit off, from scheming dorm presidents to
a guy who looks and acts more like a girl to the guy who lives with his motorcycle. This representative of the school comedy genre is often over the
top but manages to reign in the uproar to bring everything back to school
spirit, friendship, and making a family out of those life sends you.

Soryo, Fuyumi. *Mars*. Tokyopop, 1996–2000 Japan (2002–2003 U.S.). Pub-
lisher Age Rating: 13+. Age Recommendation: S. Volumes: 1–15 [T].
Genres: Romance, School Drama. Related Manga: *Mars: A Horse with No
Name* (prequel)

Anyone who loves teen romance will be glued to this tale of a reckless "bad boy" and the shy, talented teen girl who attracts his attention.
Motorcycle racer Rei's rebellious attitude and good looks make him a girl
magnet. Kira is a gifted young artist, but her fear and awkwardness make
her a target for bullies. After seeing Kira's beautiful, Klimt-inspired draw-
ings, Rei offers himself as a model—and a protector. This manga romance

literally has it all: romance, motorcycle races, bullying, haunted pasts, child abuse, friendly transvestites, murder, sociopaths, and more romance. The soap opera appeal is undeniable. In terms of content, there is a sex scene, but it's not any more explicit than many young adult novels; it is only ten pages in the three-thousand-page epic, and it's all about feelings, not titillation.

Takaya, Natsuki. *Fruits Basket*. Tokyopop, 1999–Japan (2004 U.S.). Publisher Age Rating: 13+. Age Recommendation: J. Volumes: 1–15 [T]. Genres: Fantasy, Romance, School Drama, Slice of Life. Related Anime: *Fruits Basket* (TV series)

As curses go, the Sohma family has one of the most inconvenient. The entire clan, when hugged by a member of the opposite sex will turn into specific creatures from the Chinese Zodiac. When teen Tohru ends up working as a housekeeper for dreamy Yuki (a rat), fireball Kyo (a cat), and mild Shigure (a dog), she didn't count on ending up part of a modern legend. Irrepressibly sweet and humorous, the focus in *Fruits Basket* is on family and finding out how to fit into the world. Both the manga and anime top the popularity charts for both genders (my anime club teens would watch only *Fruits Basket* if I let them), and in this case popularity and quality are both key to the series' appeal.

Tsuda, Masami. *Kare Kano: His and Her Circumstances*. Tokyopop, 1996–2005 Japan (2003 U.S.). Publisher Age Rating: Teen. Age Recommendation: S. Volumes: 1–19+ [T]. Genres: Romance, School Drama, Comedy, Slice of Life. Related Anime: *Kare Kano* (TV series)

Yukino loves attention way more than most girls. In fact, she can't feel right without it—she's the smartest student, the most beloved, and of course the most modest, At least on the outside. Her family knows her better as the slovenly praise-obsessed schemer that plots how to get the most attention at any one instant. Then Souchiro Arima shows up, her unwitting rival in school. What's a girl to do but pull out all the stops—except, what if she's starts to like Arima? Even love him? A favorite for good reason, *Kare Kano* proudly contains all the trademark silliness and relationship-driven drama of shōjo school comedies. No magic, no destiny, just human foibles and the links forged between people.

Ueda, Miwa. *Peach Girl*. Tokyopop, 1998–2004 Japan (2004–2006 U.S.). Publisher Age Rating: Teen. Age Recommendation: S. Volumes: 1–8 [T]. Genres: Romance, School Drama, Slice of Life. Related Manga: *Peach Girl: Change of Heart* (sequel). Related Anime: *Peach Girl* (TV series)

Momo is terribly aware of how she looks: blond hair and a tan she cannot get rid of in a world where dark hair and pale skin is the ideal. Her peers tease her for either being a beach bunny or a slut, although she is most certainly neither. Her "friend" Sae, actually her backstabbing rival, sports dark tresses and a pale complexion. Will Momo get the object of her affection, the quiet Toji, despite her perceived flaws, or will Sae win the day? Add in the class dreamboat, Kiley, making eyes at Momo, and you have a recipe for humor and heartache in all the right doses. The story packs in lots of drama as well—including all sorts of heartrending betrayals, threats of violence, and tearful confessions. This series doesn't feature any in-panel sex, but there are a few scenes of foreplay, and issues such as date rape are addressed.

***Ceres: Celestial Legend* by Watase Yu.**
© 1997 Yuu WATASE/Shogakukan Inc.

Watase, Yu. *Ceres: Celestial Legend.* VIZ Media, 1996–2000 Japan (2003–2006 U.S.). Publisher Age Rating: Older Teen. Age Recommendation: S, A. Volumes: 1–14 [T]. Genres: Action, Fantasy, Romance, Magical Girl. Related Anime: *Ceres: Celestial Legend* (TV series)

Aya used to be your regular teen girl singing karaoke, but when her family's dark genetic secret gets activated on her sixteenth birthday, Aya is due for a terrible shock. Now her family's trying to kill her, except for her twin brother, Aki, who has his own bitter part to play. A grim and powerful take on the magical girl tradition, *Ceres* confronts misogyny, genetic engineering, incest, and mixes it all together in the framework of the Japanese legend of the tennyo, or Celestial maidens. This series can be brutal both in fighting and in sexual threat, all stronger content than Watase Yu's usual fare. In the end, the melodrama, love story, and strong feminist bent make it appealing and worthwhile for older teens.

Yazawa, Ai. *Paradise Kiss*. Tokyopop, 2000–2003 Japan (2002–2004 U.S.). Publisher Age Rating: Older Teen. Age Recommendation: S. Volumes: 1–5 [T]. Genres: Romance, School Drama, Slice of Life. Related Anime: *Paradise Kiss* (TV series)

No matter how hard she tries, Yukari knows she will never get into the high school of her mother's dreams. She tries to propel herself forward through sheer determination, putting her own wishes on hold, until a group of misfits literally sweeps her off her feet. Fashion designers from an arts high school, pretty-boy George and his crew decide Yukari is the perfect model for their senior fashion show, but can Yukari balance school with her new escape from the mundane? Should she even try? This relatively short series packs a powerful punch. Yazawa Ai is renowned for giving shōjo conventions a shot of realism, pulling no punches about heartache, sex, and the manipulative side of love. Her very honesty is what makes this series so refreshing—although far from ideal, her characters feel very alive and accurate. Given her subject, a bit of sexual content and the pressures highlighted in the tale will suit older teens best.

Latest Promising Series

These newer series titles have just arrived in the United States, but each promises compelling reading. Teen readers have already given their stamp of approval to most, both in circulation and in discussions with me personally, while the others are quality titles waiting to find their audience. These are all slanted toward the female audience and should balance out the following list of primarily shōnen and seinen manga.

Higuri, You. *Cantarella*. GoComi! Manga, 2001–2004 Japan (2005 U.S.). Publisher Age Rating: Older Teen. Age Recommendation: S. Volumes: 1–4+ [T]. Genres: Action, Fantasy, Historical, Horror.

Power, politics, wealth and family legacy have always been an explosive mix. Fifteenth-century Italy is a time famous for a brutal and devious set of players. Cesare and Lucrezia Borgia are figures of legend—Lucrezia is a slim girl with a devious, lethal sweetness, and Cesare is her cunning, loving (perhaps too loving) older brother who is shadowed everywhere by a swordsman and a poisoner. History, though, is always written by the conquerors—what if the Borgias were not what they were reputed to be? *Cantarella*, with rich fluid art, creatively embellishes history and brings to life this complicated and treacherous world. The content is so far not so much explicit as sophisticated.

Marley. *Dokebi Bride*. Netcomics, 2005 Korea (2006 U.S.). Publisher Age Rating: 13+. Age Recommendation: S. Volumes: 2+ [K]. Genres: Fantasy, Mystery

Sunbi is born into a family of shamans. Shamans keep the balance between the human and supernatural world, so Sunbi grows up watching her grandmother negotiate with all manner of spirits. As she approaches teenhood, she discovers her spiritual heritage is both a blessing and a curse—her mother is rumored to have gone mad and killed herself, while her grandmother dealt calmly with her magical duties. When her grandmother dies, Sunbi is wrenched from her idyllic country life to live with her distant father and her new stepfamily. Balancing the spirits in a world where no one believes her will be hard, but hiding her talents and accommodating her new family will be almost impossible. This charming new manhwa is rich with Korean mythology, drawing its stories from traditional shaman practice and folklore. The art is compelling, and the story thus far is beautifully human amid all of the supernatural moments.

Mistuba, Takanashi. *Crimson Hero*. VIZ Media, 2003 Japan (2005 U.S.). Publisher Age Rating: Teen. Age Recommendation: S. Volumes: 1–3+ [T]. Genres: School Drama, Sports, Slice of Life

Nobara is anything but the demure doll her mother wants to inherit her hotel. Nobara wants nothing more than to play volleyball, and when she gets into the high school with the best volleyball team, she's elated. Then the school discontinues the girls' team. Thrown out of her house for pursuing her dream, Nobara must find a place to live, money to eat, and a way to revive a team her classmates gave up on. Nobara is a strong role model who will not give up her dreams despite obstacles but who is not untouchable. She just won't let her doubts stop her.

Mizushiro, Setona. *After School Nightmare*. Go Comi, 2000– Japan (2006– U.S.). Publisher Age Rating: Older Teen. Age Recommendation: S. Volumes: 1–6+ [T]. Genres: Fantasy, Horror, Romance, School Drama

Mashiro Ichijo is hiding a secret: he is, in fact, not really a he or a she. Male on top and female on the bottom, he's spent his whole life passing as male and can see no advantage to admitting his female side. When he's informed he has to attend a special class to graduate, a class in which students compete in a communal dreamscape to get a magical key, at first it all seems like some sort of elaborate test. In the dreamscape, however, everyone's darkest secrets are revealed, and no mater what Ichijo does, it's only a matter of time before his fellow dreamers use his secret against him. Mizushiro's breathtaking art and critique of gender roles combine to create an engaging and unsettling title not to be missed.

Mori, Kaoru. *Emma*. CMX, 2002–2006 Japan (2006 U.S.). Publisher Age Rating: Teen+. Age Recommendation: S. Volumes: 1–4+ [T]. Genres: Historical, Romance, Slice of Life.

When William, a member of the upper crust in Victorian London, prepares to visit his strict former nanny at her home, things don't start out well. He gets bashed in the nose by the door before he gets a chance to knock. Then he looks up and sees Emma, a housemaid. From this one moment, Mori builds a meticulously researched and drawn Victorian romance to rival the classics. Emma and William court timidly and sweetly, but the reality of society's disapproval is palpable on every page. Can they truly break free and find happiness, no matter what they both must sacrifice? A simple art style, beautifully expressive, amplifies the quiet emotion and measured pace of the drama, creating a delicious tension.

Ninomiya, Tomoko. *Nodame Cantabile*. Del Rey Manga, 2002–2005 Japan (2005 U.S.). Publisher Age Rating: 16+. Age Recommendation: S, A. Volumes: 1–7+ [T]. Genres: School Drama, Comedy, Slice of Life, Music

Music is a tough thing to write about, but when it's done right, readers crave an included soundtrack so that they can hear the characters' performances. College student Shoichi is determined to be a conductor, but his arrogant, unforgiving attitude hasn't won him any friends. His neighbor Nodame is a complete slob but plays the most alluring if totally unschooled piano pieces. What happens when these two meet both personally and musically is anyone's guess, but you know the music will be something you wish you could hear. Ninomiya's artwork is looser and less articulated than many manga, and the free style suits the story well.

Shin, Ji-Sang. *Chocolat*. Ice Kunion, 2002– Korea (2003 U.S.). Publisher Age Rating: Teen. Age Recommendation: J. Volumes: 1–7+ [K]. Genres: Romance, School Drama, Comedy

Kum-ji is dead set on getting close to her favorite boy band, DDL. Desperate to find a way into the pop idol world, she decides to be sneaky: she joins the fan club of DDL's biggest rivals in the pop scene, Yo-I. Suddenly, she's managed to attract the attention of E-Soh, the pretty but bratty member of Yo-I, as well as make contact with DDL's dreamy lead singer, Jin-Ryu. In the fangirl world, pretending to love one band just to get to another is an unforgivable scheme—and Kum-ji's secret is about to come out.

Toyoda, Minoru. *Love Roma*. Del Rey Manga, 2003 Japan (2005 U.S.). Publisher Age Rating: Teen. Age Recommendation: S. Volumes: 1–4 [T]. Genres: Romance, School Drama, Comedy

Every once in a while, you want a story that's ordinary, no flying princesses, no dashing knights (or demons), and no chirping sidekick. When the blunt, honest, and slightly awkward Hoshino confesses his love for Negishi, she reacts the way any girl who's never been asked out before would: stuttering, flattered, and not quite sure whether this guy is really the guy she wants to try out this whole dating thing with. *Love Roma*'s art is intentionally simple and clear, almost childlike, but the content is amusingly, affectionately teen.

NANA by Yazawa Ai.
© 1999 by Yazawa Manga Seisakusho/SHUEISHA, Inc.

Yazawa, Ai. *NANA*. VIZ Media, 2000 Japan (2005 U.S.). Publisher Age Rating: Older Teen. Age Recommendation: S, A. Volumes: 1–3+ [T]. Genres: Romance, Slice of Life. Related Anime: *NANA* (TV series), *NANA* (live action film)

Two girls named Nana meet on a train heading to Tokyo—one nursing a broken heart and aiming to make it as a punk rock musician while the other is rejoining her boyfriend and embraces life in the big city. A realistic romantic drama, Nana concentrates on how love, sisterhood, and serendipity can make lasting impact on a life. Yazawa Ai's artwork is immediately recognizable with its slender figures and dramatic style, and as one of the most popular titles in Japan, it's already a hit through serialization in *Shōo Beat*.

Yoshinaga, Fumi. *Antique Bakery*. Digital Manga, 2000–2002 Japan (2005–2006 U.S.). Publisher Age Rating: 16+. Age Recommendation: S, A. Volumes: 1–4 [T]. Genres: Comedy, Slice of Life

With a priceless antique tea cup in hand, at the *Antique Bakery* you can enjoy world-class pastries (described in mouth-watering detail). You may also get a glimpse of the eclectic staff: a scruffy but savvy owner, a boxer turned sous-chef, a bumbling bodyguard maitre d', and a "demonically charming" gay master pastry chef. The key to this series is the humorous and dramatic escapades of both the staff and the customers all drawn with expressive, elegant lines. Although the series starts off light, the last two volumes move into dramatic territory.

Top Classics

Given that the comic market was originally aimed at adult men, you'll note that many of the classic titles are shōnen or seinen manga and most are more adult than the previous lists. This should be balanced by the previous list, slanted toward female readers, but all of these are classics in the medium. These tales continue to be popular and have wide appeal for manga fans interested in the progression of the format.

CLAMP. *X/1999*. VIZ Media, 1992–2002 Japan. (2002–2005 U.S. 2nd ed.). Publisher Age Rating: Older Teen. Age Recommendation: S, A. Volumes: 1–18 [F]. Genres: Action, Fantasy, Apocalypse. Related Manga: *Tokyo Babylon, Tsubasa: RESERVoir CHRoNICLE*. Related Anime: *X* (TV series), *X* (movie), *Tokyo Babylon* (OVA)

    Apocalyptic battle over the planet, check. Superpowered, intimately connected teenagers, check. Intricate plots and elaborate betrayals, check. Pretty boys, check. *X/1999* is the ultimate epic battle shōjo manga masquerading as a shōnen action series. What makes it more shōjo is that despite the great responsibility of all the players to either save or doom the planet, the motivations for all characters are intensely personal, approaching selfish, and their relationships drive the vast battleground rather than any grander concerns. *X/1999*'s art cements CLAMP's early reputation for striking character design and a dramatic sense of layout—the pages are dripping with flower petals, blood, and melodrama. The violence is what pushes this to being best for older teens and adults.

Junji, Ito. *Uzumaki*. VIZ Media, 1998 Japan (2001–2002 U.S.). Publisher Age Rating: Adult. Age Recommendation: S, A. Volumes: 1–3 [F]. Genres: Fantasy, Horror, Mystery. Related Anime: *Uzumaki* (live action movie)

    Most hauntings are by spirits or ghouls, but a shape possesses the rural Japanese town of Kurozu-cho: the spiral. As townspeople start succumbing to bewitching images and are contorted into snail-shell shapes, high school girl Kirie tries desperately to stop the advance of the madness. The suspense, wreckage, and eventual numbness experienced by the townsfolk are not easy to stomach, but Ito is a master of horror who knows how to manipulate and enthrall his audience.

Kasuhiro, Otomo. *Akira*. Dark Horse/Digital Manga, 1982–1990 Japan (2000–2002 U.S.). Publisher Age Rating: 14+. Age Recommendation: S, A. Volumes: 1–6 [F]. Genres: Action, Science Fiction, Apocalypse. Related Anime: *Akira* (movie)

Kaneda and Tetsuo are best friends trying to survive in a post-apocalyptic neo-Tokyo in 2030. Members of a biker gang, the two are pulled into a situation involving secret scientific experiments, extraordinary psychic powers, a conniving government, and a military losing its ability to maintain order. At the center of it all is Akira, a psychic so powerful, he's been kept in stasis for more than thirty years; but he will soon awaken. Vast in scale and melodrama but personal in its focus, *Akira* is an undisputed classic. The violence keeps the series aimed at adult audiences, but the cyberpunk vision is both jarring and beguiling decades after it was first released.

Kazuo, Koike. *Lone Wolf and Cub*. Dark Horse/Digital Manga, 1970–1976 Japan (2000–2002 U.S.). Publisher Age Rating: Mature. Age Recommendation: A. Volumes: 1–28 [F]. Genres: Action, Historical, Military

A disgraced samurai, or rōnin, and his three-year-old son travel the countryside trying to survive. Once a high-ranking executioner of the Tokugawa court, Ogami Otti was politically disgraced, his wife murdered, and forced to take up the trade of an assassin. Emotions simmer throughout the whole story, but within the story of Ogami's bitter revenge for his dishonor is a fragile, fleeting portrait of a man and his young son finding peace where they can. Goseki Kojima's fluid and expressive art perfectly complements the tender and the harsh scenes.

Nakazawa, Keiji. *Barefoot Gen*. Last Gasp Publishing, 1973–1974 Japan (2004 U.S.). Publisher Age Rating: None. Age Recommendation: S. Volumes: 1–4+ [T]. Genres: Historical, Slice of Life. Related Anime: *Barefoot Gen* (movie)

A landmark series that has recently been reprinted in excellent new editions, *Barefoot Gen* is a partially autobiographical tale of a young teen boy, his mother, and his little sister experiencing and surviving the atomic bombing of Hiroshima. The style may appear dated to readers used to today's titles, but the eloquence and horror contained in Nakazawa's images never lose their emotional impact.

Shirow, Masamune. *Ghost in the Shell*. Dark Horse/Digital Manga, 1991 Japan (2004 U.S.). Publisher Age Rating: Mature. Age Recommendation: A. Volumes: 1 [T] 2nd ed. Genres: Action, Science Fiction, Mecha, Military. Related Manga: *Ghost in the Shell 2: Man-Machine Interface* (sequel),

Ghost in the Shell: Stand Alone Complex. Related Anime: *Ghost in the Shell* (movie), *Ghost in the Shell 2: Innocence* (movie), *Ghost in the Shell: Stand Alone Complex* (TV series)

In a future where bodies are artificial and only your soul, or your "ghost" defines your humanity, how do you know what is human and what is not? What happens when you can hack into people—especially now that people, machines, and networks are merging into one and the same thing? This landmark manga follows Section 9, the secret military security force designated to deal with cyber crimes and espionage. The second edition restores previously cut material, including a graphic sex scene that makes this a strictly adult content title. However, the true boundary pushing is in the complex political and technological landscape, beautifully rendered, and the gruff camaraderie of the agents who try to tame the virtual whirlwind. The films and TV series are smash hits, so many teens seek out the original inspiration.

Takahashi, Rumiko. *Maison Ikkoku.* VIZ Media, 1980–1987 Japan (2003–2006 U.S. 2nd ed.). Publisher Age Rating: Older Teen. Age Recommendation: S, A. Volumes: 1–15 [T] 2nd ed. Genres: Comedy, Slice of Life, Romance. Related Anime: *Maison Ikkoku* (TV series)

Godai has never been particularly lucky—he's failed the college entrance exams three times, and he's living in a ramshackle apartment building with a pack of interfering neighbors who drink, talk, and give advice freely (especially when it's not wanted). Now he's falling for his cute new landlady—but although she seems equally smitten, she's a recent widow trying to come to terms with her loss. A classic romantic comedy for older teens and adults, much of the comedy hinges on the pair's inability to express themselves, their drunken escapades, and their well-meaning but bizarre neighbors.

Takemiya, Keiko. *To Terra.* Vertical, 1977–1980 Japan (2007– U.S.). Publisher Age Rating: None. Age Recommendation: S. Volumes: 1–4 [T]. Genre: Science Fiction

Considered part of the famous female manga creator group the Fabulous Forty-Niners, Takemiya took shōjo manga to a new territory with her epic, *To Terra.* In the distant future, Earth has been made all but uninhabitable because of humanity's pollution and abuse. Mankind, in an effort to salvage the destroyed planet, has created a regimented society. All people are programmed as soon as they hit puberty to follow the orders of the government. They work all their lives to restore Earth, ensuring future generations will one day get to go home. There are renegades, however—the powerful telepaths known as Mu, a new evolution of true humanity. Young Jomy, caught between both sides, must choose between what he has always believed and what his newfound psychic abilities are telling him.

Cover of *Maison Ikkoku*.
© Rumiko Takahashi SHOGAKUKAN 1982.

Tezuka, Osamu. *Buddha*. Vertical, 1972–1983 Japan (2003–2005 U.S.). Publisher Age Rating: None. Age Recommendation: S, A. Volumes: 1–8 [T] . Genres: Historical, Slice of Life

An ambitious and ultimately breathtaking work, Tekuza's biography of Buddha pulls all of his trademark mastery of the manga format into one epic work. Tezuka's style seems especially cartoony to today's manga fans, with comical caricatures in side characters and wide-eyed heroes, but once readers get past their initial reaction, they'll discover the eloquence of Tezuka's work. The Vertical editions are expertly produced and give this work its due. Given the setting and people of the work, there is incidental nudity, but sparse detail.

Tohru, Fujisawa. *GTO: Great Teacher Onizuka*. Tokyopop, 1997–2002 Japan (2002–2005 U.S.). Publisher Age Rating: Older Teen. Age Recommendation: S, A. Volumes: 1–25 [T]. Genres: School Drama, Comedy, Slice of Life. Related Anime: *Great Teacher Onizuka* (TV series)

Onizuka Eikichi is a sexually frustrated virgin ex-biker determined to land a job that gets him a chance at cute girls. His bad boy posturing covers the fact that he is, at heart, a good guy, and although his tactics may appall parents and administrators, his students love him. He even manages to teach valuable lessons among all the brawling, peeping, and expletive-peppered rants. The language and sexual humor make this a title for older teens at least, but it remains one of the most popular of its kind.

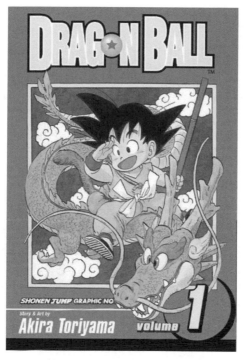

***Dragon Ball* by Toriyama Akira.**
© 1984 by BIRD STUDIO/SHUEISHA Inc.

Toriyama, Akira. *Dragon Ball*. VIZ Manga 1984–1995 Japan (2003–2005 U.S.) Publisher Age Rating: Teen. Age Recommendation: S. Volumes: 1–16 [T]. Genres: Action, Fantasy, Comedy. Related Manga: *Dragon Ball Z* (sequel). Related Anime: *Dragon Ball* (TV series)

    Dragon Ball is another remix of *Journey to the West*, and it manages to mix together robots, magical thunderclouds, monkey boys, dragons, quests, and lots of jokes into one crazy, fun, fractured myth. From the anime series, many readers expect this series to be for kids, but it's decidedly teen with oodles of panty jokes, partial nudity, and scatological humor. It's undeniably funny, which is why it remains so popular. Sometimes inane humor is what suits your mood.

Top Anime Titles for Teens

    Anime lists are no less subjective than manga lists, and this list has been built from my experiences running my library's manga and anime club for the past two years. I've tried to present a variety of what's available in anime as well as acknowledge the favorites of my audience and club. These are the titles the teens requested (in some cases, over and over again), along with a few titles they were skeptical about but, in the end, embraced.

All of the anime listed in the previous section as related titles to manga are also worth considering for anime screenings. Remember anime television shows tend to be tamer in terms of explicit sensual, sexual, or violent content than the related manga. This can be important when recommending between the two media. For example, the television series of *GetBackers* is fine for teens, but the manga's more explicit violence and occasional near nudity make it most appropriate for older teens and adult.

There are always new titles coming out—ICv2 (http://www.icv2.com) and the Anime News Network (http://www.animenewsnetwork.com) are great places to keep track of the popular titles and read reviews of the latest.

The Top Club Selections

.hack//SIGN. Bandai, 2003–2005, TV series (26 episodes, 25 minutes running time), 7 DVDs. Publisher Age Rating: 13+. Age Recommendation: J. Genres: Action, Fantasy, Science Fiction, Mystery

> One of the original installments released at the same time as a manga and video game series addressing other aspects, *.hack//SIGN* envelopes viewers in the World, the most popular online role-playing game on the planet. There is something wrong though—Subaru, a player, cannot log out of the game. Nor does he feel like a player—he feels real. While hints of what's happening in the real world only filter through occasionally, the bulk of this series takes place in the World's environment of quests, heroes, rules, and hidden programs. The power of the story resides in the connections the players make as they reveal why they play, what they want to do, and how they might all come together to solve the true mysteries of the game.

Cowboy Bebop. Bandai, 2001–2002, TV series (26 episodes, 25 minutes running time), 6 DVDs. Publisher Age Rating: 16+. Age Recommendation: S, A. Genres: Action, Science Fiction, Comedy

> Three bounty hunters are working in the space around and on Mars trying to make a buck (or a wulong) by capturing wanted criminals, but their own histories, hijinks, and reluctant morality always seem to get in the way. *Cowboy Bebop* is a landmark series for fans a generation back, but the jazz-scored combo science fiction/noir western still absorbs audiences. Spike's laissez-faire style, Jet's grumbling big brother attitude, and Faye's sassy fire liven up a show that can turn from slapstick to tense action on a dime. The related film makes a great introduction for new viewers, although the violence is a tad more explicit than in the series.

Fruits Basket. FUNimation, 2002–2003, TV series (26 episodes, 24 minutes running time), 4 DVDs. Publisher Age Rating: 13+. Age Recommendation: S. Genres: Fantasy, Romance, School Drama, Comedy

Based on the equally popular manga, the anime series brings to life the zodiac-cursed Sohma family and their confidant Tohru in all their sweetness, rivalry, and affection. The series soundtrack is a favorite, and the animation is a fine example of today's anime fare.

Fullmetal Alchemist. FUNimation, 2005–, TV series (51 episodes, 24 minutes running time), 11 DVDs. Publisher Age Rating: 13+. Age Recommendation: S. Genres: Action, Fantasy, Science Fiction, Military, Mystery

Following the twists and turns of the Elric brothers' quest for the elusive Philosopher's Stone, this anime has a bit of everything: wacky humor, brotherly love, political conspiracies, and deliciously evil villains. The animation is top notch, and an equally admired film follows the series.

GetBackers. ADV Films, 2004–2005, TV series (49 episodes, 26 minutes running time), 10 DVDs. Publisher Age Rating: 15+. Age Recommendation: S. Genres: Action, Fantasy, Comedy, Mystery

Ban and Ginji each have hidden powers. Ginji can harness electricity in a fight, and Ban has a super-strong grip and can create convincing illusions that last for exactly one minute. Together they work as the GetBackers, who will get back anything, anywhere, for a price. Or they *would* work if anyone deigned to hire them. As with characters in any action series, both Ban and Ginji have pasts that eventually come back to haunt them, but the high energy action keeps everything barreling along. The banter between the heroes reminds everyone how much they actually care about each other, and the inventiveness of the fighting, especially with Ban's talent, make the whole ride tons of fun.

Kya Kara Maoh! Geneon, 2005–2006, TV series (78 episodes, 23 minutes running time), 9 DVDs. Publisher Age Rating: 13+. Age Recommendation: S. Genres: Fantasy, Comedy

When thinking of being transported to a fantasy world, most of us don't think about getting there through plumbing. No one is more surprised than Shibuya when, after being shoved into a toilet by bullies, he emerges into a world where he is proclaimed by a bevy of bishōnen to be their long lost Demon king. In no time and after many misunderstandings, he's managed to get involved in a war, get engaged to another guy, and storm a pirate ship with a crew attired in typical school girl uniforms (and nary a snicker from anyone). Ridiculous and laugh-out-loud funny, *Kya Kara Maoh!* also displays a fine sense of justice, loyalty, and reluctant heroism.

Paranoia Agent. Geneon, 2004–2005, TV miniseries (13 episodes, 25 minutes running time), 4 DVDs. Publisher Age Rating: 16+. Age Recommendation: S, A. Genres: Fantasy, Mystery

A student known only as Li'l Slugger starts viciously attacking isolated pedestrians with a golden baseball bat. The police are stumped, the rumors are flying, and the victims are all tenuously connected. Venturing into an exploration of how people make themselves victims to escape deeper-seated problems, *Paranoia Agent* is a creepily compelling journey into mass psychology and the power of rumor, fear, and willful ignorance. There is little truly explicit violence, but the unnerving subject and a bit of sexual content make this title best for older teen and adult viewers.

Princess Tutu. ADV Films, 2002–, TV series (38 episodes, 25 minutes running time), 6 DVDs. Publisher Age Rating: 13+. Age Recommendation: J. Genres: Fantasy, Romance, Magical Girl, Comedy

A duck transforms into a girl, then into a superheroine ballerina, and then back again—and all the transformations have the same mission: to save the prince who has no heart. The core story of how important all emotions are, from good to bad, is fleshed out with snippets of ballet music and history in each episode. The reality of the story, as lorded over by the creepy Drosselmeyer of Nutcracker origins, is anybody's guess. Any girl who's fallen in love with ballet as an art and as a source of stories will adore this series.

Read or Die. Studio Deen, 2003, OVA (3 episodes, 24 minutes running time), 1 DVD. Publisher Age Rating: 13+. Age Recommendation: S. Genres: Action, Fantasy, Comedy, Mystery. Related Anime: *Read or Die* (TV series)

Anyone who's ever felt compelled to finish those last two pages of a great book while walking down the street will love Yomiko Readman. She's a complete book hound who spends her life happily buried under piles of books while ignoring everything else. She's also a secret agent working for the British government who can control paper, making everything from giant paper airplanes to attacking missiles. Part booklover's dream, part super spy story, the original *Read or Die* OVA is short, but extremely fun.

Samurai Champloo. Bandai, 2005–2006. TV series (26 episodes, 24 minutes running time), 7 DVDs. Publisher Age Rating: 16+. Age Recommendation: S, A. Genres: Action, Historical, Comedy

When Mugen and Jin first meet, they recognize a kindred spirit: all they want to do is fight each other, preferably to the death. Too bad ditzy waitress Fuu gets in the way. When Fuu helps the two out, she blackmails them into helping her find a samurai who smells of sunflowers—but the true story here is the unstable partnership that develops between all three. Famous for its freestyle remix of samurai legends and hip-hop culture, the entire series is crammed full of fun references. The language, a bit of foreplay, and violence make it best for older teens.

Spirited Away. Studio Ghibli, Disney/Buena Vista, 2001, feature film (125 minutes running time), 1 DVD. Publisher Age Rating: PG. Age Recommendation: M. Genre: Fantasy

Thirteen-year-old Chihiro is bored and annoyed. As her family makes their way to their new home, she cannot believe she must leave everything familiar behind. Little does she know what's in store. When her parents take a wrong road, the family ends up in thrall to the witch Yubaba, the strict owner of a bathhouse intended only for gods and spirits. Chihiro must find a way to win back her parents and her own freedom, all the while dodging Yubaba's clever traps and exploring the amazing world usually hidden from human sight. This Academy Award–winning film opens up a rich world of mythology from Japan and beyond, and Miyazaki's trademark director's eye makes the whole story as enchanting as the spirits.

Tokyo Godfathers. Columbia-Tristar, 2004, feature film (92 minutes running time), 1 DVD. Publisher Age Rating: NR. Age Recommendation: S. Genres: Comedy, Slice of Life

When homeless Miyuki, Gin, and Hana (a runaway, drunkard, and former drag queen) find an abandoned baby, they know they must return her to her parents. Unfortunately for them, that task proves far more difficult than predicted. This sweet Christmastime tale is a departure from Kon Satoshi's usual psychological dark fare. An unabashed valentine to creating families and finding home, it is a perfect film for seasoned fans and newbies alike.

Voices of a Distant Star. ADV Films, 2002, short film (25 minutes running time), 1 DVD. Publisher Age Rating: 13+. Age Recommendation: J. Genres: Action, Science Fiction, Romance, Military, Mecha

When Mikako leaves to become the pilot of a giant robot ship, fighting the good fight at the other end of the solar system, she leaves her boyfriend, Noboru, behind. The two try to text message to keep in touch, but as the distance stretches across space, the time between messages increases. An unusual and heartbreaking love story, this thirty-minute anime dresses itself up in mecha technology only to punch the viewer in the gut with the sheer hopelessness of the dwindling relationship. Gorgeous animation and the open-ended story inspire great discussions.

The Unexpected Anime Hits

Boogiepop Phantom. Right Stuf, 2000, TV miniseries (12 episodes, 25 minutes running time), 4 DVDs. Publisher Age Rating: 13+. Age Recommendation: S. Genres: Fantasy, School Drama, Horror, Mystery

Jumping back and forth in time, and thus requiring close attention, *Boogiepop Phantom* investigates an outbreak of disturbing incidents in one city. Five years ago, there was a serial killer stalking the streets, and now … no one's sure. Boogiepop is a phantom protector, or maybe the killer, and each student lives through his or her own private horror. Deliciously spooky, this series is not for everyone, but the production values catch everyone's attention along with the unique style of storytelling and multilayered sound and images.

Gankutsuou: The Count of Monte Cristo. Geneon, 2005–, TV series (24 episodes, 24 minutes running time), 6 DVDs. Publisher Age Rating: 16+. Age Recommendation: S. Genres: Science Fiction, Mystery

The Count of Monte Cristo is a tale of long-simmering revenge—and so is *Gankutsuou*, but nothing else is quite the same between the two tales. The count is an alien; the story is told by his prey, the naïve Albert; and the world is a collision of future technology with nineteenth-century trimmings. The story is inventive even as it echoes its source, but the animation is an astounding whirl of patterns, lights, and lines that show off the latest trends in animation.

Ghost in the Shell: Stand Alone Complex. Bandai, 2002–2004, TV series (52 episodes, 25 minutes running time), 7 DVDs each season. Publisher Age Rating: 13+. Age Recommendation: S, A. Genres: Action, Science Fiction, Military, Mecha, Mystery

In a spin-off from the original manga and film, *Stand Alone Complex* takes the premise of Section 9 and turns it into a more traditional police drama than its more philosophically fixated sources. All of the original characters are here, but in the series you have the time to build a truly complicated political atmosphere as well as strong camaraderie among the tight-knit crew. A careful melding of computer-generated imaging and handdrawn characters make the whole world alive and believable.

Kino's Journey. ADV Films, 2003, TV miniseries (13 episodes, 24 minutes running time), 4 DVDs. Publisher Age Rating: 13+. Age Recommendation: S. Genre: Fantasy

Kino, a sharpshooting traveler accompanied by a gruff-talking motorbike, follows the belief that traveling is the ideal and thus stays only three days in any one place. Each episode leads Kino from place to place, myth to myth, and lesson to lesson. A meditative and thought-provoking series, although not for die-hard action fans, *Kino's Journey* asks big questions using symbolism, fairy-tale structures, and evocative animation.

Witch Hunter Robin. Bandai, 2004, TV series (26 episodes, 24 minutes running time), 6 DVDs. Publisher Age Rating: 13+. Age Recommendation: S. Genres: Action, Fantasy, Science Fiction, Military, Mystery

Witches, or users of mental powers, are a real threat. The special STN-J division tracks and captures witches to try to harness and understand them. Robin is a novice agent, but unlike her peers, she uses her unique powers against what she is beginning to realize are her own kind. Gothic, terse, and occasionally obscure, the world of *Witch Hunter Robin* is an intriguing mix of old-fashioned military drama, supernatural battle, and theological puzzle.

Appendix A

Vocabulary

Akihabara—in the northeastern Chiyoda ward of Tokyo, Akihabara is an area famous as a mecca for anything and everything electronic. Originally the place to get radio parts right after World War II, today it is plastered with brilliant neon signs and has been all but taken over by otaku. Manga and anime books and films, toys, tie-ins, and dōjinshi (fan comics) are everywhere, and you can find a store to suit any interest. Here also are the manga cafes, or the shops offering free coffee, Internet access, and shelves of manga to read for a nominal fee (Macias 2004). As an example from the manga and anime series *Genshiken* shows, a trip to Akihabara is an initiation for newly confessed otaku.

Anime—Refers to animated films produced in Japan. The word itself comes from the word *animeshōn*, a translation of the English word "animation." This term encompasses all animated titles including feature films, television shows, and original video animation (OVA) released to the home entertainment market.

Anime music videos (AMV)—AMVs are anime clips edited together to match a particular song. AMVs are one of many ways fans use their favorite media to create and are frequently shown at anime conventions.

Baths and bathing—Bathing among the family, not always segregated by gender, is a time-honored custom in Japan and a way to grab a little family time while still getting something practical done. Historically, community baths in towns were the way to hear the news of the town, meet up with your neighbors, and hang out. Baths are not quite as common as they were up until the 1950s, but they are still a common form of relaxation, taken while on vacation or after a particularly hard day (Ueda 1994).

293

Bishōjo—Literally, "beautiful girls." Bishōjo are female characters designed to appeal to guys, complete with large breasts, tiny waists, and clinging outfits.

Bishōnen—Literally, "beautiful young men." Bishōnen are male characters designed to appeal to girls, identified by fine features, tall and slender frames, and fine features. Bishōnen are not always willowy and may sport a more muscled physique, but they are always beautiful.

BL—An acronym for "boy's love." BL is the most inclusive term for manga and anime portraying romances between two men, customarily written by women for girls and women. BL stories cover the full range of explicitness and audience.

Blood type—In Japan, blood type is similar to one's astrological sign in the United States—it denotes personality and likely strengths and weaknesses. Compatibility is also a factor, as Type A matches best with A or AB, B with B or AB, O with O and AB, and AB with all four. This tradition arose in the 1930s, when blood types were first accurately identified, and grew over time to be a national tradition.

Bushidō—Literally, "the way of the warrior." Developed in during the Feudal eras, bushidō was formalized during the Tokugawa Era (1600–1867).

Chibi, or super-deformed (SD)—The exaggerated and simplified form characters take on in a heightened emotional state. From the noun *chibi*, which is a slang term referring to a short person or child (similar to the English runt).

CLAMP—A four-woman artistic team that came from the dōjinshi market to become some of the most popular and admired manga creators. Famous for impeccable layout, engaging fantasy, and intelligent plots, their stories range from the classic (*Cardcaptor Sakura*) to the experimental (*Clover*).

Confucianism—Confucianism influenced Japanese culture as soon as Chinese concepts and ideas traveled into Japan through diplomatic envoys and visits to the Chinese court during the Heian era (794–1185). The ideals of Confucianism—social harmony, filial piety, and loyalty—were essentially institutionalized by the Tokugawa (1600–1867) shogunate to keep the country in line and at peace. Confucianism is not a religion but a set of rules for society.

Cosplay—Shortened from "costume play," cosplay is the creation and display of costumes representing favorite characters from manga, anime, and video games. Cosplay may also refer to events designed to shown off such costumes, including masquerades and skits, and is also used as a verb, as in, "Are you going to cosplay this year?"

Daimyō—Daimyō were the local lords during the feudal and Tokugawa eras. The emperor and shoguns were above daimyō, and the samurai, peasants, merchants, and artisans were all lower in status. Samurai were loyal to their daimyō.

Diet Building—The Kokkai, or the Diet building, home of Japan's parliament, is another fixture of Tokyo that often appears in manga and anime, as in *Ghost in the Shell: Stand Alone Complex* and *X/1999*.

Dōjinshi—Comics produced by fans outside of the traditional publishing industry.

Ecchi—An alternate term for hentai, the word comes from the English letter "h." Ecchi is somewhat gentler than hentai or ero content, usually indicating rampant fan service rather than truly explicit content.

Ennichi—Feast days are held on special days according to Buddhist or Shintō traditions. During summertime, it is customary to don *yukata*, or light-weight cotton kimono, to attend a festival.

Ero—From erotic, ero is the term for erotic manga. Ero and hentai are often used interchangeably, although ero indicates a more artistic intention, whereas hentai may be less artful and more simply pornographic.

Fabulous 49ers—Including Hagio Moto, Ōshima Yumiko, Yamagishi Ryoko, and Takemiya Keiko, this team of female manga creators paved the way for shōjo manga, both in terms of capturing the audience and proving that women could succeed in manga at the same level as their male counterparts. Also known as the Fabulous 24 Group.

Fan fiction—Fan fiction is fiction inspired by published sources written by fans for other fans. Although fan fiction started as fan-produced collections at fan conventions, today most fan fiction is written, critiqued, and published on the Internet.

Fan service—Fan service indicates elements in manga or anime that do not further the plot or develop characters but simply exist to pander to fans. The panty shots, cleavage close-ups, and pinups common in shōnen and seinen manga contain a lot of fan service, but it can also be found in the extended shots of robots in mecha titles.

Fansub—An anime title that has been translated and subtitled by fans for fans. Traditionally, fansubs were exchanged via traded VHS tapes, but today fans download fansubs of anime soon after the title is available in Japan from the Internet.

Fuji—Fuji-san, or Mt. Fuji, is by far the most famous and most beloved landmark in Japan. Japan's highest mountain, officially an active volcano, Fuji-san is a majestic presence in the landscape. Climbing Fuji-san is both a pilgrimage and a pleasure, with tens of thousands of people climbing it in July and August every year (Kodansha International 1999).

Geisha—Geisha represent a long tradition of paid companionship. Geisha today are women educated from early childhood to converse, play traditional music, and perform traditional dances. They are highly trained, and their current rarity and accomplishment make their prices astronomical, so being entertained by a geisha is a special experience, and a high honor if it is on someone else's tab. The role of a geisha is not comparable to that of a prostitute; instead their duties are to ease the way for their guests to make conversation, do business, and enjoy themselves. Historically, male geisha did exist, but today there are very few men in the profession (Poitras 1999).

Gekiga—Literally, "dramatic pictures." This genre of manga is defined by mature content and appeal. It may include explicit violence and sensuality as well as complicated and morally murky plotlines.

Giri—Giri defines the conduct expected from society in relation to others and is driven by social expectations and hundreds of years of tradition. The loyalty of a samurai to his lord, family members helping each other, and coworkers offering advice to new and subordinate colleagues all exemplify giri.

Go—Go started as an ancient strategy board game using black and white stones alternately placed on a wooden board. It is mentioned in *The Tale of Genji* and during the Tokugawa Era (1600–1867), four professional Go schools were established. Today there are four hundred professional players who make their living through competitions, and the game claims millions of fans in Japan and beyond. Go is most popular among senior citizens, but the popularity of the manga and anime *Hikaru no Go* has revived the game for younger generations (Kodansha International 1999).

GothLoli—GothLoli refers to the fashion of striving to look like a combination of a little girl, a goth, and a porcelain doll. GothLoli gear features Victorian-style bonnets, gowns, and shoes complete with an abundance of lace and ruffles and usually includes accessories such as a stuffed bear or a large, beribboned hat. Women and teens who dress this way are not automatically pandering to rorikon men. GothLoli is considered by some to be a reaction against the previous kogal culture by reversing the tanned, mature look kogals prefer. The bulk of manga characters who follow this fashion are girls who prefer fantasy to reality, as in *Dazzle*, *Doll*, *Beautiful People*, and *Kamikaze Girls*.

Hakama—Hakama are trousers, usually worn by men, worn tied over kimono or haori (short coats)—they are so loose that they are often mistaken for skirts. The freedom of hakama made them ideal for samurai, and many of the traditional martial arts still have hakama as part of their uniform, from kendō to kyūdō as seen in *Alice 19th*.

Haori—When the weather turns colder, people wear haori, or short coats varying from hip to knee length, over their kimono, or they turn to wearing the heavier-weight version of a kimono, a tanzen.

Harajuku—The Harajuku area, in the Shibuya district, boasts rows of fashion stores and a variety of young people showing off their latest fashion statements (Poitras 1999). The area is the playground of the kogals in *GALS!* To see the variety of fashions and attitudes on display, check out Aoki Shoichi's photo essay collections *Fruits* and *Fresh Fruits*.

Hara-kiri—*See* **Seppuku.**

Harem manga and anime—In a typical harem title, a crowd of lovely young ladies surrounds an ordinary guy, and all of them compete for his affections. These titles contain a higher level of fan service and sexual slapstick than romantic comedies.

Hentai—Literally, pervert or perverted. Hentai manga is pornographic manga and may be used interchangeably with ero to indicate a manga or anime's explicit sexual content. Hentai is reputed to be less artful than ero manga.

Honorifics—Honorifics are commonly used at the end of a person's name to indicate the status in age, gender, and social standing of the addressee and their relative position to the speaker. There are two major types of speech: informal plain speech and customary polite speech. Plain speech is most often used with immediate family members, close friends, and children. On top of this, there are the traditional three levels of honorifics added on to names and nouns.

Hostess/host clubs—The modern, cheaper version of paid companionship originating from geisha. The hostess's job is to be company for customers, puffing up their egos, relaxing them, and providing a pretty girl on their arm for the evening. Hostesses are not prostitutes, and there are strict rules against sleeping with customers. Host clubs operate on the same idea with male hosts for customers rather than women. *Ouran High School Host*

Club pokes fun at the whole tradition by having students start their very own host club for high school girls looking for charming, handsome dates.

Hot springs—The Japanese islands have a variety of hot springs that have long been held to not only provide a relaxing getaway but are also believed to have health benefits. Visiting hot springs is a common reason for a vacation, and the areas surrounding hot springs have built up many modern resorts (Kodansha International 1999). In *Ranma 1/2*, hero Ranma is cursed after a fall into a magical spring. Because of the nature of the curse, hot springs and baths are triggers for the curse. In the anime *Samurai Champloo*, the trio Mugen, Jin, and Fuu all relax in hot springs while on their travels.

Josei—Literally, "woman." This term distinguishes the audience for manga aimed at women aged eighteen and up. Josei manga include many of the traditions of shōjo titles but the content is more mature in terms of explicitness and complexity.

Juku (cram school)—To pass progressively more rigorous exams to get into middle and high school, private special classes are held after school to help students compete both in their regular curriculum and on exams. Cram school is featured in almost every manga and anime involving school.

Kabuki—Kabuki began in the seventeenth century when a female attendant at a Shintō shrine led a mostly female company in performances of comedies and sensual dances for the public near Kyoto. Because the performers were selling their bodies as well as their talents, the government quickly forbade women from performing, but kabuki continued starring young men. Ironically, during the subsequent eras, kabuki actors were known to be the equivalent of geisha for female courtiers, their sexual favors bought once the performance was through. Kabuki today consists of three types of performance: elaborate historical plays, more realistic domestic plays, and dances (Kodansha International 1999).

Kami—According to Shintō beliefs, natural elements such as the wind, moon, sun, mountains, and trees are all kami, as are the variety of spirits and gods believed to have created the world. Animal spirits of all kinds can be kami, as shown in the film *Princess Mononoke*.

Karaoke—Karaoke music is recorded specifically for karaoke sing-alongs, and sentimental old standards, known as *enka*, are perpetual favorites alongside the latest pop hits. Fans rent out soundproof booths equipped with individual stereo systems and microphones for smaller parties. Many people also own personal karaoke systems, used among the family or for small get-togethers and parties (Ueda 1994). Karaoke is one of the most popular pastimes, and this activity features in almost every modern manga somewhere along the way.

Kazuo Koike—The author of the classic *Lone Wolf and Cub*, Kazuo exemplifies gekiga and seinen manga with tough heroes, brutal plotlines, and visionary art. Artist Kojima Goseki's sketchy and impressionist style suits Kazuo's complex stories perfectly.

Kimono—Kimono and their accoutrements are a recognizable symbol of Japan, known for their elegant lines and brilliant colors and patterns. Traditionally kimono are long robes worn by both men and women, with women's robes being typically more colorful than men's. Kimonos are always worn with the left side overlapping the right (corpses are the opposite, which when manga is flipped makes for an odd visual) (Poitras 1999). *Obi* are the sashes worn by both sexes to secure the kimono, and women's are usually wider and more elaborately designed than men's. As in CLAMP's one-shot volume *The One I Love*, sometimes wearing a traditional outfit can indicate a shift in emotional state, in that case an expression of affection and reconciliation. In *Fruits Basket*, one of the many members of the transforming Sohma family prefers wearing a kimono around the house so much that heroine Tohru remarks on how nice he looks when he wears a Western style suit.

Kogals—Kogals struggle to meet Western standards of beauty by tanning their skin, bleaching their hair blond, and wearing the most expensive couture clothing they can buy. They are presented in attitude as brash, tacky, and blunt about their consumerism. Kogals claim Harajuku as their stomping ground, a section of the Shibuya shopping district in Western Tokyo. The hilarious and good-spirited *GALS!* is all about the kogal culture, although happily its heroine Ran espouses a philosophy of valuing oneself rather than depending on external judgments. Momo in *Peach Girl* is often mistaken for a kogal, here used as a negative term that implies she's both an airhead and a slut, simply because she has light hair and dark skin.

Kōhai—In school, kōhai is an underclassman, and in other organizations, a junior member. The term is most often used in school dramas or in corporate environments.

Kon Satoshi—A challenging anime director, Kon has led a number of anime's recent classic projects, including the unsettling, Hitchcockian *Perfect Blue*, the endearing *Tokyo Godfathers*, and the imaginative but dark miniseries *Paranoia Agent*.

Kyoto—For almost a thousand years up to 1868, Kyoto was the capital of Japan, originally known as Heiankyo and the jewel of the Heian era's glittering court. The city was planned along Chinese inspirations and remains famous for traditional architecture and heritage.

Loli-con or **roricon**—*Rorikon*, or loli-con, refers to the sexualization of and obsession with prepubescent girls, a disturbing trend among male otaku in Japan and a vibrant part of the male dōjinshi fan culture. It's unknown whether this trend condones the rare leap between fiction and reality, but in terms of fashion, it has created an intriguing style, GothLoli (Schodt 1996).

Magical girl—A fantasy subgenre, magical girl manga and anime are possibly the closest answer Japan has to the American superhero tradition. An ordinary girl discovers magical powers that she must use to save herself, her family, her friends, and, usually, the world. Magical girl stories are defined by including transformations and costume changes for the heroine's use of her powers.

Mah-jongg—Mah-jongg, familiar from Chinese traditions, is a popular board game in Japan, consisting of using tiles to create sequences and sets. Unlike the impression from U.S. pop culture that mah-jongg is a game enjoyed by older women, in Japan mah-jongg is mainly played by men.

Manga—Print comics in Japan. The word simply translates as "comics," and covers all printed matter from three-hundred-page magazines printed weekly and monthly to the tankobon, or bound volumes, available at newsstands, manga stores, and bookstores.

Manga-ka—The title given to all manga creators.

Matsuri—The general name for festivals celebrated throughout the year. They may be religious or secular, and depending on the occasion, they may feature floats, parades, costumes, or fireworks.

Mecha—The subgenre of science fiction manga and anime that deal specifically with giant robot technology, usually controlled by human pilots.

Miyazaki Hayao—Currently the most recognized anime director worldwide, Miyazaki is the artist behind *My Neighbor Totoro*, *Princess Mononoke*, and *Spirited Away*, which won the Academy Award for Best Animated Feature in 2003.

Moe—Literally, "budding." Moe refers to a recent trend in male dōjinshi and otaku tastes creating stories about protecting young, often prepubescent girls. Stories range from courtly protection to pornographic escapades.

Nakazawa Keiji—Nakazawa is notable as one of the few manga or anime creators to address World War II directly in his manga, inspired by his own experiences surviving the nuclear bombing of Hiroshima, *Barefoot Gen*.

Ninjō—Ninjō are the personal feelings any person might express including love, sorrow, affection, and sympathy.

No—Derived from Buddhist traditions and Chinese influences, No started in the fourteenth century and is the oldest form of theater in Japan. Performances are more like a solemn religious observance than a piece of theater. No seeks to illuminate the basic Buddhist concept that existence is only as it is perceived and thus is not permanent. The actor dances, sings, and gestures deliberately and stylistically (Kodansha International 1999). The anime *Otogi Zoshi* features a character in the Hciankyo court, Mansairaku, known for his No performances that are seen frequently throughout the series.

Obi—The sashes worn by both sexes to secure their kimono; women's are usually wider and more elaborately designed than men's. Traditionally unmarried women wore obi tied in the back, while married women tie obi in front, but today most women wear obi tied, in any number of elaborate ways, in the back.

Oni—The general term for demons or evil spirits. Oni were originally benevolent spirits, but in current usage, the term is used for grotesque, evil spirits.

Osaka—Osaka is the third largest city in Japan and the major center for trade and manufacturing. Osaka is defined by its touristy atmosphere, full of flashy shops and restaurants. The Osakan love of baseball is legendary (and gently mocked in *Tsubasa: RESERVoir CHRoNICLE*). People from Osaka are unkindly noted for their regional accent. In manga and anime translations, they are often given pronounced U.S. Southern accents to imply the regional shift in accent. This shift, as seen in *Peacemaker* and *Azumanga Daioh*, can be quite startling, as samurai appear to be speaking with Georgia accents, but the connotations are similar enough to make the convention common.

Otaku—In the past, this term referred to a very formal address for "you," similar to the French *vous* or German *sie*. At this point in Japan, the term means a nerd or geek and has a negative spin. In the United States, this term has been adopted and reclaimed by anime and manga fans without the negative connotation and is frequently used for self-identification with pride.

Otomo Katsuhiro—The creator behind both the manga and anime *Akira*, Otomo's dark visions were some of the first to make an impact in the United States. Recently, Otomo has continued to explore the intersection of man, technology, and ambition in the anime films *Metropolis* and *Steamboy*.

Otsu-e—Pictures that were a talisman for travelers. They first appeared outside the town of Otsu. Otsu-e represent one of many historical influences on today's manga and anime art and popularity.

OVA—Acronym for original video animation, or those anime released in the home video market rather than via television or as films. OVAs are often, but not always, titles that are not expected to have the popular acceptance and demand that produce feature films or television shows and may feature the more risqué and cult genres and stories.

Pachinko—Pachinko is one of the most popular solitary games enjoyed across Japan, especially by young businessmen. Pachinko is essentially a pinball game turned on its side to play vertically. Metal balls are propelled by levers to the top of the machine and then proceed toward the bottom via gravity. Along the way, the balls are impeded by small metal pins that change their path, and the goal is to get the ball into a winning hole rather than lose it to the bottom of the machines. If you win, you get more balls. Balls are officially exchanged for small prizes, but are also often illegally exchanged for cash, making pachinko a small-time form of gambling. The game's appeal rests in being a game one can play both easily and without interacting with others, thus providing a mental break for the overwhelmed (Ueda 1994). Pachinko not only appears in manga as a pastime, as in You Higuri's *Earthian*, but also has its own booming subgenre of manga, from simple competition manga to the more bizarre erotic pachinko manga aimed at the businessmen who are the game's biggest fans (Gravett 2004).

Rōnin—A masterless samurai, or a warrior that has lost his lord due to death or dishonor. Rōnin are favorite heroes of historical manga and anime because they combine the strict code of a warrior with the allure of an outsider.

Rori-con—*See* **Loli-con**

Sakura—Cherry trees or petals. Cherry blossoms and petals represent fleeting youth and beauty and are often used as symbols in manga and anime to accentuate a character or a moment in the plot.

Samurai—Members of an elite warrior class who for centuries were at the top of the food chain with only their lords, or *daimyō*, and the emperor above them. They were established at the beginning of the Kamakura Era (around 1185) as a specific rank in society, and helped maintain military rule in Japan for more than two hundred years. In the late 1500s, Toyotomi Hideyoshi, one of three lords who eventually unified Japan, recreated the samurai as a carefully defined class with special privileges. Hideyoshi ordered that all of the peasantry be stripped of their swords. The samurai wore two swords, a long and a short sword, as a sign of their station.

Scanlation—Manga not yet available in the United States that has been digitally scanned, the text translated and replaced with English text, all by fans for other fans. Fans largely distribute scanlations over the Internet.

Screentones—The patterns, shades of gray, and most shading in manga are created from screentones. Screentones are traditionally sheer sheets of adhesive plastic that can be cut and affixed to the finished manga page. Today there are also digital Screentones used in image editing programs.

Seinen—Literally, young men. This term distinguishes the audience for men's or seinen manga. Seinen continue many of the common genres from shōnen manga, but the content becomes more mature in terms of explicitness and complexity.

Senpai or sempai—In school, an upperclassmen, and in organizations, a senior member. The term is most often used in school dramas or in corporate environments.

Seppuku (also known as **hara-kiri**)—Ritual suicide, traditionally performed by a samurai. The act is highly ritualized and requires the warrior to slice open his belly and, once he is finished, a fellow samurai, his second, completes the act by severing his head.

Sequential art—The format of all comics including comic strips, comic books, and graphic novels. The format is predominantly defined by images used in sequence to tell a story, and text bubbles and sound effects are expected elements.

Shibuya—The Shibuya ward as a whole is famous for being a hotspot for young adults, and thus it is featured in many modern teen and young adult manga and anime. Shibuya is full of shopping, entertainment, and hangouts including karaoke establishments and pachinko parlors.

Shinigami—Literally, "death god." The term is not specifically used in Shintō, but in popular media, there are many types of shinigami, from the humanoid creatures in *Death Note* to the just warriors of *Bleach.*

Shinjuku—Shinjuku and nearby Aoyama are the business centers of Tokyo, marked by many of the skyscrapers in the city's skyline. The Tokyo Metropolitan Government Offices are a grand local landmark. Shinjuku's train station is the busiest in the city and is near many of the city's entertainment districts (Kodansha International 1999).

Shintō—Literally "the way of the gods," Shintō is the native religion of Japan. There is no single major religious text, no supreme god, but countless gods and spirits called kami, and a sense of purity and impurity rather than the Christian concept of sin. Shintō is a gathering together of myths and traditions, formally collected in the eighth century, that emphasizes the close relationship between man and nature, a sense of family lineage traced back to original kami, and the celebration of festivals as major religious holidays.

Shirow Masamune—Shirow is best know for creating *Ghost in the Shell*, the manga that exemplifies the complex and dark view of man, machine, and cyborg technology.

Shōgi—Shōgi is another board game and is reputedly similar to chess, both originating from the same Indian game. Shōgi has two players, forty pieces, and the object is to checkmate your opponent's king. The major difference between Western chess and shōgi is that captured pieces can be used in play again on the capturer's side (Ministry of Internal Affairs and Communications 1999). In the *Cowboy Bebop* TV series, two main bounty hunters, Spike and Jet, are often observed playing shōgi and, fittingly, quoting Zun Tsu's *The Art of War* at each other.

Shōjo—Literally, "girl(s)." This term distinguishes the audience for girl's, or shōjo, manga. Shōjo manga is usually defined by a concentration on emotion and relationships. As with the counterpoint shōnen manga, shōjo manga has its own set of character types, conventions, and typical genres, ranging from romance to science fiction.

Shōjo-ai—Literally, "girl's love." Manga and anime exploring romances between two girls or women. As with shōnen-ai, the term can imply a more romantic, less explicit story, with the related term yuri indicating more sexually explicit stories.

Shōnen—Literally, "boy(s)." This term distinguishes the audience for boy's, or shōnen, manga. Shōnen manga is often distinguished by storylines that concentrate on action, humor, honor, and social obligation.

Shōnen-ai—Literally, "boy's love." This term, now outdated in Japan, was used to identify romances between two boys or men written by women for women and girls. These stories were traditionally more romantic than sexually explicit—in the United States, yaoi is often used to refer to the more explicit stories.

Shota—This term represents the reverse of loli-con (or rori-con) and refers to the sexualization of young, prepubescent boys. Most of this occurs in dōjinshi and is more a part of hardcore otaku culture than mainstream manga publication.

Steampunk—A speculative tradition of fiction that takes an antiquated technology, such as the steam engine, and extrapolates an alternate world where that technology became the dominant achievement and source of power. Airships and dirigibles feature in many fantastical manga and anime, as with *Last Exile* and *Elemental Gelade*. The recent film *Steamboy* imagined an alternate 1880s London obsessed with steam power.

Takahashi Rumiko—A multimillionaire manga legend, Takahashi is responsible for hit after hit: *Maison Ikkoku, Ranma 1/2*, and *Inuyasha*. Her titles appeal across audiences and genre definitions, and she is famous for maintaining an all-female studio.

Tankobon—The bound collections of manga originally serialized in magazine form. Essentially the same as the trade paperbacks or graphic novels collected from U.S. comics originally printed in comic book form.

Tezuka Osamu—Tezuka is appropriately known as the grandfather of Japanese manga and anime—his work defined both formats in their establishment in the 1950s. His character design, cinematic visuals, and extended storylines continue to affect manga and anime production today.

Toba-e—Named after Bishop Toba, the creator of the *Choju Giga* or Animal Scrolls, Toba e were collections of cartoons popular in the twelfth century.

Tokyo—Tokyo, Japan's capital city, is one of the most common locations in manga and anime. Tokyo, Kyoto, and Osaka are all on the island of Honshu, as is most of Japan's population of 127 million. As author Patrick Drazen describes it, Japan is half of the population of the U.S. squeezed into Washington, Oregon, and California. Tokyo itself is home to more than 12 million people, or 10 percent of the entire population, and if you take in the surrounding urban sprawl, the number raises to 25 million (Kodansha International 1999). Tokyo has a long history as a city, but it is its modern incarnation that is most often seen—the unique districts that divide the city are key references in dialogue and background. Famous districts include Shinjuku and Shibuya.

Tokyo Tower—Aside from the districts, there are a number of buildings that are emblematic of the city, like the Eiffel Tower in Paris or Big Ben in London. Tokyo Tower, 100 feet higher than the Eiffel Tower it resembles, is the highest building in Tokyo and provides two observation decks for spectacular views of the city (Poitras 1999). Tokyo Tower appears prominently in *Tokyo Babylon* as the scene of one ghost's suicide, among many other Tokyo-based manga.

Ueno Park—Ueno Park in Tokyo is a major landmark often referenced or seen in manga. The park hosts a zoo, a temple, and a number of museums. This is also where many Tokyo residents stake out their spaces every spring for *hanami*, or the boisterous picnics and parties held to watch the cherry blossoms fall (Poitras 1999).

Ukiyo-e—Literally, "floating world pictures." Ukiyo-e were woodblock prints created from the 1600s on. Noted for elegant layout and eventually rich colors, they remained in popular demand all the way through the Tokugawa Era (1600–1867).

Visual kei—Japan's music scene contains a group of bands defined as *visual kei*, or "visual type," groups. These acts do what their name implies– they grab the public's attention through dramatic costumes and visuals, which usually means striking makeup, gender-bending, costumes, and spectacles on stage and in video. The music itself is usually pop or pop-rock.

Yakuza—The general term for organized crime in Japan, similar to the traditional Sicilian-based mafia in the United States. The yakuza have their own rituals and traditions, some borrowed from samurai culture, and are dramatic figures in manga and anime.

Yaoi—Literally, "no climax no punchline, no meaning." From "yama nashi, ochi nashi, imi nashi." The term in Japan is mainly for dōjinshi romances between two male characters, of all levels of explicitness. In the United States, the term is associated with the more explicit male–male romances.

Yukata—Yukata are light cotton kimono worn during the hot summer months, and in modern manga, these are often the kimono worn to summer festivals, as in *Yotsuba&!* and *XXXholic*.

Yuri—Literally, "lily" The term is used for romances between two women or girls. Unlike shōjo-ai, the term implies more explicit content.

Appendix B

Frequently Asked Questions

What is sequential art?

Sequential art is the term for stories presented in the traditional comic art format— thus anything from the newspaper comic strips to comic books to graphic novels use sequential art to tell their tales. Sequential art is most often marked by the use of panels and text bubbles.

What is manga?

Manga (pronounced mahn guh with a hard" "g") is the general term for Japanese print comics, the equivalent of comic books and graphic novels in the United States. You may also hear the related term, *manhwa* (mahn-hwah), which refers to Korean print comics.

What is anime?

Anime (pronounced ah-nee may) is the general term for Japanese animated work, including television shows, movies, and direct-to-video releases.

Why anime and manga?

Both anime and manga have a rich, distinct visual storytelling style. Anime is often related to manga—the two industries inspire each other and often create related titles together. Both are also much more common in Japan than their counterparts in the United States and are a dominant part of Japanese pop culture. Manga is used for everything from titles on how to do your job to biographies of famous figures to best-selling fiction. Both formats are great fun—not to mention fascinating in terms of looking at different cultures, translation methods, history, and language.

What would I gain from reading manga or watching anime?

As with other media, graphic novels embody a different kind of literacy than traditional text, and in this world where TV, the Internet, and multimedia are increasingly the mode by which information is distributed, visual literacy is a vital tool for everyone to master. More specifically, manga presents not only a different way of telling a story, but also a window into a different and rich culture. Reading manga and watching anime frequently inspires readers to read Japanese mythology, learn to speak Japanese, and investigate the country's history.

I've heard that anime and manga are full of schoolgirls, revealing outfits, and swordfights—is this true?

Although schoolgirls and samurai are common characters, the way they are represented depends on the intended audience. Unlike in the U.S. where many comics and animated films are aimed at and are appropriate for younger readers and viewers, both manga and anime are produced for a variety of audiences and age ranges, from girls to boys, toddlers to adults. In fact, a much wider variety of titles are produced than in the United States as these two media. The variety of titles can be compared to the productions on U.S. television or films: yes, there are titles produced that contain sex and violence, but these are intended for an adult audience. By no means do all or even most anime and manga titles fall into this category.

Is it true that girls like manga? Do only girls like manga, or do boys like it too?

Traditionally, similar to U.S. comics, boys and men were the biggest consumers of both manga and anime. Recently there has been a lot of press about how manga draws in girls. This is true: girls read manga, and more girls read manga than traditionally read U.S. or Western comics. However, the audience is still very diverse, and because manga and anime are created for all genders and ages, boys are just as likely to be fans as girls.

What is up with the giant eyes?

Most simply, manga and anime characters have unrealistically large eyes because they learned to cartoon from Western cartoons. Think back to the cartoon characters of the 1930s and 1940s: Betty Boop, Mickey Mouse, Felix the Cat, Popeye. When Japanese creators started cartooning, our own Western comic strips and cartoons inspired them, so they started from models that had large eyes. Over time, eye shape and size came to mean something: for example, wide eyes indicates purity and innocence, and narrow, squinting eyes indicate villainy and cruelty.

Why are there so many giant robots?

Like the tradition of superheroes here in the United States, a subgenre focused on giant robots, called mecha, is very popular in Japan. Technology and all of its forms are interesting to Japanese creators (remember who created Nintendo and our tiniest cell phones) and robots are often featured in manga and anime. Most of the time it's a way to talk about the links and problems between man and machine, but the other angle is very simple: you can sell toy robots.

Are women objectified in manga and anime?

Most cultures, our own included, still have a long way to go toward equal and realistic representations of women in media. Japanese manga and anime have their share of fantastic anatomy and images of women devoted to titillating male readers. Unlike in the United States, however, Japanese manga and anime creators aim their work at a particular audience: so, boys' and men's comics have women in skimpy outfits and peeks at panties (a common joke in Japan). By the same token, though, in girls' and women's comics, there are pinups of lovely young men. This tradition, called fan service, is part and parcel of all manga and anime production, but considering our own comics, television, and films, these images are at about the same level as our own at each age level. In a perfect world, no one would be objectified—but until we reach that point, manga and anime are no worse than Western media.

How can I find out more about anime and manga?

There are a number of great resources both in print and on the Web. Here are a few titles and Web sites to get you started.

Print Resources

The Anime Companion: What's Japanese in Japanese Animation? by Gilles Poitras

A dictionary of anything and everything you might see in anime, from gestures to food — a whole lot of fun to browse through, not to mention informative.

Anime Essentials: Everything a Fan Needs to Know by Gilles Poitras

A short guide to all of the ins and outs of anime, from the films themselves to the fan communities.

Anime Explosion: The What? Why? And Wow! Of Japanese Animation by Patrick Drazen

An enlightening book that covers the trends and common stories in anime, explaining in detail the links between anime and Japanese culture.

Manga! Manga!: The World of Japanese Comics by Frederick L. Schodt

One of the first books to thoroughly explore manga, covering everything from its history to common motifs—again, there is some adult content as Schodt addresses manga for all age ranges including adults.

Manga: 60 Years of Japanese Comics by Paul Gravett

A visually engrossing book on the variety and history of Japanese manga. The breadth of the topic means that this book includes some adult content, but it is definitely not to be missed if you want to see visual examples of manga.

Web Resources

The Librarian's Guide to Anime and Manga
http://www.koyagi.com/Libguide.html

A great place to start, full of vocabulary, definitions, frequently asked questions, and recommended titles.

No Flying, No Tights
http://www.noflyingnotights.com

Visit author Robin Brenner's site to find out a bit more about graphic novels in general, as well as to find reviews of new manga series.

The Parent's Guide to Anime
http://www.abcb.com/parents/

A useful list of titles with short reviews, commentary, and ratings according to the Motion Picture Association of America standards.

The Anime Companion Online Supplement
http://www.koyagi.com/ACPages/ACmain.html

The supplement to Mr. Poitras's book cited earlier.

Bibliography

Recommended Further Reading

Print Resources

Allison, Anne. *Permitted and Prohibited Desires: Mothers, Comics, and Censorship in Japan*. Berkeley: University of California Press, 2000.

Aoki, Shoichi. *Fruits*. Boston: Phaidon Press, 2001.

———. *Fresh Fruits*. Boston: Phaidon Press, 2005.

Bernabe, Marc. *Japanese in Mangaland: Learning the Basics*. Tokyo: Japan Publications Trading, 2004.

Buruma, Ian. *Behind the Mask: On Sexual Demons, Sacred Mothers, Transvestites, Gangsters, Drifters, and Other Japanese Cultural Heroes*. New York: New American Library, 1984.

Clements, Jonathan, and Helen McCarthy. *The Anime Encyclopedia: A Guide to Japanese Animation Since 1917*. Berkeley, CA: Stone Bridge Press, 2001.

Comickers Magazine. *Japanese Comickers: Draw Anime and Manga Like Japan's Hottest Artists*. New York: Collins Design, 2003.

Drazen, Patrick. *Anime Explosion: The What? Why? & Wow! of Japanese Animation*. Berkeley, CA: Stone Bridge Press, 2003.

Eisner, Will. *Comics and Sequential Art*. Tamarac, FL: Poorhouse Press, 1994.

Gorman, Michele. *Getting Graphic! Using Graphic Novels to Promote Literacy with Preteens and Teens*. Worthington, OH: Linworth, 2003.

Gravett, Paul. *Manga: Sixty Years of Japanese Comics*. London: Laurence King, 2004.

Gresh, Lois H., and Robert Weinberg. *The Science of Anime: Mecha-Noids and AI-Super-Bots*. Berkeley, CA: Thunder's Mouth Press, 2005.

Griepp, Milton, ed. *ICv2 Retailers Guide to Graphic Novels* 7 (2006).

———. *ICv2 Retailers Guide to Anime and Manga* 13 (2006).

Kardy, Glenn, and Chihiro Hattori. *Kanji De Manga Special Box Set*. Saitama, Japan: Japanime, 2006.

Kinsella, Sharon. *Adult Manga: Culture and Power in Contemporary Japanese Society*. Richmond, UK: Curzon Press, 2000.

Kodansha International. *Japan: Profile of a Nation,* rev. ed. Tokyo: Kodansha International, 1999.

Krashen, Stephen. *The Power of Reading: Insights from the Research*. Westport, CT: Libraries Unlimited, 2004.

Ledoux, Trish, ed. *Anime Interviews: The First Five Years of Animerica Anime and Manga Monthly (1992–97)*. San Francisco: Cadence Books, 1997.

Lehmann, Timothy. *Manga: Masters of the Art*. Scranton, PA: Collins Design, 2005.

Lenhard, Amanda, and Mary Madden. "Pew Internet Life Survey: Teen Content Creators and Consumers." November, 2005. Washington, DC: Pew Internet and American Life Project. Available at http://www.pewinternet.org.

Lenhard, Amanda, and Mary Madden. "Pew Internet Life Survey: Teens and Technology." July, 2005. Washington, DC: Pew Internet and American Life Project. http://www.pewinternet.org

Lyga, Allyson, and Barry Lyga. *Graphic Novels in Your Media Center: A Definitive Guide*. Westport, CT: Libraries Unlimited, 2004.

Macias, Patrick, and Tomohiro Machiyama. *Cruising the Anime City: An Otaku Guide to Neo Tokyo*. Berkeley, CA: Stone Bridge Press, 2004.

McCloud, Scott. *Understanding Comics: The Invisible Art*. Northampton, MA: Kitchen Sink Press, 1993.

Murakami, Takashi, ed. *Little Boy: The Arts of Japan's Exploding Subculture*. New Haven, CT: Yale University Press, 2005.

Napier, Susan J. *Anime from Akira to Princess Mononoke: Experiencing Contemporary Japanese Animation*. New York: Palgrave, 2000.

Patten, Fred. *Watching Anime, Reading Manga: 25 Years of Essays and Reviews*. Berkeley: Stone Bridge Press, 2004.

Poitras, Gilles. *The Anime Companion: What's Japanese in Japanese Animation?* Berkeley, CA: Stone Bridge Press, 1999.

———. *The Anime Companion 2: More What's Japanese in Japanese Animation?* Berkeley, CA: Stone Bridge Press, 2005.

———. *Anime Essentials: Everything a Fan Needs to Know*. Berkeley, CA: Stone Bridge Press, 2001.

Robertson, Jennifer. *Takarazuka: Sexual Politics and Popular Culture in Modern Japan*. Berkeley: University of California Press, 1998.

Schodt, Frederik L. *Dreamland Japan: Writings on Modern Manga*. Berkeley, CA: Stone Bridge Press, 1996.

———. *Manga! Manga! The World of Japanese Comics*. Tokyo: Kodansha International, 1983.

Sugiyama, Rika. *Comic Artists—Asia: Manga Manhwa Manhua*. New York: Collins Design, 2004.

Suzuki, Takao. *Words in Context: A Japanese Perspective on Language and Culture*. Tokyo: Kodansha International, 2001.

"Teen Reader Survey." By Robin Brenner. April, 2006. A report prepared by No Flying, No Tights, Arlington, MA. http://www.noflyingnotights.com.

Thorn, Matt. "Girls and Women Getting Out of Hand: The Pleasure and Politics of Japan's Amateur Comics Community." In *Fanning the Flames: Fans and Consumer Culture in Contemporary Japan*. Albany: State University of New York Press, 2004.

Ueda, Atsushi, ed. *The Electronic Geisha: Exploring Japan's Popular Culture*. Translated by Miriam Eguchi. Tokyo: Kodansha International, 1994.

Articles

"Amazing Anime: *Princess Mononoke* and Other Wildly Imaginative Films Prove That Japanese Animation Is More than Just Pokémon." *Time* 154, no. 21 (1999): 94.

Black, R.W. "Access and Affiliation: The Literacy and Composition Practices of English Language Learners in an Online Fan Fiction Community." *Journal of Adolescent and Adult Literacy* 49, no. 2 (2005): 118-28.

Cha, Ariana Eunjun. "Harry Potter and the Copyright Lawyer: Use of Popular Characters Puts 'Fan Fiction' Writers in Gray Area." *The Washington Post*, Wednesday, 18 June 2003, sec. A, p. 1.

Cha, Kai-Ming. "Yaoi Manga: What Girls Like?" *Publishers Weekly* 252, no. 10 (2005): 44.

Fletcher-Spear, Kristin, and Kat Kan. "The Anime-ted Library." *Voice of Youth Advocates* (April 2005).

ICv2. "CMX Bowlderizes Tenjho Tenge Manga." http://www.icv2.com/articles/news/6528.html March 07, 2005 (accessed September 30, 2006).

———. "Shoujo Sales Soaring: Go! Comi Goes Back to Press." http://www.icv2.com/articles/news/8462.html March 28, 2006 (accessed April 4, 2006).

———. "TokyoPop Signs Alliance with HarperCollins for Co-Publishing and Distribution." http://www.icv2.com/articles/news/8430.html March 28, 2006 (accessed April 28, 2006).

Japan External Trade Organization. "Japanese Animation Goes Global." http://www.jetro.go.jp/en/market/trend/topic/2004_07_anime.html (accessed April 28, 2006).

Japan. Ministry of Internal Affairs and Communications. "Historical Statistics of Japan." 2002. http://www.stat.go.jp/english/data/chouki/index.htm (accessed April 28, 2006).

Japan. Ministry of Internal Affairs and Communications. "Japan in Figures." 2006. http://www.stat.go.jp/english/data/figures/index.htm (accessed April 28, 2006).

"Japanese Sound Effects and What They Mean." Oop-ack.com. http://www.oop-ack.com/ (accessed on April 28, 2006).

MacDonald, Heidi. "Manga Sales Grow; So Do Worries; Despite Concerns about Title Glut, Quality and Censorship, Manga and Anime Sales Continue to Boom." *Publishers Weekly* 251, no. 11 (2004): 29.

McGray, Douglas. "Japan's Gross National Cool." *Foreign Policy* (May 2002): 44.

"Manga Bonanza." *Publishers Weekly* 251, no. 49 (2004): 38.

"Manga for Girls," *New York Times Book Review*, October 2005.

Moore, Rebecca C. "All Shapes of Hunger: Teenagers and Fan Fiction." *Voice of Youth Advocates* (April 2005).

Reid, Calvin. "Manga Sells Anime—and Vice Versa." *Publishers Weekly* 251, no. 42 (2004): 30.

Roth, Daniel. "It's ... Profitmon! From *Pokémon* to *Full Metal Panic*, the Anime Industry Is Doing Everything the Rest of Show Biz Isn't: Embracing Technology, Coddling Fans—and Making a Killing." *Fortune* 152, no. 12 (2005): 100.

Versaci, Rocco. "How Comic Books Can Change the Way Our Students See Literature: One Teacher's Perspective." *English Journal* (November 2001): 61–67.

Online Resources

AMV. http://www.animemusicvideos.org/home/home.php (accessed April 27, 2006).

Anime News Network. http://animenewsnetwork.com (accessed April 27, 2006).

Fanfiction.net. http://www.fanfiction.net (accessed April 28, 2006).

ICv2. http://icv2.com/index.html (accessed April 27, 2006).

Katie Bair's Petting Zoo Wig Design. http://www.katiebair.com/wigs.html (accessed on April 28, 1996).

Wikipedia. http://www.wikipedia.org (accessed April 27, 2006).

Japanese Manga Series

(U.S. publication dates and U.S. distributors used)

Aida, Yu. *Gunslinger Girl*. 6+ vols. Houston: ADV Manga, 2005-present.

Aihara, Mika. *Hot Gimmick*. 12 vols. San Francisco: VIZ Media, LLC, 2005-2006.

Akamatsu, Ken. *Love Hina*. 14 vols. Los Angeles: TokyoPop, 2002-2003.

———. *Negima*. 14+ vols. New York: Del Ray, 2004-present.

Akino, Matsuri. *Pet Shop of Horrors*. 10 vols. Los Angeles: TokyoPop, 2003-2005.

Aoki, Yuya. *GetBackers*. 31+ vols. Los Angeles: TokyoPop, 2004-present.

Arakawa, Hiromu. *Fullmetal Alchemist*. 13+ vols. San Francisco: Viz Media, LLC, 2005-present.

Azumah, Kiyohiko. *Azumanga Daioh*. 4 vols. Houston: ADV Manga, 2003-2004.

———. *Yotsuba&!* 4 vols. Houston: ADV Manga, 2005-present.

Chrono, Nanae. *Peace Maker Kurogane*. 5 vols. Houston: ADV Manga, 2004-present.

CLAMP. *Angelic Layer*. 5 vols. Los Angeles: TokyoPop, 2002-2003.

———. *Clover*. 4 vols. Los Angeles: TokyoPop, 2001-2002.

———. *Legal Drug*. 3 vols. Los Angeles: TokyoPop, 2004-2005.

———. *Magic Knight Rayearth*. 3 vols. Los Angeles: TokyoPop, 2003.

———. *The One I Love*. Los Angeles: TokyoPop, 2004.

———. *Tokyo Babylon*. 7 vols. Los Angeles: TokyoPop, 2004-2005.

———. *Tsubasa: RESERVoir CHRoNICLE*. 11+ vols. New York: Del Ray, 2004-current.

———. *X/1999*. 18 vols. San Francisco: VIZ Media, LLC, 2003-2005.

———. *XXXholic*. 8+ vols. New York: Del Ray, 2004-present.

Endo, Minari. *Dazzle*. 2+ vols. Los Angeles: TokyoPop, 2006-present.

Fujii, Mihona. *Gals*. 10 vols. New York: CMX Manga, 2005-present.

Gatoh, Shoji. *Full Metal Panic!* 9 vols. Houston: ADV Manga, 2003-2006.

Hakase, Mizuki. *The Demon Ororon*. 4 vols. Los Angeles: TokyoPop, 2004.

Hamazaki, Tatsuya. *.hack/Legend of the Twilight*. 3 vols. Los Angeles: TokyoPop, 2003-2004.

Hatori, Bisco. *Ouran High School Host Club*. 7+ vols. San Francisco: Viz Media, LLC, 2005-present.

Hayakawa, Tomoko. *The Wallflower.* 15+ vols. New York: Del Ray, 2004-present.

Higuchi, Daisuke. *Whistle!* 13+ vols. San Francisco: VIZ Media, LLC, 2004-present.

Higuri, You. *Cantarella.* 10+ vols. Agoura Hills, CA: Go!Media Entertainment, 2005-present.

Higuri, You. *Gorgeous Carat.* 4 vols. Los Angeles: BLU, 2006-present.

Hotta, Yumi. *Hikaru No Go.* 23 vols. San Francisco: VIZ Media, LLC, 2004-present.

Inada, Shiho. *Ghost Hunt.* 9+ vols. New York: Del Ray, 2005-present.

Inoue, Santa. *Tokyo Tribes.* 11 vols. Los Angeles: TokyoPop, 2004-present.

Kamijiyo, Akimine. *Samurai Deeper Kyo.* 37+ vols. Los Angeles: TokyoPop, 2003-present.

Kamio, Yoko. *Boys Over Flowers.* 36 volumes. San Francisco: VIZ Media, LLC, 2003-present.

Kanesada, Yukio. *Kamikaze Girls.* San Francisco: VIZ Media, LLC, 2006.

Kannagi, Satoru. *Only the Ring Finger Knows.* Gardena, CA: Digital Manga Publishing, 2006.

Kawahara, Yumiko. *Dolls.* 4 vols. San Francisco: VIZ Media, LLC, 2004-2005.

Kawai, Chigusa. *La Esperança* 5 vols. Gardena, CA: Digital Manga Publishing, 2005-present.

Kawai, Toko. *Our Everlasting.* 2 vols. Gardena, CA: Digital Manga Publishing, 2005-2006.

Kinoshita, Sakura. *Tactics.* 4 vols. Houston: ADV Manga, 2004-present.

Kio, Shimoko. *Genshiken.* 6+ vols. New York: Del Ray, 2005-present.

Kishimoto, Masashi. *Naruto.* 32 vols. San Francisco: VIZ Media, LLC, 2003-present.

Kitoh, Mohito. *Shadow Star Narutaru.* 12 vols. Milwaukee: Dark Horse, 2001-present.

Koike, Kazuo. *Lone Wolf and Cub.* 28 vols. Milwaukee: Dark Horse, 2000-2002.

Kouga, Yun. *Earthian*. 5 vols. Los Angeles: BluManga, 2005-present.

———. *Loveless*. 6 vols. Los Angeles: TokyoPop, 2006-present.

Kubotite. *Bleach*. 23+ vols. San Francisco: VIZ Media, LLC, 2004-present.

Masamune, Shirow. *Ghost in the Shell*. Milwaukee: Dark Horse, 2004.

Matoh, Sanami. *Fake*. 7 vols. Los Angeles: TokyoPop, 2003-2004.

Matsushita, Yoko. *Descendants of Darkness*. 11 vols. San Francisco: VIZ Media, LLC, 2004-present.

Mihara, Mitsukazu. *Beautiful People*. Los Angeles: TokyoPop, 2006.

Minekura, Kazuya. *Saiyuki*. 9 vols. Los Angeles: TokyoPop, 2004-2005.

Miyamoto, Yuki. *Café Kichijouji de*. 3 vols. Gardena, CA: Digital Manga Publishing, 2005-2006.

Miyazaki, Hayao. *Nausicaä of the Valley of the Wind*. 7 vols. San Francisco: VIZ Media, LLC, 2004.

Mizushiro, Setona. *X-Day*. 2 vols. Los Angeles: TokyoPop, 2003.

Momochi, Reiko. *Confidential Confessions*. 6 vols. Los Angeles: TokyoPop, 2003-2005.

Monkey Punch. *Lupin III*. 14 vols. Los Angeles: TokyoPop, 2002-2004.

Moriyama, Daisuke. *Chrono Crusade*. 8 vols. Houston: ADV Manga, 2004-2006.

Murakami, Maki. *Gravitation*. 12 vols. Los Angeles: TokyoPop, 2003-2006.

Nakajo, Hisaya. *Hana-Kimi*. 23 vols. San Francisco: VIZ Media, LLC, 2004-present.

Nakazawa, Keiji. *Barefoot Gen*. 4 vols. San Francisco: Last Gasp Publishing, 2004-2005.

Nanami, Shingo. *Kamui*. 8 vols. Los Angeles: Broccoli Books, 2005-present.

Nasu, Yukie. *Here is Greenwood*. 11 vols. San Francisco: VIZ Media, LLC, 2004-present.

Nightow, Nasuhiro. *Trigun*. 2 vols. Gardena, CA: Digital Manga Publishing, 2003.

———. *Trigun Maximum*. 11 vols. Gardena, CA: Digital Manga Publishing, 2004-present.

Nishimori, Hiroyuki. *Cheeky Angel*. 14 vols. San Francisco: VIZ Media, LLC, 2004-2006.

Nishiyama, Yuriko. *Dragon Voice*. 11 vols. Los Angeles: TokyoPop, 2004-present.

Nonaka, Eiji. *Cromartie High School*. 16+ vols. Los Angeles: TokyoPop, 2005-present.

Oda, Eiichiro. *One Piece*. 41+ vols. San Francisco: VIZ Media, LLC, 2003-present.

Ohashi, Kaoru. *Sengoku Nights*. 2 vols. Los Angeles: TokyoPop, 2006.

Okuda, Hitoshi. *Tenchi Muyo!* 12 vols. San Francisco: VIZ Media, LLC, 1997-present.

Ooba, Tsugumi. *Death Note*. 10+ vols. San Francisco: VIZ Media, LLC, 2005-present.

Otomo, Katsuhiro. *Akira*. 6 vols. Milwaukee: Dark Horse, 2000–2002.

Quick, Jen Lee. *Off*beat*. 1+ vols. Los Angeles: TokyoPop, 2005.

Rikodou, Koushi. *Excel Saga*. 14 vols. San Francisco: VIZ Media, LLC, 2003-present.

Sadamoto, Yoshiyuki. *Neon Genesis Evangelion*. 9 vols. San Francisco: VIZ Media, LLC, 1998-2004.

Saijyo, Shinji. *Iron Wok Jan!*. 27 vols. Fremont: DrMaster Publications, 2002-present.

Saito, Takao. *Golgo 13*. 13 vols. San Francisco: VIZ Media, LLC, 2006–present.

Sakurazawa, Erica. *Angel*. Los Angeles: TokyoPop, 2003.

———. *Between the Sheets*. Los Angeles: TokyoPop, 2003.

Seino, Shizura. *Girl Got Game*. 10 vols. Los Angeles: TokyoPop, 2004–2005.

Shiozu, Shura. *Eerie Queerie*. 4 vols. Los Angeles: TokyoPop, 2004.

Sorya, Fuyumi. *Mars*. 15 vols. Los Angeles: TokyoPop, 2002–2003.

Sugisaki, Yukiro. *D.N.Angel*. 10 vols. Los Angeles: TokyoPop, 2004–2005.

Takahashi, Rumiko. *Inuyasha*. 43+ vols. San Francisco: VIZ Media, LLC, 2003–present.

———. *Maison Ikkoku*. 15 vols. Los Angeles: TokyoPop, 2003–2006.

———. *Ranma 1/2*. 38 vols. San Francisco: VIZ Media, LLC, 2003–present.

Takami, Koushon. *Battle Royale*. Los Angeles: TokyoPop, 2003–present.

Takanashi, Mitsuba. *Crimson Hero*. 5+ vols. San Francisco: VIZ Media, LLC, 2005–present.

Takaya, Natsuki. *Fruits Basket*. 19 vols. Los Angeles: TokyoPop, 2004–present.

Takeuchi, Mick. *Her Majesty's Dog*. 10 vols. Agoura Hills, CA: Go! Media Entertainment, 2005–present.

Tezuka, Osamu. *Astro Boy*. 23 vols. Milwaukee: Dark Horse, 2002–2004.

———. *Buddha*. 8 vols. New York: Vertical, 2003–2005.

Toriyama, Akira. *Dragon Ball*. 42 vols. San Francisco: VIZ Media, LLC, 2000–present.

———. *Dragon Ball Z*. 26 vols. San Francisco: VIZ Media, LLC, 2003–present.

Tsuda, Masami. *Kare Kano*. 21 vols. Los Angeles: TokyoPop, 2003–present.

Ueda, Miwa. *Peach Girl*. 18 vols. Los Angeles: TokyoPop, 2003–present.

Vin, Lee. *Crazy Love Story*. 5 vols. Los Angeles: TokyoPop, 2004–2006.

Watanabe, Taeko. *Kare Kano*. 21 vols. San Francisco: VIZ Media, LLC, 2003–2006.

Watase, Yu. *Alice 19th*. 7 vols. San Francisco: VIZ Media, LLC, 2003–2004.

———. *Ceres: Celestial Legend*. 14 vols. San Francisco: VIZ Media, LLC, 2003–2006.

———. *Fushigi Yugi*. 18 vols. San Francisco: VIZ Media, LLC, 1999–2006.

Watsuki, Nobuhiro. *Rurouni Kenshin*. 28 vols. San Francisco: VIZ Media, LLC, 2003–present.

Yazawa, Ai. *Nana*. 15+ vols. San Francisco: VIZ Media, LLC, 2005–present.

———. *Paradise Kiss*. 5 vols. Los Angeles: TokyoPop, 2002–2005.

Yoshinaga, Fumi. *Antique Bakery*. 4 vols. Gardena, CA: Digital Manga Publishing, 2005–2006.

Yoshizumi, Wataru. *Ultra Maniac*. 5 vols. San Francisco: VIZ Media, LLC, 2005–2006.

Yu, Lee Young. *Kill Me, Kiss Me*. 5 vols. Los Angeles: TokyoPop, 2004–2005.

Yuki, Kaori. *Angel Sanctuary*. 20 vols. San Francisco: VIZ Media, LLC, 2004–present.

Anime

(original Japanese air dates used)

Akira. Directed by Katsuhiro Otomo. Akira Committee Company, 1988.

Cowboy Bebop. Directed by Hiroyuki Okiura, Shinichiro Watanabe and Tensei Okamura. Sony Pictures (Japan), 2001.

Cowboy Bebop. Series directed by Shinichiro Watanabe. Bandai Visual, 1998–1999.

Cromartie High School. Series directed by Hiroaki Sakurai. Bandai Visual, 2003–2004.

GetBackers. Series directed by Kazuhiro Furuhasi. Kodansha Ltd., 2002–2003.

Ghost in the Shell. Directed by Mamoru Oshii. Bandai Visual, 1995.

Ghost in the Shell 2: Innocence. Directed by Mamoru Oshii. Bandai Visual, 2004.

Ghost in the Shell: Stand Alone Complex. Series directed by Kenji Kamayama. Bandai Visual, 2002–2005.

Grave of the Fireflies. Directed by Isao Takahata. Studio Ghibli, 1988.

Gravion. Series directed by Masami Obari. Gonzo Digimation, 2002.

Gravion Zwei. Series directed by Masami Obari. Gonzo Digimation, 2004.

Howl's Moving Castle. Directed by Hayao Miyazaki. Studio Ghibli, 2004.

Madlax. Series directed by Koichi Mashimo. Victor Entertainment, Inc., 2004.

Magical Play. Series directed by Hiroki Hayashi. Magicaland Magic Union, 2001–2002.

My Neighbor Totoro. Directed by Hayao Miyazaki. Studio Ghibli, 1988.

Nausicaä of the Valley of the Wind. Directed by Hayao Miyazaki. Studio Ghibli, 1984.

Neon Genesis Evangelion. Series directed by Hideaki Anno. Gainax, 1995–1996.

Otogi Zoshi. Series directed by Mizuho Nishikubo. Production I.G., 2004–2005.

Paranoia Agent. Series directed by Satoshi Kon. WoWow, Inc., 2004.

Peacemaker. Series directed by Tomohiro Hirata. Gonzo Digimation, 2003–2004.

Princess Mononoke. Directed by Hayao Miyazaki. Studio Ghibli, 1997.

Princess Nine. Series directed by Tomomi Mochizuki. ADV Films, 1998.

Princess Tutu. Series directed by Junichi Sato and Shuogo Kawamato. Film Makers, 2002.

Revolutionary Girl Utena. Series directed by Kunihiko Ikuhara. SoftX, 1997.

Robotech. Series directed by Robert Barron. Harmony Gold, Ltd., 1985–1986.

Rurouni Kenshin. Series directed by Kazuhiro Furuhashi. Fuji Television Network, 1996–1998.

Sailor Moon. Series directed by Junichi Sato and Kunihiko Ichuhara. Cloverway International, 1992–1993.

Samurai Champloo. Series directed by Shinichiro Wanatabe. Fuji TV, 2004.

Samurai X: Trust and Betrayal. Directed by Kazuhiro Furuhashi. Studio DEEN, 1999.

Shadowstar Narutaru. Series directed by Toshiaki Iino. Planet, 2003.

Speed Racer. Series directed by Tatsuo Yoshida. Tatsunoko Productions Co., Ltd., 1967–1968.

Steamboy. Directed by Katsuhiro Otomo. *Steamboy* Committee, 2004.

Super Dimensional Fortress Macross. Series directed by Noburo Ishiguro. Mainichi Broadcasting System, 1982–983.

Vampire Hunter D: Bloodlust. Directed by Yoshiaki Kawajiri. BMG Funhouse, 2000.

Wolf's Rain. Series director by Tensai Okamura. Bandai Visual, 2003.

Creator and Title Index

Subject Index

About the Author

ROBIN E. BRENNER is the Teen Librarian at the Brookline Public Library in Massachusetts. She has created and leads a successful Japanese manga and anime club for teens. She is a member of the ALA/YALSA Great Graphic Novels for Teens Selection List Committee, a list she was chosen to help establish, coauthored the RUSA graphic novel reviewing guidelines and the "Getting Graphic at Your Library" workshop guidelines, is one of the judges for the 2007 Eisner awards, reviews manga for *Booklist*, reviews Japanese anime for *Video Librarian*, and she regularly speaks and conducts workshops on graphic novels, manga, and anime. She also hosts a Web site on graphic novels, www.noflyingnotights.com, and two sister sites (Sidekicks, for children thru age 12; and the Lair, for adults).